BARAKAMON

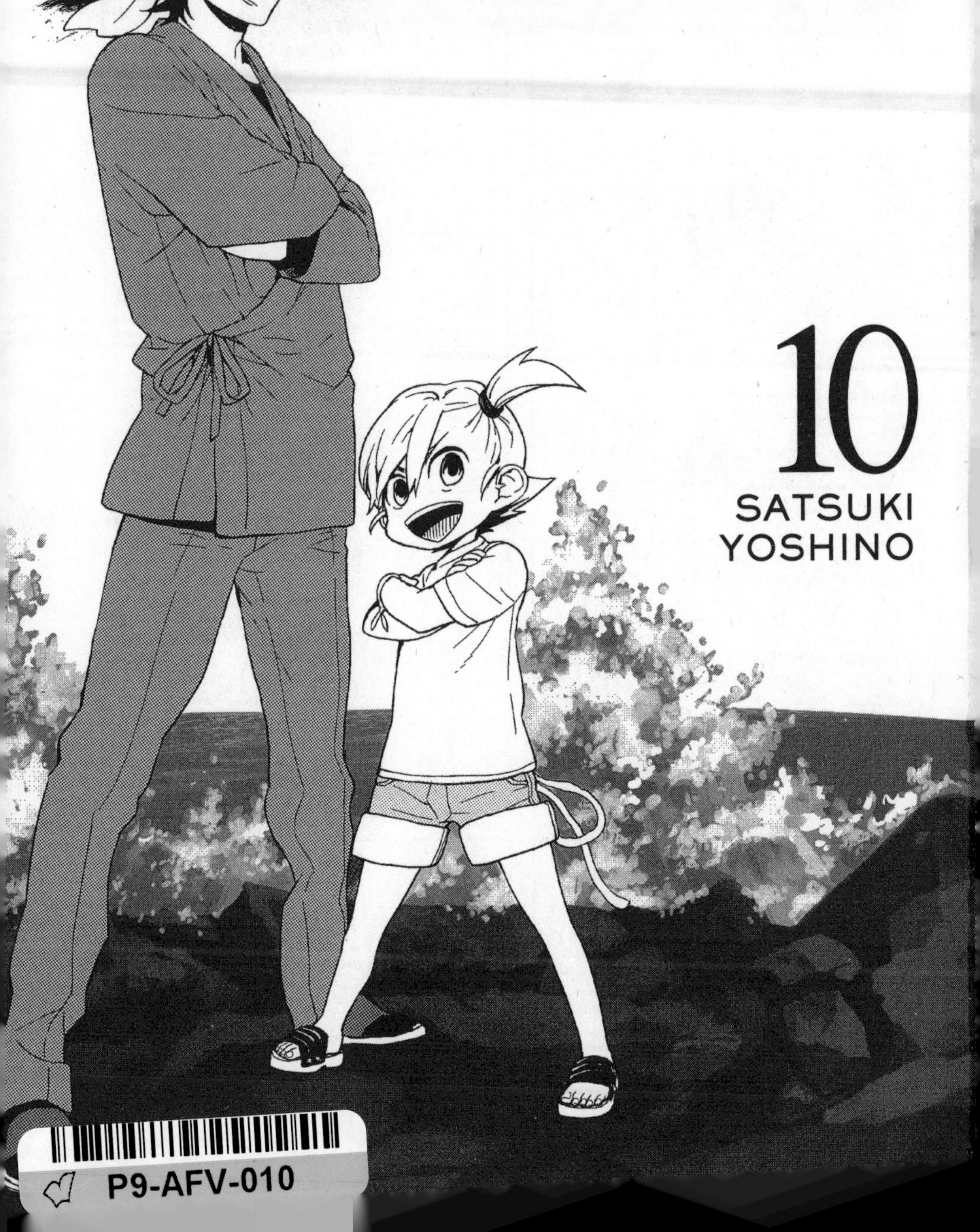

10

SATSUKI YOSHINO

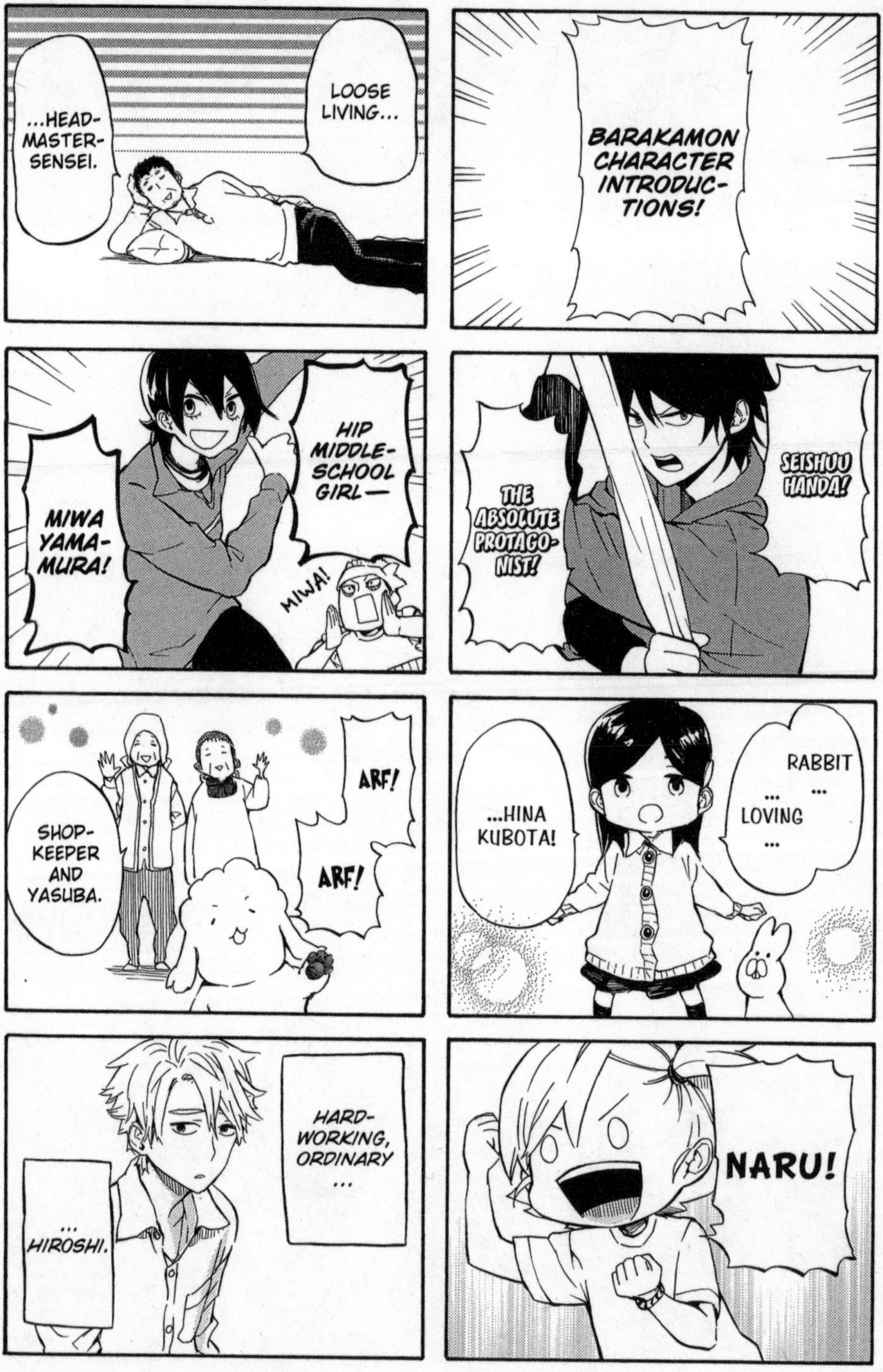
BARAKAMON CHARACTER INTRODUCTIONS!
LOOSE LIVING...
...HEAD-MASTER-SENSEI.
SEISHUU HANDA!
THE ABSOLUTE PROTAGONIST!
HIP MIDDLE-SCHOOL GIRL—
MIWA YAMAMURA!
MIWA!
RABBIT ... LOVING ...
...HINA KUBOTA!
ARF!
ARF!
SHOP-KEEPER AND YASUBA.
NARU!
HARD-WORKING, ORDINARY ...
... HIROSHI.

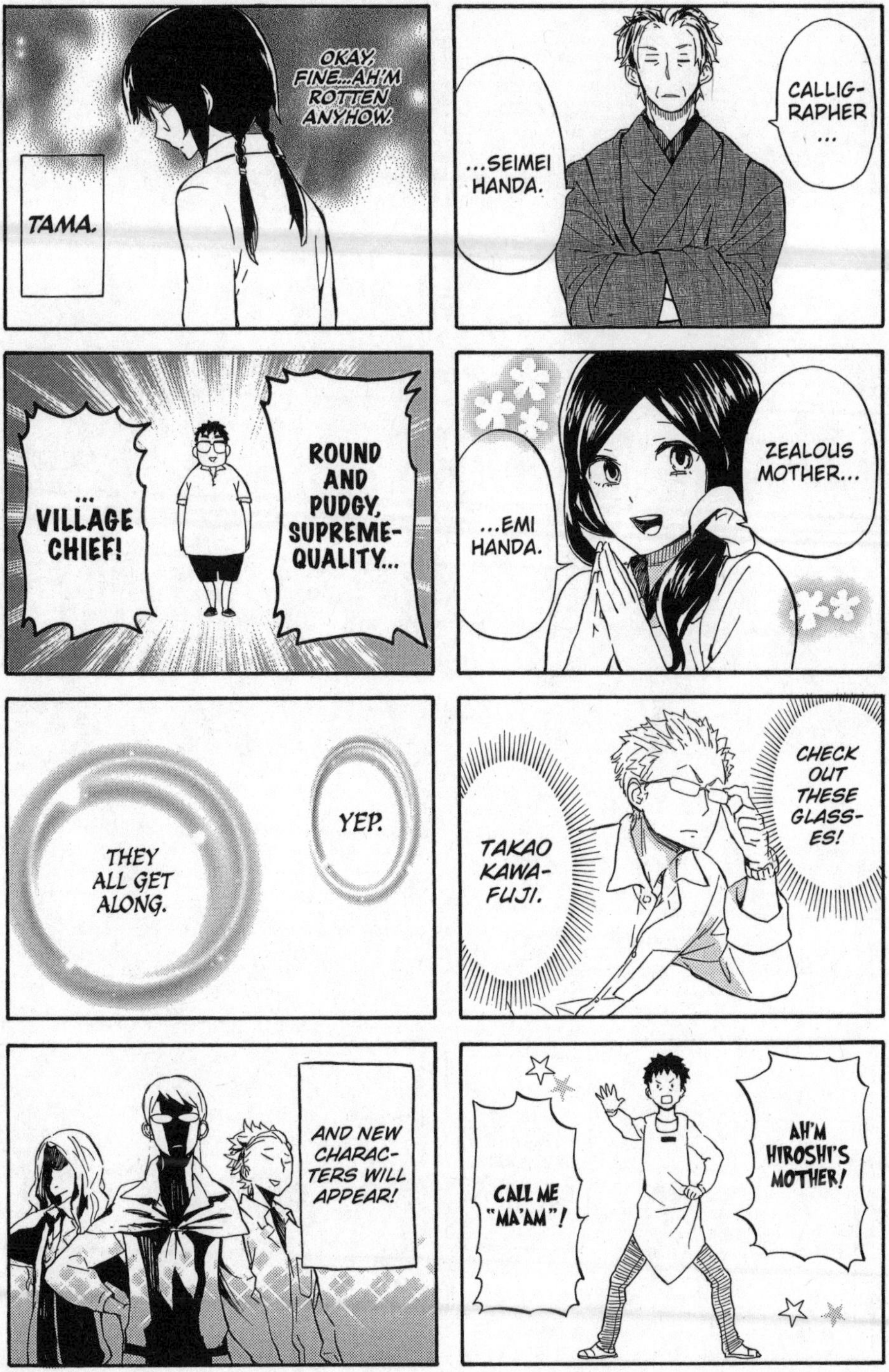
CALLIGRAPHER...
...SEIMEI HANDA.
OKAY, FINE...AH'M ROTTEN ANYHOW.
TAMA.
ZEALOUS MOTHER...
...EMI HANDA.
ROUND AND PUDGY, SUPREME-QUALITY...
...VILLAGE CHIEF!
CHECK OUT THESE GLASSES!
TAKAO KAWAFUJI.
YEP.
THEY ALL GET ALONG.
AH'M HIROSHI'S MOTHER!
CALL ME "MA'AM"!
AND NEW CHARACTERS WILL APPEAR!

Contents

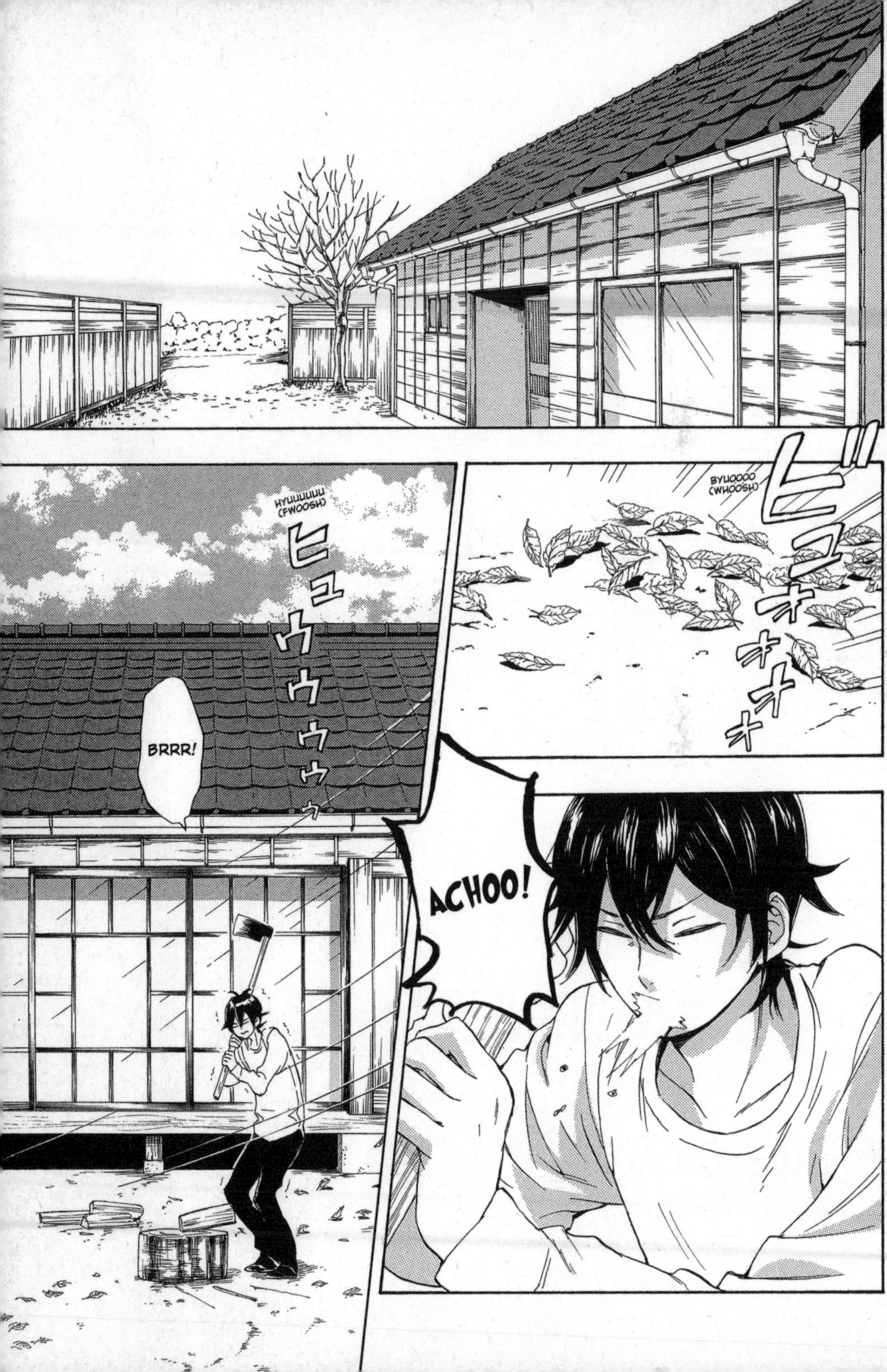
BYUOOOO (WHOOSH)
ビュオォォォ
ACHOO!
HYUUUUUU (FWOOSH)
ヒュウウウウゥ
BRRR!

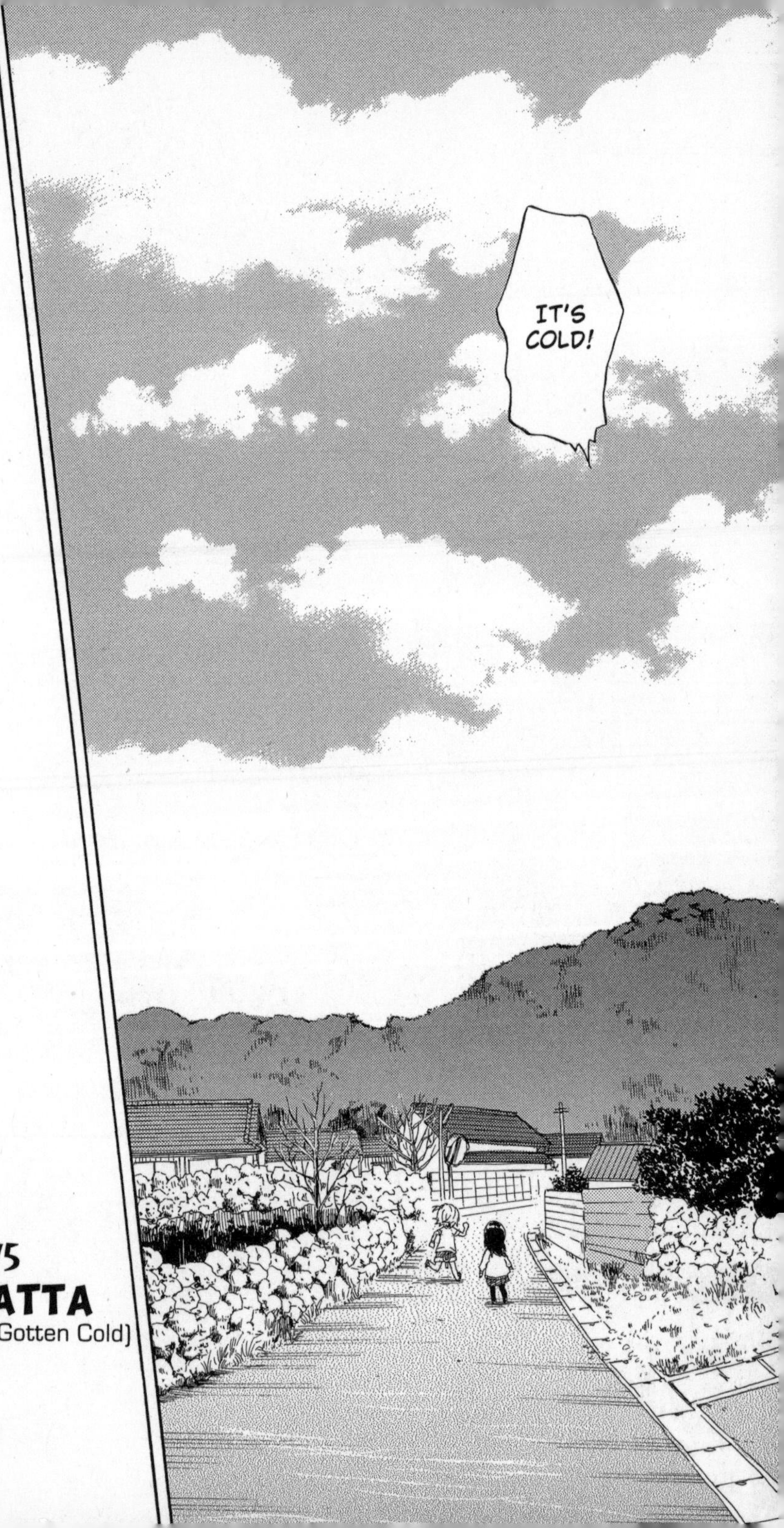
IT'S COLD!

Act. 75
SABUNATTA
(Translation: It's Gotten Cold)

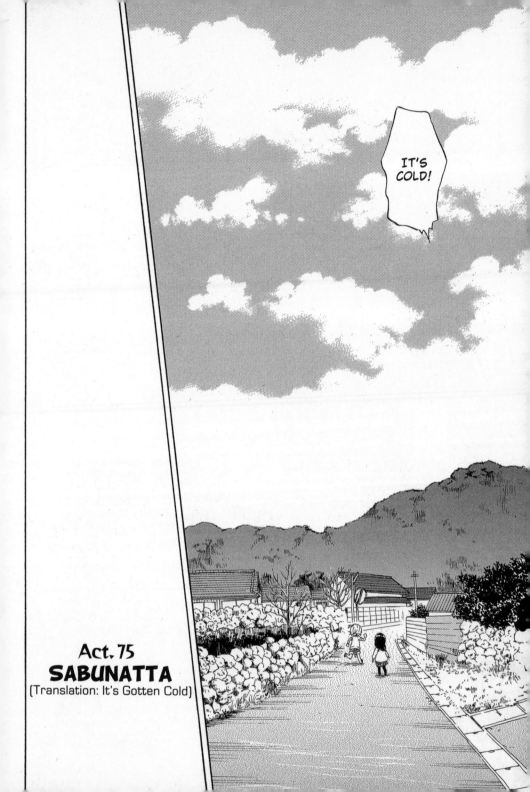

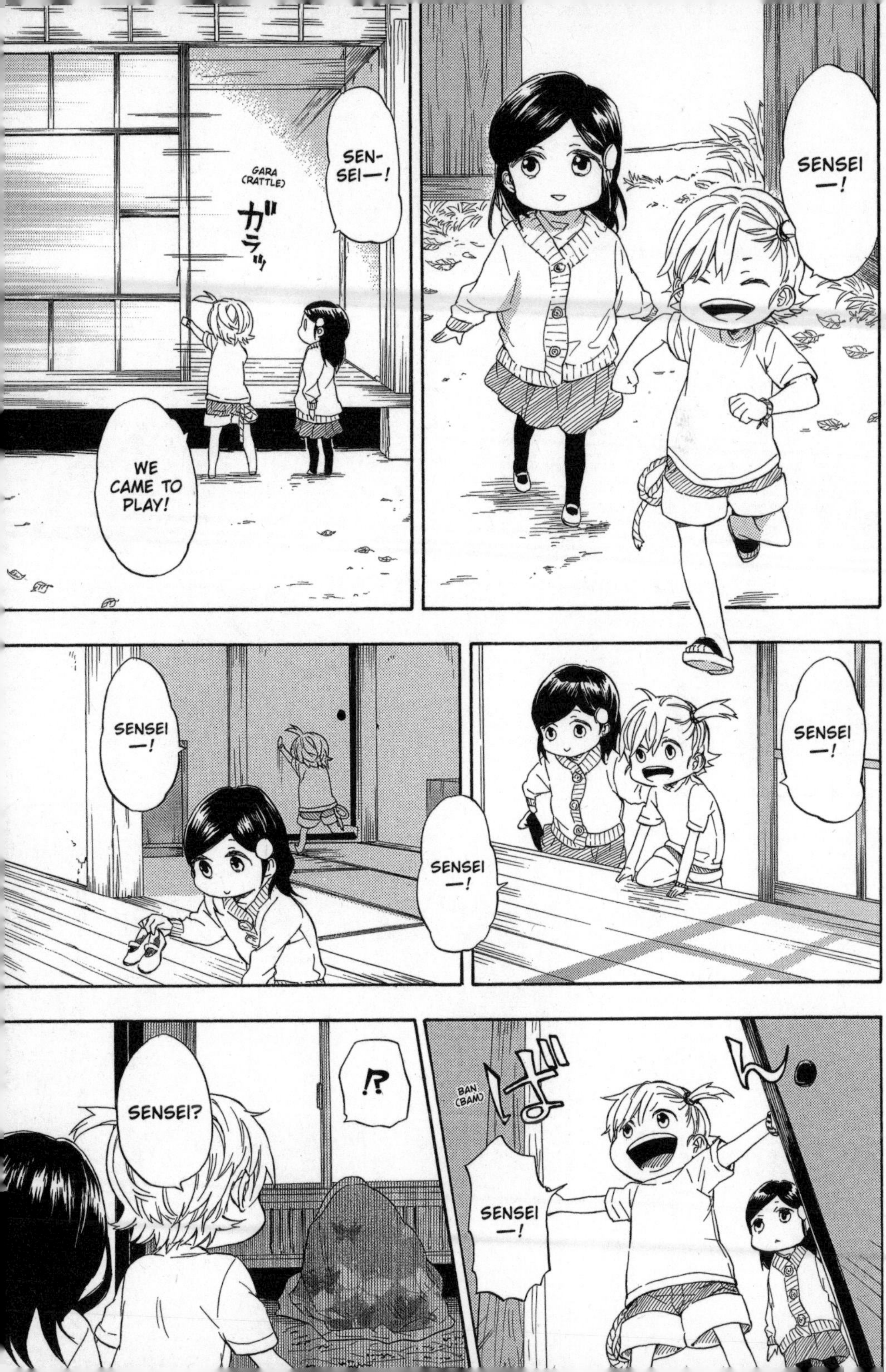
SENSEI—!
SEN-SEI—!
GARA (RATTLE)
ガラッ
WE CAME TO PLAY!
SENSEI—!
SENSEI—!
SENSEI—!
BAN (BAM)
ばん
SENSEI—!
!?
SENSEI?

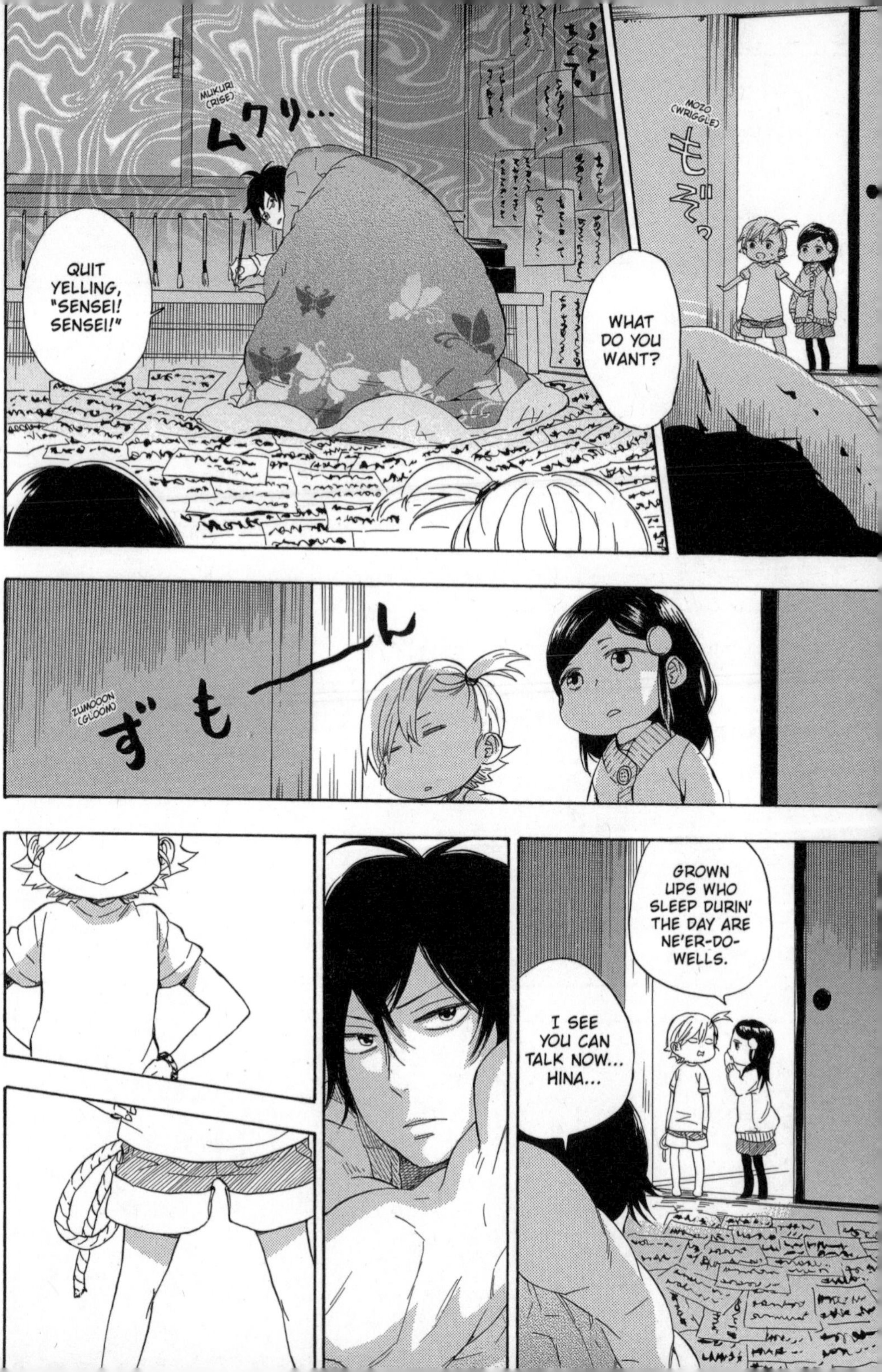
MOZO (WRIGGLE)
もぞっ
MUKURI (RISE)
ムクリ…
WHAT DO YOU WANT?
QUIT YELLING, "SENSEI! SENSEI!"
ZUMOOON (GLOOM)
ずもーーん
GROWN UPS WHO SLEEP DURIN' THE DAY ARE NE'ER-DO-WELLS.
I SEE YOU CAN TALK NOW... HINA...

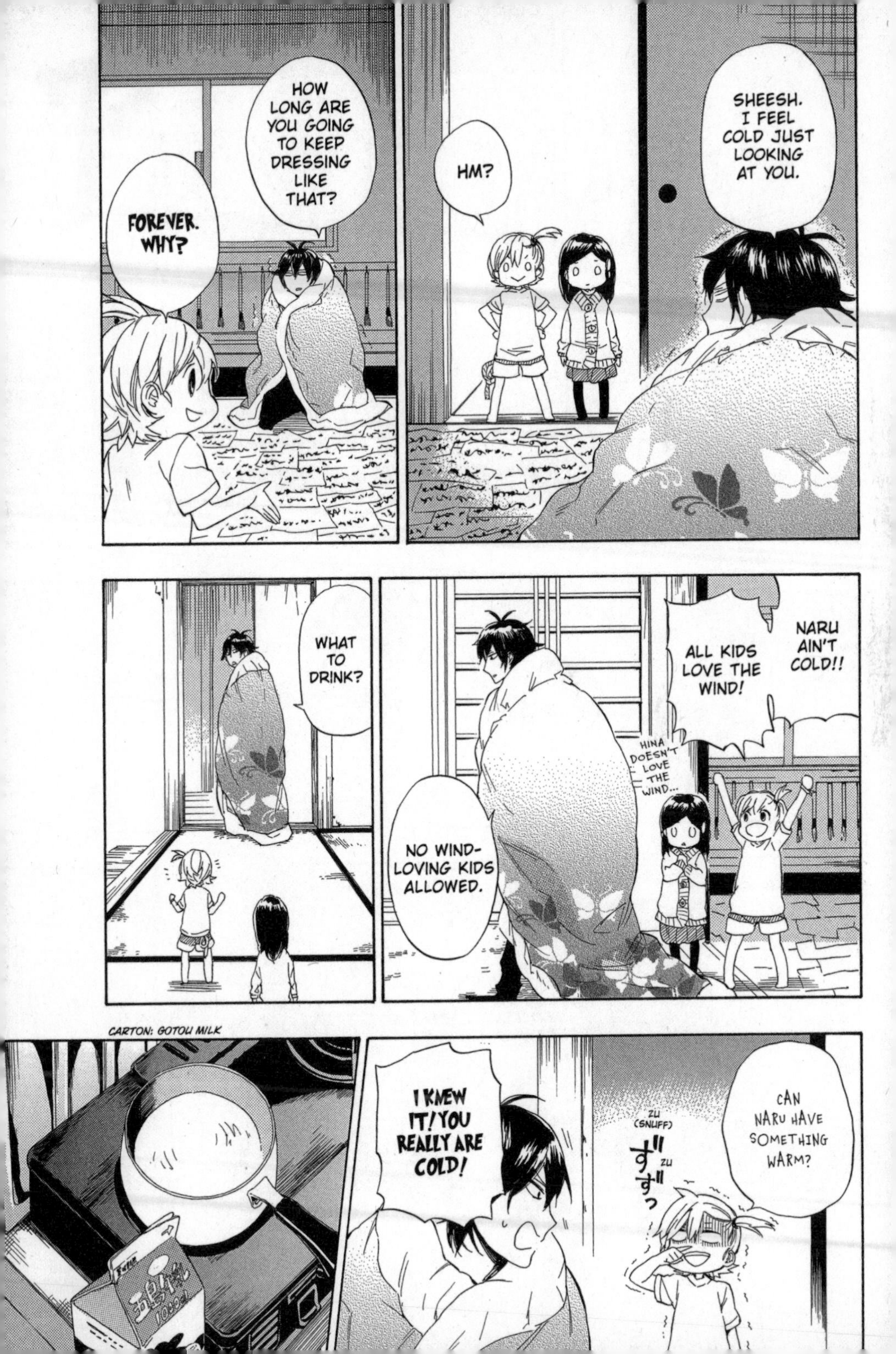
SHEESH. I FEEL COLD JUST LOOKING AT YOU.
HM?
HOW LONG ARE YOU GOING TO KEEP DRESSING LIKE THAT?
FOREVER. WHY?
NARU AIN'T COLD!!
ALL KIDS LOVE THE WIND!
HINA DOESN'T LOVE THE WIND...
NO WIND-LOVING KIDS ALLOWED.
WHAT TO DRINK?
CAN NARU HAVE SOMETHING WARM?
ZU (SNUFF)
ずずっ
ZU
I KNEW IT! YOU REALLY ARE COLD!
CARTON: GOTOU MILK

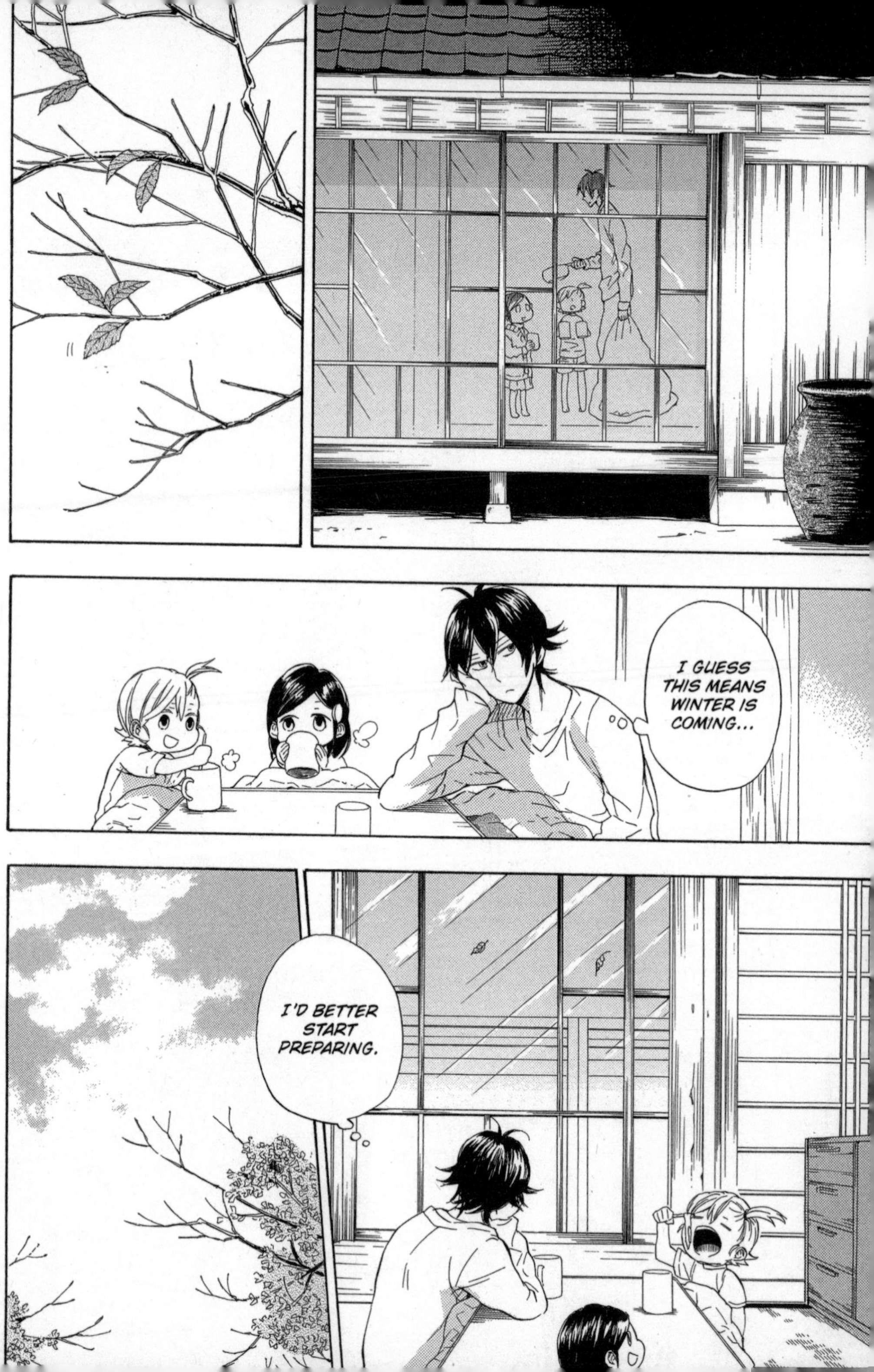
I GUESS THIS MEANS WINTER IS COMING...
I'D BETTER START PREPARING.

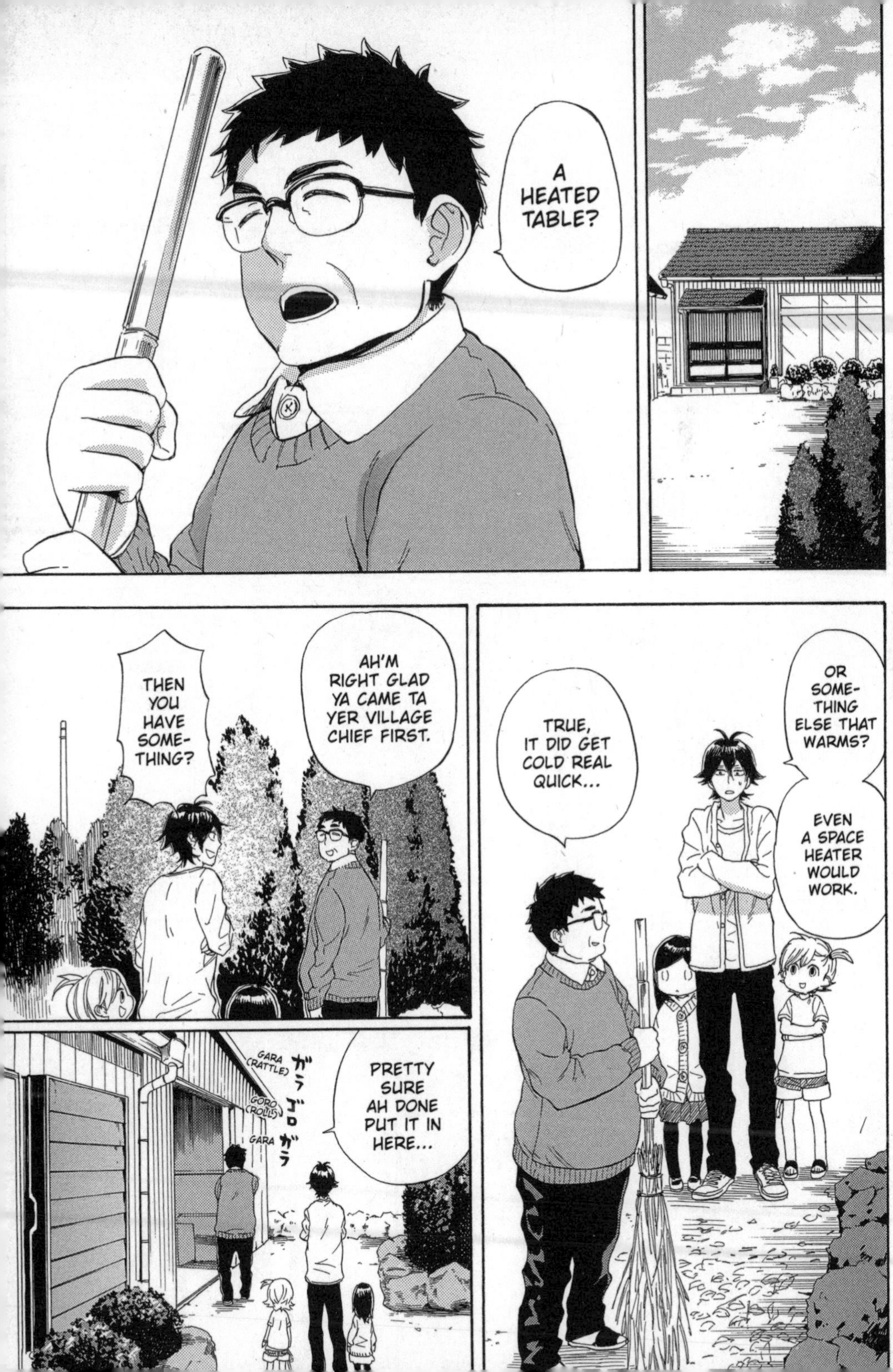
A HEATED TABLE?
OR SOME-THING ELSE THAT WARMS?
EVEN A SPACE HEATER WOULD WORK.
TRUE, IT DID GET COLD REAL QUICK...
AH'M RIGHT GLAD YA CAME TA YER VILLAGE CHIEF FIRST.
THEN YOU HAVE SOME-THING?
PRETTY SURE AH DONE PUT IT IN HERE...
ガラ GARA (RATTLE)
ゴロ GORO (ROLLS)
ガラ GARA

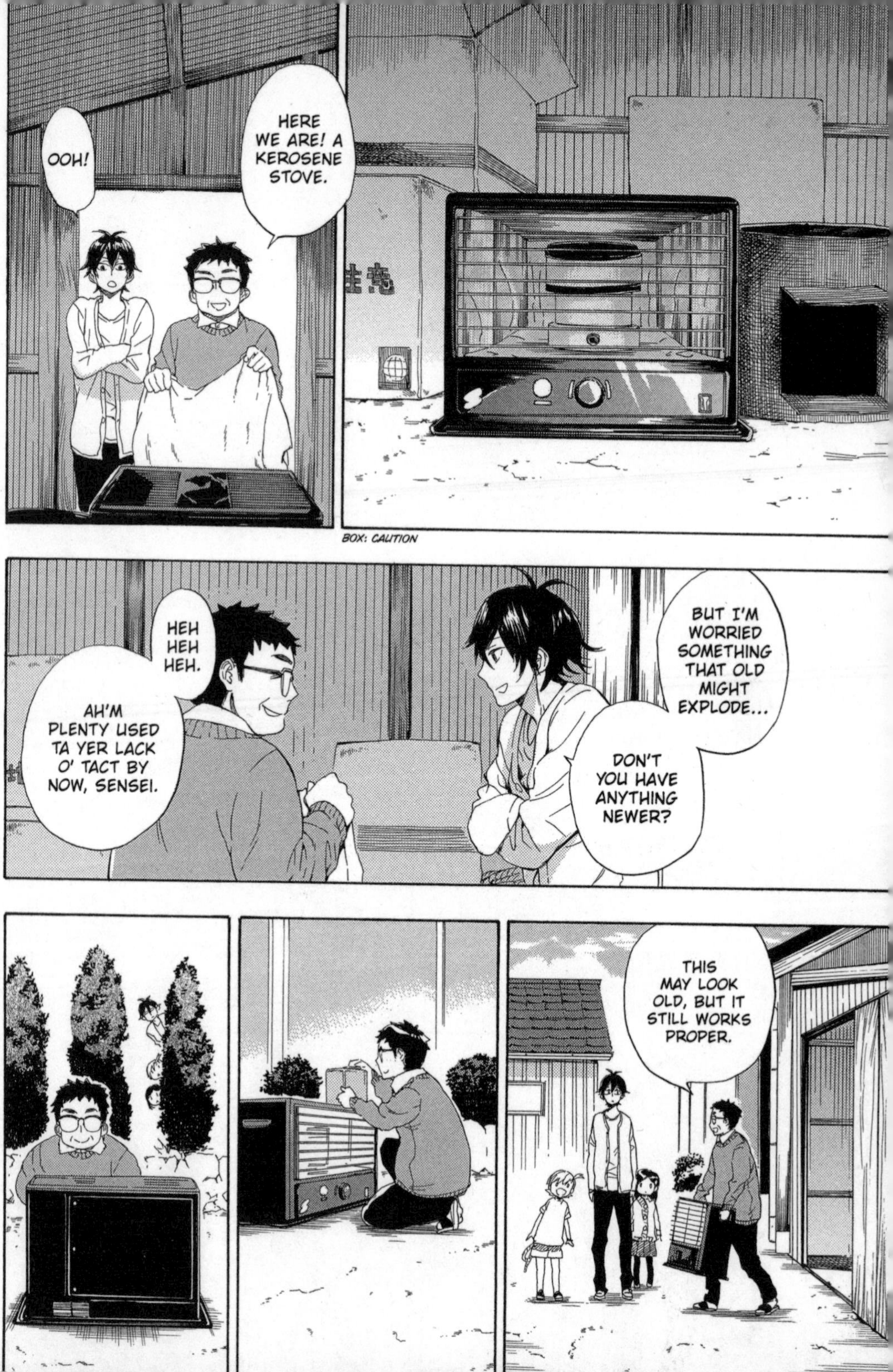
BOX: CAUTION
HERE WE ARE! A KEROSENE STOVE.
OOH!
BUT I'M WORRIED SOMETHING THAT OLD MIGHT EXPLODE...
DON'T YOU HAVE ANYTHING NEWER?
HEH HEH HEH.
AH'M PLENTY USED TA YER LACK O' TACT BY NOW, SENSEI.
THIS MAY LOOK OLD, BUT IT STILL WORKS PROPER.

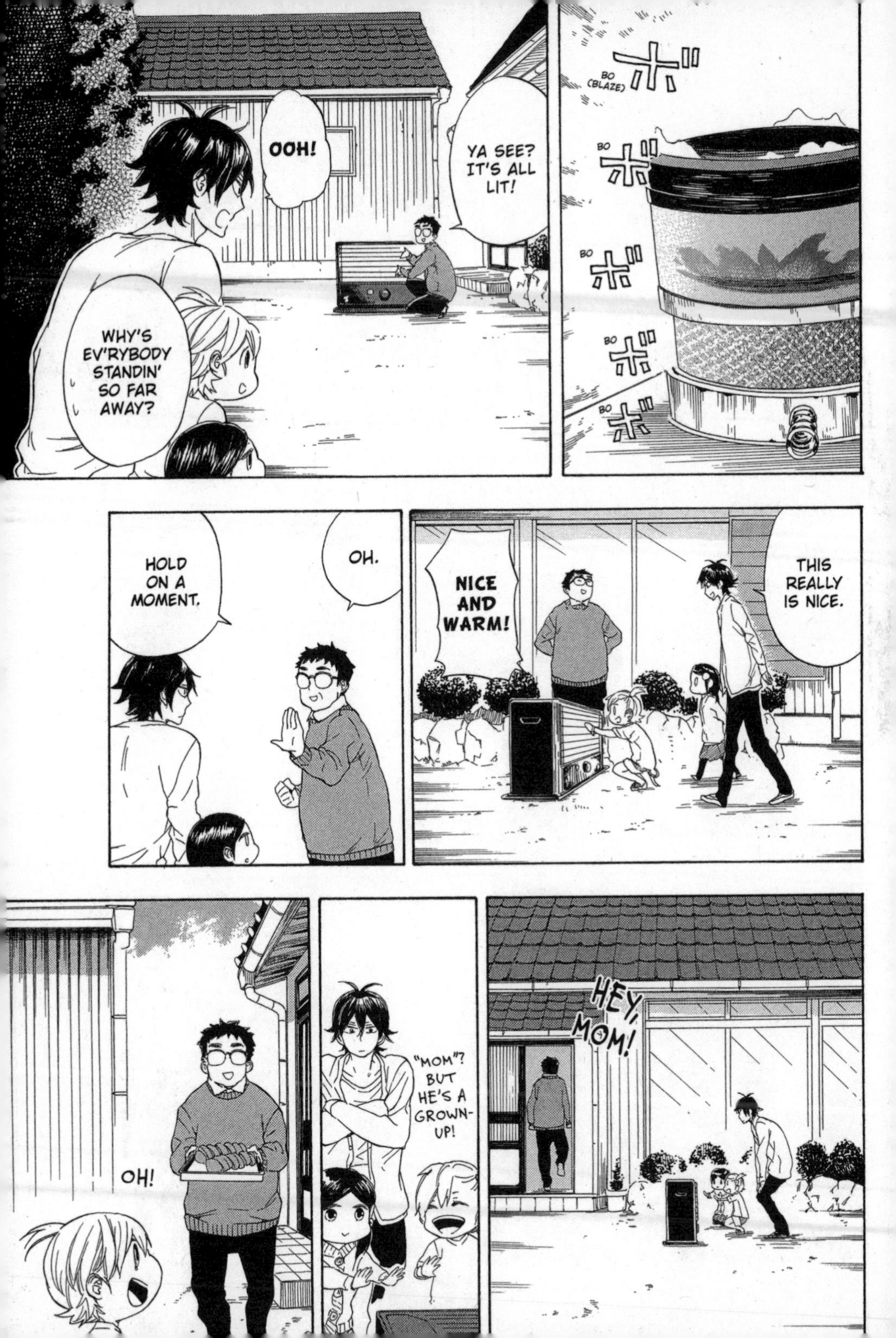
BO (BLAZE) ボ
BO ボ
BO ボ
BO ボ
BO ボ
YA SEE? IT'S ALL LIT!
OOH!
WHY'S EV'RYBODY STANDIN' SO FAR AWAY?
THIS REALLY IS NICE.
NICE AND WARM!
OH.
HOLD ON A MOMENT.
HEY, MOM!
"MOM"? BUT HE'S A GROWN-UP!
OH!

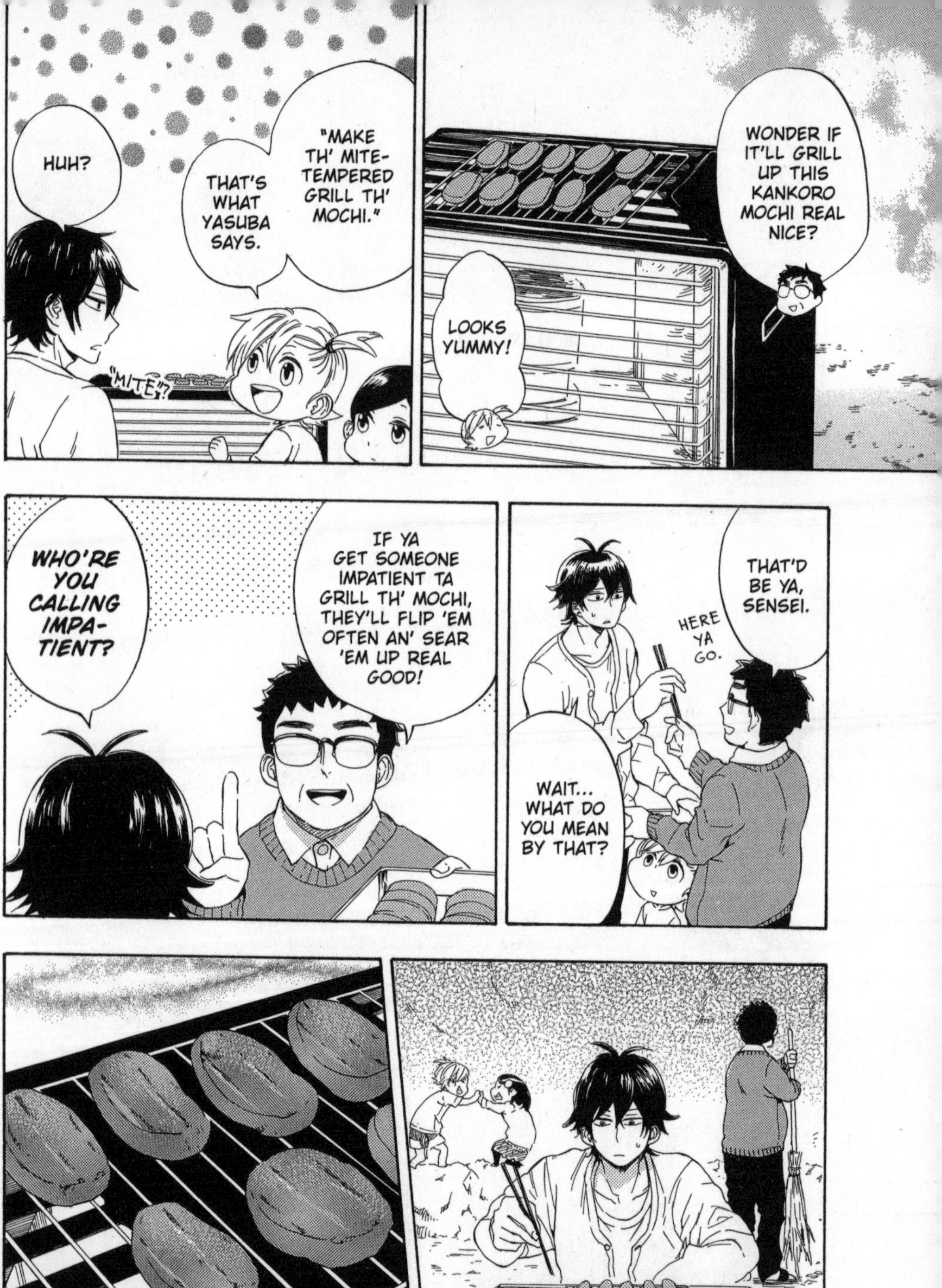
WONDER IF IT'LL GRILL UP THIS KANKORO MOCHI REAL NICE?
LOOKS YUMMY!
"MAKE TH' MITE-TEMPERED GRILL TH' MOCHI."
THAT'S WHAT YASUBA SAYS.
HUH?
"MITE"?
THAT'D BE YA, SENSEI.
HERE YA GO.
WAIT... WHAT DO YOU MEAN BY THAT?
IF YA GET SOMEONE IMPATIENT TA GRILL TH' MOCHI, THEY'LL FLIP 'EM OFTEN AN' SEAR 'EM UP REAL GOOD!
WHO'RE YOU CALLING IMPATIENT?

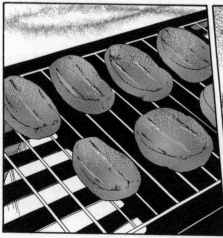

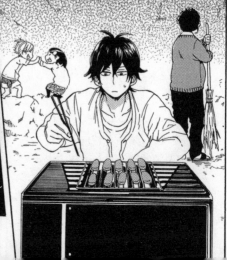

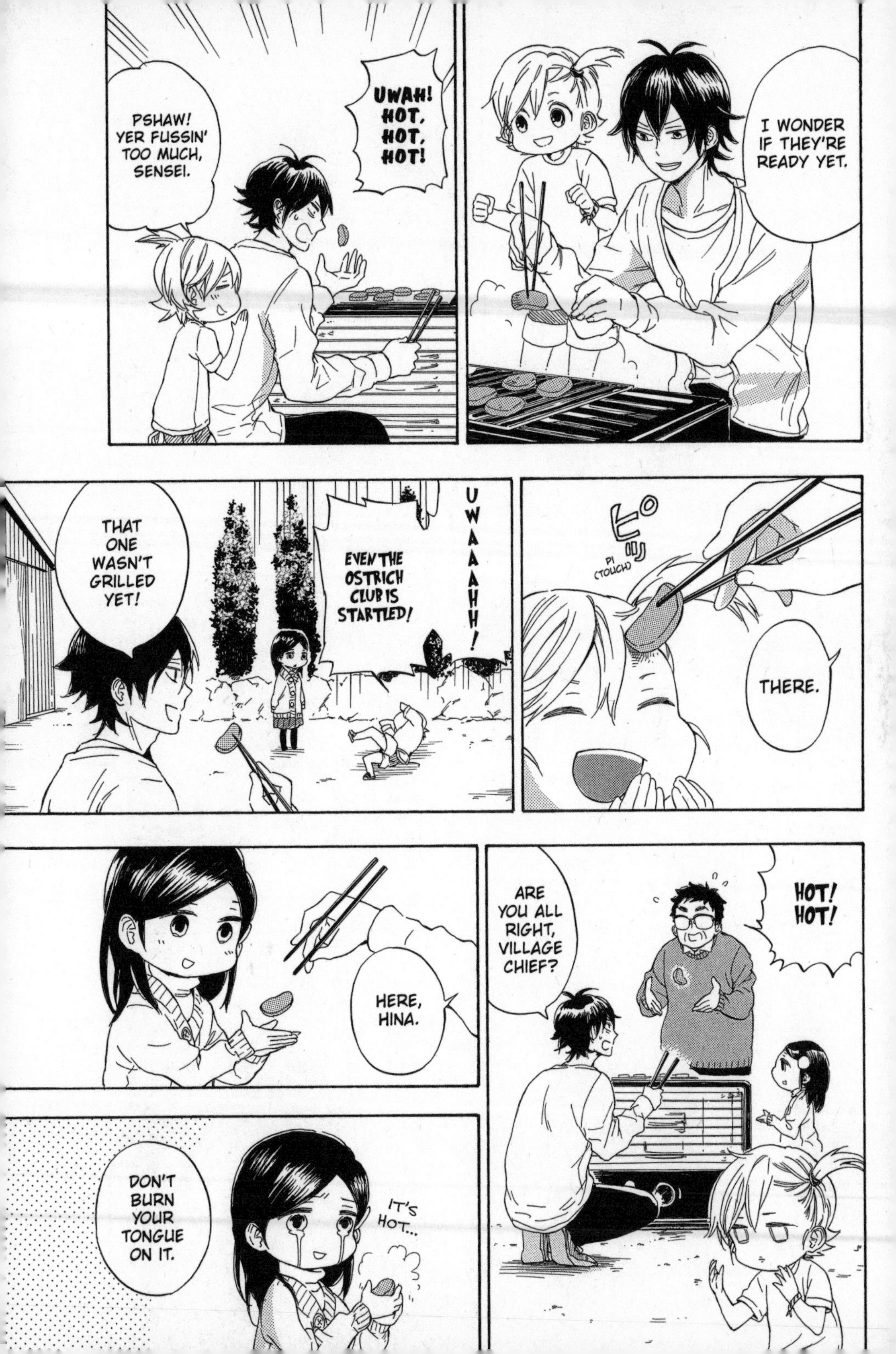
I WONDER IF THEY'RE READY YET.
UWAH! HOT, HOT, HOT!
PSHAW! YER FUSSIN' TOO MUCH, SENSEI.
ピッ
PI (TOUCH)
THERE.
UWAAAAHH!
EVEN THE OSTRICH CLUB IS STARTLED!
THAT ONE WASN'T GRILLED YET!
HOT! HOT!
ARE YOU ALL RIGHT, VILLAGE CHIEF?
HERE, HINA.
DON'T BURN YOUR TONGUE ON IT.
IT'S HOT...

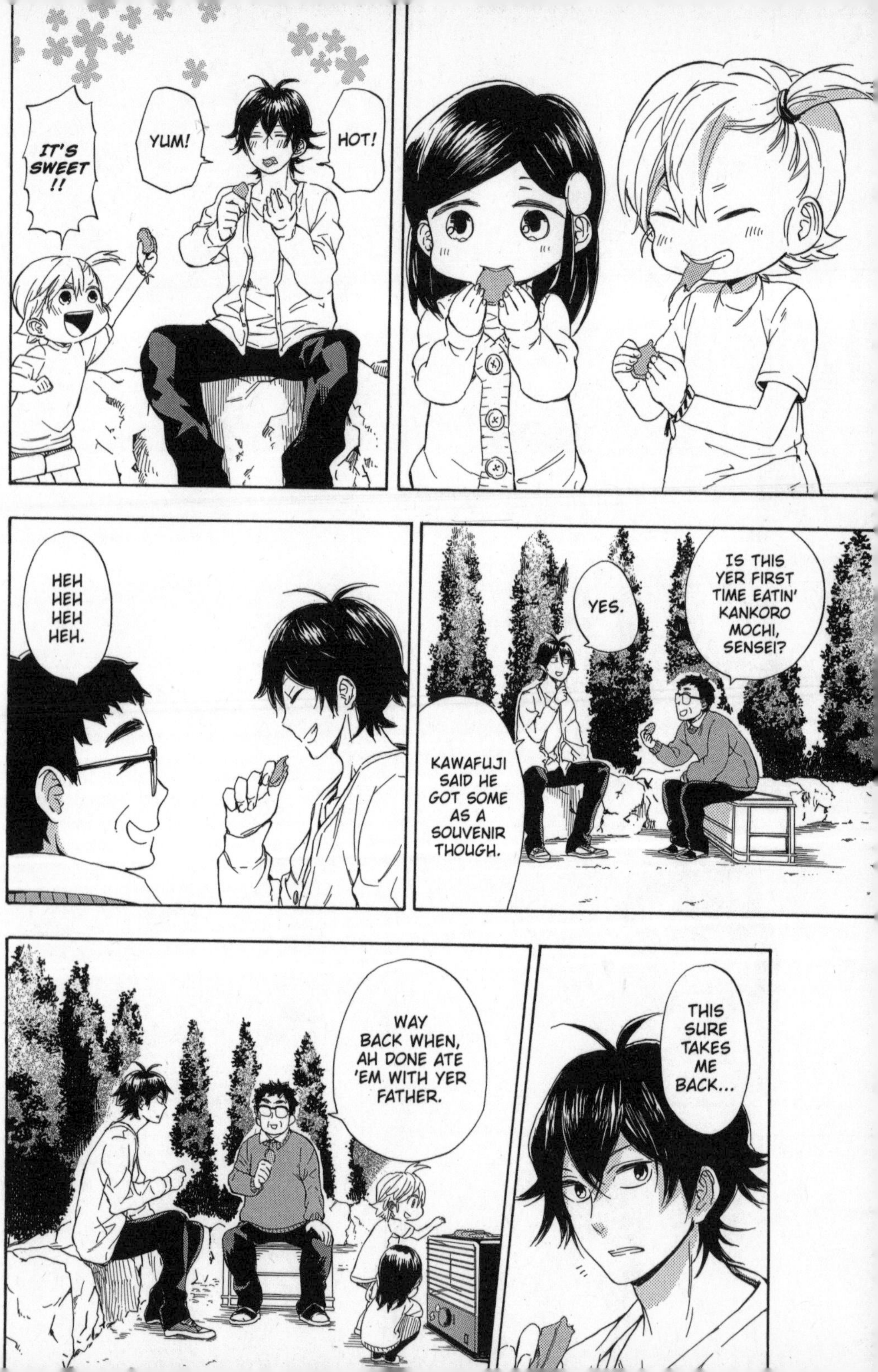
HOT!
YUM!
IT'S SWEET !!
IS THIS YER FIRST TIME EATIN' KANKORO MOCHI, SENSEI?
YES.
KAWAFUJI SAID HE GOT SOME AS A SOUVENIR THOUGH.
HEH HEH HEH HEH.
THIS SURE TAKES ME BACK...
WAY BACK WHEN, AH DONE ATE 'EM WITH YER FATHER.

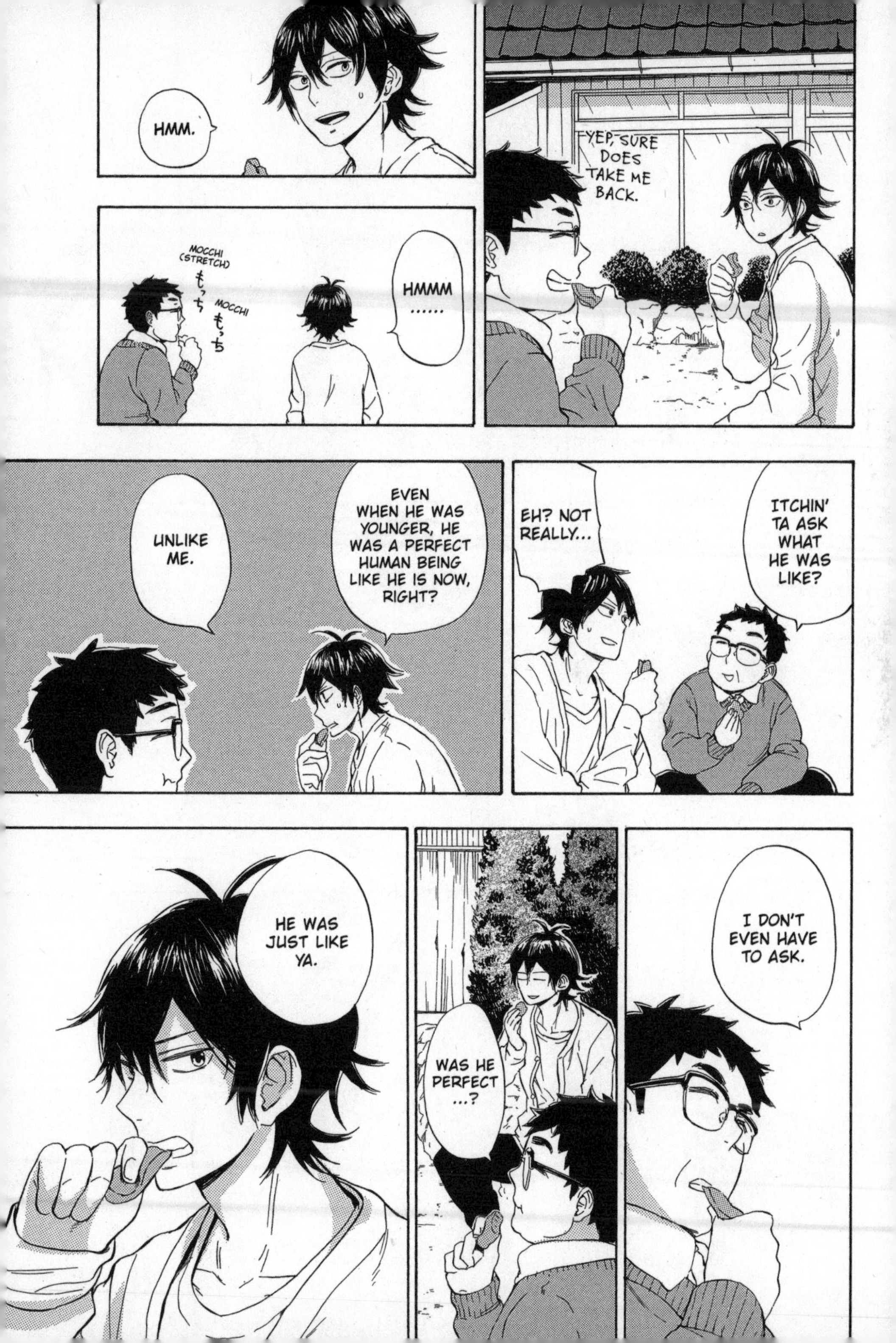
YEP, SURE DOES TAKE ME BACK.
HMM.
HMMM ......
MOCCHI (STRETCH) もっち
MOCCHI もっち
ITCHIN' TA ASK WHAT HE WAS LIKE?
EH? NOT REALLY...
EVEN WHEN HE WAS YOUNGER, HE WAS A PERFECT HUMAN BEING LIKE HE IS NOW, RIGHT?
UNLIKE ME.
I DON'T EVEN HAVE TO ASK.
WAS HE PERFECT ...?
HE WAS JUST LIKE YA.

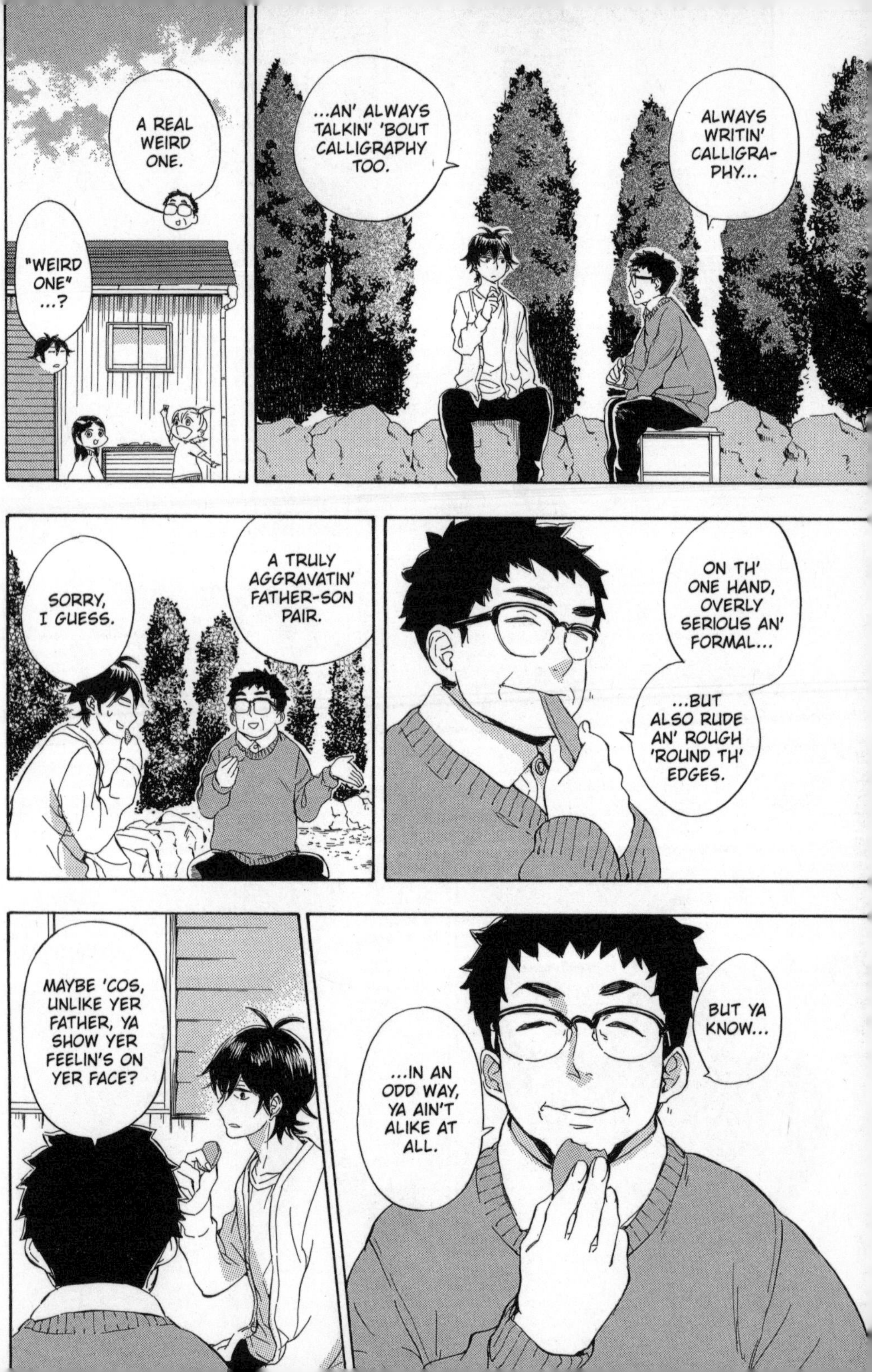
ALWAYS WRITIN' CALLIGRA-PHY...
...AN' ALWAYS TALKIN' 'BOUT CALLIGRAPHY TOO.
A REAL WEIRD ONE.
"WEIRD ONE" ...?
ON TH' ONE HAND, OVERLY SERIOUS AN' FORMAL...
...BUT ALSO RUDE AN' ROUGH 'ROUND TH' EDGES.
A TRULY AGGRAVATIN' FATHER-SON PAIR.
SORRY, I GUESS.
BUT YA KNOW...
...IN AN ODD WAY, YA AIN'T ALIKE AT ALL.
MAYBE 'COS, UNLIKE YER FATHER, YA SHOW YER FEELIN'S ON YER FACE?

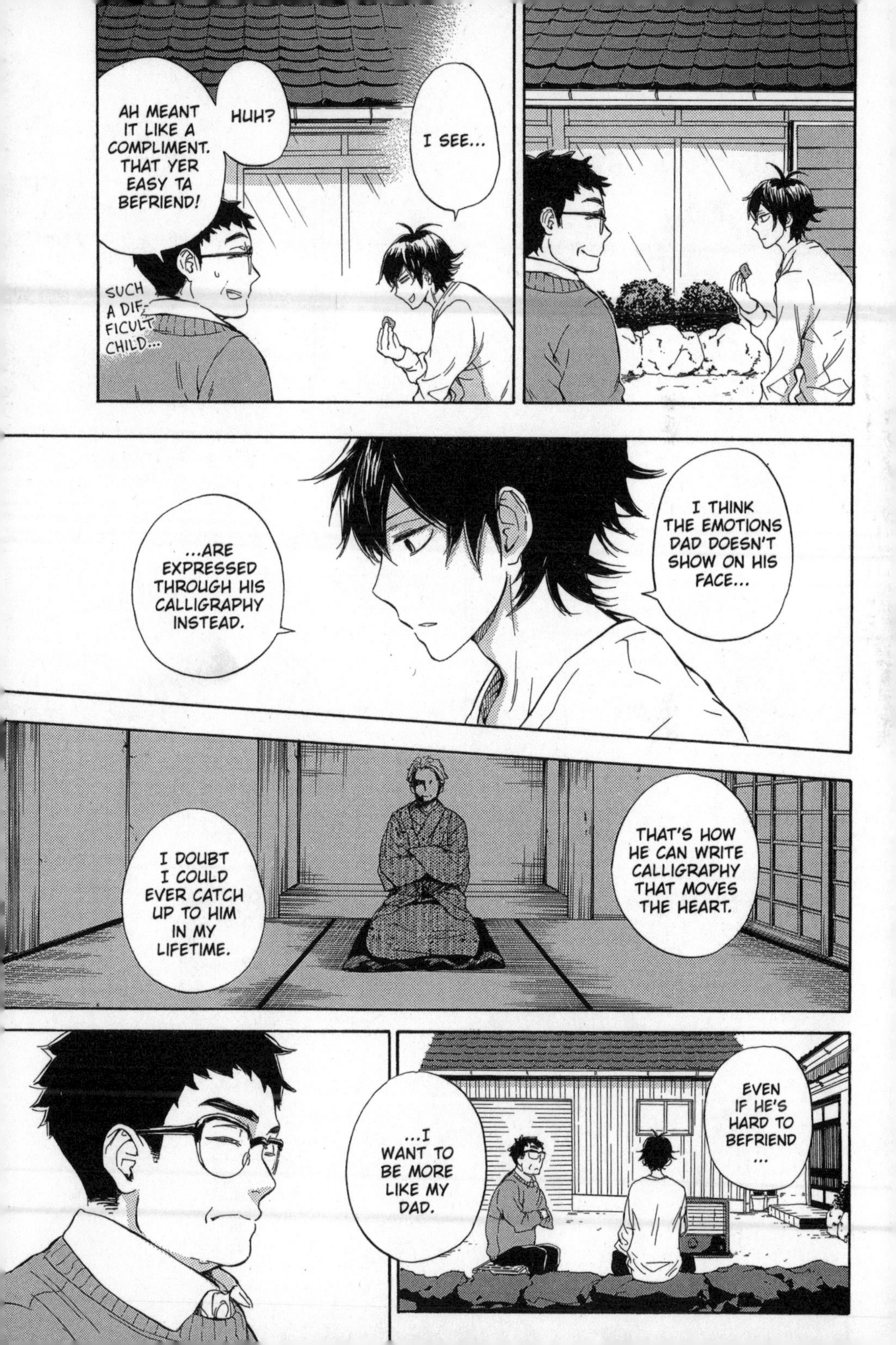
I SEE...
HUH?
AH MEANT IT LIKE A COMPLIMENT. THAT YER EASY TA BEFRIEND!
SUCH A DIF-FICULT CHILD...
I THINK THE EMOTIONS DAD DOESN'T SHOW ON HIS FACE...
...ARE EXPRESSED THROUGH HIS CALLIGRAPHY INSTEAD.
THAT'S HOW HE CAN WRITE CALLIGRAPHY THAT MOVES THE HEART.
I DOUBT I COULD EVER CATCH UP TO HIM IN MY LIFETIME.
EVEN IF HE'S HARD TO BEFRIEND...
...I WANT TO BE MORE LIKE MY DAD.

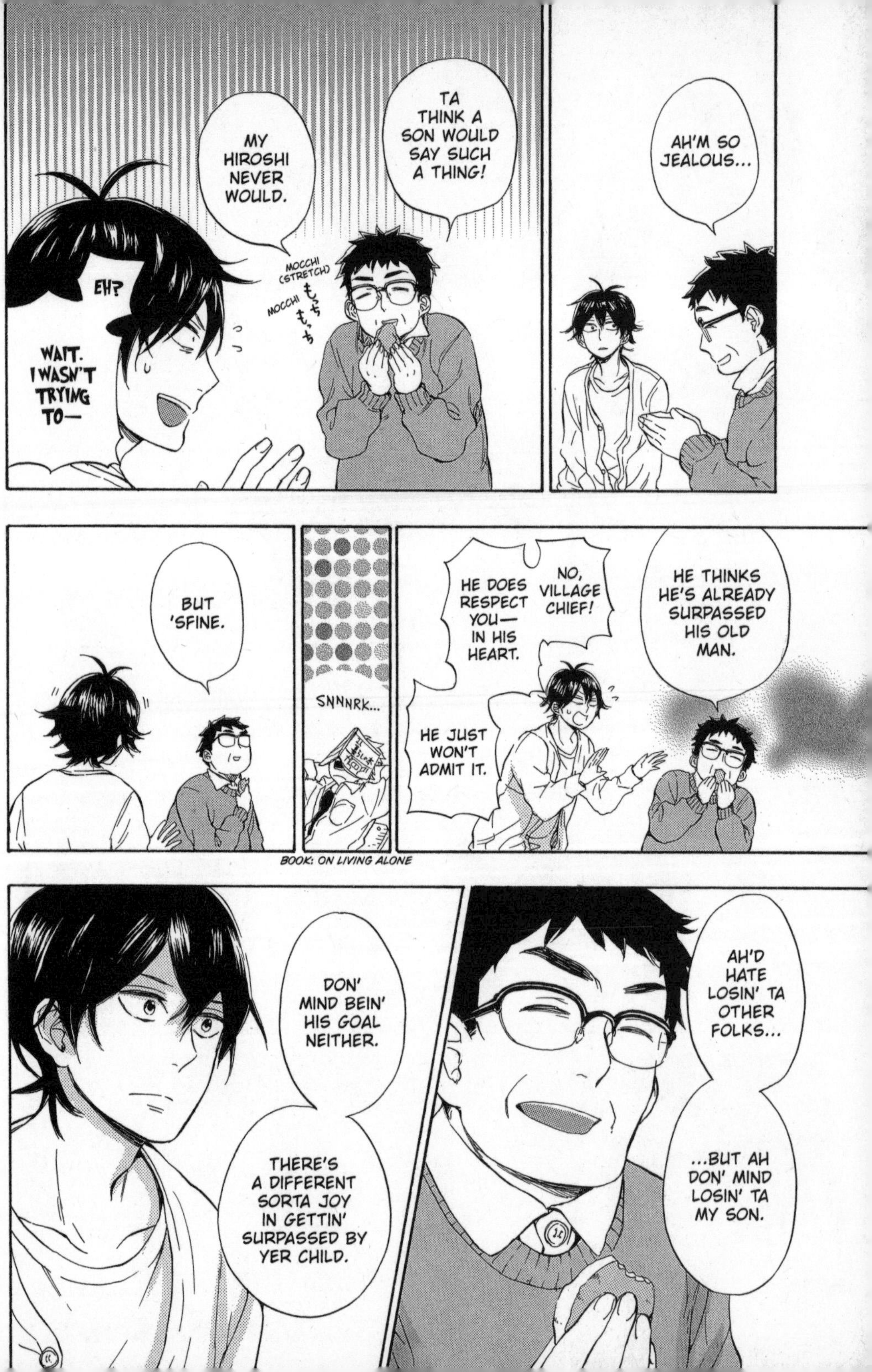
AH'M SO JEALOUS...
TA THINK A SON WOULD SAY SUCH A THING!
MY HIROSHI NEVER WOULD.
MOCCHI (STRETCH) もっち
MOCCHI もっち
EH?
WAIT. I WASN'T TRYING TO—
HE THINKS HE'S ALREADY SURPASSED HIS OLD MAN.
NO, VILLAGE CHIEF!
HE DOES RESPECT YOU— IN HIS HEART.
HE JUST WON'T ADMIT IT.
SNNNRK...
BOOK: ON LIVING ALONE
BUT 'SFINE.
AH'D HATE LOSIN' TA OTHER FOLKS...
...BUT AH DON' MIND LOSIN' TA MY SON.
DON' MIND BEIN' HIS GOAL NEITHER.
THERE'S A DIFFERENT SORTA JOY IN GETTIN' SURPASSED BY YER CHILD.

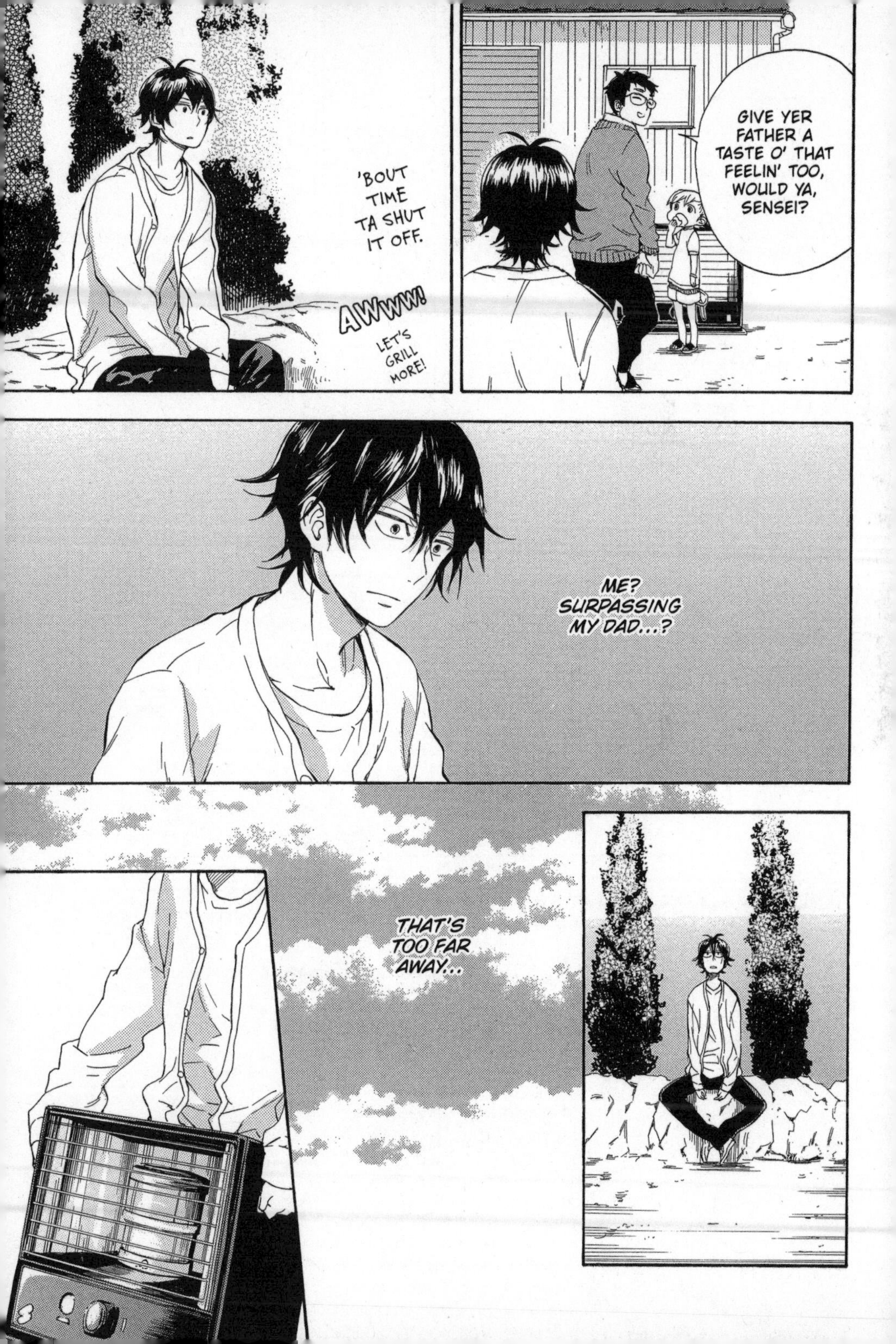
GIVE YER FATHER A TASTE O' THAT FEELIN' TOO, WOULD YA, SENSEI?
'BOUT TIME TA SHUT IT OFF.
AWWW!
LET'S GRILL MORE!
ME? SURPASSING MY DAD...?
THAT'S TOO FAR AWAY...

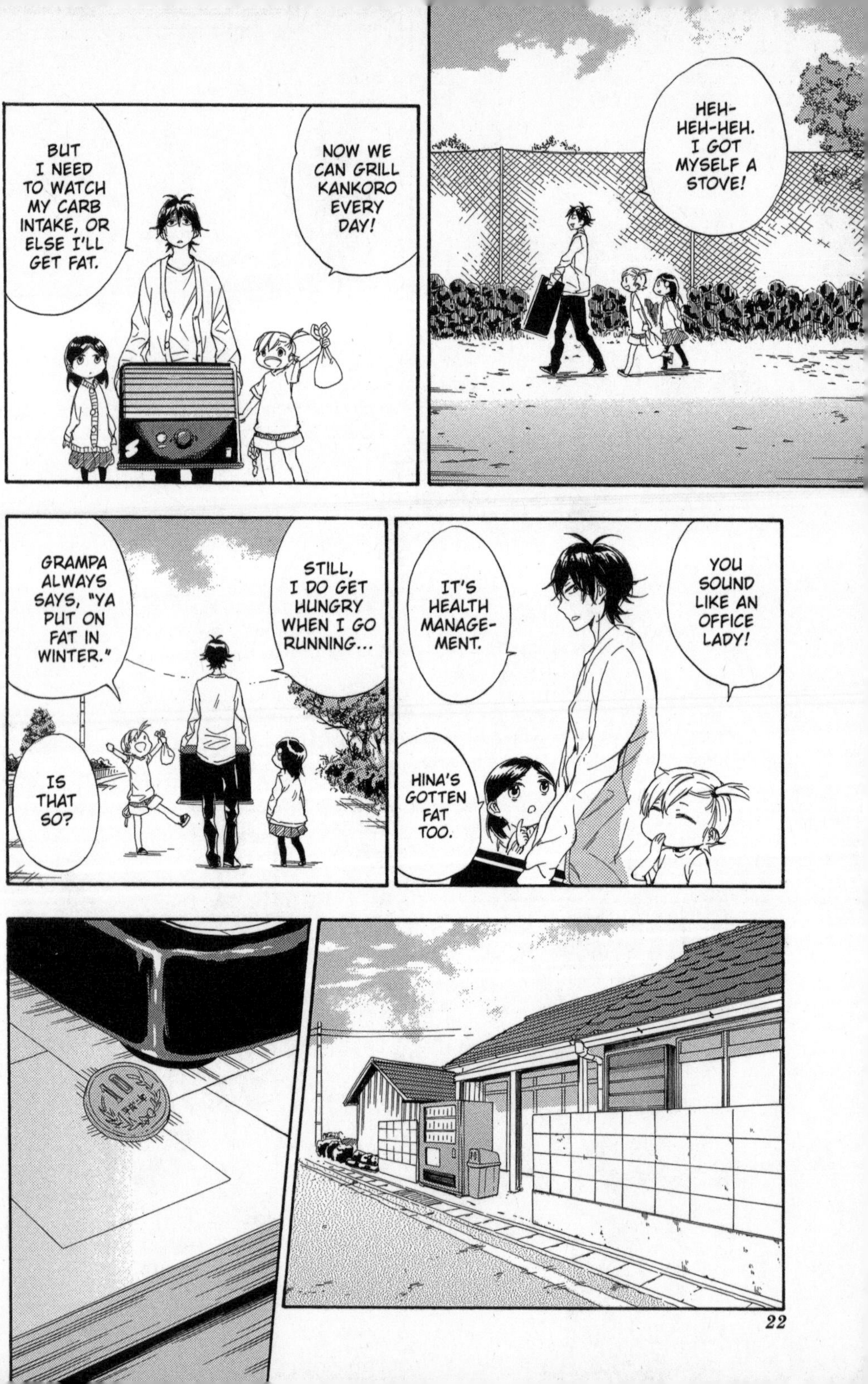
HEH-HEH-HEH. I GOT MYSELF A STOVE!
NOW WE CAN GRILL KANKORO EVERY DAY!
BUT I NEED TO WATCH MY CARB INTAKE, OR ELSE I'LL GET FAT.
YOU SOUND LIKE AN OFFICE LADY!
IT'S HEALTH MANAGE-MENT.
HINA'S GOTTEN FAT TOO.
STILL, I DO GET HUNGRY WHEN I GO RUNNING...
GRAMPA ALWAYS SAYS, "YA PUT ON FAT IN WINTER."
IS THAT SO?

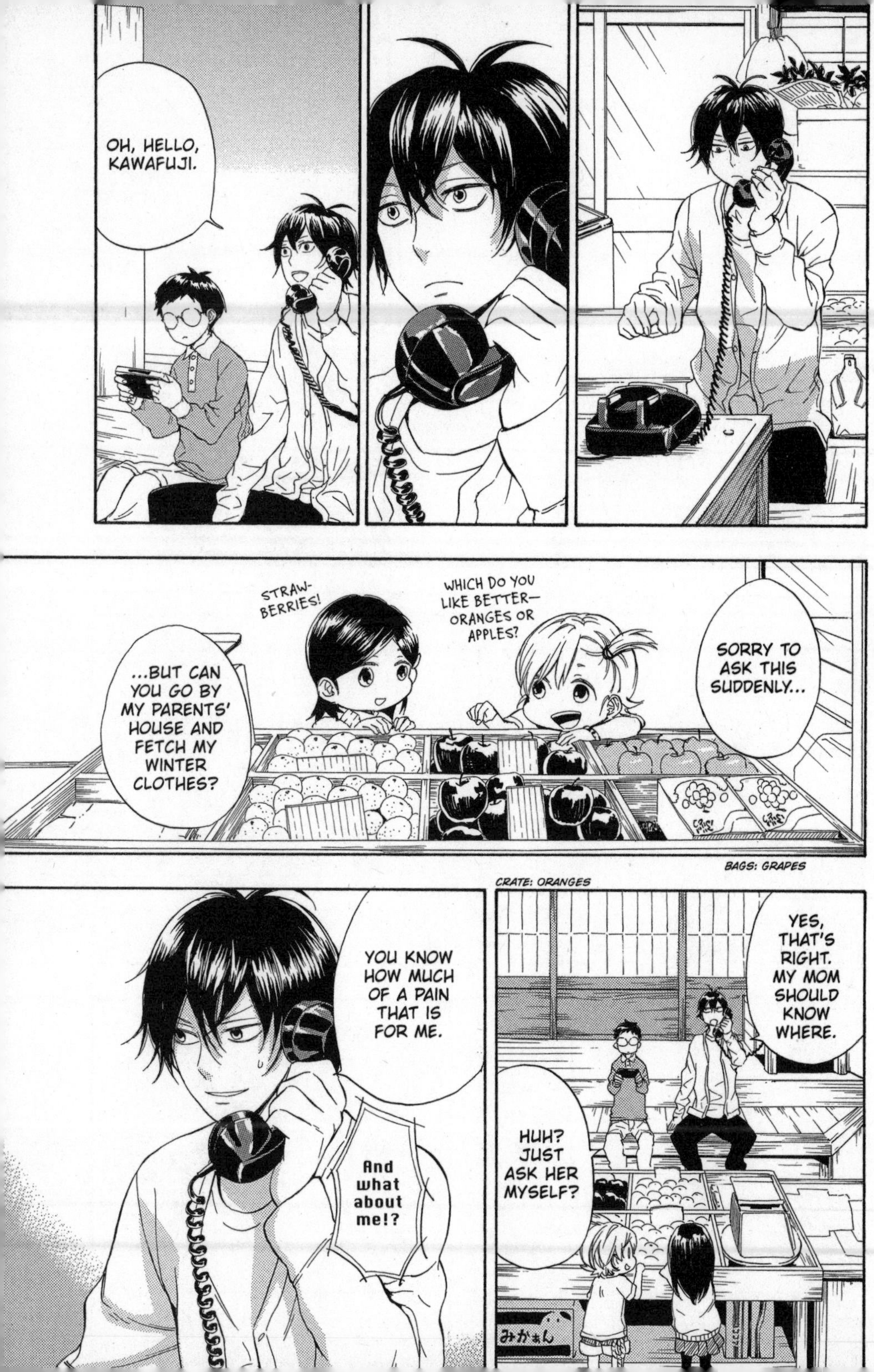
OH, HELLO, KAWAFUJI.
SORRY TO ASK THIS SUDDENLY...
WHICH DO YOU LIKE BETTER—ORANGES OR APPLES?
STRAW-BERRIES!
...BUT CAN YOU GO BY MY PARENTS' HOUSE AND FETCH MY WINTER CLOTHES?
YES, THAT'S RIGHT. MY MOM SHOULD KNOW WHERE.
HUH? JUST ASK HER MYSELF?
みかん
YOU KNOW HOW MUCH OF A PAIN THAT IS FOR ME.
And what about me!?

BAGS: GRAPES

CRATE: ORANGES

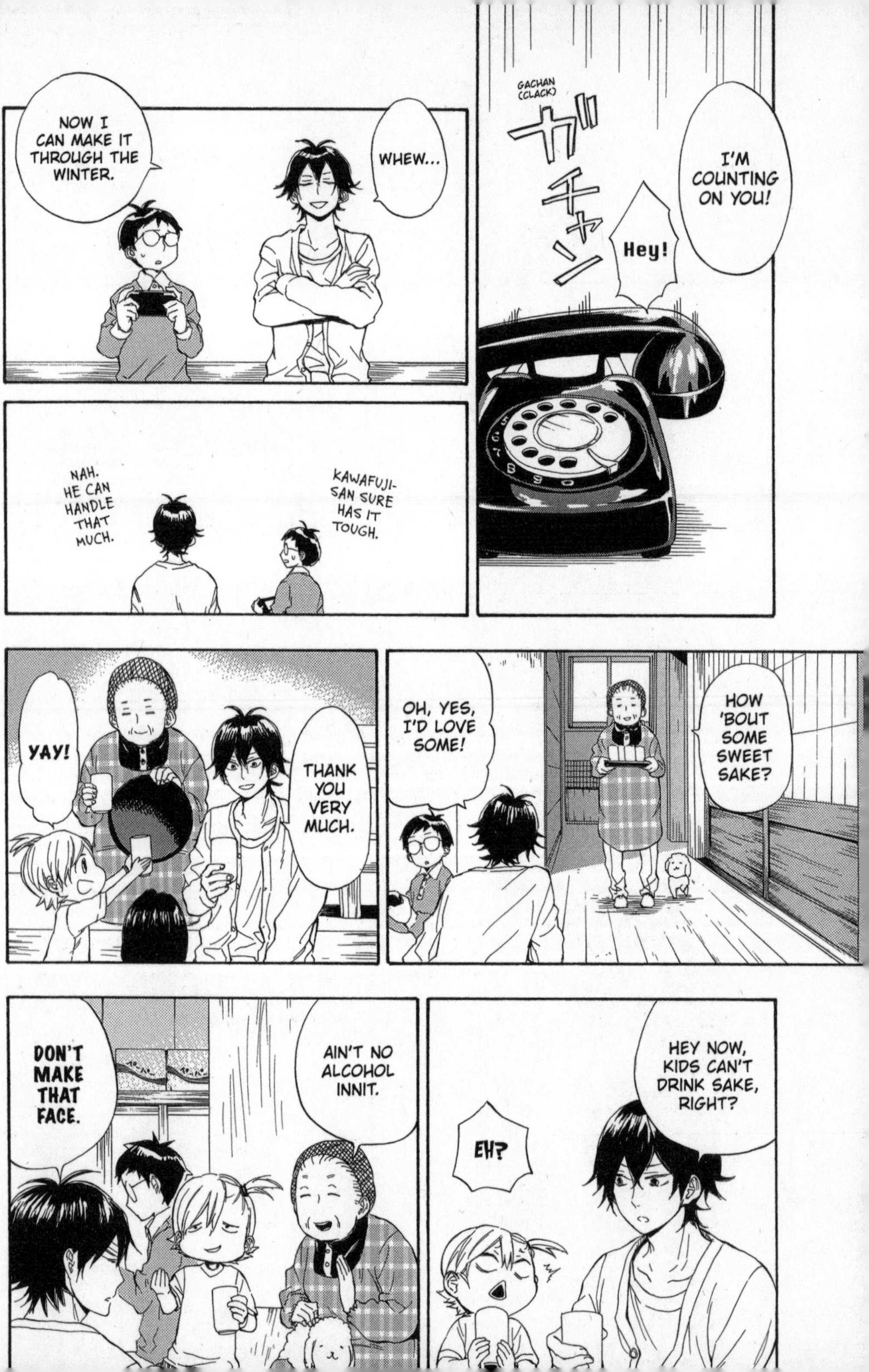
I'M COUNTING ON YOU!
GACHAN (CLACK)
Hey!
WHEW...
NOW I CAN MAKE IT THROUGH THE WINTER.
KAWAFUJI-SAN SURE HAS IT TOUGH.
NAH. HE CAN HANDLE THAT MUCH.
HOW 'BOUT SOME SWEET SAKE?
OH, YES, I'D LOVE SOME!
THANK YOU VERY MUCH.
YAY!
HEY NOW, KIDS CAN'T DRINK SAKE, RIGHT?
EH?
AIN'T NO ALCOHOL INNIT.
DON'T MAKE THAT FACE.

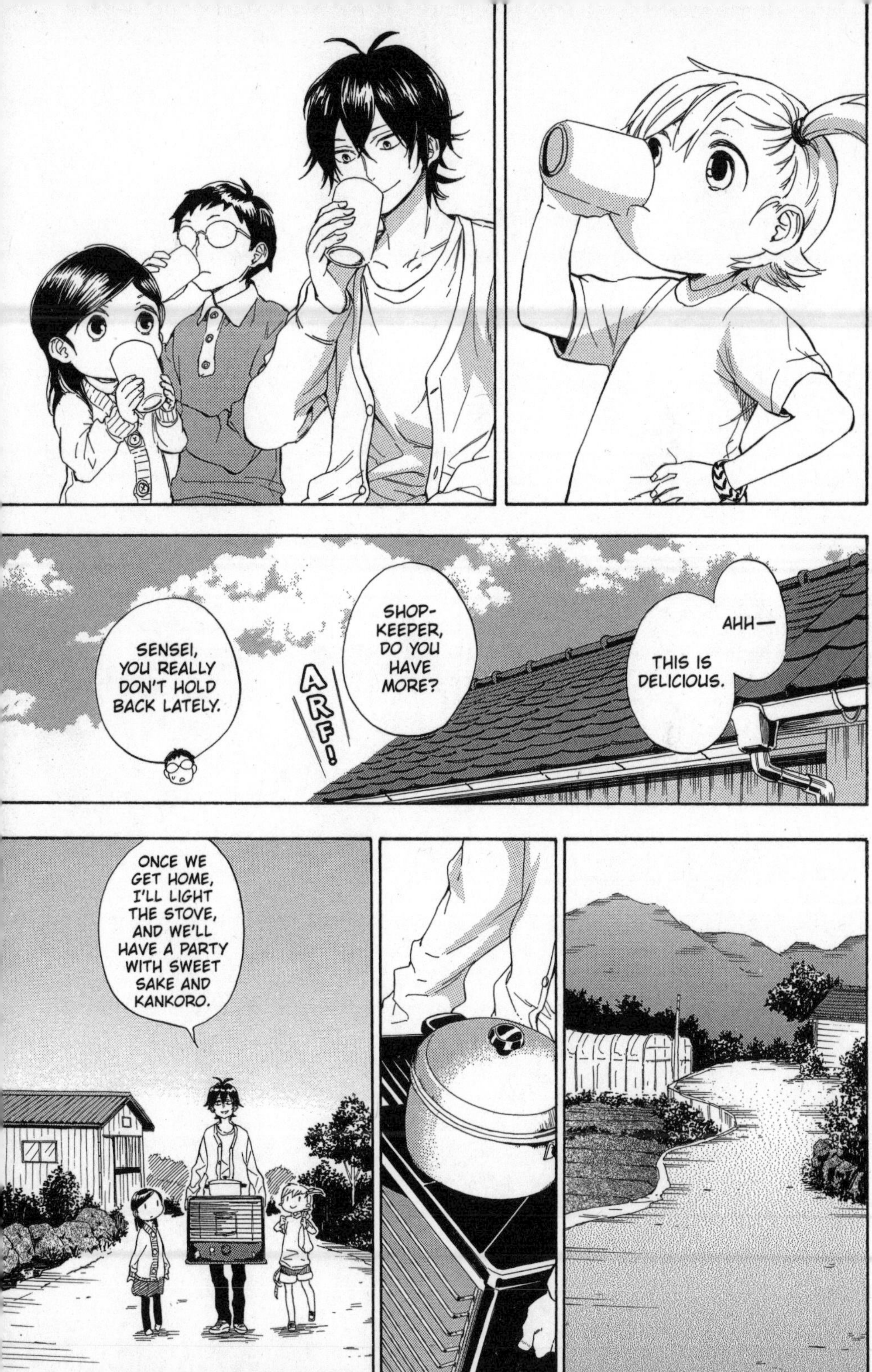
AHH—
THIS IS DELICIOUS.
SHOP-KEEPER, DO YOU HAVE MORE?
ARF!
SENSEI, YOU REALLY DON'T HOLD BACK LATELY.
ONCE WE GET HOME, I'LL LIGHT THE STOVE, AND WE'LL HAVE A PARTY WITH SWEET SAKE AND KANKORO.

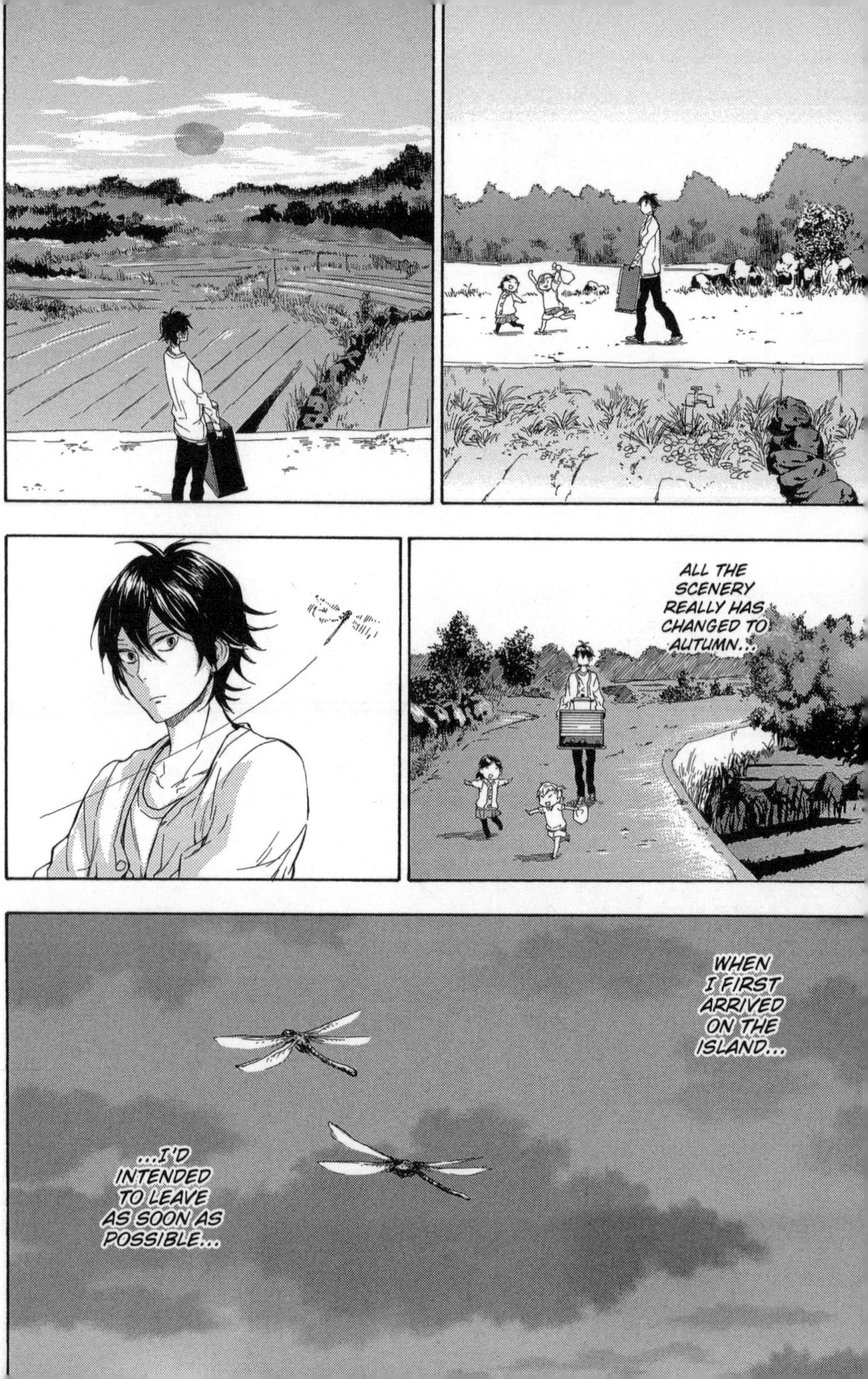
ALL THE SCENERY REALLY HAS CHANGED TO AUTUMN...
WHEN I FIRST ARRIVED ON THE ISLAND...
...I'D INTENDED TO LEAVE AS SOON AS POSSIBLE...

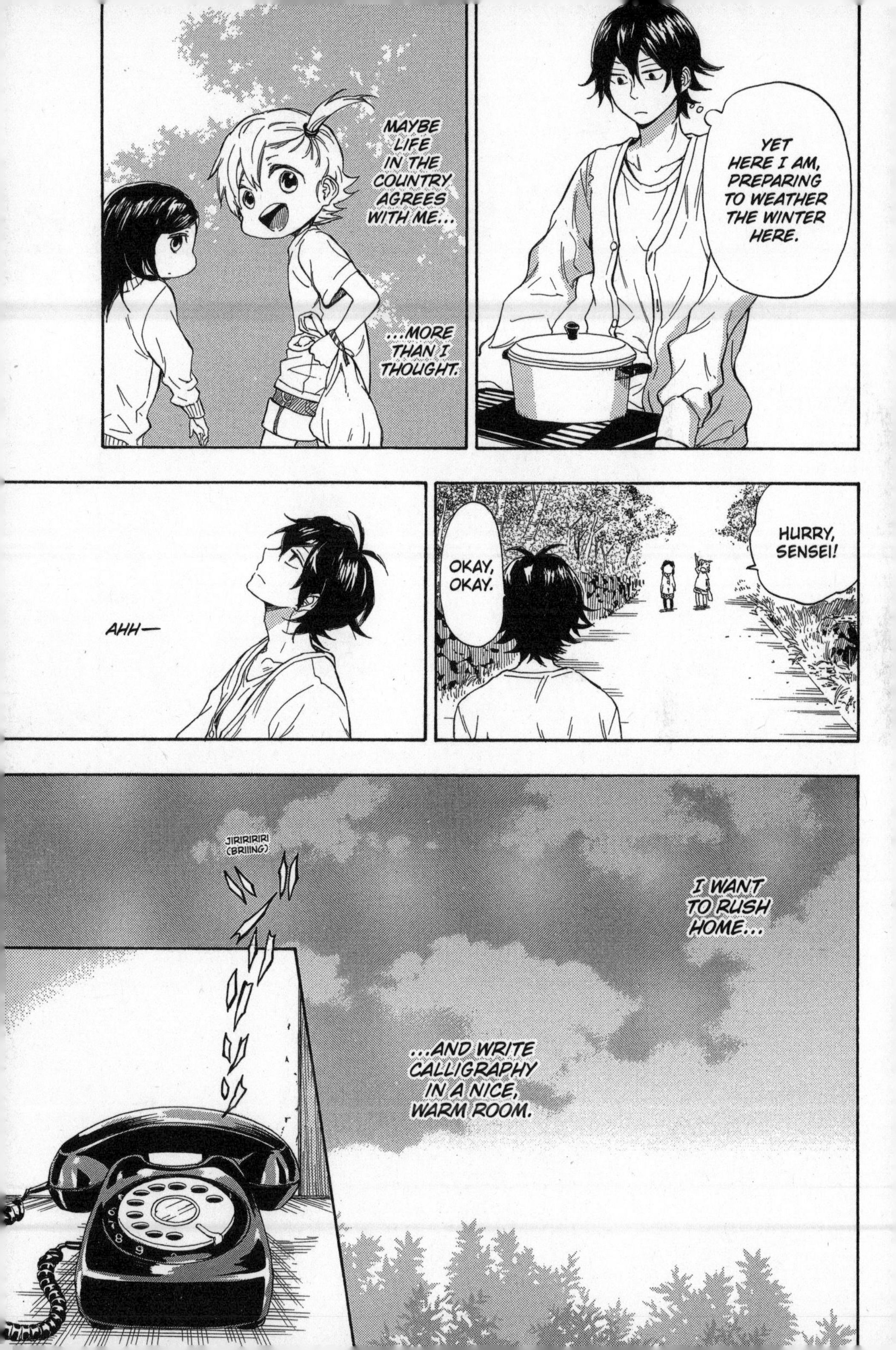
YET HERE I AM, PREPARING TO WEATHER THE WINTER HERE.
MAYBE LIFE IN THE COUNTRY AGREES WITH ME...
...MORE THAN I THOUGHT.
HURRY, SENSEI!
OKAY, OKAY.
AHH—
I WANT TO RUSH HOME...
JIRIRIRIRI (BRIIING)
...AND WRITE CALLIGRAPHY IN A NICE, WARM ROOM.

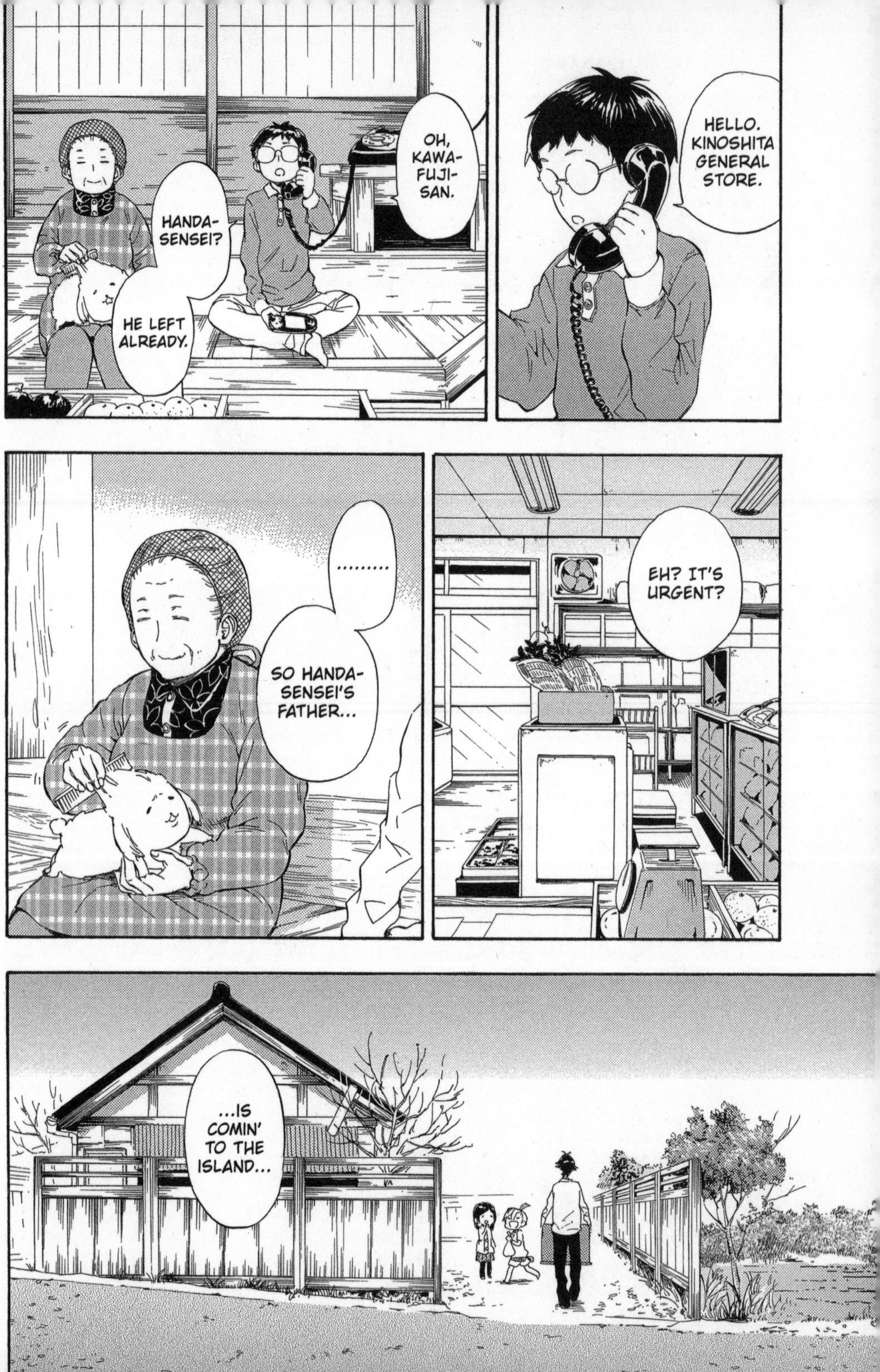
HELLO. KINOSHITA GENERAL STORE.
OH, KAWA-FUJI-SAN.
HANDA-SENSEI?
HE LEFT ALREADY.
EH? IT'S URGENT?
....
SO HANDA-SENSEI'S FATHER...
...IS COMIN' TO THE ISLAND...

BONUS

KANKORO MOCHI'S GRILLED!
SWEET SAKE'S WARM AND READY!
NOW IT'S LIKE...THE WEATHER'S HOT AGAIN ...

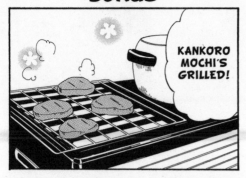

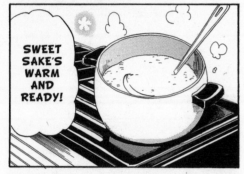

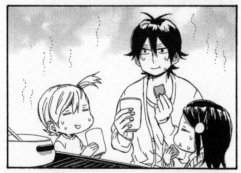

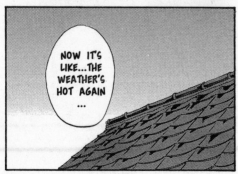

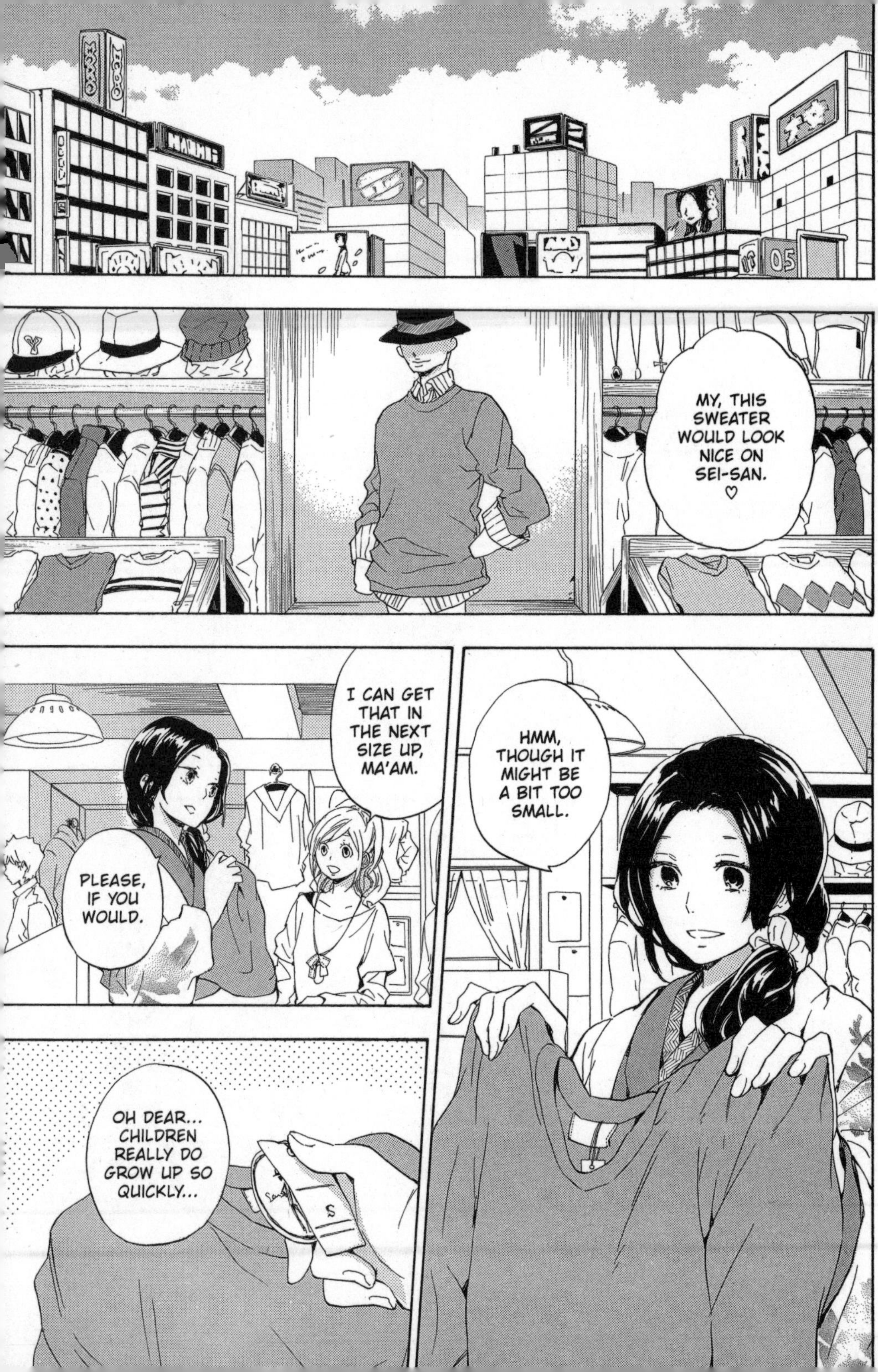
MY, THIS SWEATER WOULD LOOK NICE ON SEI-SAN. ♡
HMM, THOUGH IT MIGHT BE A BIT TOO SMALL.
I CAN GET THAT IN THE NEXT SIZE UP, MA'AM.
PLEASE, IF YOU WOULD.
OH DEAR... CHILDREN REALLY DO GROW UP SO QUICKLY...

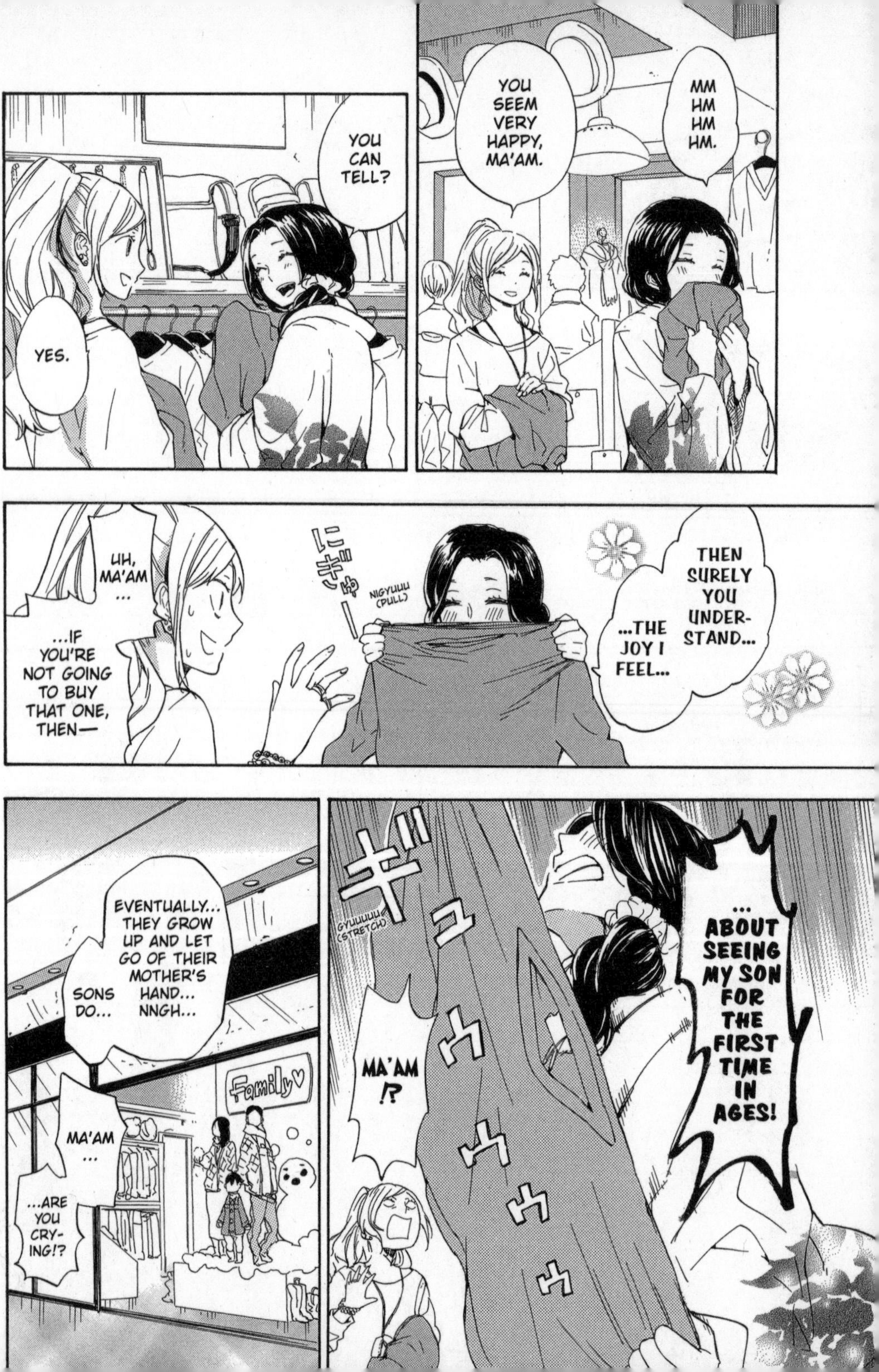
MM HM HM HM.
YOU SEEM VERY HAPPY, MA'AM.
YOU CAN TELL?
YES.
THEN SURELY YOU UNDERSTAND...
...THE JOY I FEEL...
にぎゅー
NIGYUUU (PULL)
UH, MA'AM ...
...IF YOU'RE NOT GOING TO BUY THAT ONE, THEN—
... ABOUT SEEING MY SON FOR THE FIRST TIME IN AGES!
ギュウウウウ
GYUUUUUU (STRETCH)
MA'AM !?
EVENTUALLY... THEY GROW UP AND LET GO OF THEIR MOTHER'S HAND... NNGH...
SONS DO...
Family♡
MA'AM ...
...ARE YOU CRY-ING!?

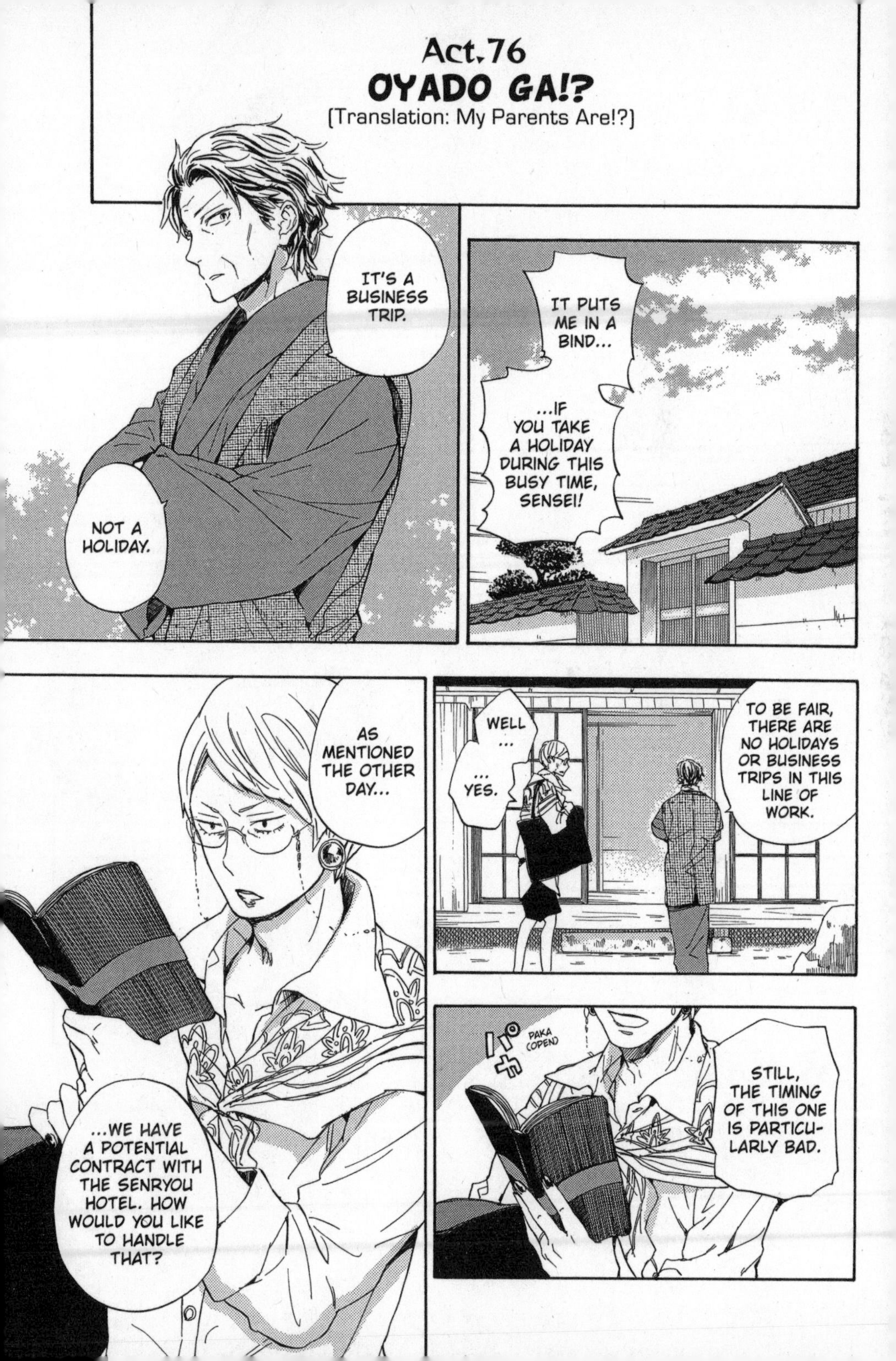
Act.76
OYADO GA!?
[Translation: My Parents Are!?]
IT PUTS ME IN A BIND...
...IF YOU TAKE A HOLIDAY DURING THIS BUSY TIME, SENSEI!
IT'S A BUSINESS TRIP.
NOT A HOLIDAY.
TO BE FAIR, THERE ARE NO HOLIDAYS OR BUSINESS TRIPS IN THIS LINE OF WORK.
WELL...
...YES.
STILL, THE TIMING OF THIS ONE IS PARTICULARLY BAD.
PAKA (OPEN)
AS MENTIONED THE OTHER DAY...
...WE HAVE A POTENTIAL CONTRACT WITH THE SENRYOU HOTEL. HOW WOULD YOU LIKE TO HANDLE THAT?

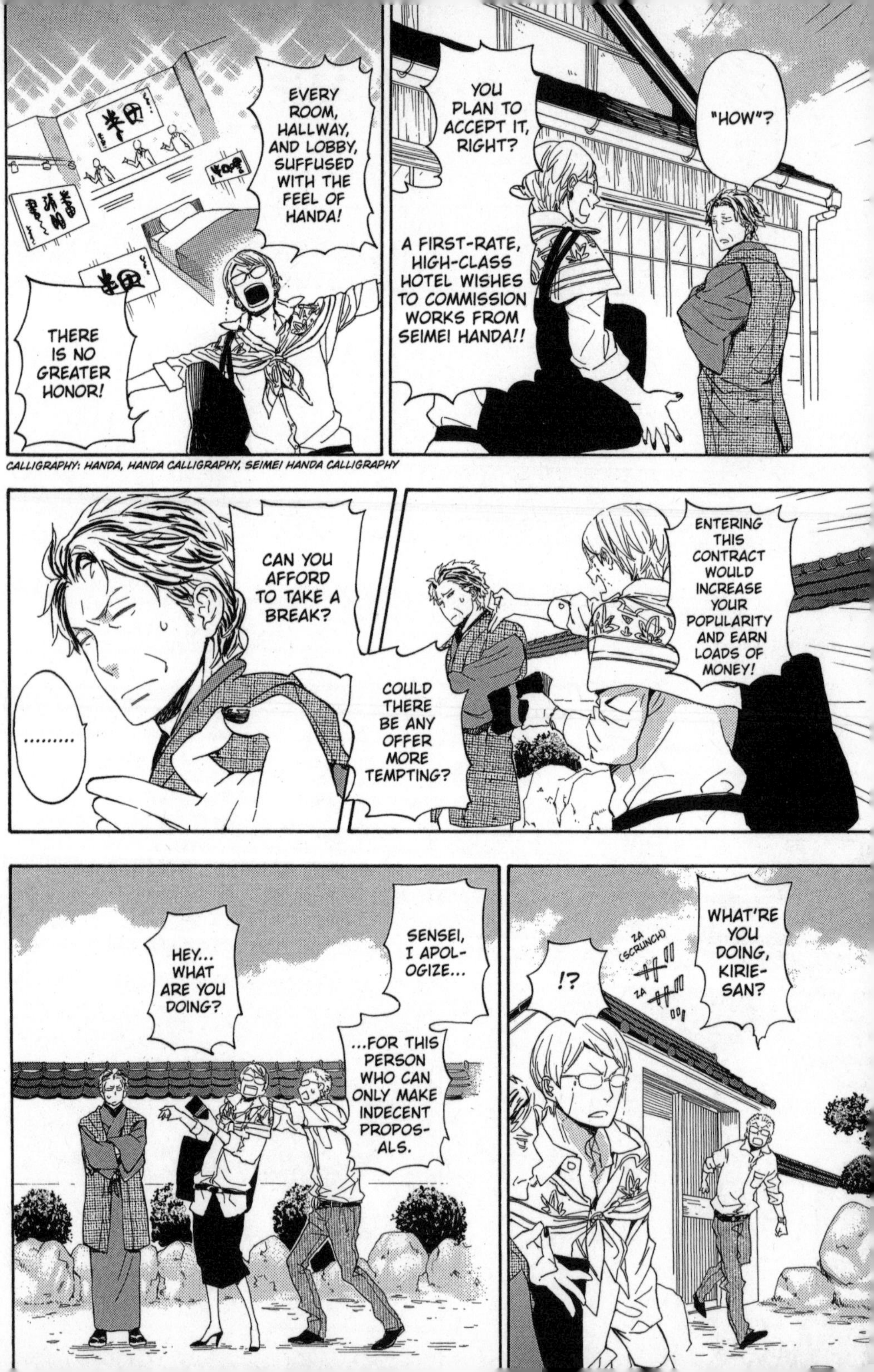
"HOW"?
YOU PLAN TO ACCEPT IT, RIGHT?
A FIRST-RATE, HIGH-CLASS HOTEL WISHES TO COMMISSION WORKS FROM SEIMEI HANDA!!
EVERY ROOM, HALLWAY, AND LOBBY, SUFFUSED WITH THE FEEL OF HANDA!
THERE IS NO GREATER HONOR!
CALLIGRAPHY: HANDA, HANDA CALLIGRAPHY, SEIMEI HANDA CALLIGRAPHY
ENTERING THIS CONTRACT WOULD INCREASE YOUR POPULARITY AND EARN LOADS OF MONEY!
CAN YOU AFFORD TO TAKE A BREAK?
COULD THERE BE ANY OFFER MORE TEMPTING?
....
WHAT'RE YOU DOING, KIRIE-SAN?
ZA (SCRUNCH)
ZA
!?
SENSEI, I APOLOGIZE...
...FOR THIS PERSON WHO CAN ONLY MAKE INDECENT PROPOSALS.
HEY... WHAT ARE YOU DOING?

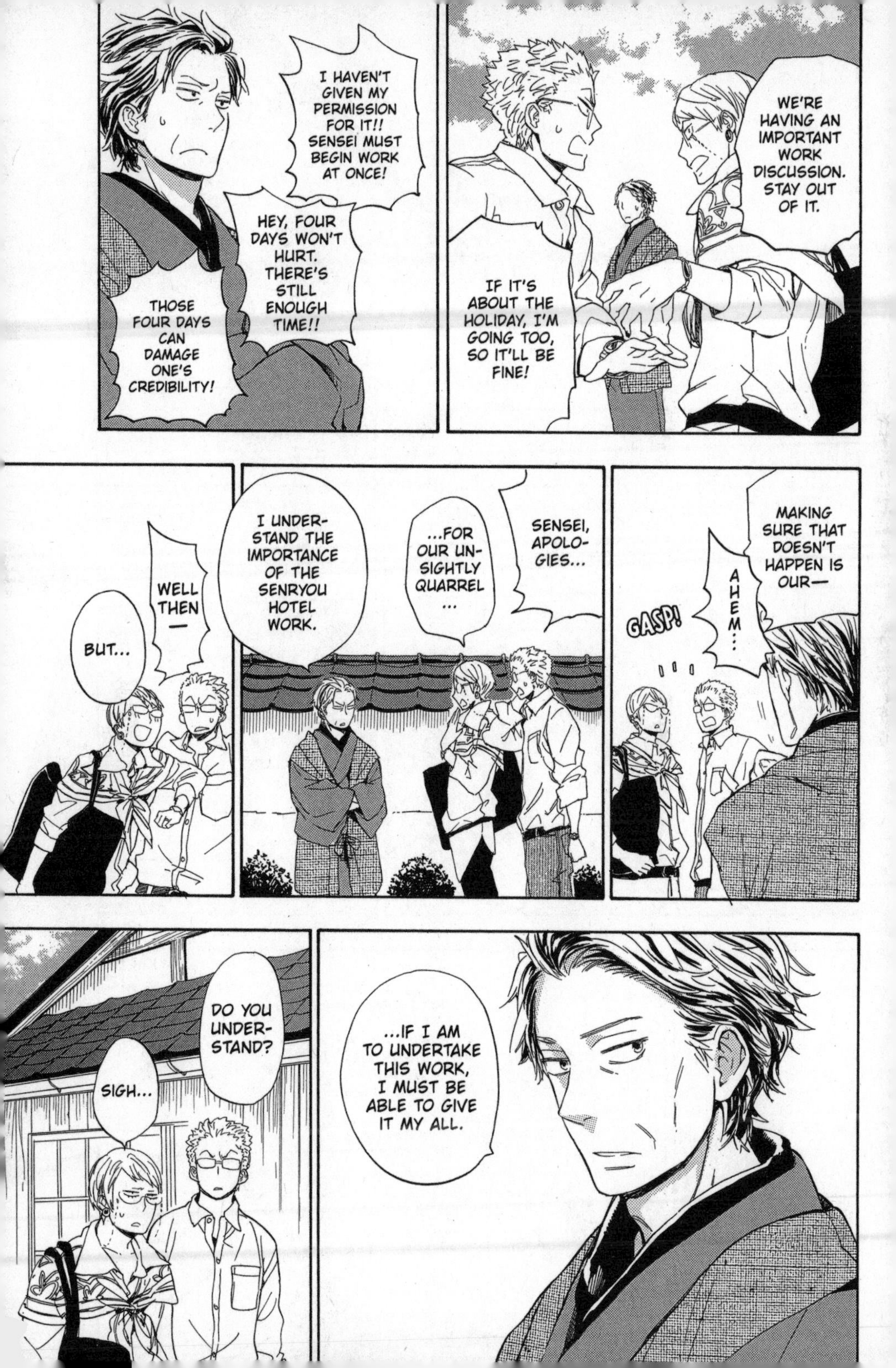
WE'RE HAVING AN IMPORTANT WORK DISCUSSION. STAY OUT OF IT.
IF IT'S ABOUT THE HOLIDAY, I'M GOING TOO, SO IT'LL BE FINE!
I HAVEN'T GIVEN MY PERMISSION FOR IT!! SENSEI MUST BEGIN WORK AT ONCE!
HEY, FOUR DAYS WON'T HURT. THERE'S STILL ENOUGH TIME!!
THOSE FOUR DAYS CAN DAMAGE ONE'S CREDIBILITY!
MAKING SURE THAT DOESN'T HAPPEN IS OUR—
AHEM...
GASP!
SENSEI, APOLOGIES...
...FOR OUR UNSIGHTLY QUARREL...
I UNDERSTAND THE IMPORTANCE OF THE SENRYOU HOTEL WORK.
WELL THEN—
BUT...
...IF I AM TO UNDERTAKE THIS WORK, I MUST BE ABLE TO GIVE IT MY ALL.
DO YOU UNDERSTAND?
SIGH...

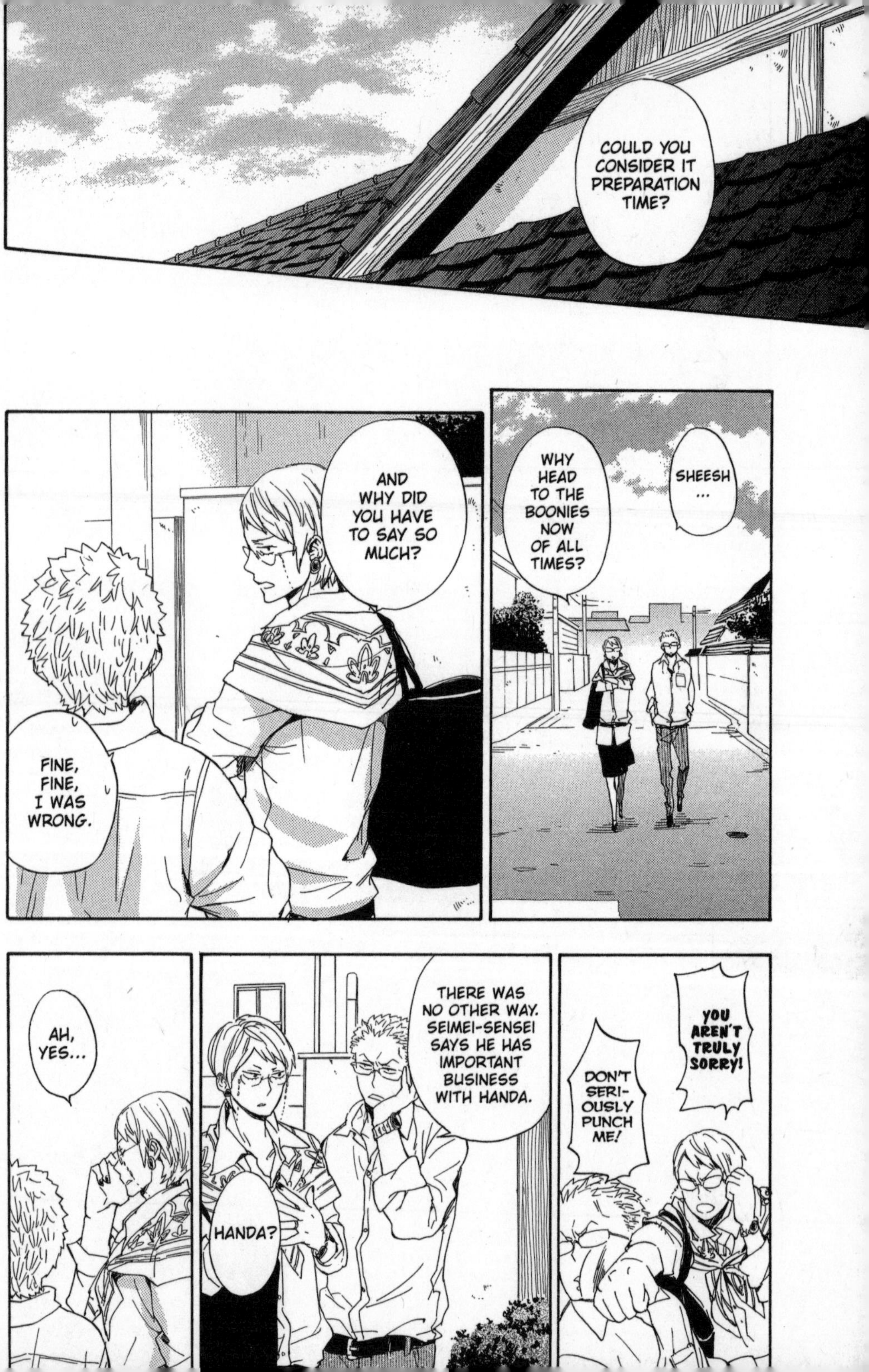
COULD YOU CONSIDER IT PREPARATION TIME?
SHEESH...
WHY HEAD TO THE BOONIES NOW OF ALL TIMES?
AND WHY DID YOU HAVE TO SAY SO MUCH?
FINE, FINE, I WAS WRONG.
YOU AREN'T TRULY SORRY!
DON'T SERIOUSLY PUNCH ME!
THERE WAS NO OTHER WAY. SEIMEI-SENSEI SAYS HE HAS IMPORTANT BUSINESS WITH HANDA.
HANDA?
AH, YES...

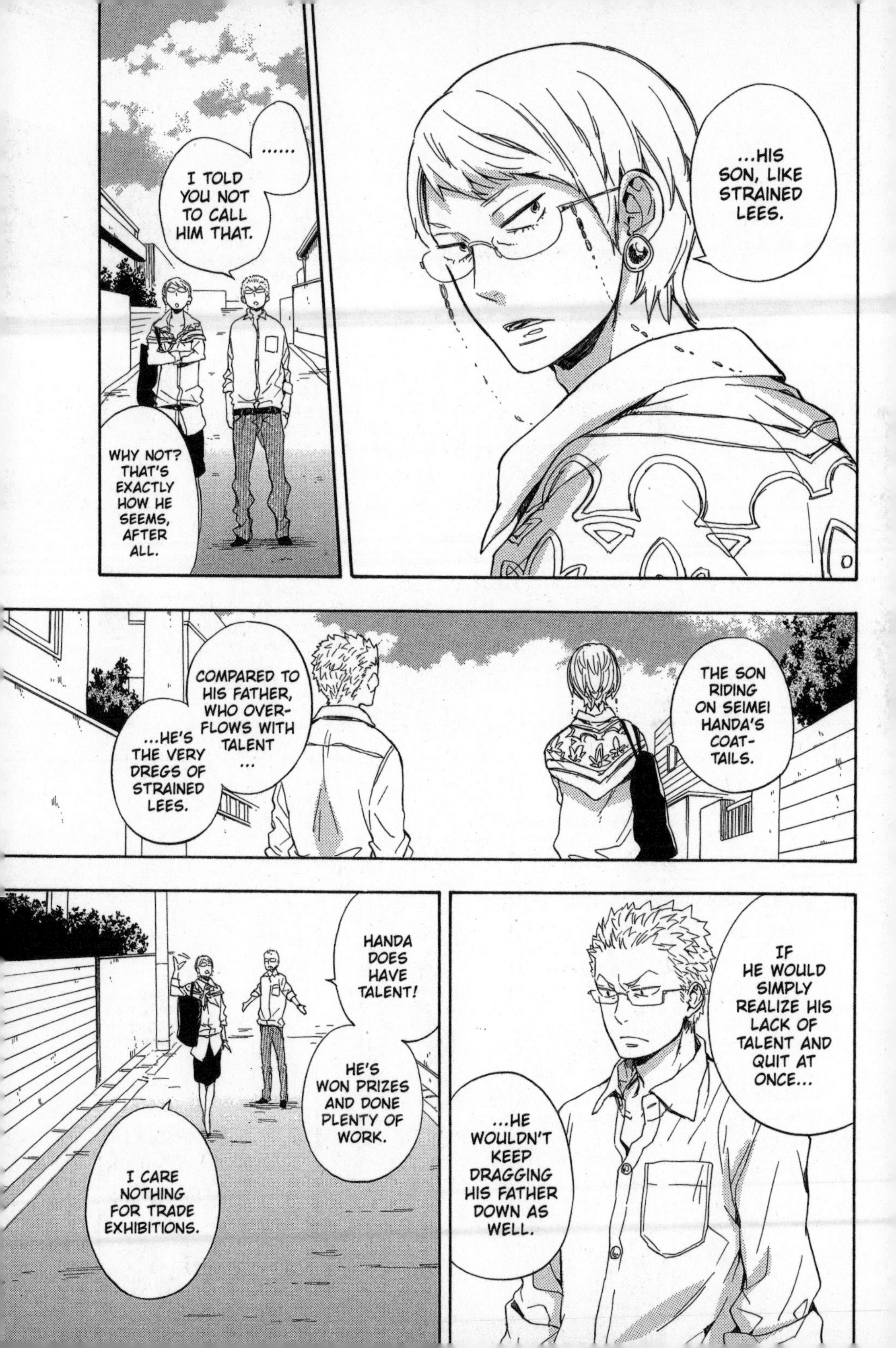
...HIS SON, LIKE STRAINED LEES.
......
I TOLD YOU NOT TO CALL HIM THAT.
WHY NOT? THAT'S EXACTLY HOW HE SEEMS, AFTER ALL.
THE SON RIDING ON SEIMEI HANDA'S COAT-TAILS.
COMPARED TO HIS FATHER, WHO OVER-FLOWS WITH TALENT...
...HE'S THE VERY DREGS OF STRAINED LEES.
IF HE WOULD SIMPLY REALIZE HIS LACK OF TALENT AND QUIT AT ONCE...
...HE WOULDN'T KEEP DRAGGING HIS FATHER DOWN AS WELL.
HANDA DOES HAVE TALENT!
HE'S WON PRIZES AND DONE PLENTY OF WORK.
I CARE NOTHING FOR TRADE EXHIBITIONS.

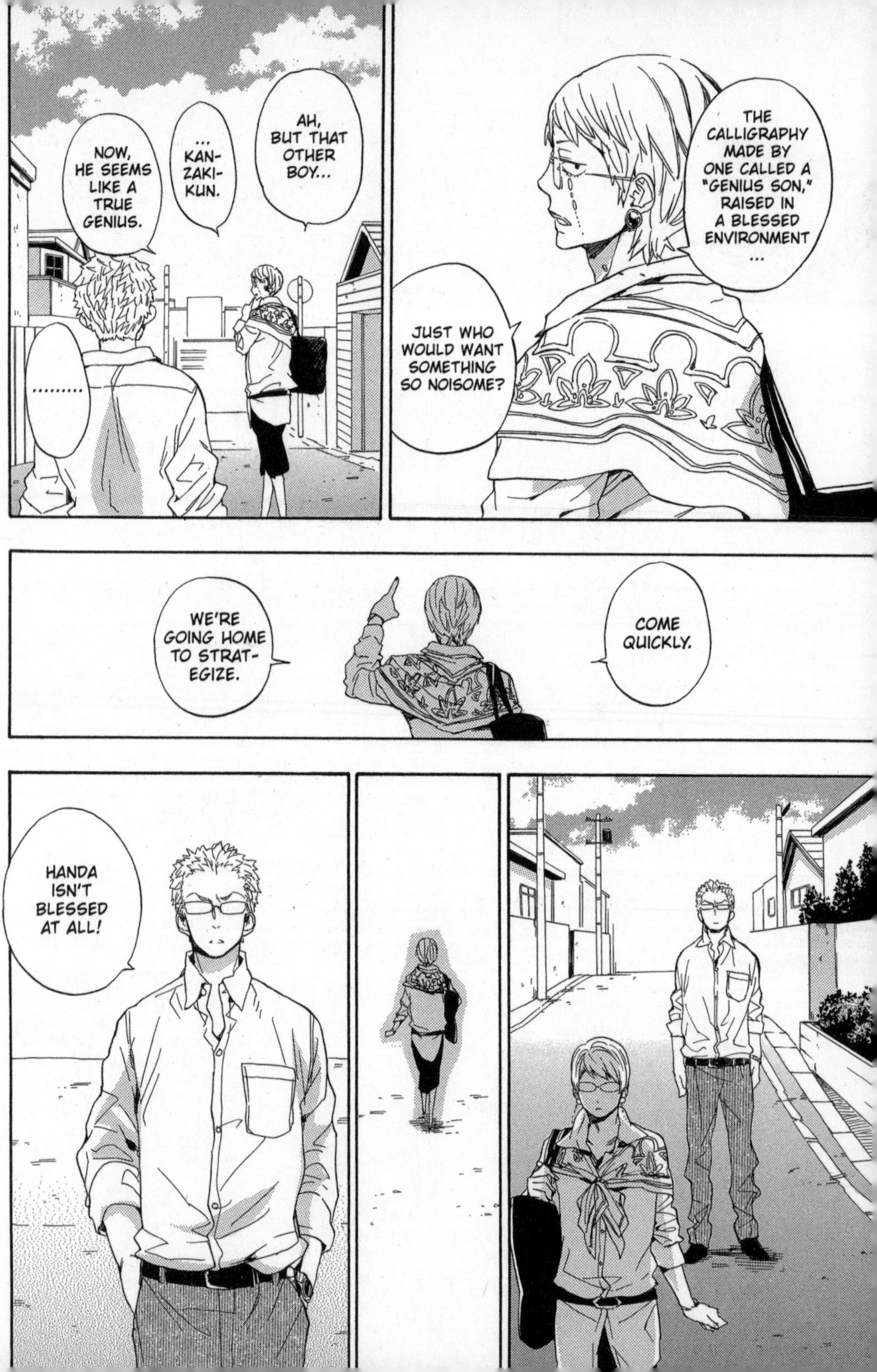
THE CALLIGRAPHY MADE BY ONE CALLED A "GENIUS SON," RAISED IN A BLESSED ENVIRONMENT ...
JUST WHO WOULD WANT SOMETHING SO NOISOME?
AH, BUT THAT OTHER BOY...
... KAN-ZAKI-KUN.
NOW, HE SEEMS LIKE A TRUE GENIUS.
....
COME QUICKLY.
WE'RE GOING HOME TO STRAT-EGIZE.
HANDA ISN'T BLESSED AT ALL!

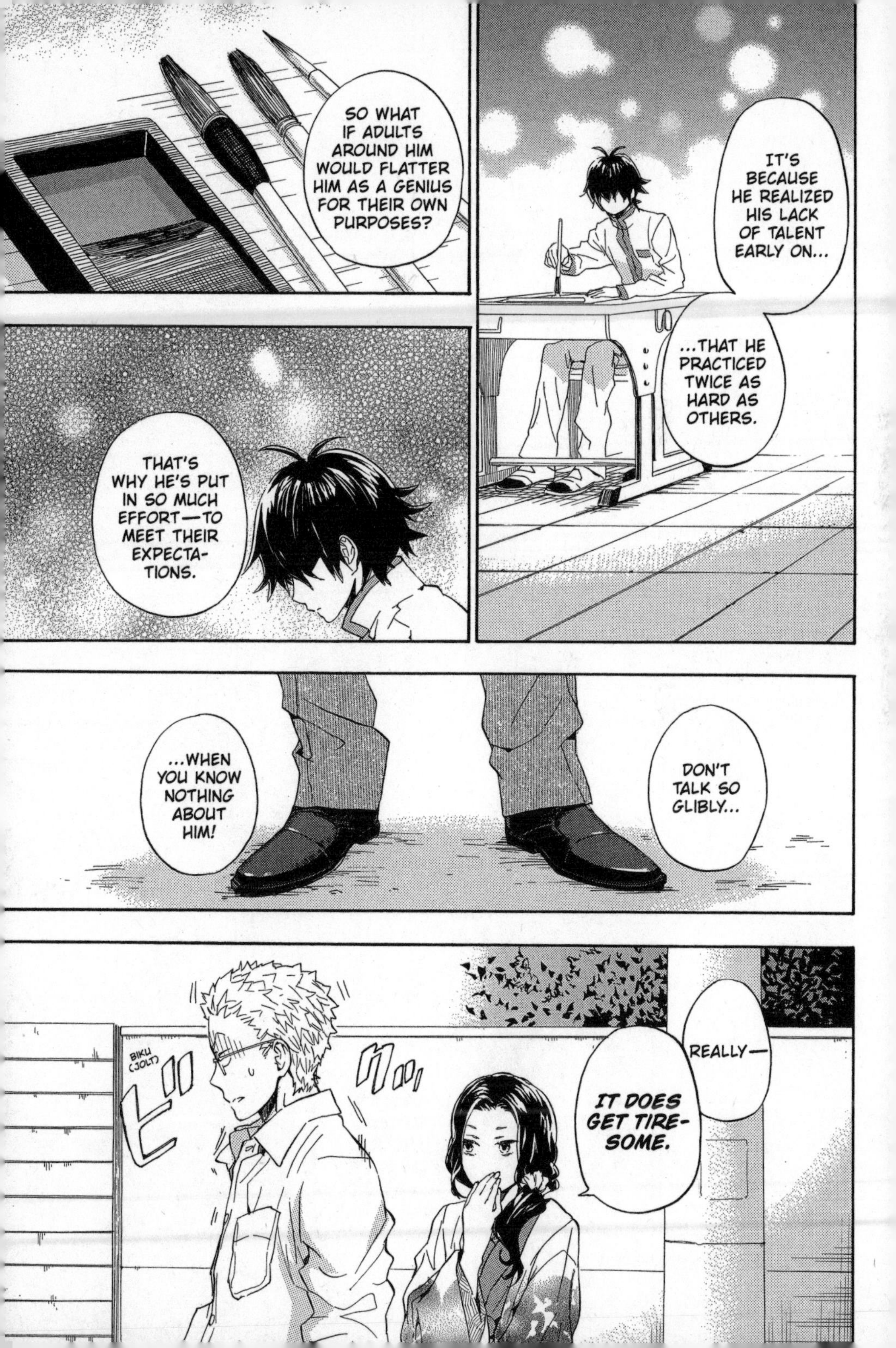
IT'S BECAUSE HE REALIZED HIS LACK OF TALENT EARLY ON...
...THAT HE PRACTICED TWICE AS HARD AS OTHERS.
SO WHAT IF ADULTS AROUND HIM WOULD FLATTER HIM AS A GENIUS FOR THEIR OWN PURPOSES?
THAT'S WHY HE'S PUT IN SO MUCH EFFORT—TO MEET THEIR EXPECTATIONS.
DON'T TALK SO GLIBLY...
...WHEN YOU KNOW NOTHING ABOUT HIM!
REALLY—
IT DOES GET TIRESOME.
BIKU (JOLT)

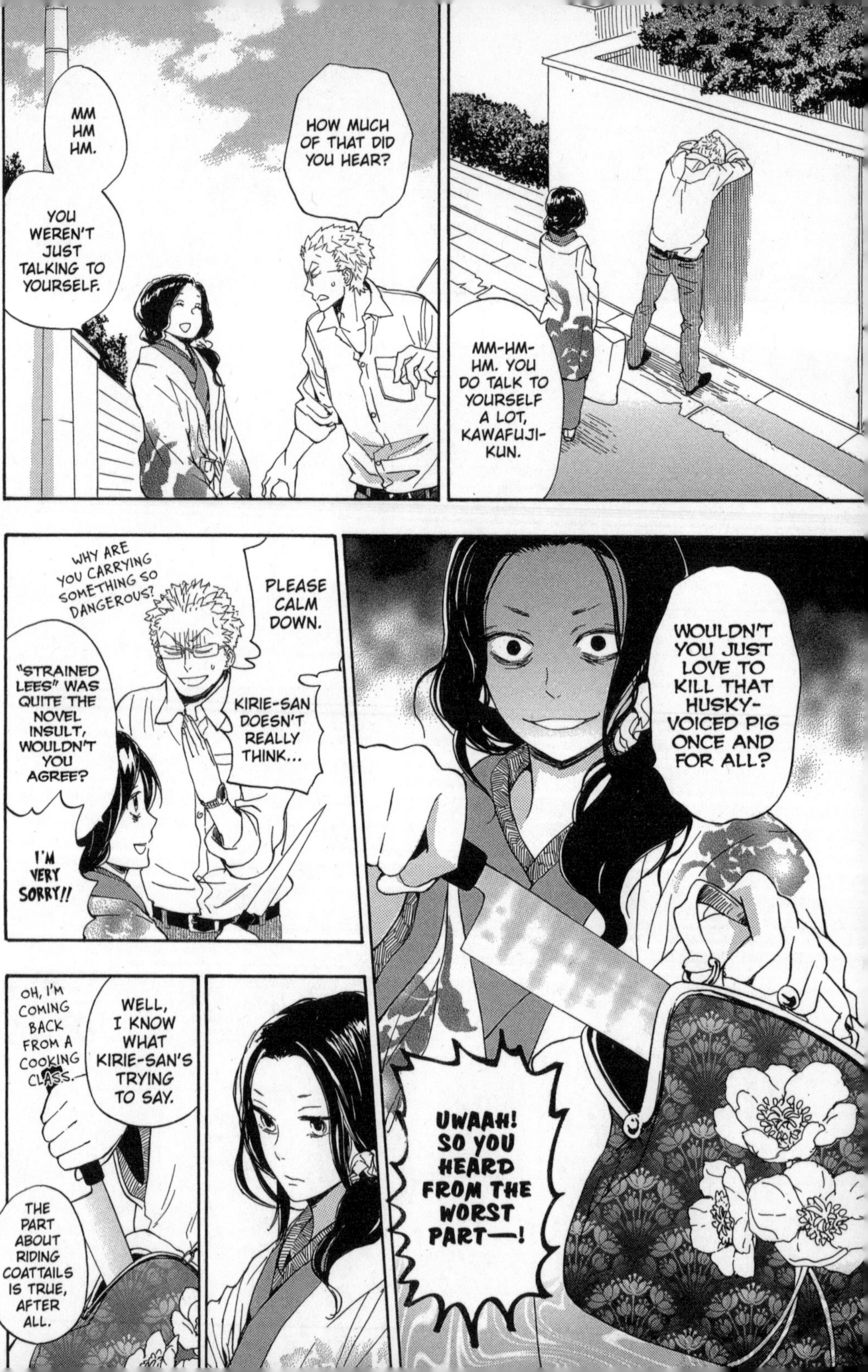
MM-HM-HM. YOU DO TALK TO YOURSELF A LOT, KAWAFUJI-KUN.
HOW MUCH OF THAT DID YOU HEAR?
MM HM HM.
YOU WEREN'T JUST TALKING TO YOURSELF.
WOULDN'T YOU JUST LOVE TO KILL THAT HUSKY-VOICED PIG ONCE AND FOR ALL?
UWAAH! SO YOU HEARD FROM THE WORST PART—!
PLEASE CALM DOWN.
WHY ARE YOU CARRYING SOMETHING SO DANGEROUS?
KIRIE-SAN DOESN'T REALLY THINK...
"STRAINED LEES" WAS QUITE THE NOVEL INSULT, WOULDN'T YOU AGREE?
I'M VERY SORRY!!
WELL, I KNOW WHAT KIRIE-SAN'S TRYING TO SAY.
OH, I'M COMING BACK FROM A COOKING CLASS.
THE PART ABOUT RIDING COATTAILS IS TRUE, AFTER ALL.

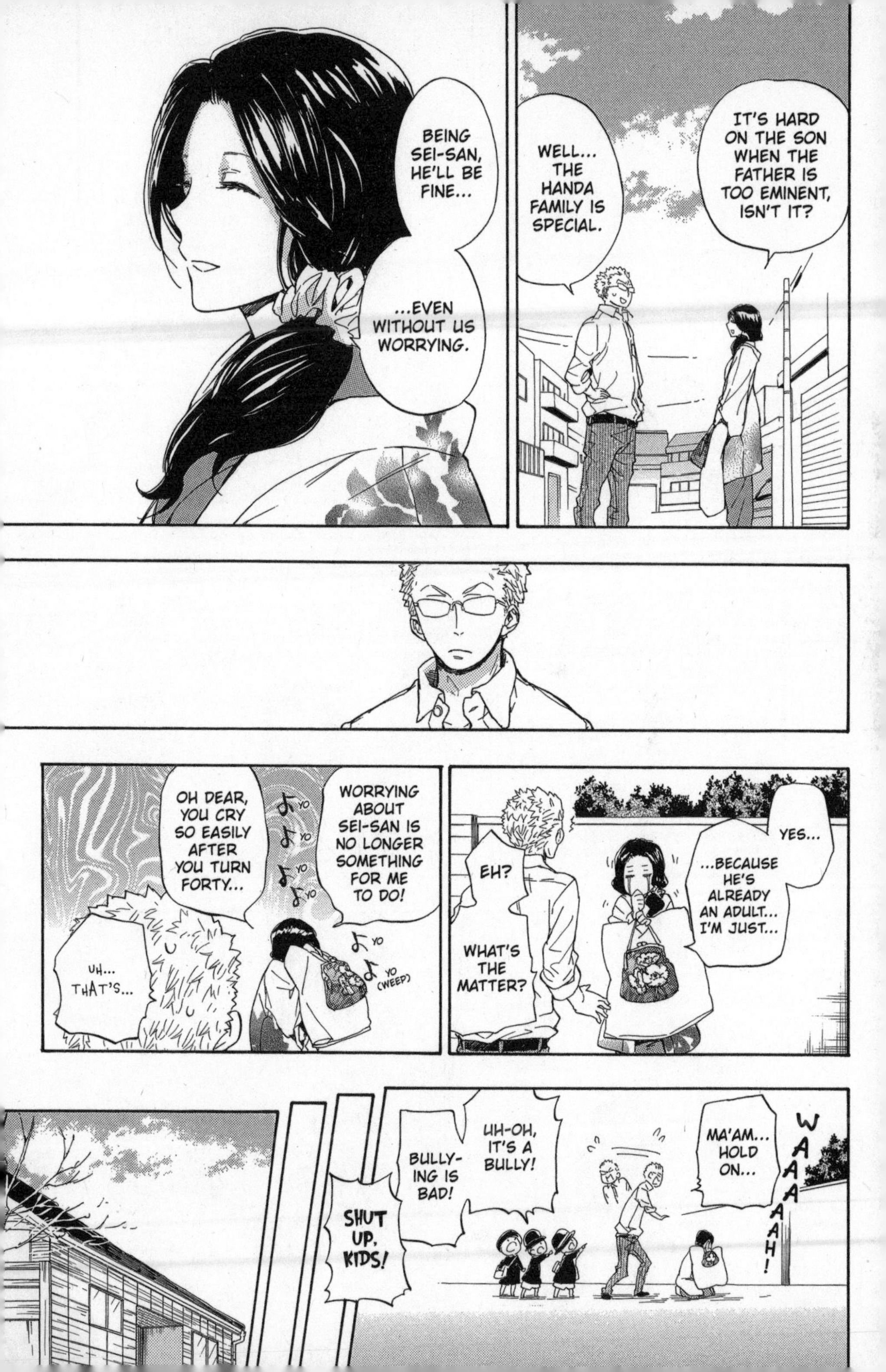
IT'S HARD ON THE SON WHEN THE FATHER IS TOO EMINENT, ISN'T IT?
WELL... THE HANDA FAMILY IS SPECIAL.
BEING SEI-SAN, HE'LL BE FINE...
...EVEN WITHOUT US WORRYING.
YES...
...BECAUSE HE'S ALREADY AN ADULT... I'M JUST...
EH?
WHAT'S THE MATTER?
WORRYING ABOUT SEI-SAN IS NO LONGER SOMETHING FOR ME TO DO!
YO YO YO YO YO YO (WEEP)
OH DEAR, YOU CRY SO EASILY AFTER YOU TURN FORTY...
UH... THAT'S...
WAAAAAH!
MA'AM... HOLD ON...
UH-OH, IT'S A BULLY!
BULLY-ING IS BAD!
SHUT UP, KIDS!

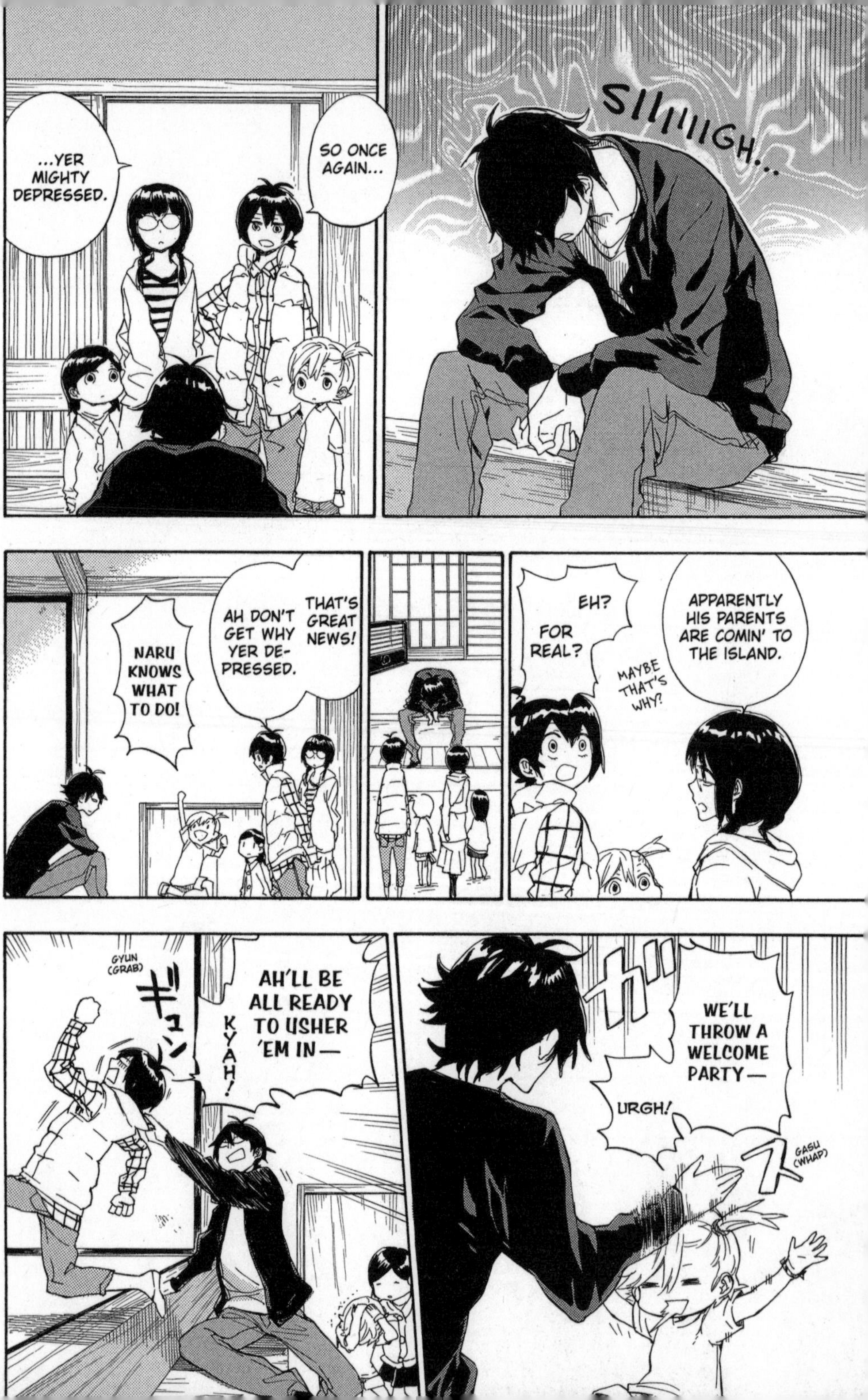
SIIIIIGH...
SO ONCE AGAIN...
...YER MIGHTY DEPRESSED.
APPARENTLY HIS PARENTS ARE COMIN' TO THE ISLAND.
MAYBE THAT'S WHY?
EH? FOR REAL?
THAT'S GREAT NEWS!
AH DON'T GET WHY YER DE-PRESSED.
NARU KNOWS WHAT TO DO!
WE'LL THROW A WELCOME PARTY—
URGH!
GASU (WHAP)
AH'LL BE ALL READY TO USHER 'EM IN—
KYAH!
GYUN (GRAB)

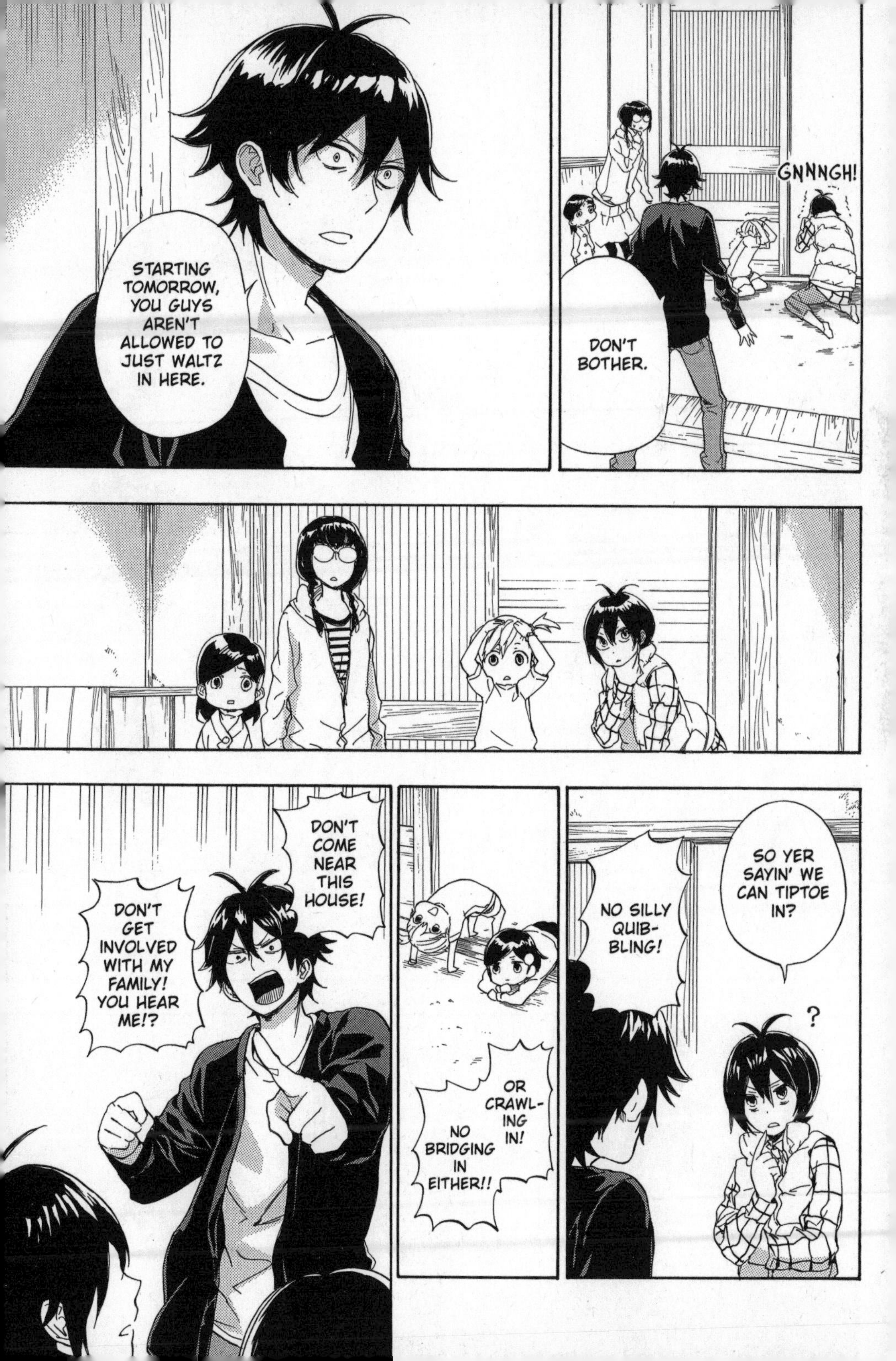
GNNNGH!
DON'T BOTHER.
STARTING TOMORROW, YOU GUYS AREN'T ALLOWED TO JUST WALTZ IN HERE.
SO YER SAYIN' WE CAN TIPTOE IN?
?
NO SILLY QUIB-BLING!
OR CRAWL-ING IN!
NO BRIDGING IN EITHER!!
DON'T COME NEAR THIS HOUSE!
DON'T GET INVOLVED WITH MY FAMILY! YOU HEAR ME!?

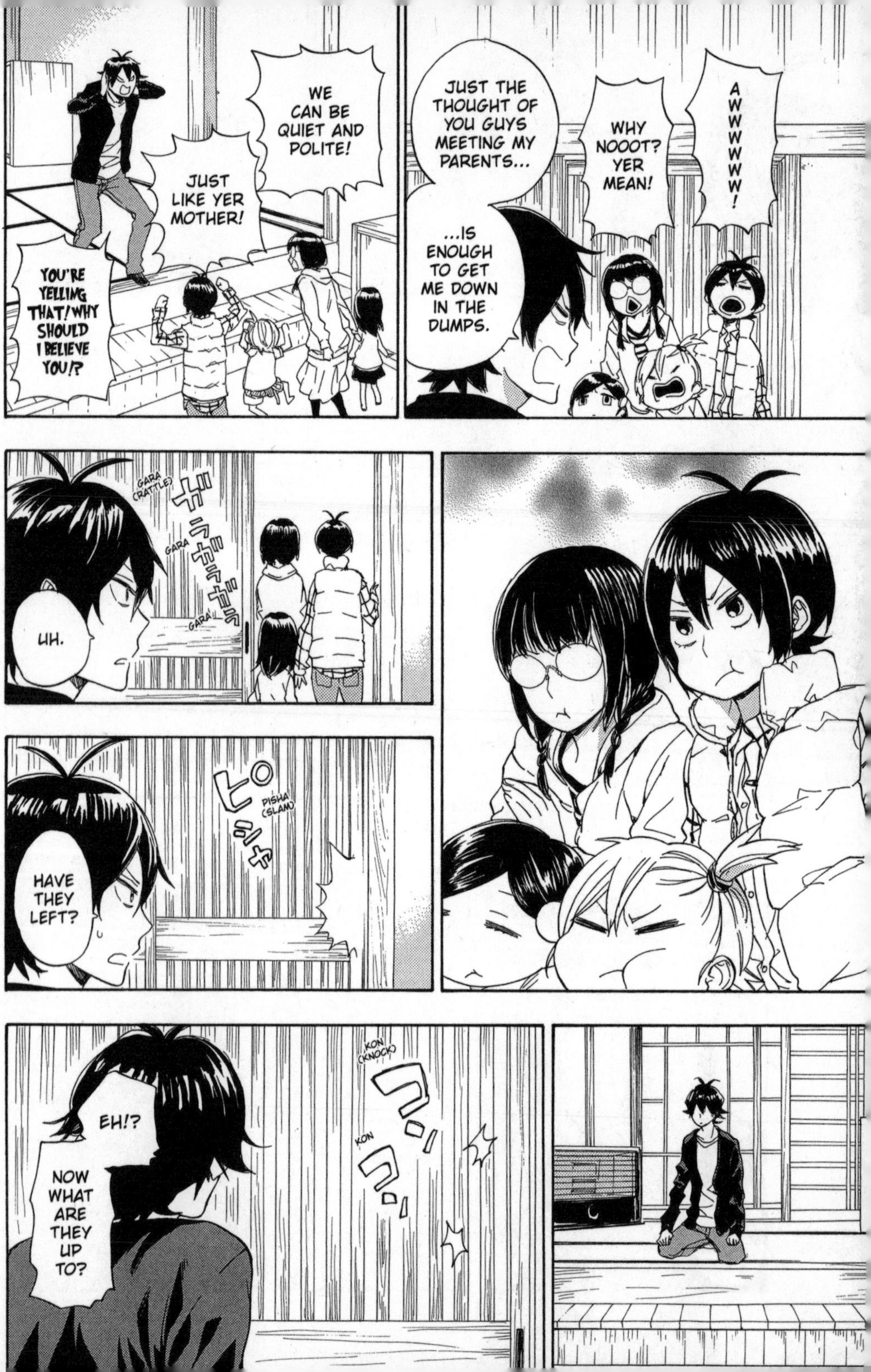
AWWWWWW!
WHY NOOOT? YER MEAN!
JUST THE THOUGHT OF YOU GUYS MEETING MY PARENTS...
...IS ENOUGH TO GET ME DOWN IN THE DUMPS.
WE CAN BE QUIET AND POLITE!
JUST LIKE YER MOTHER!
YOU'RE YELLING THAT! WHY SHOULD I BELIEVE YOU!?
GARA (RATTLE)
GARA
GARA
UH.
PISHA (SLAM)
HAVE THEY LEFT?
KON (KNOCK)
KON
EH!?
NOW WHAT ARE THEY UP TO?

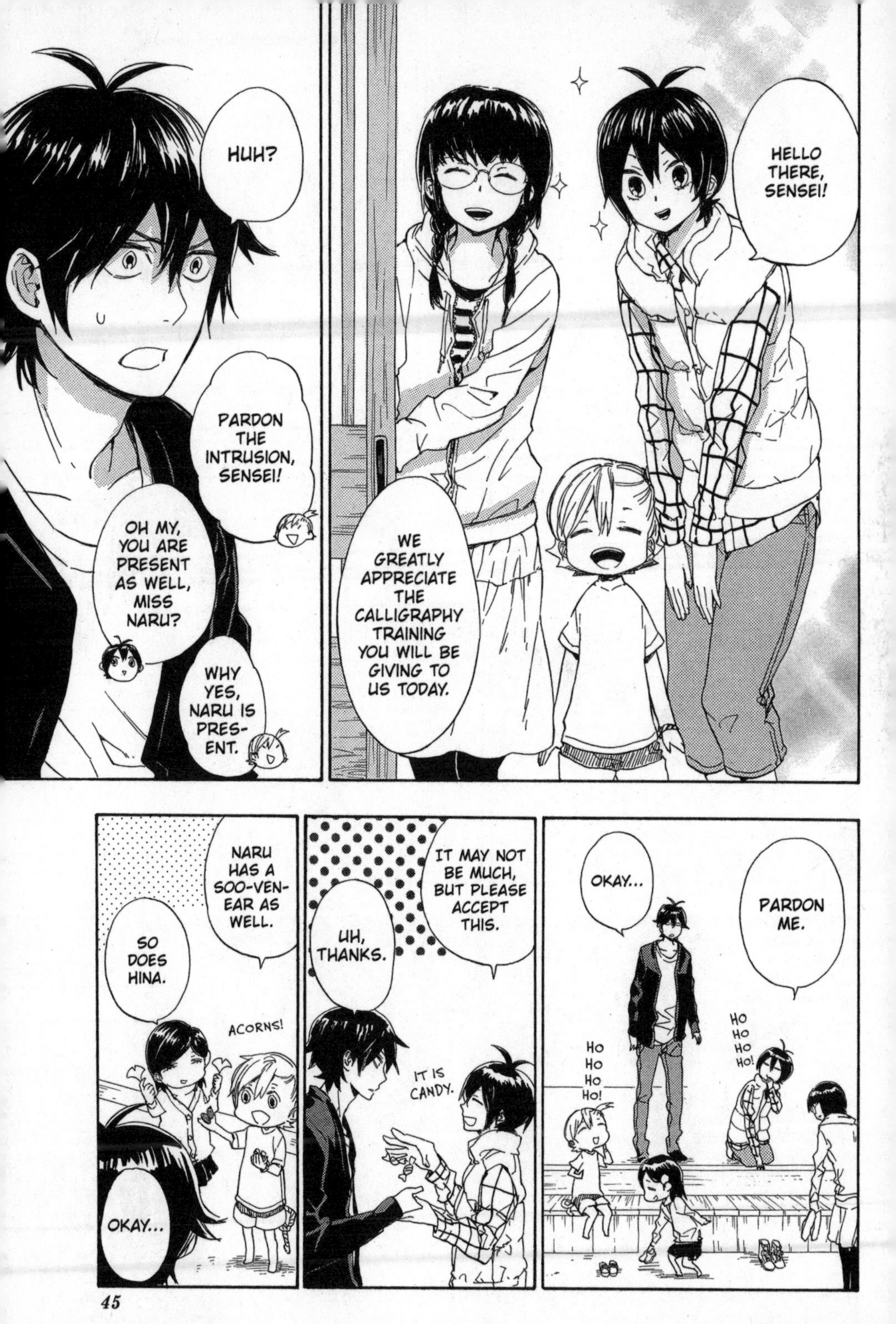
HELLO THERE, SENSEI!
WE GREATLY APPRECIATE THE CALLIGRAPHY TRAINING YOU WILL BE GIVING TO US TODAY.
HUH?
PARDON THE INTRUSION, SENSEI!
OH MY, YOU ARE PRESENT AS WELL, MISS NARU?
WHY YES, NARU IS PRES-ENT.
PARDON ME.
OKAY...
HO HO HO HO!
HO HO HO HO!
IT MAY NOT BE MUCH, BUT PLEASE ACCEPT THIS.
UH, THANKS.
IT IS CANDY.
NARU HAS A SOO-VEN-EAR AS WELL.
SO DOES HINA.
ACORNS!
OKAY...

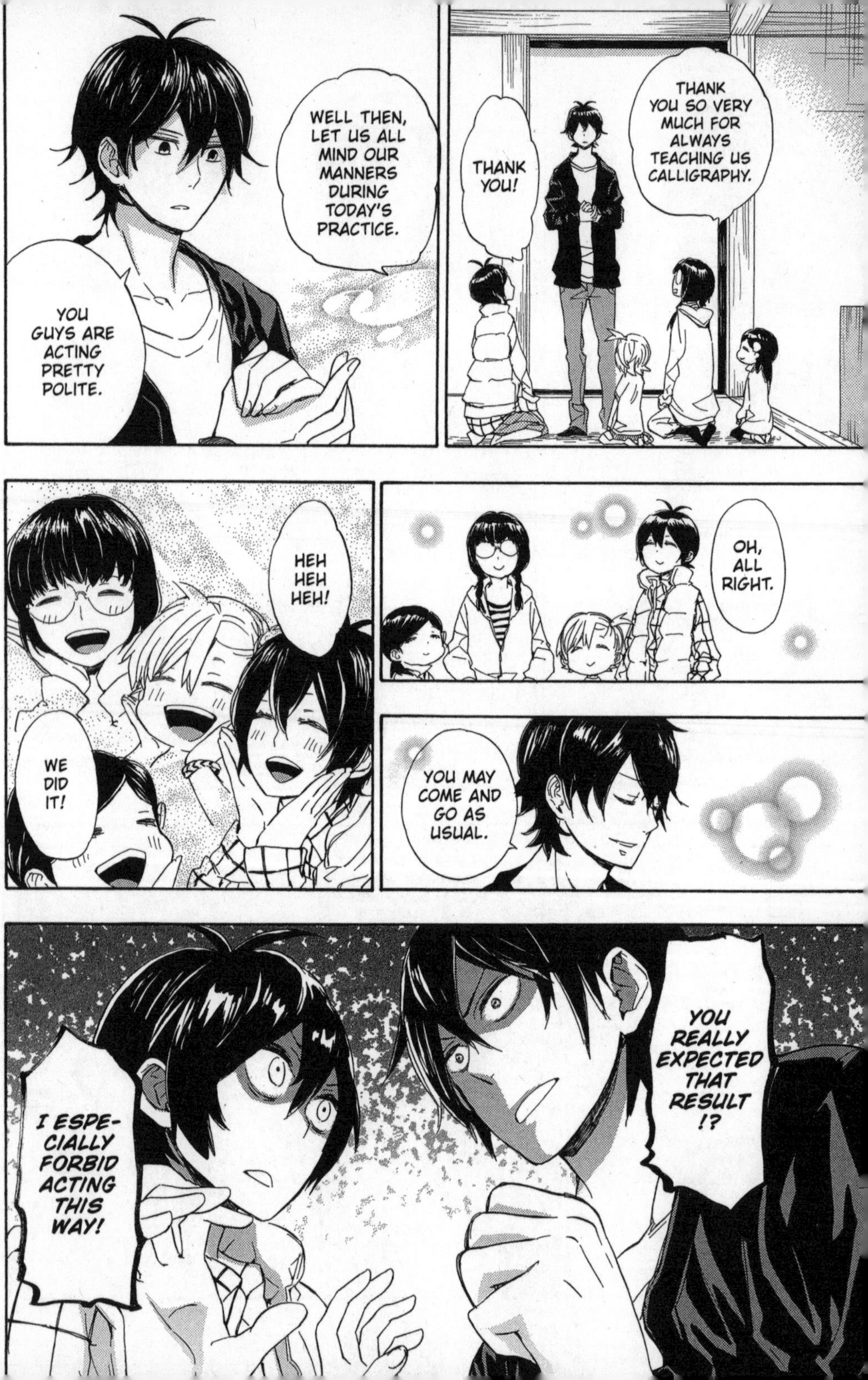
THANK YOU SO VERY MUCH FOR ALWAYS TEACHING US CALLIGRAPHY.
THANK YOU!
WELL THEN, LET US ALL MIND OUR MANNERS DURING TODAY'S PRACTICE.
YOU GUYS ARE ACTING PRETTY POLITE.
OH, ALL RIGHT.
YOU MAY COME AND GO AS USUAL.
HEH HEH HEH!
WE DID IT!
YOU REALLY EXPECTED THAT RESULT!?
I ESPECIALLY FORBID ACTING THIS WAY!

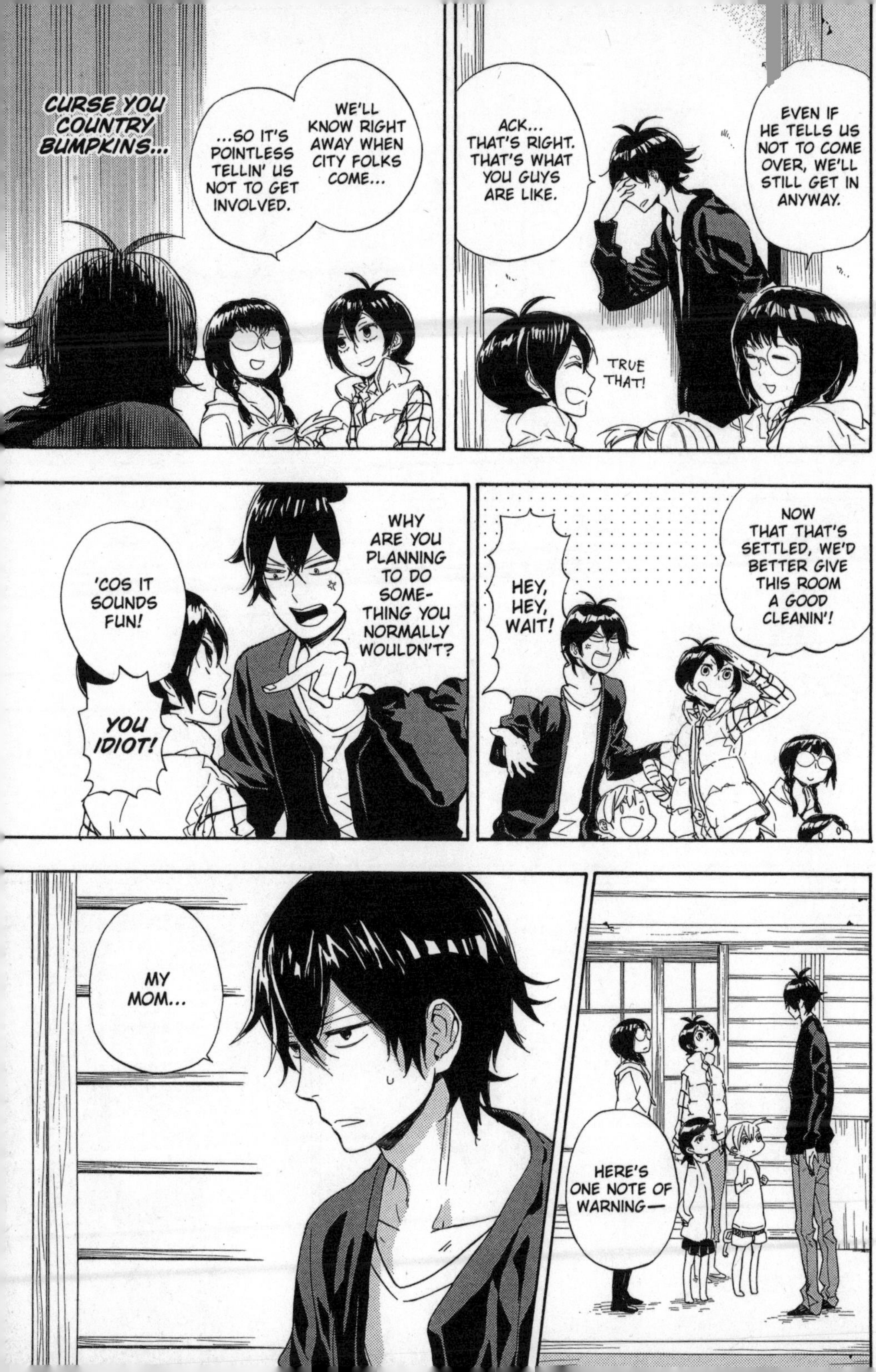
EVEN IF HE TELLS US NOT TO COME OVER, WE'LL STILL GET IN ANYWAY.
ACK... THAT'S RIGHT. THAT'S WHAT YOU GUYS ARE LIKE.
TRUE THAT!
WE'LL KNOW RIGHT AWAY WHEN CITY FOLKS COME...
...SO IT'S POINTLESS TELLIN' US NOT TO GET INVOLVED.
CURSE YOU COUNTRY BUMPKINS...
NOW THAT THAT'S SETTLED, WE'D BETTER GIVE THIS ROOM A GOOD CLEANIN'!
HEY, HEY, WAIT!
WHY ARE YOU PLANNING TO DO SOME-THING YOU NORMALLY WOULDN'T?
'COS IT SOUNDS FUN!
YOU IDIOT!
HERE'S ONE NOTE OF WARNING—
MY MOM...

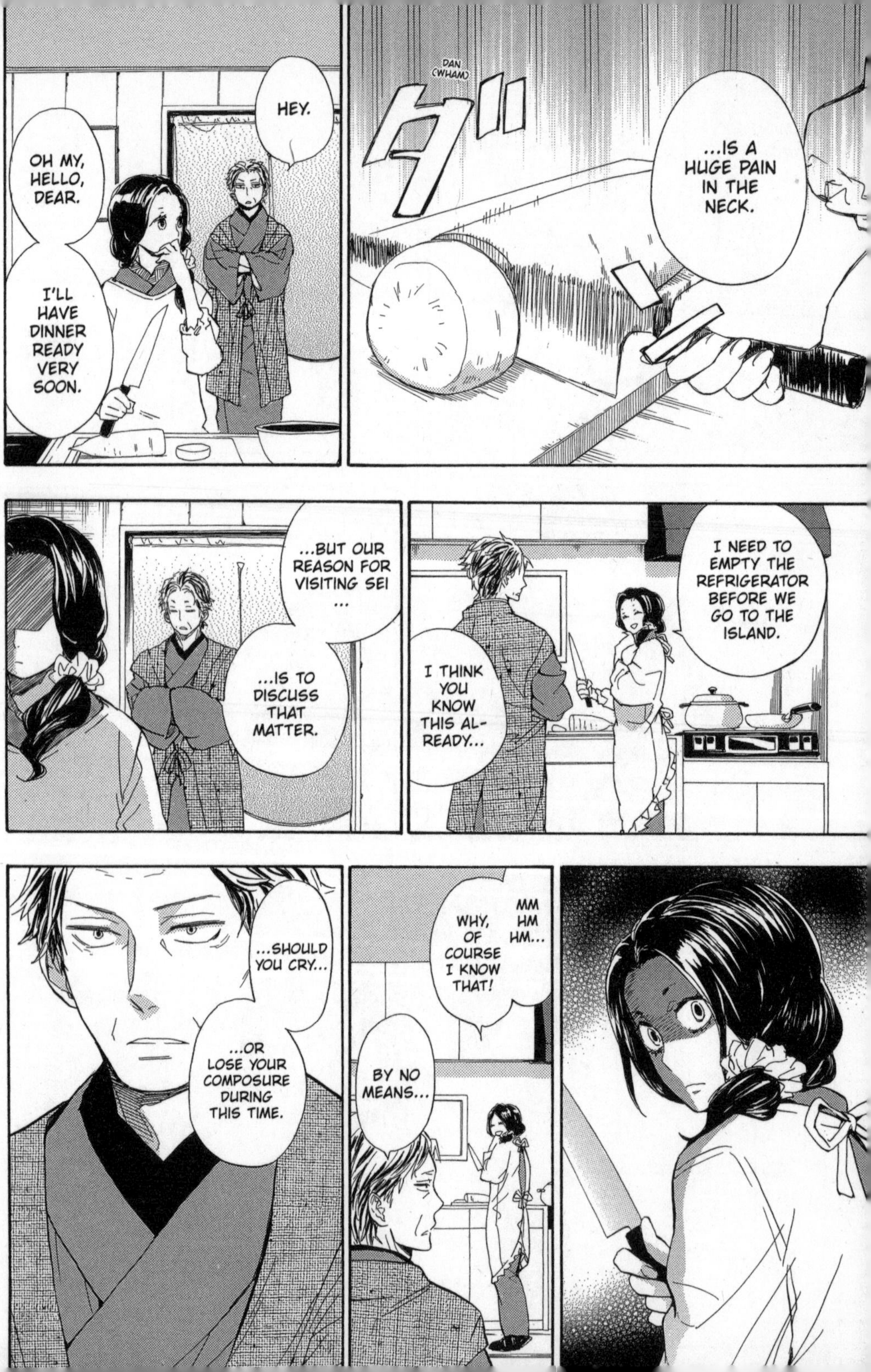
DAN (WHAM)
...IS A HUGE PAIN IN THE NECK.
HEY.
OH MY, HELLO, DEAR.
I'LL HAVE DINNER READY VERY SOON.
I NEED TO EMPTY THE REFRIGERATOR BEFORE WE GO TO THE ISLAND.
I THINK YOU KNOW THIS AL-READY...
...BUT OUR REASON FOR VISITING SEI ...
...IS TO DISCUSS THAT MATTER.
MM HM HM...
WHY, OF COURSE I KNOW THAT!
BY NO MEANS...
...SHOULD YOU CRY...
...OR LOSE YOUR COMPOSURE DURING THIS TIME.

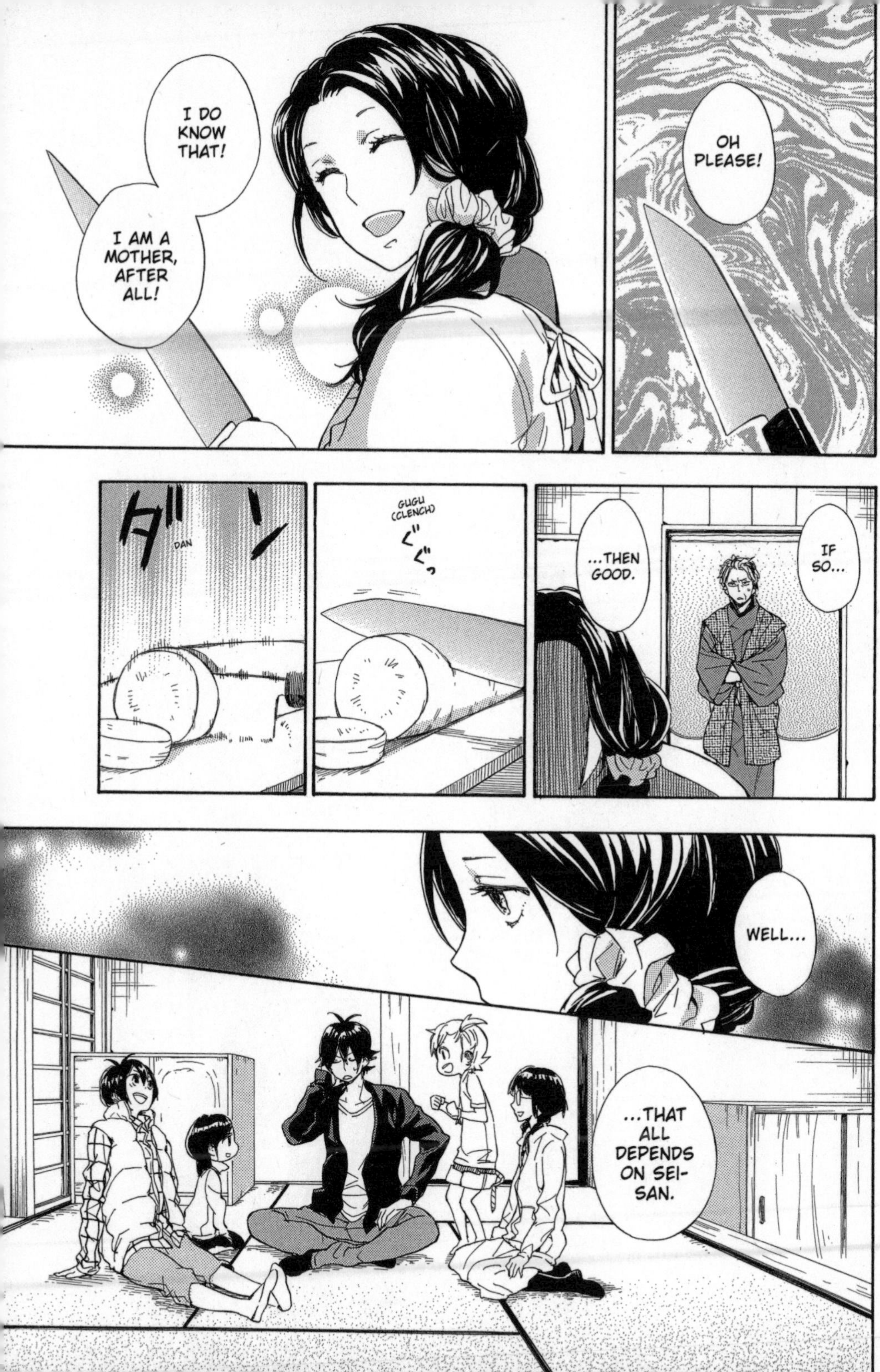
OH PLEASE!
I DO KNOW THAT!
I AM A MOTHER, AFTER ALL!
IF SO...
...THEN GOOD.
GUGU (CLENCH)
ぐぐっ
ダン
DAN
WELL...
...THAT ALL DEPENDS ON SEI-SAN.

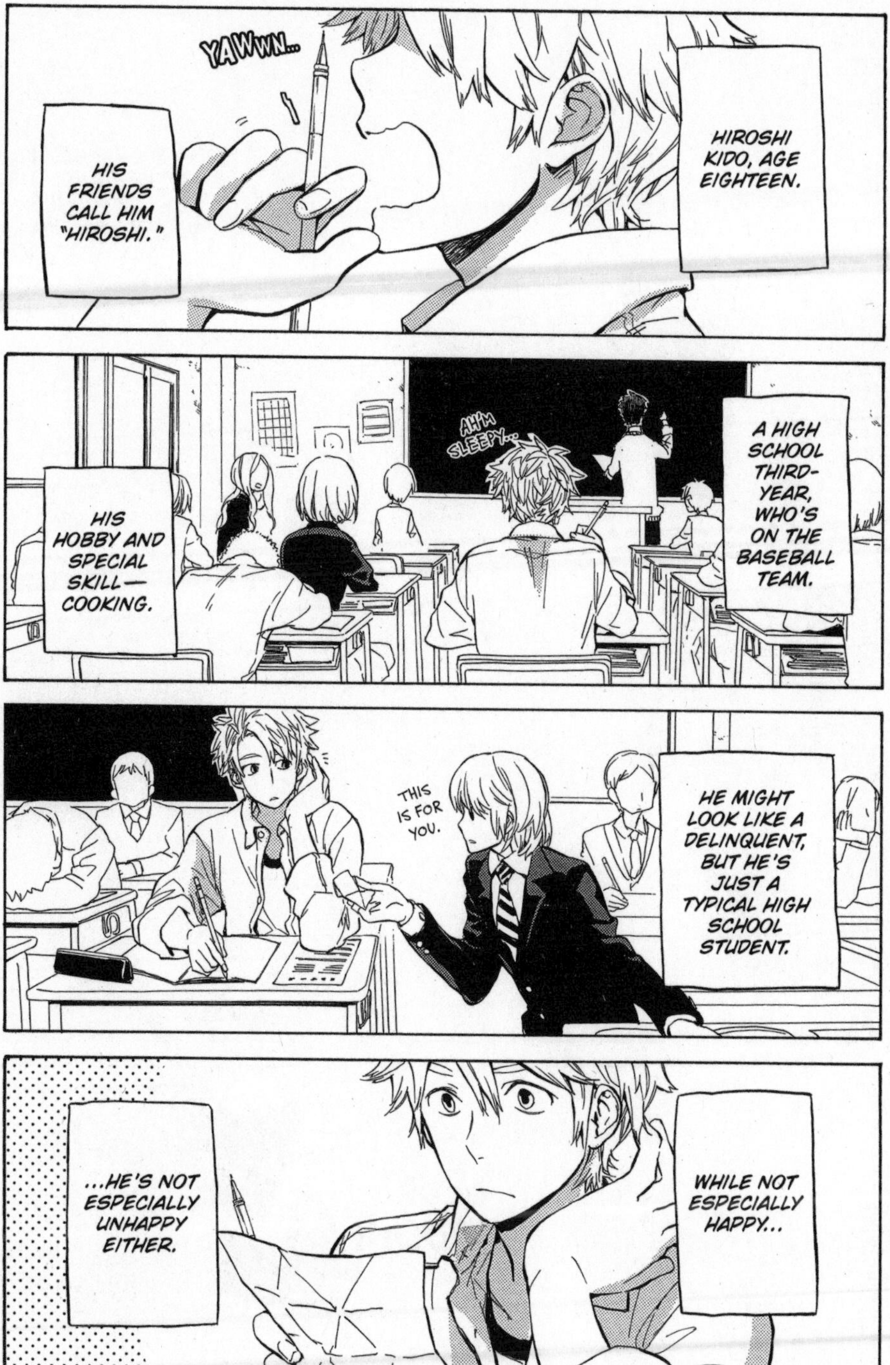
HIROSHI KIDO, AGE EIGHTEEN.
YAWWN...
HIS FRIENDS CALL HIM "HIROSHI."
A HIGH SCHOOL THIRD-YEAR, WHO'S ON THE BASEBALL TEAM.
AH'M SLEEPY...
HIS HOBBY AND SPECIAL SKILL—COOKING.
HE MIGHT LOOK LIKE A DELINQUENT, BUT HE'S JUST A TYPICAL HIGH SCHOOL STUDENT.
THIS IS FOR YOU.
WHILE NOT ESPECIALLY HAPPY...
...HE'S NOT ESPECIALLY UNHAPPY EITHER.

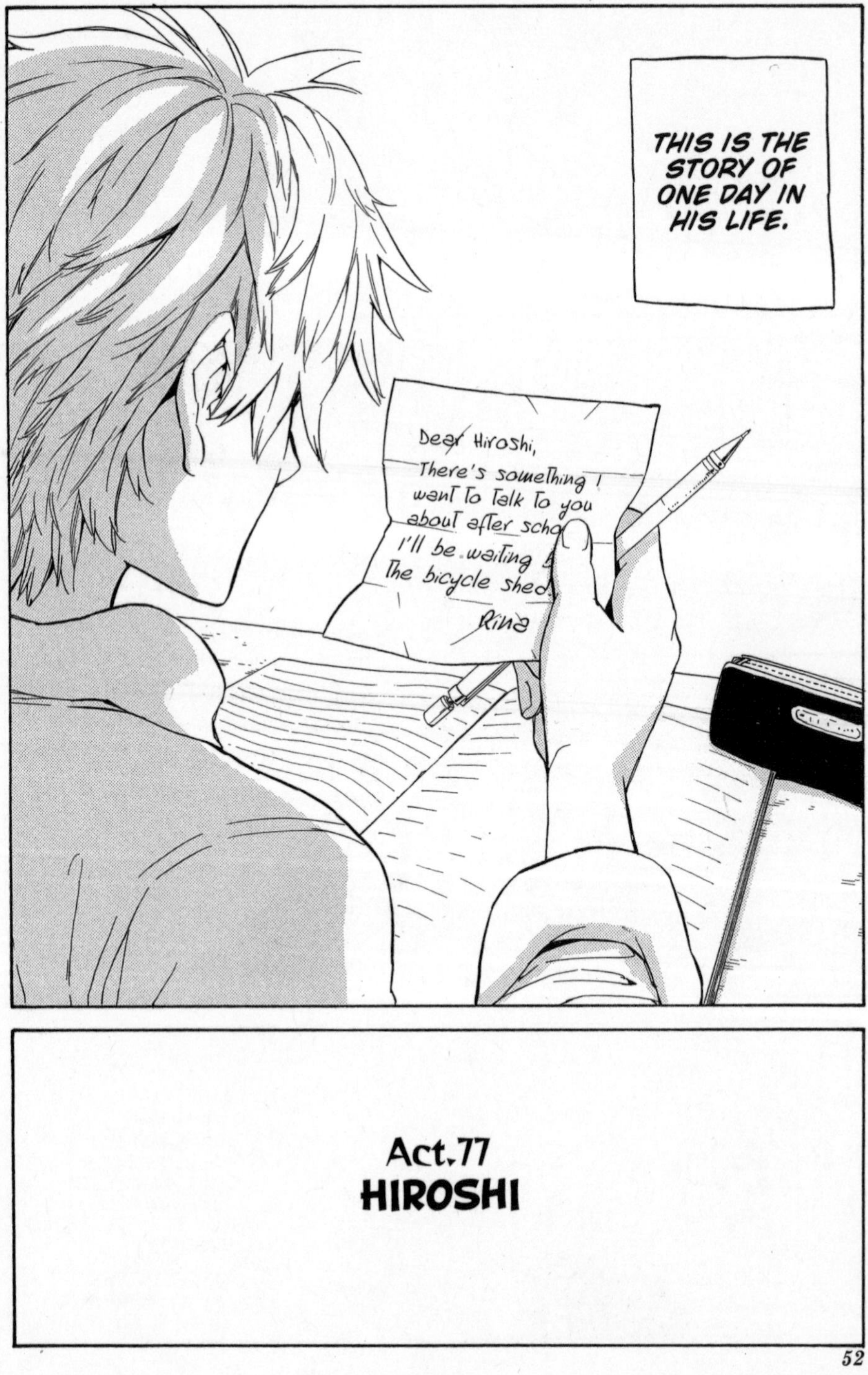
THIS IS THE STORY OF ONE DAY IN HIS LIFE.
Dear Hiroshi,
There's something I want to talk to you about after scho
I'll be waiting
The bicycle shed.
Rina

Act.77

HIROSHI

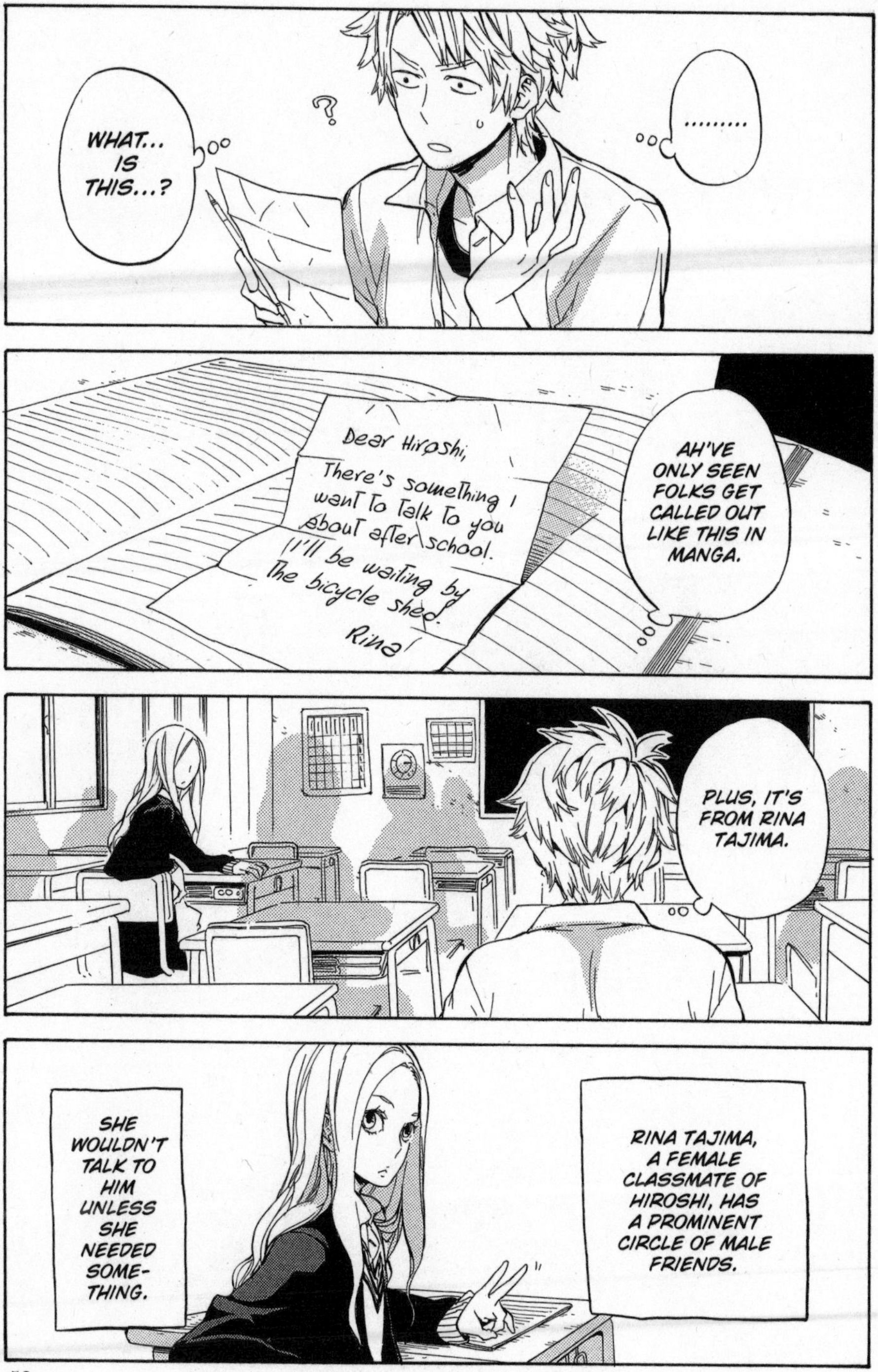
....
WHAT... IS THIS...?
AH'VE ONLY SEEN FOLKS GET CALLED OUT LIKE THIS IN MANGA.
Dear Hiroshi, There's something I want to talk to you about after school. I'll be waiting by the bicycle shed. Rina
PLUS, IT'S FROM RINA TAJIMA.
RINA TAJIMA, A FEMALE CLASSMATE OF HIROSHI, HAS A PROMINENT CIRCLE OF MALE FRIENDS.
SHE WOULDN'T TALK TO HIM UNLESS SHE NEEDED SOME-THING.

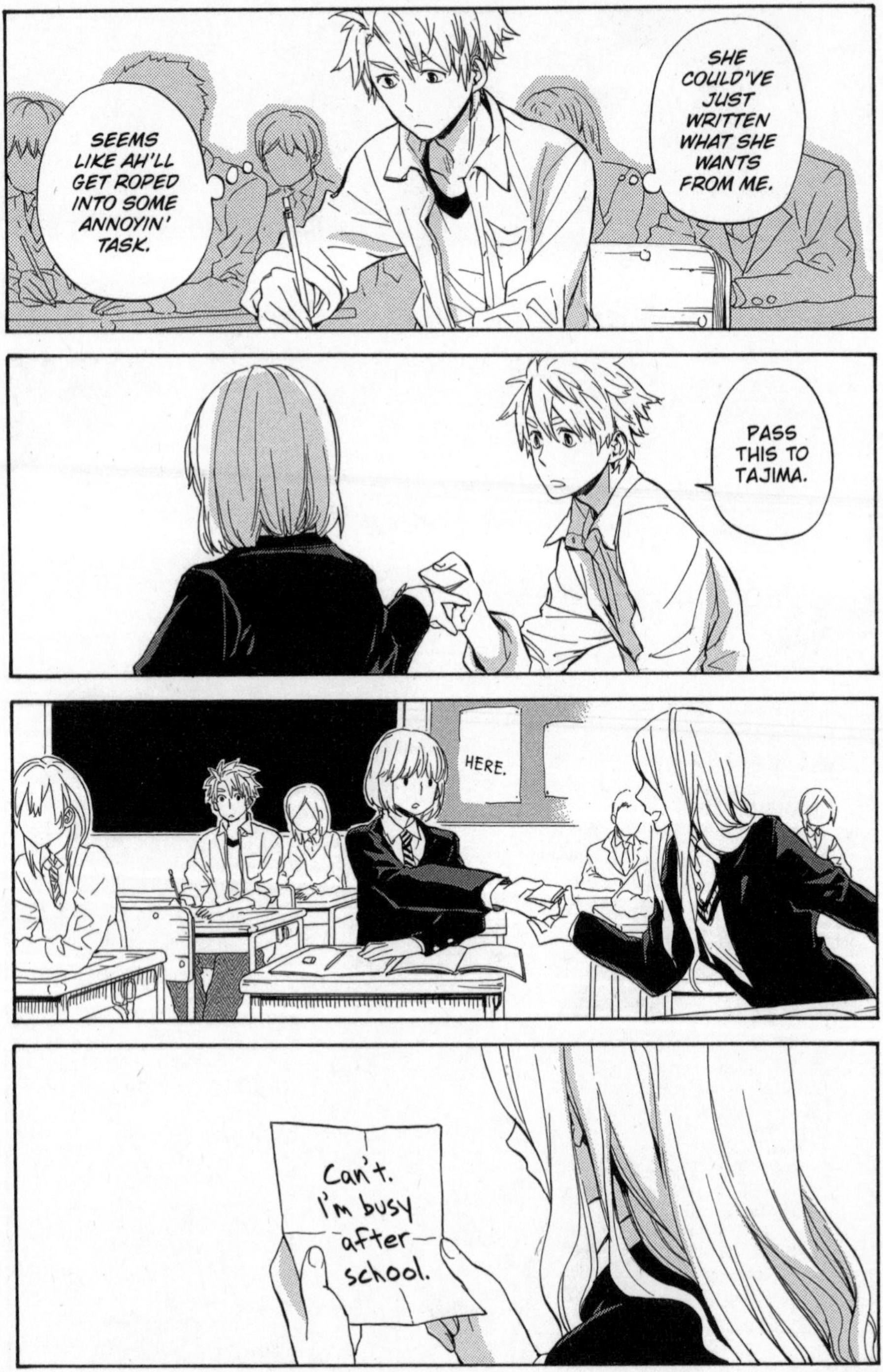
SHE COULD'VE JUST WRITTEN WHAT SHE WANTS FROM ME.
SEEMS LIKE AH'LL GET ROPED INTO SOME ANNOYIN' TASK.
PASS THIS TO TAJIMA.
HERE.
Can't. I'm busy after school.

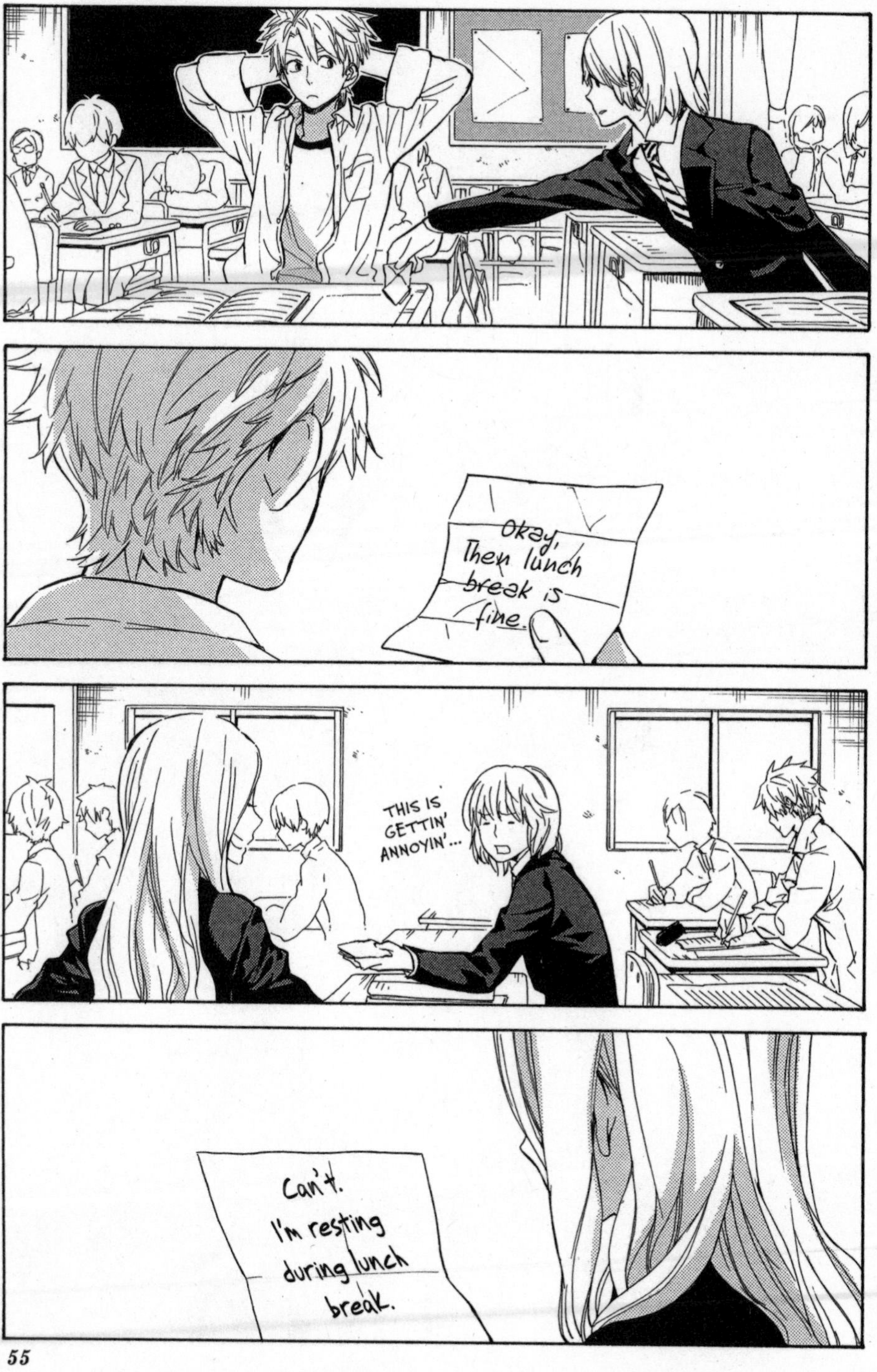
Okay, Then lunch break is fine.
THIS IS GETTIN' ANNOYIN'...
Can't. I'm resting during lunch break.

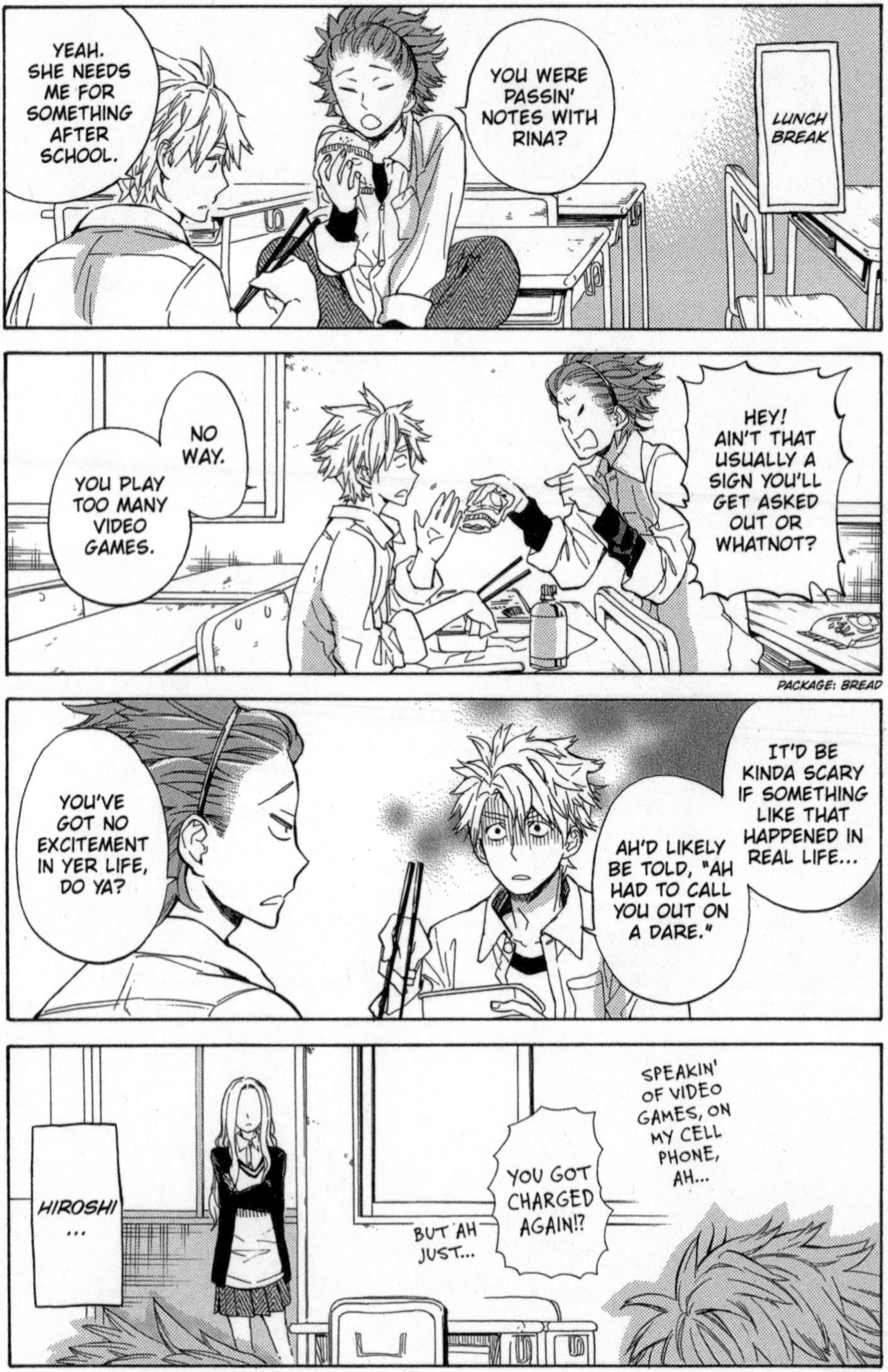
LUNCH BREAK
YOU WERE PASSIN' NOTES WITH RINA?
YEAH. SHE NEEDS ME FOR SOMETHING AFTER SCHOOL.
HEY! AIN'T THAT USUALLY A SIGN YOU'LL GET ASKED OUT OR WHATNOT?
NO WAY.
YOU PLAY TOO MANY VIDEO GAMES.
PACKAGE: BREAD
IT'D BE KINDA SCARY IF SOMETHING LIKE THAT HAPPENED IN REAL LIFE...
AH'D LIKELY BE TOLD, "AH HAD TO CALL YOU OUT ON A DARE."
YOU'VE GOT NO EXCITEMENT IN YER LIFE, DO YA?
SPEAKIN' OF VIDEO GAMES, ON MY CELL PHONE, AH...
YOU GOT CHARGED AGAIN!?
BUT AH JUST...
HIROSHI ...

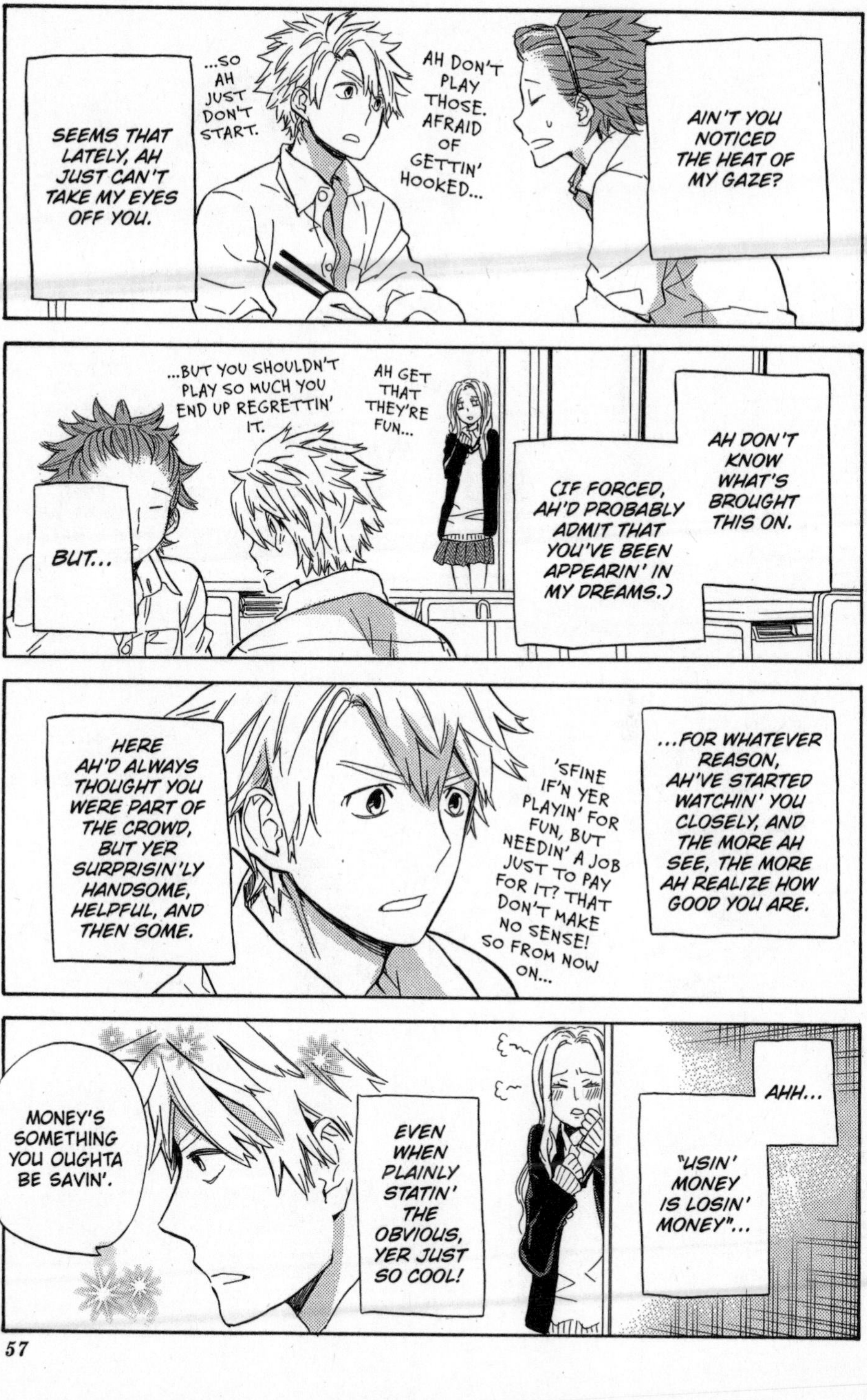
AIN'T YOU NOTICED THE HEAT OF MY GAZE?
AH DON'T PLAY THOSE. AFRAID OF GETTIN' HOOKED...
...SO AH JUST DON'T START.
SEEMS THAT LATELY, AH JUST CAN'T TAKE MY EYES OFF YOU.
AH DON'T KNOW WHAT'S BROUGHT THIS ON.
(IF FORCED, AH'D PROBABLY ADMIT THAT YOU'VE BEEN APPEARIN' IN MY DREAMS.)
AH GET THAT THEY'RE FUN...
...BUT YOU SHOULDN'T PLAY SO MUCH YOU END UP REGRETTIN' IT.
BUT...
...FOR WHATEVER REASON, AH'VE STARTED WATCHIN' YOU CLOSELY, AND THE MORE AH SEE, THE MORE AH REALIZE HOW GOOD YOU ARE.
'SFINE IF'N YER PLAYIN' FOR FUN, BUT NEEDIN' A JOB JUST TO PAY FOR IT? THAT DON'T MAKE NO SENSE! SO FROM NOW ON...
HERE AH'D ALWAYS THOUGHT YOU WERE PART OF THE CROWD, BUT YER SURPRISIN'LY HANDSOME, HELPFUL, AND THEN SOME.
AHH...
"USIN' MONEY IS LOSIN' MONEY"...
EVEN WHEN PLAINLY STATIN' THE OBVIOUS, YER JUST SO COOL!
MONEY'S SOMETHING YOU OUGHTA BE SAVIN'.

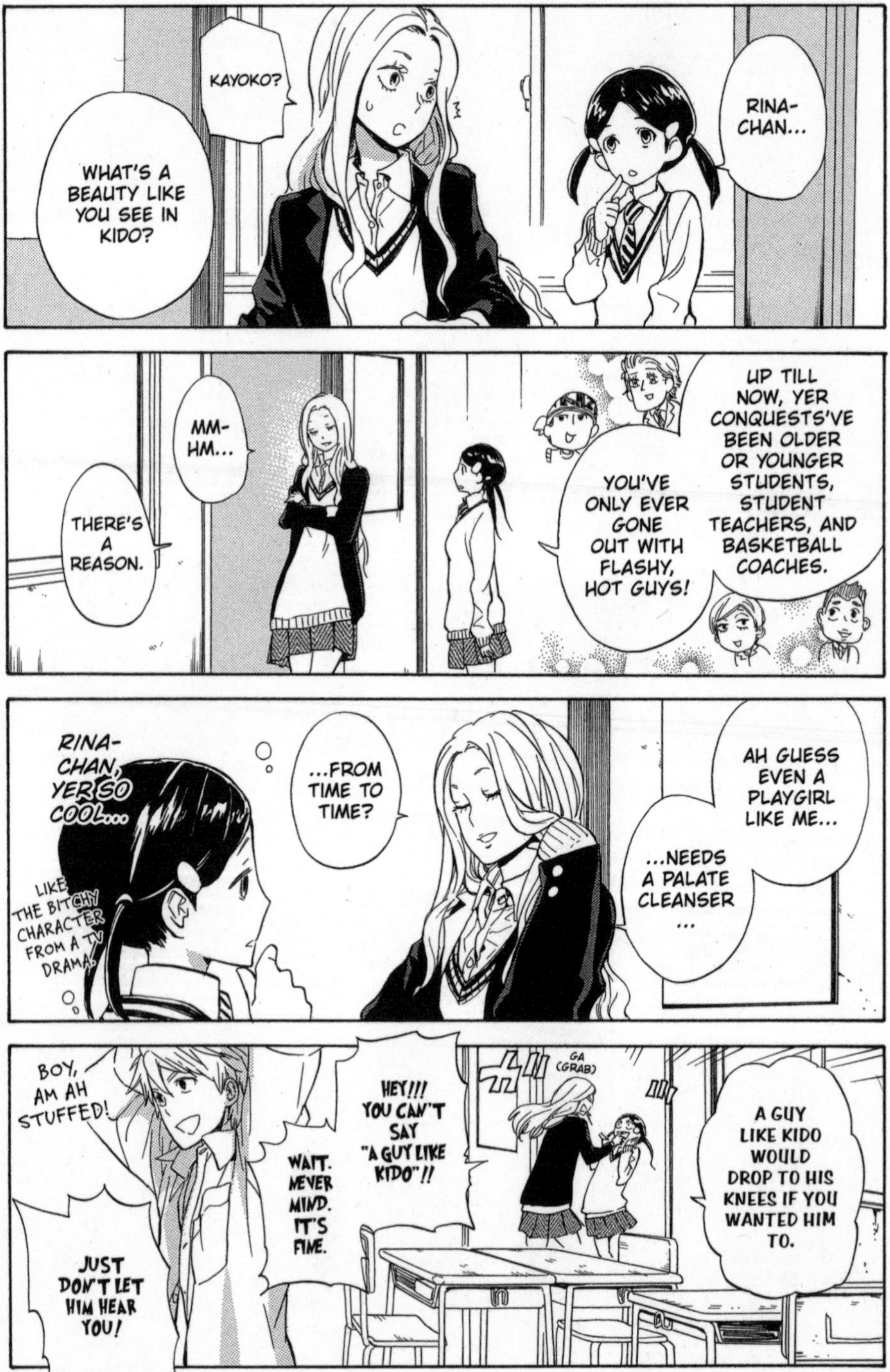
RINA-CHAN...
KAYOKO?
WHAT'S A BEAUTY LIKE YOU SEE IN KIDO?
UP TILL NOW, YER CONQUESTS'VE BEEN OLDER OR YOUNGER STUDENTS, STUDENT TEACHERS, AND BASKETBALL COACHES.
YOU'VE ONLY EVER GONE OUT WITH FLASHY, HOT GUYS!
MM-HM...
THERE'S A REASON.
AH GUESS EVEN A PLAYGIRL LIKE ME...
...NEEDS A PALATE CLEANSER ...
...FROM TIME TO TIME?
RINA-CHAN, YER SO COOL...
LIKE THE BITCHY CHARACTER FROM A TV DRAMA.
A GUY LIKE KIDO WOULD DROP TO HIS KNEES IF YOU WANTED HIM TO.
GA (GRAB)
HEY!!! YOU CAN'T SAY "A GUY LIKE KIDO"!!
WAIT. NEVER MIND. IT'S FINE.
BOY, AM AH STUFFED!
JUST DON'T LET HIM HEAR YOU!

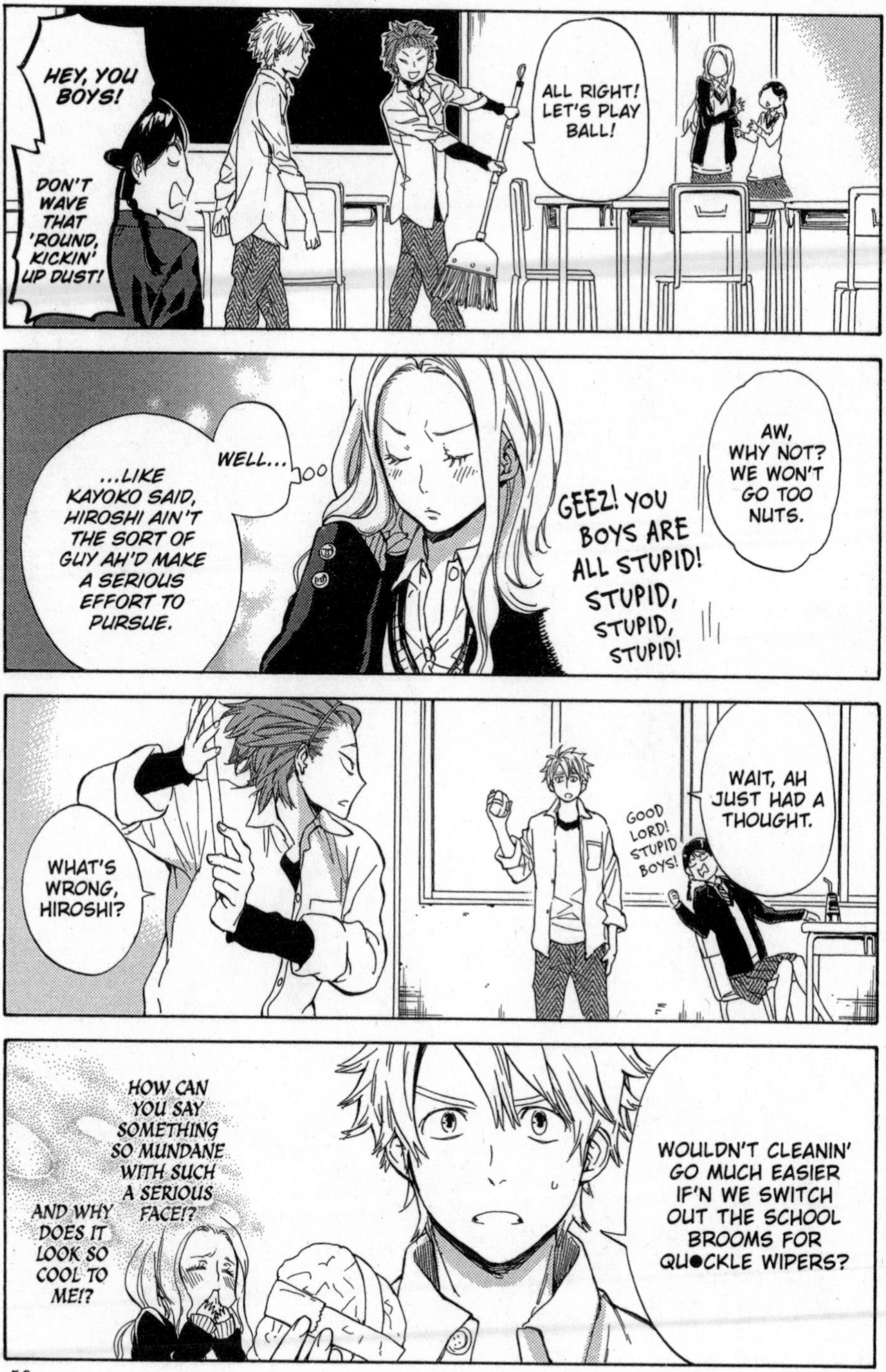
ALL RIGHT! LET'S PLAY BALL!
HEY, YOU BOYS!
DON'T WAVE THAT 'ROUND, KICKIN' UP DUST!
AW, WHY NOT? WE WON'T GO TOO NUTS.
GEEZ! YOU BOYS ARE ALL STUPID! STUPID, STUPID, STUPID!
WELL...
...LIKE KAYOKO SAID, HIROSHI AIN'T THE SORT OF GUY AH'D MAKE A SERIOUS EFFORT TO PURSUE.
WAIT, AH JUST HAD A THOUGHT.
GOOD LORD! STUPID BOYS!
WHAT'S WRONG, HIROSHI?
WOULDN'T CLEANIN' GO MUCH EASIER IF'N WE SWITCH OUT THE SCHOOL BROOMS FOR QU●CKLE WIPERS?
HOW CAN YOU SAY SOMETHING SO MUNDANE WITH SUCH A SERIOUS FACE!?
AND WHY DOES IT LOOK SO COOL TO ME!?

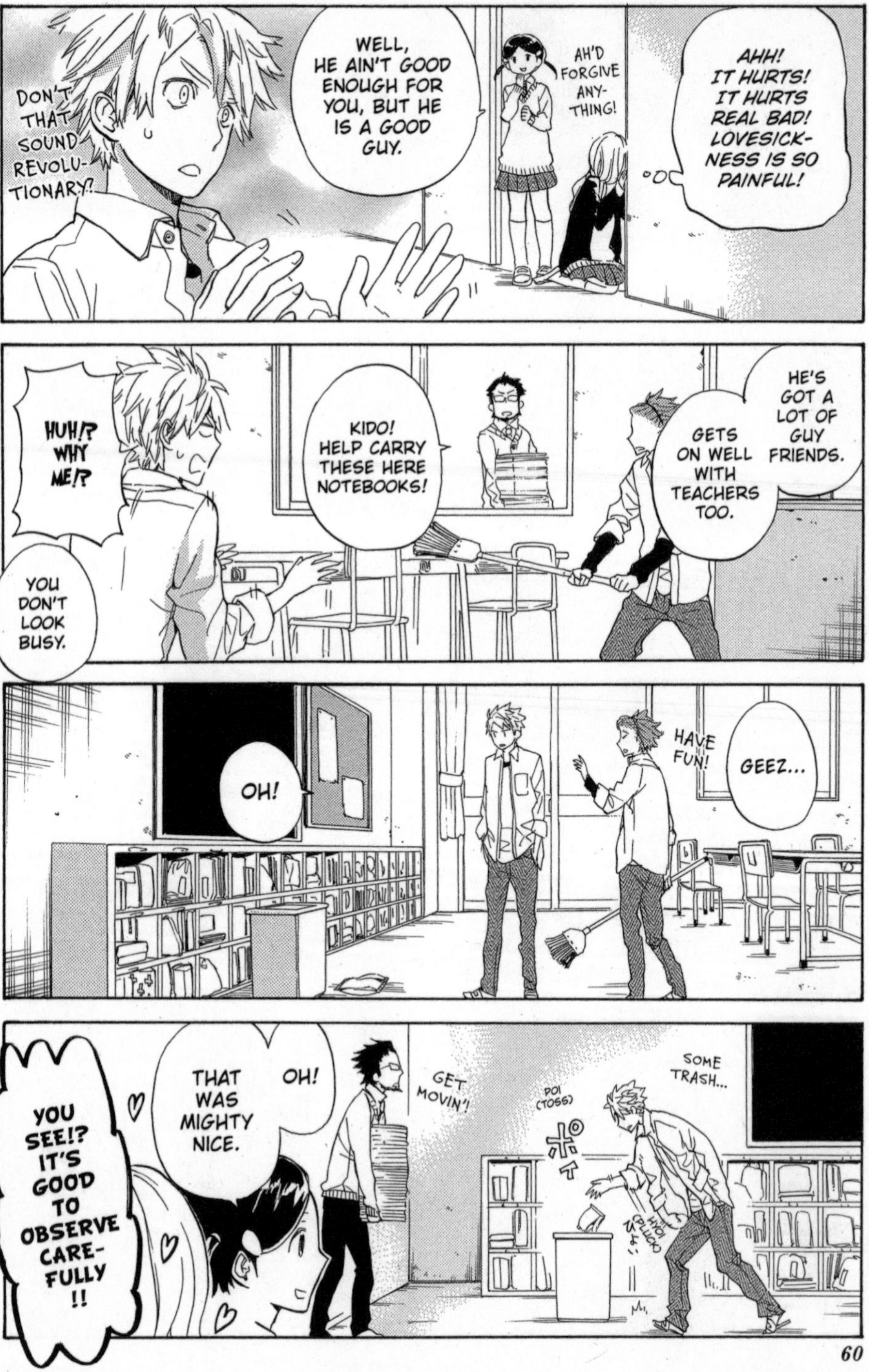
AHH! IT HURTS! IT HURTS REAL BAD! LOVESICKNESS IS SO PAINFUL!
AH'D FORGIVE ANYTHING!
WELL, HE AIN'T GOOD ENOUGH FOR YOU, BUT HE IS A GOOD GUY.
DON'T THAT SOUND REVOLUTIONARY!?
HE'S GOT A LOT OF GUY FRIENDS.
GETS ON WELL WITH TEACHERS TOO.
KIDO! HELP CARRY THESE HERE NOTEBOOKS!
HUH!? WHY ME!?
YOU DON'T LOOK BUSY.
GEEZ...
HAVE FUN!
OH!
SOME TRASH...
HYOI (PLUCK)
ひょい
POI (TOSS)
ポイ
GET MOVIN'!
OH!
THAT WAS MIGHTY NICE.
YOU SEE!? IT'S GOOD TO OBSERVE CAREFULLY!!

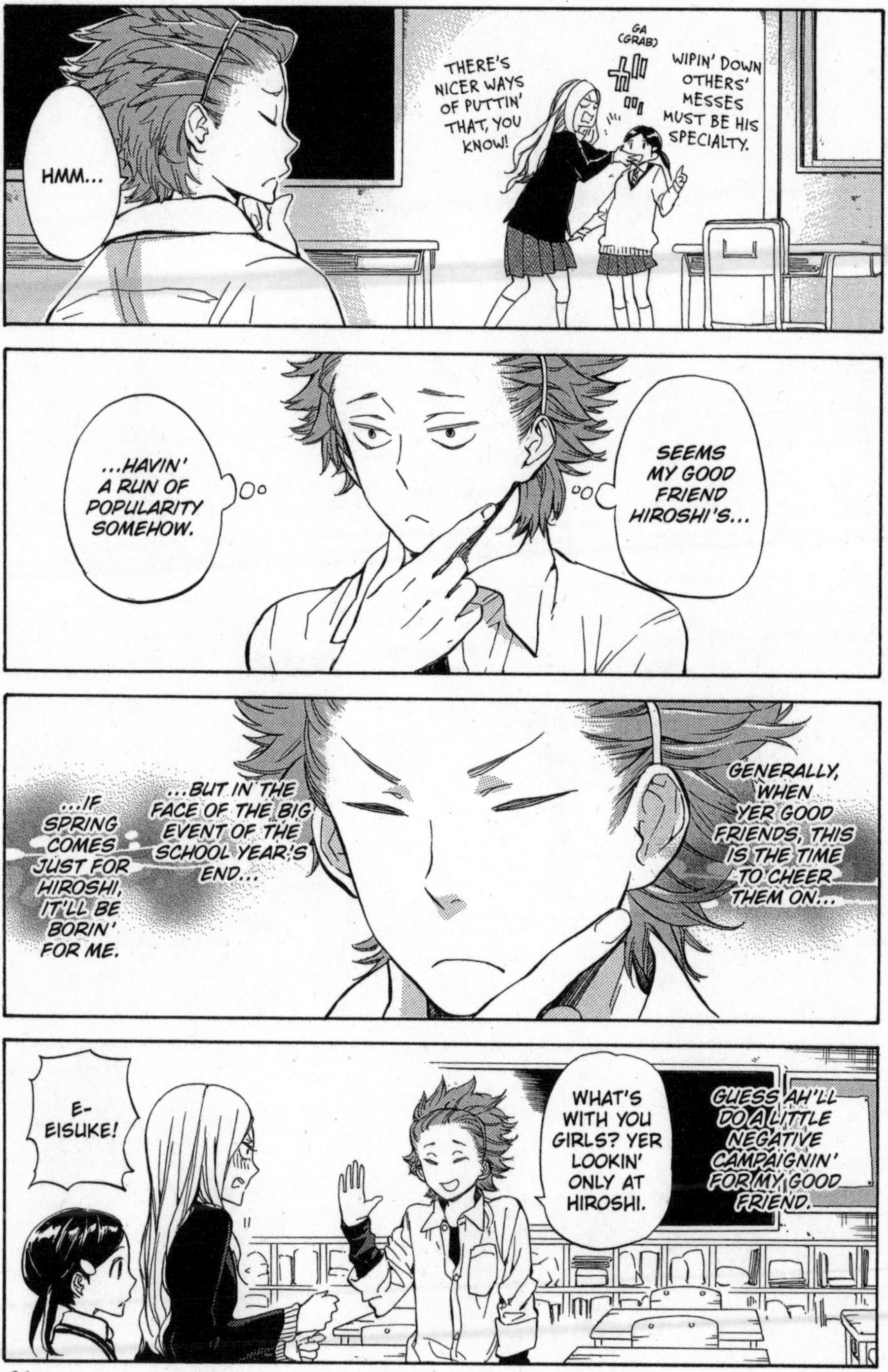
WIPIN' DOWN OTHERS' MESSES MUST BE HIS SPECIALTY.
GA (GRAB)
THERE'S NICER WAYS OF PUTTIN' THAT, YOU KNOW!
HMM...
SEEMS MY GOOD FRIEND HIROSHI'S...
...HAVIN' A RUN OF POPULARITY SOMEHOW.
GENERALLY, WHEN YER GOOD FRIENDS, THIS IS THE TIME TO CHEER THEM ON...
...BUT IN THE FACE OF THE BIG EVENT OF THE SCHOOL YEAR'S END...
...IF SPRING COMES JUST FOR HIROSHI, IT'LL BE BORIN' FOR ME.
GUESS AH'LL DO A LITTLE NEGATIVE CAMPAIGNIN' FOR MY GOOD FRIEND.
WHAT'S WITH YOU GIRLS? YER LOOKIN' ONLY AT HIROSHI.
E-EISUKE!

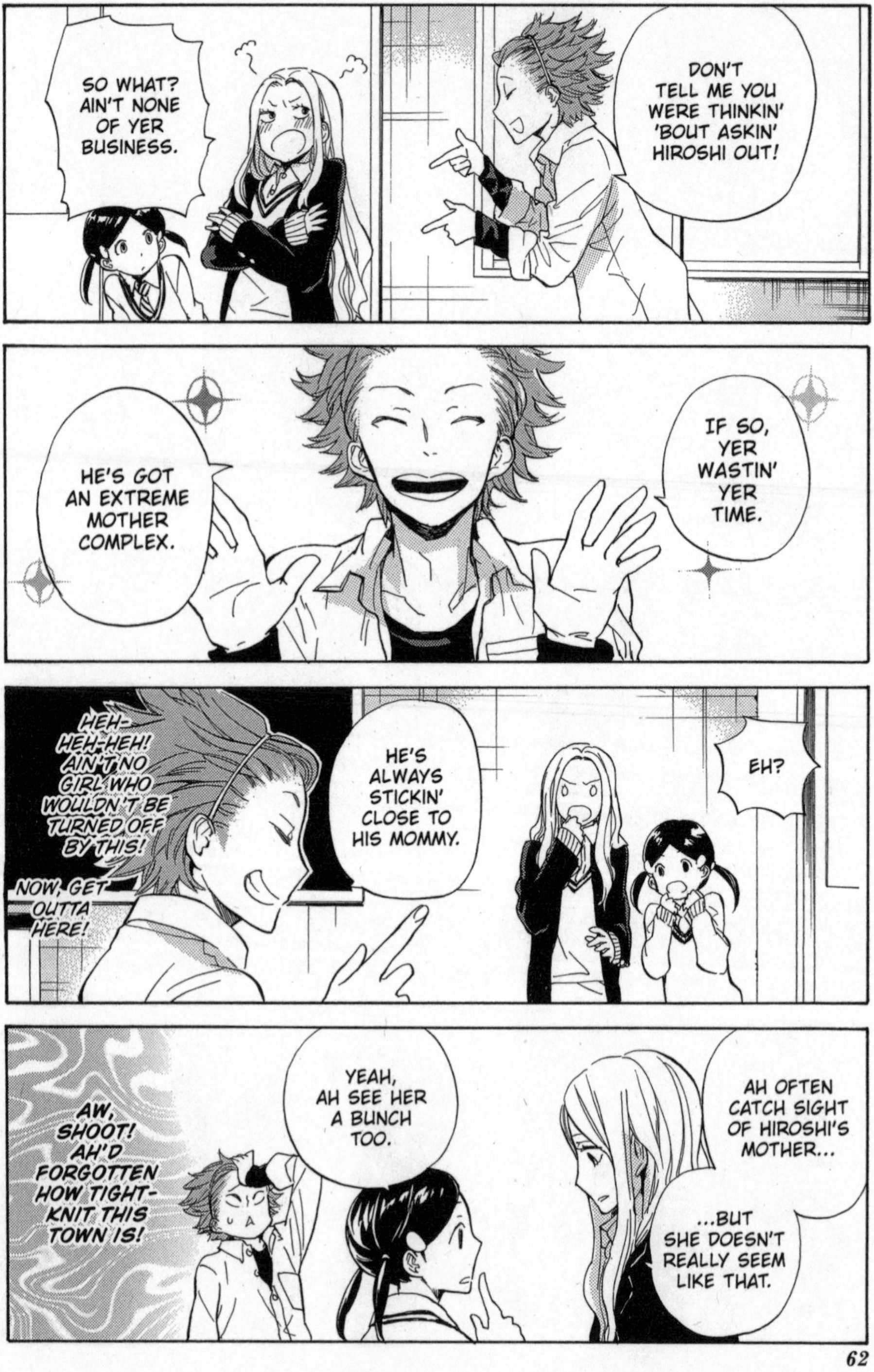
DON'T TELL ME YOU WERE THINKIN' 'BOUT ASKIN' HIROSHI OUT!
SO WHAT? AIN'T NONE OF YER BUSINESS.
IF SO, YER WASTIN' YER TIME.
HE'S GOT AN EXTREME MOTHER COMPLEX.
EH?
HE'S ALWAYS STICKIN' CLOSE TO HIS MOMMY.
HEH-HEH-HEH! AIN'T NO GIRL WHO WOULDN'T BE TURNED OFF BY THIS!
NOW, GET OUTTA HERE!
AH OFTEN CATCH SIGHT OF HIROSHI'S MOTHER...
...BUT SHE DOESN'T REALLY SEEM LIKE THAT.
YEAH, AH SEE HER A BUNCH TOO.
AW, SHOOT! AH'D FORGOTTEN HOW TIGHT-KNIT THIS TOWN IS!

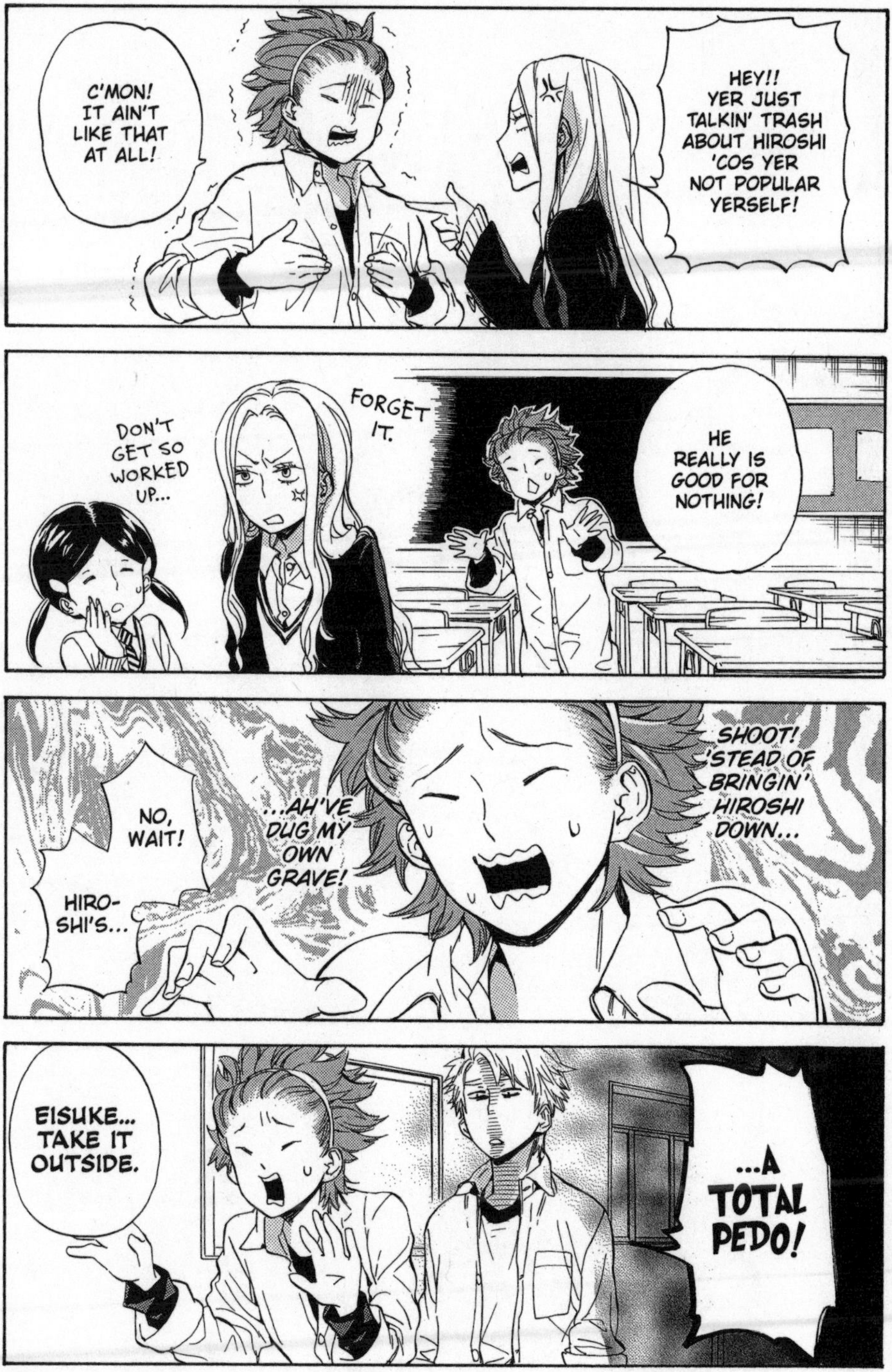
HEY!! YER JUST TALKIN' TRASH ABOUT HIROSHI 'COS YER NOT POPULAR YERSELF!
C'MON! IT AIN'T LIKE THAT AT ALL!
HE REALLY IS GOOD FOR NOTHING!
FORGET IT.
DON'T GET SO WORKED UP...
SHOOT! 'STEAD OF BRINGIN' HIROSHI DOWN...
...AH'VE DUG MY OWN GRAVE!
NO, WAIT!
HIRO-SHI'S...
...A TOTAL PEDO!
EISUKE... TAKE IT OUTSIDE.

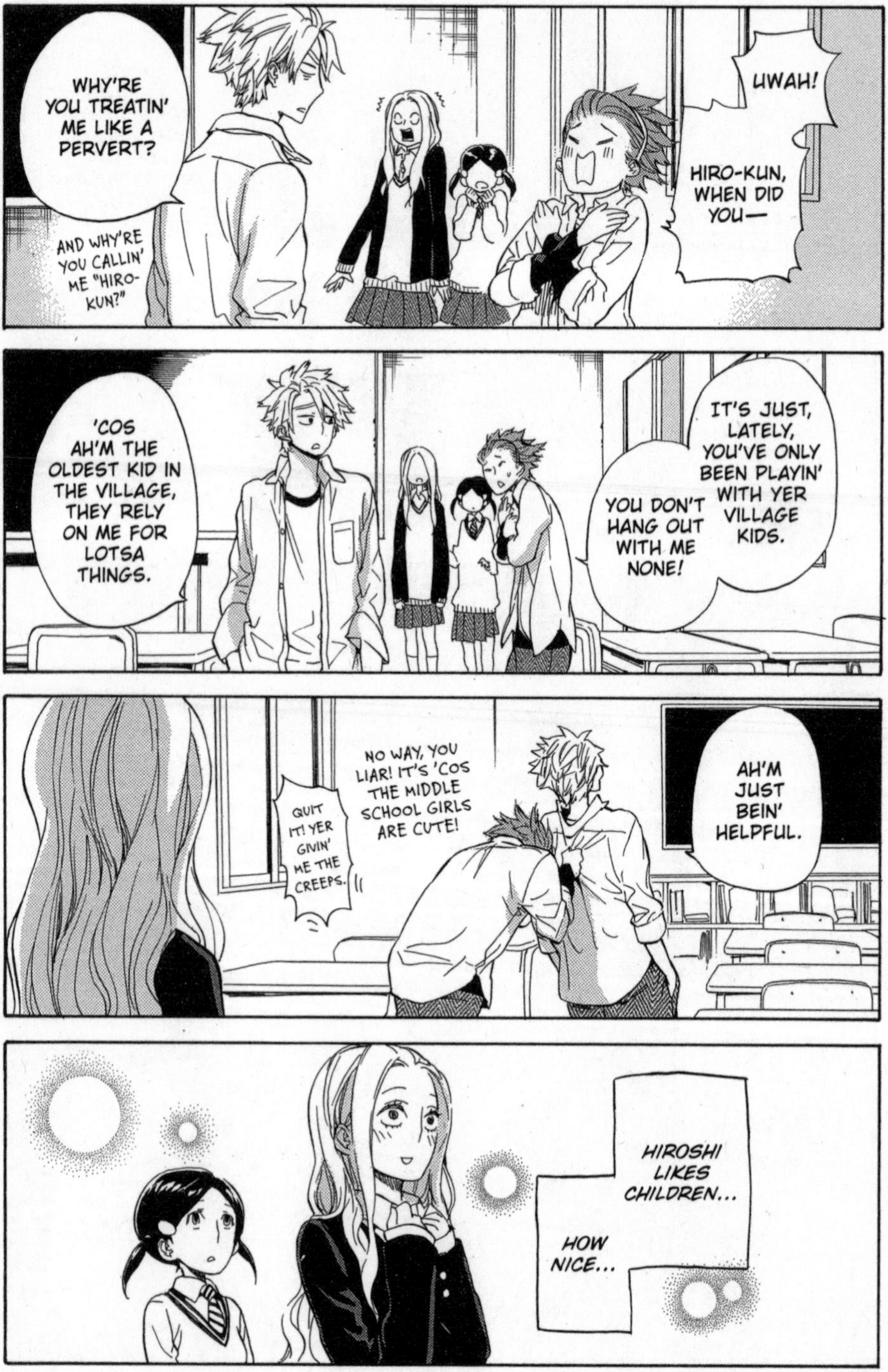
UWAH!
HIRO-KUN, WHEN DID YOU—
WHY'RE YOU TREATIN' ME LIKE A PERVERT?
AND WHY'RE YOU CALLIN' ME "HIRO-KUN?"
IT'S JUST, LATELY, YOU'VE ONLY BEEN PLAYIN' WITH YER VILLAGE KIDS.
YOU DON'T HANG OUT WITH ME NONE!
'COS AH'M THE OLDEST KID IN THE VILLAGE, THEY RELY ON ME FOR LOTSA THINGS.
AH'M JUST BEIN' HELPFUL.
NO WAY, YOU LIAR! IT'S 'COS THE MIDDLE SCHOOL GIRLS ARE CUTE!
QUIT IT! YER GIVIN' ME THE CREEPS.
HIROSHI LIKES CHILDREN...
HOW NICE...

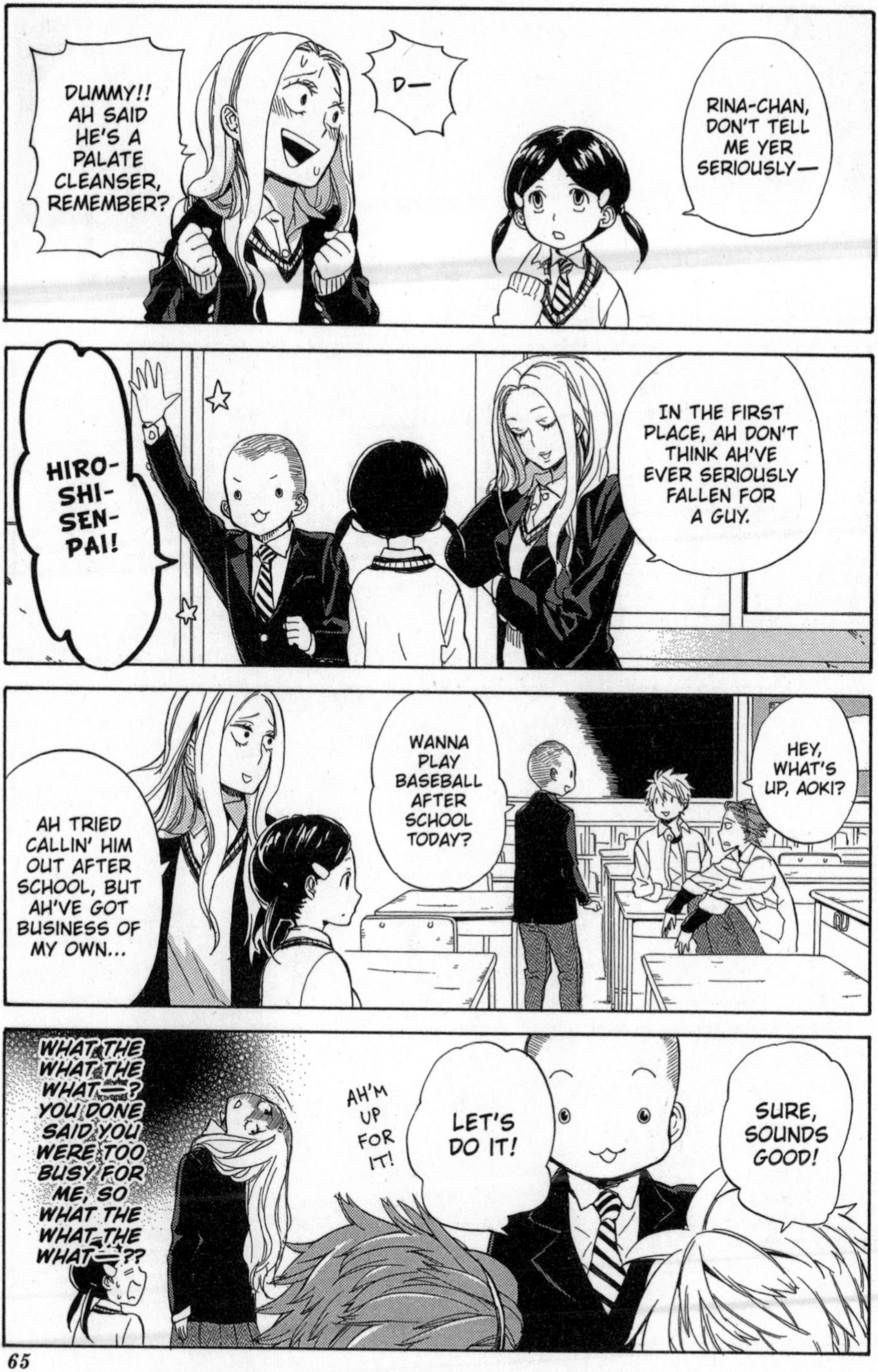
RINA-CHAN, DON'T TELL ME YER SERIOUSLY—
D—
DUMMY!! AH SAID HE'S A PALATE CLEANSER, REMEMBER?
IN THE FIRST PLACE, AH DON'T THINK AH'VE EVER SERIOUSLY FALLEN FOR A GUY.
HIRO-SHI-SEN-PAI!
HEY, WHAT'S UP, AOKI?
WANNA PLAY BASEBALL AFTER SCHOOL TODAY?
AH TRIED CALLIN' HIM OUT AFTER SCHOOL, BUT AH'VE GOT BUSINESS OF MY OWN...
SURE, SOUNDS GOOD!
LET'S DO IT!
AH'M UP FOR IT!
WHAT THE WHAT THE WHAT—? YOU DONE SAID YOU WERE TOO BUSY FOR ME, SO WHAT THE WHAT THE WHAT—??

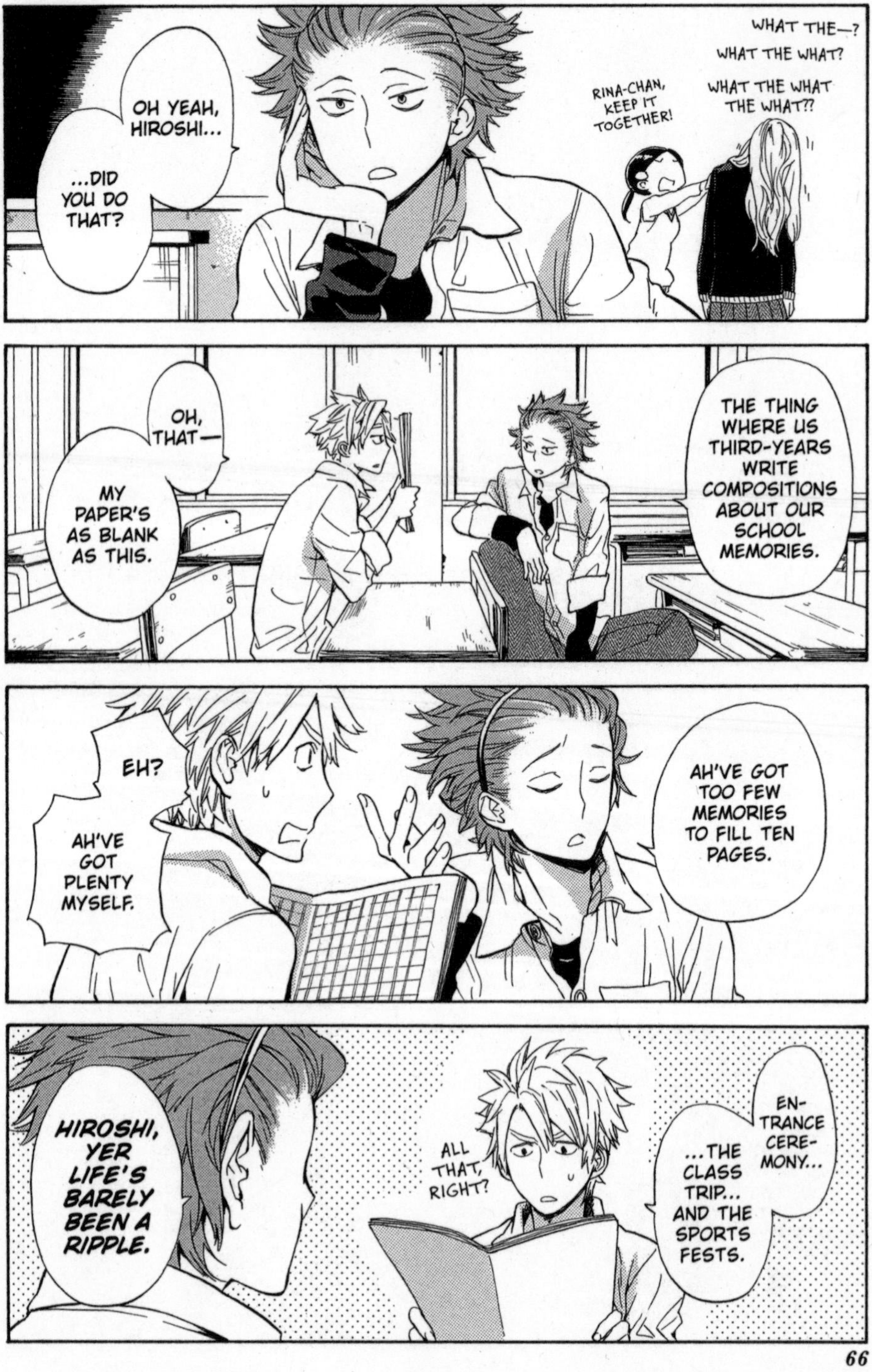
WHAT THE—?
WHAT THE WHAT?
WHAT THE WHAT THE WHAT??
RINA-CHAN, KEEP IT TOGETHER!
OH YEAH, HIROSHI...
...DID YOU DO THAT?
THE THING WHERE US THIRD-YEARS WRITE COMPOSITIONS ABOUT OUR SCHOOL MEMORIES.
OH, THAT—
MY PAPER'S AS BLANK AS THIS.
AH'VE GOT TOO FEW MEMORIES TO FILL TEN PAGES.
EH?
AH'VE GOT PLENTY MYSELF.
EN-TRANCE CERE-MONY...
...THE CLASS TRIP... AND THE SPORTS FESTS.
ALL THAT, RIGHT?
HIROSHI, YER LIFE'S BARELY BEEN A RIPPLE.

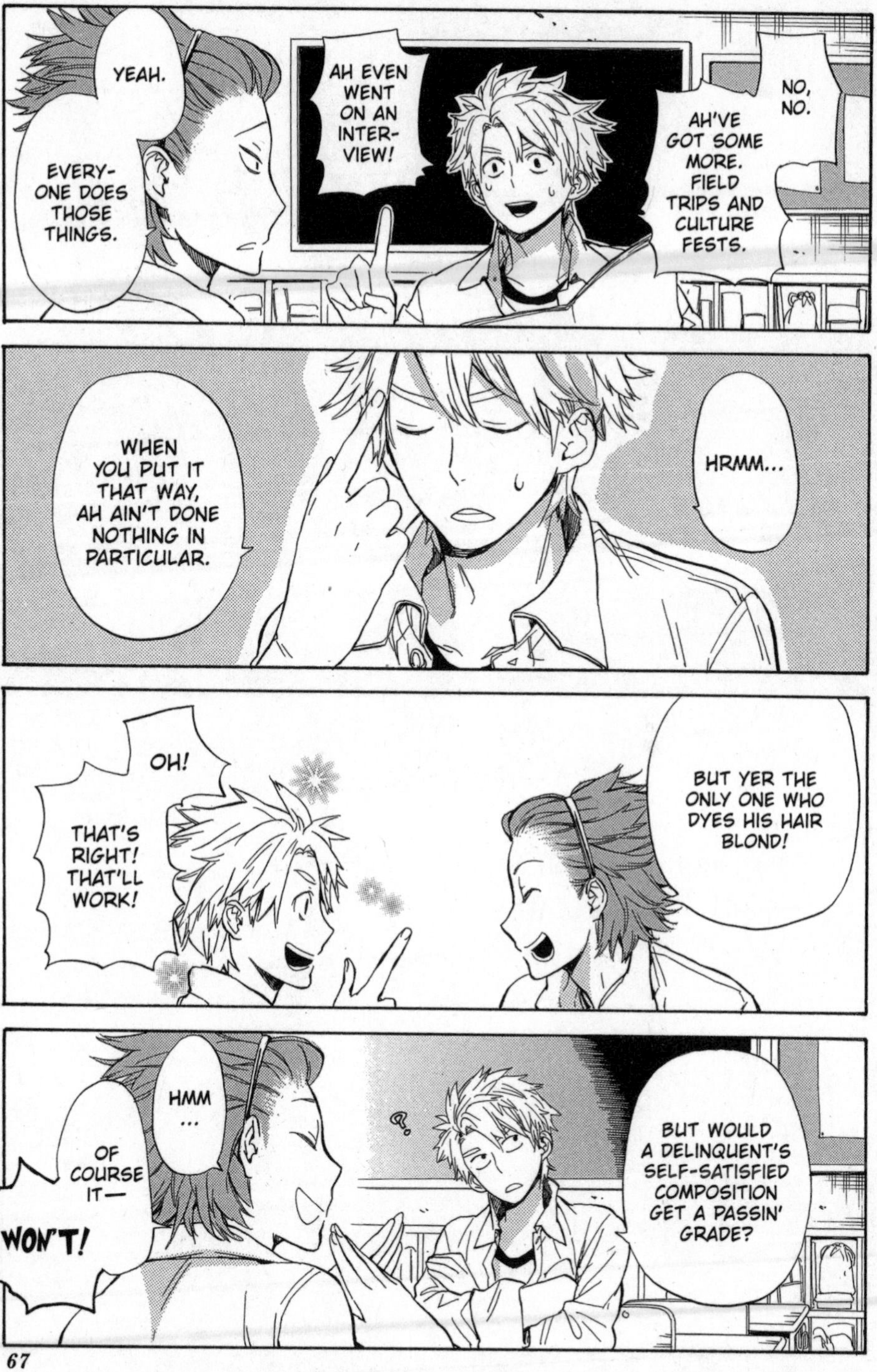
NO, NO.
AH'VE GOT SOME MORE. FIELD TRIPS AND CULTURE FESTS.
AH EVEN WENT ON AN INTERVIEW!
YEAH.
EVERYONE DOES THOSE THINGS.
HRMM...
WHEN YOU PUT IT THAT WAY, AH AIN'T DONE NOTHING IN PARTICULAR.
BUT YER THE ONLY ONE WHO DYES HIS HAIR BLOND!
OH!
THAT'S RIGHT! THAT'LL WORK!
BUT WOULD A DELINQUENT'S SELF-SATISFIED COMPOSITION GET A PASSIN' GRADE?
HMM...
OF COURSE IT—
WON'T!

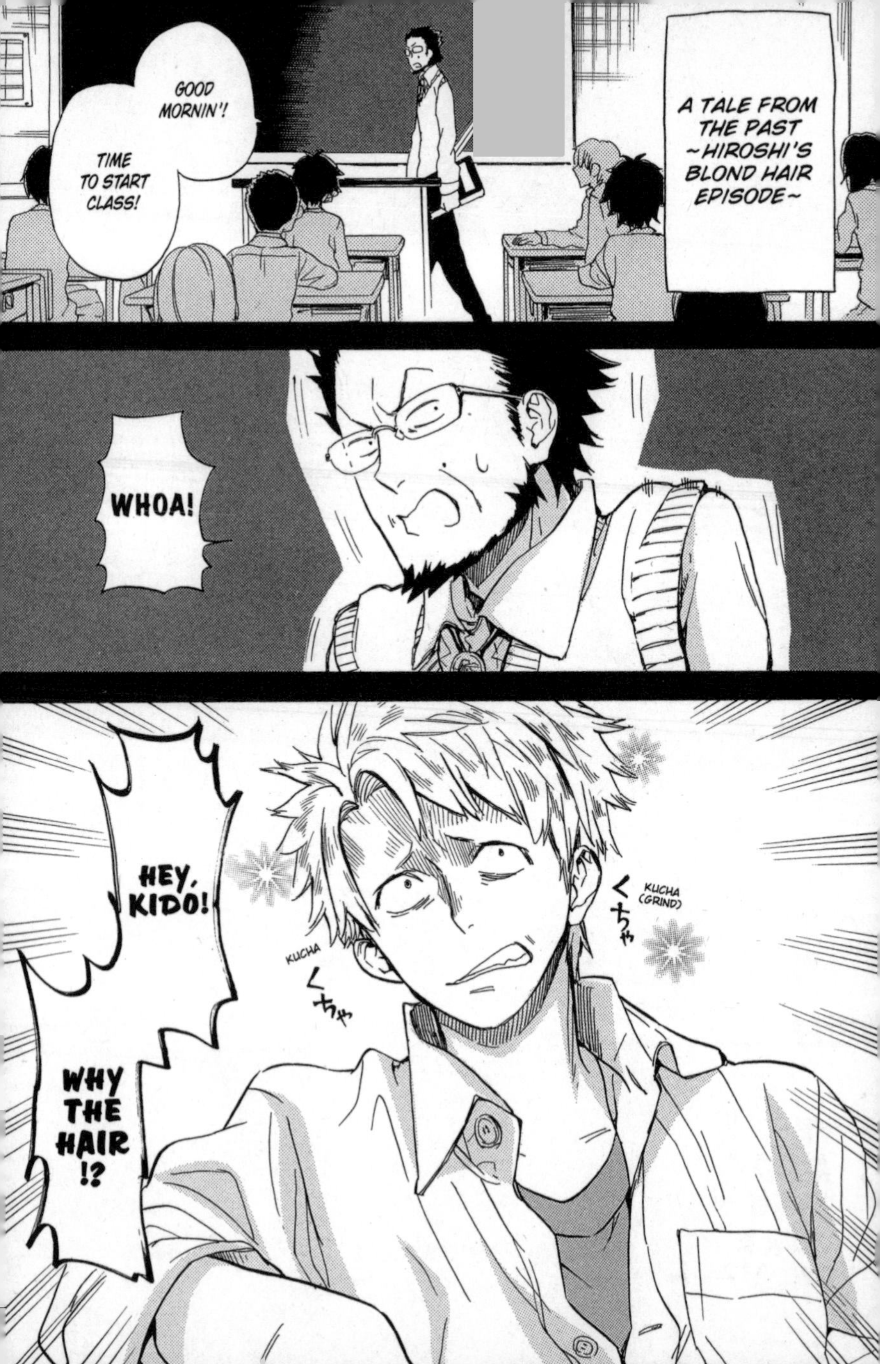
A TALE FROM THE PAST ~HIROSHI'S BLOND HAIR EPISODE~
GOOD MORNIN'!
TIME TO START CLASS!
WHOA!
HEY, KIDO!
WHY THE HAIR!?
くちゃ
KUCHA (GRIND)
KUCHA
くちゃ

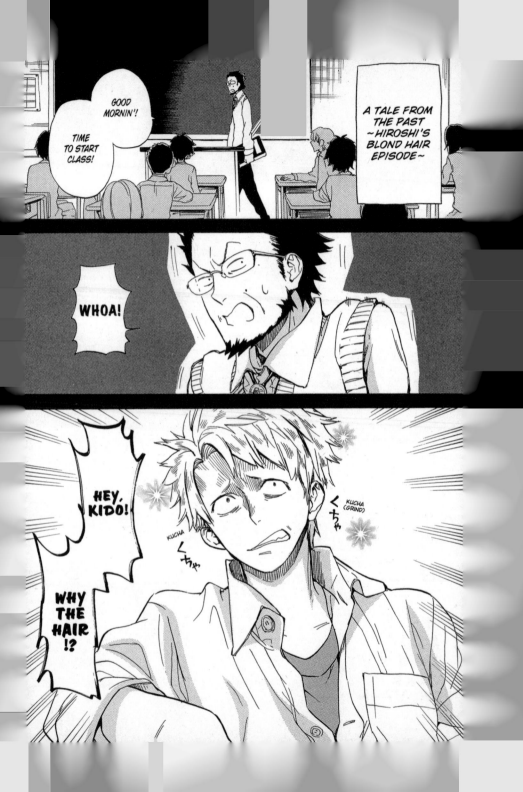

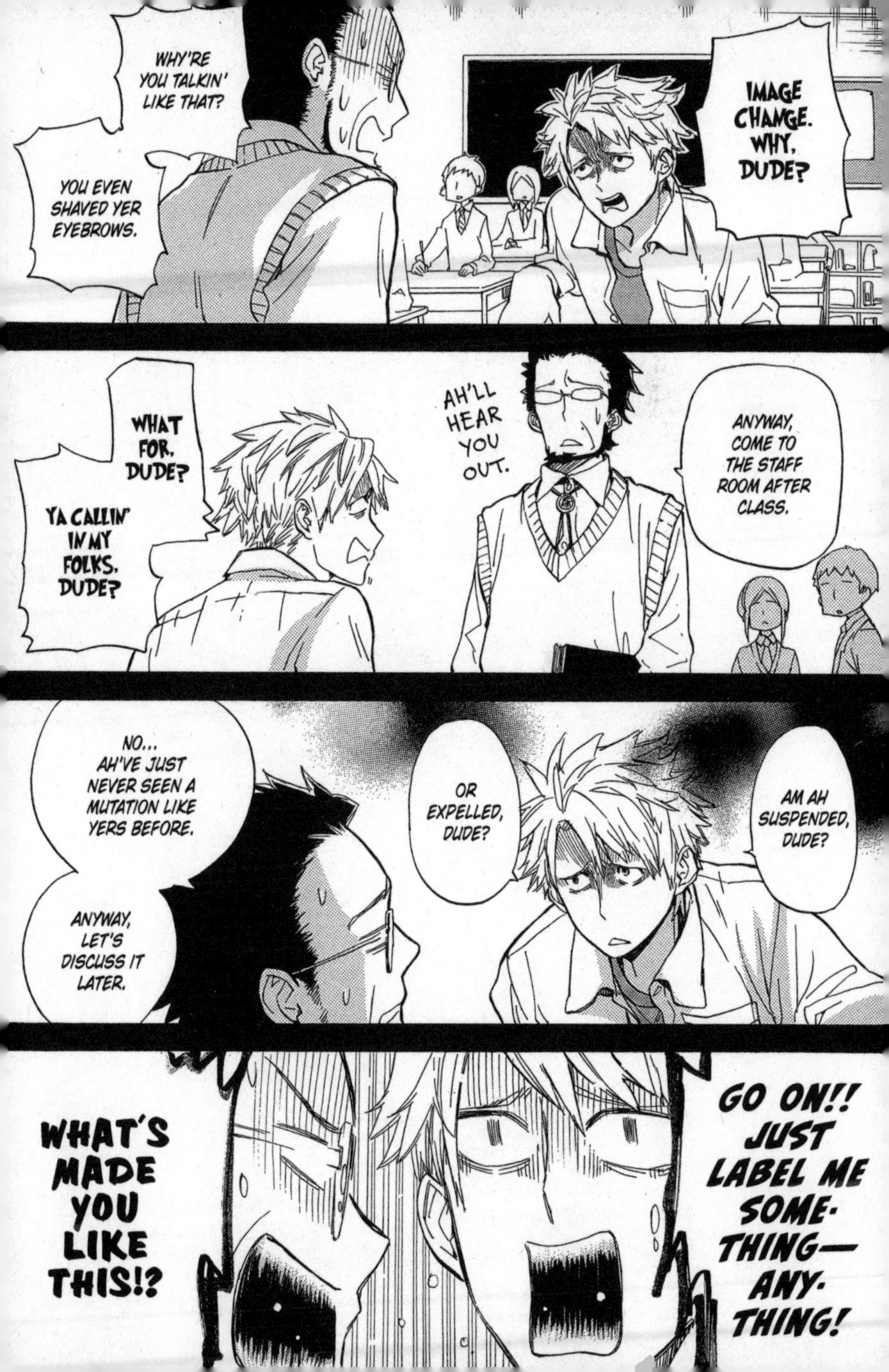
IMAGE CHANGE. WHY, DUDE?
WHY'RE YOU TALKIN' LIKE THAT?
YOU EVEN SHAVED YER EYEBROWS.
ANYWAY, COME TO THE STAFF ROOM AFTER CLASS.
AH'LL HEAR YOU OUT.
WHAT FOR, DUDE?
YA CALLIN' IN MY FOLKS, DUDE?
AM AH SUSPENDED, DUDE?
OR EXPELLED, DUDE?
NO... AH'VE JUST NEVER SEEN A MUTATION LIKE YERS BEFORE.
ANYWAY, LET'S DISCUSS IT LATER.
GO ON!! JUST LABEL ME SOME-THING—ANY-THING!
WHAT'S MADE YOU LIKE THIS!?

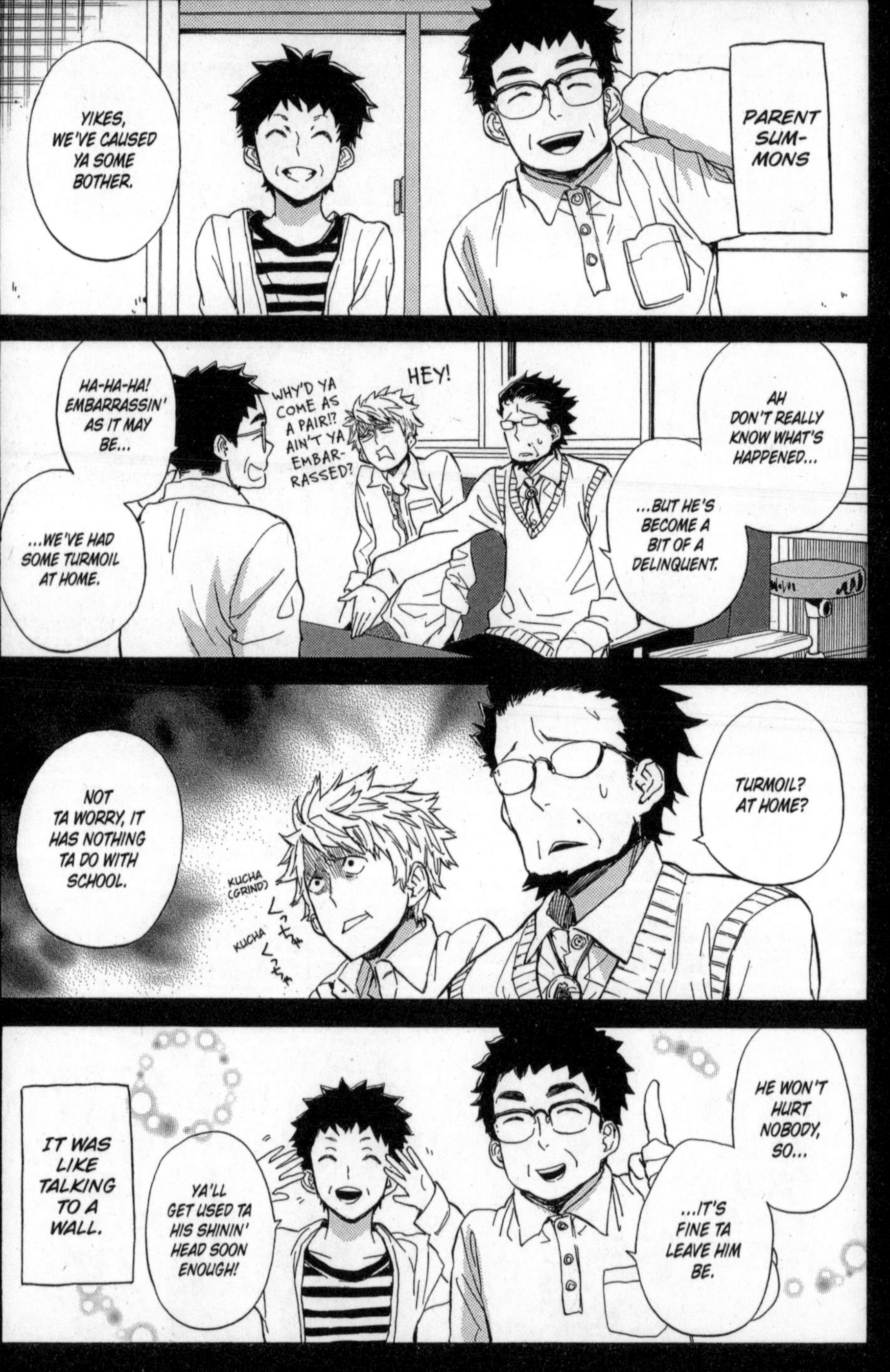
PARENT SUM-MONS
YIKES, WE'VE CAUSED YA SOME BOTHER.
AH DON'T REALLY KNOW WHAT'S HAPPENED...
...BUT HE'S BECOME A BIT OF A DELINQUENT.
HEY!
WHY'D YA COME AS A PAIR!? AIN'T YA EMBAR-RASSED?
HA-HA-HA! EMBARRASSIN' AS IT MAY BE...
...WE'VE HAD SOME TURMOIL AT HOME.
TURMOIL? AT HOME?
KUCHA (GRIND)
KUCHA
NOT TA WORRY, IT HAS NOTHING TA DO WITH SCHOOL.
HE WON'T HURT NOBODY, SO...
...IT'S FINE TA LEAVE HIM BE.
YA'LL GET USED TA HIS SHININ' HEAD SOON ENOUGH!
IT WAS LIKE TALKING TO A WALL.

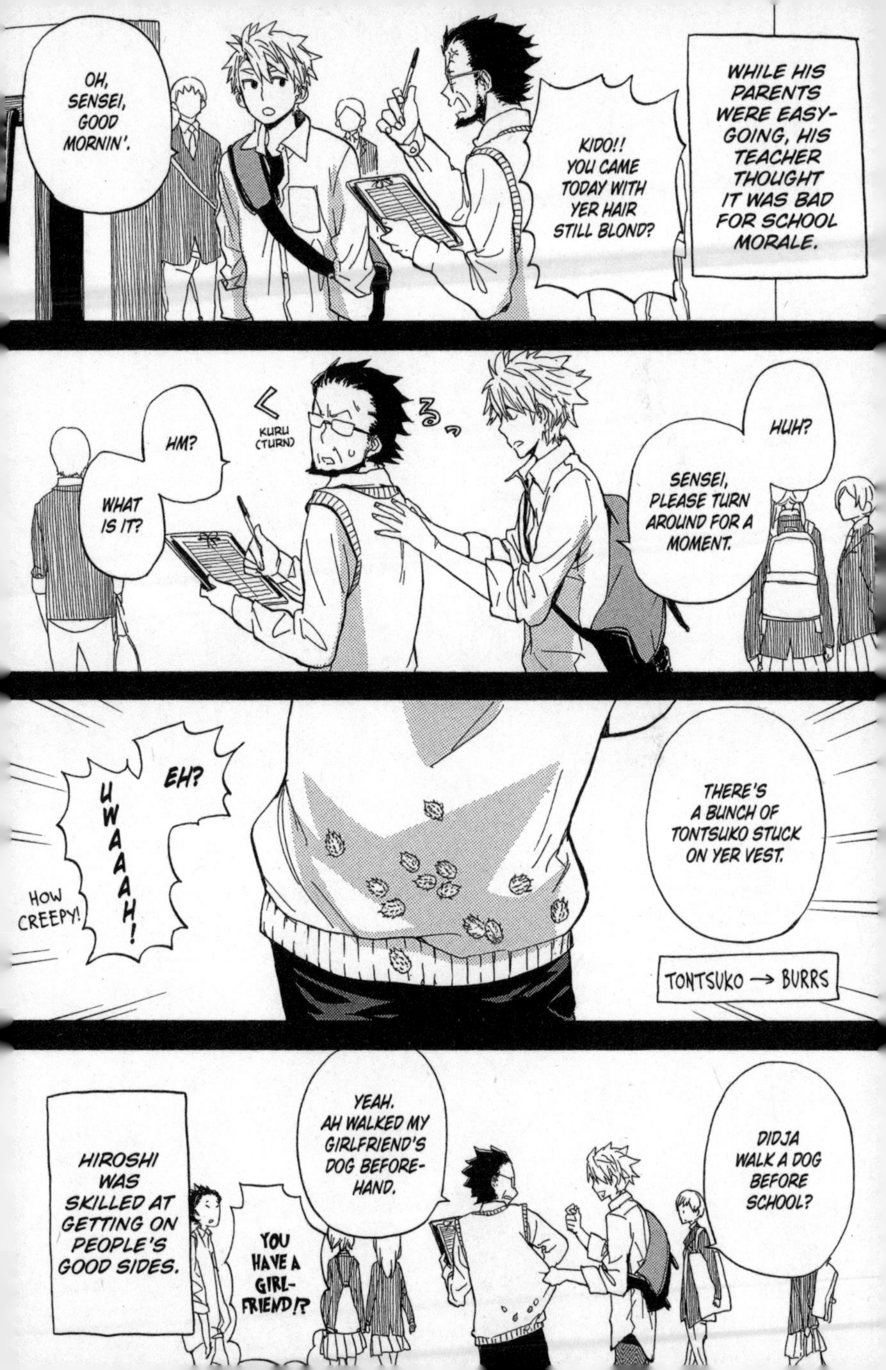
WHILE HIS PARENTS WERE EASYGOING, HIS TEACHER THOUGHT IT WAS BAD FOR SCHOOL MORALE.
KIDO!! YOU CAME TODAY WITH YER HAIR STILL BLOND?
OH, SENSEI, GOOD MORNIN'.
HUH?
SENSEI, PLEASE TURN AROUND FOR A MOMENT.
KURU (TURN)
HM?
WHAT IS IT?
THERE'S A BUNCH OF TONTSUKO STUCK ON YER VEST.
TONTSUKO → BURRS
EH?
UWAAAAH!
HOW CREEPY!
DIDJA WALK A DOG BEFORE SCHOOL?
YEAH. AH WALKED MY GIRLFRIEND'S DOG BEFOREHAND.
YOU HAVE A GIRLFRIEND!?
HIROSHI WAS SKILLED AT GETTING ON PEOPLE'S GOOD SIDES.

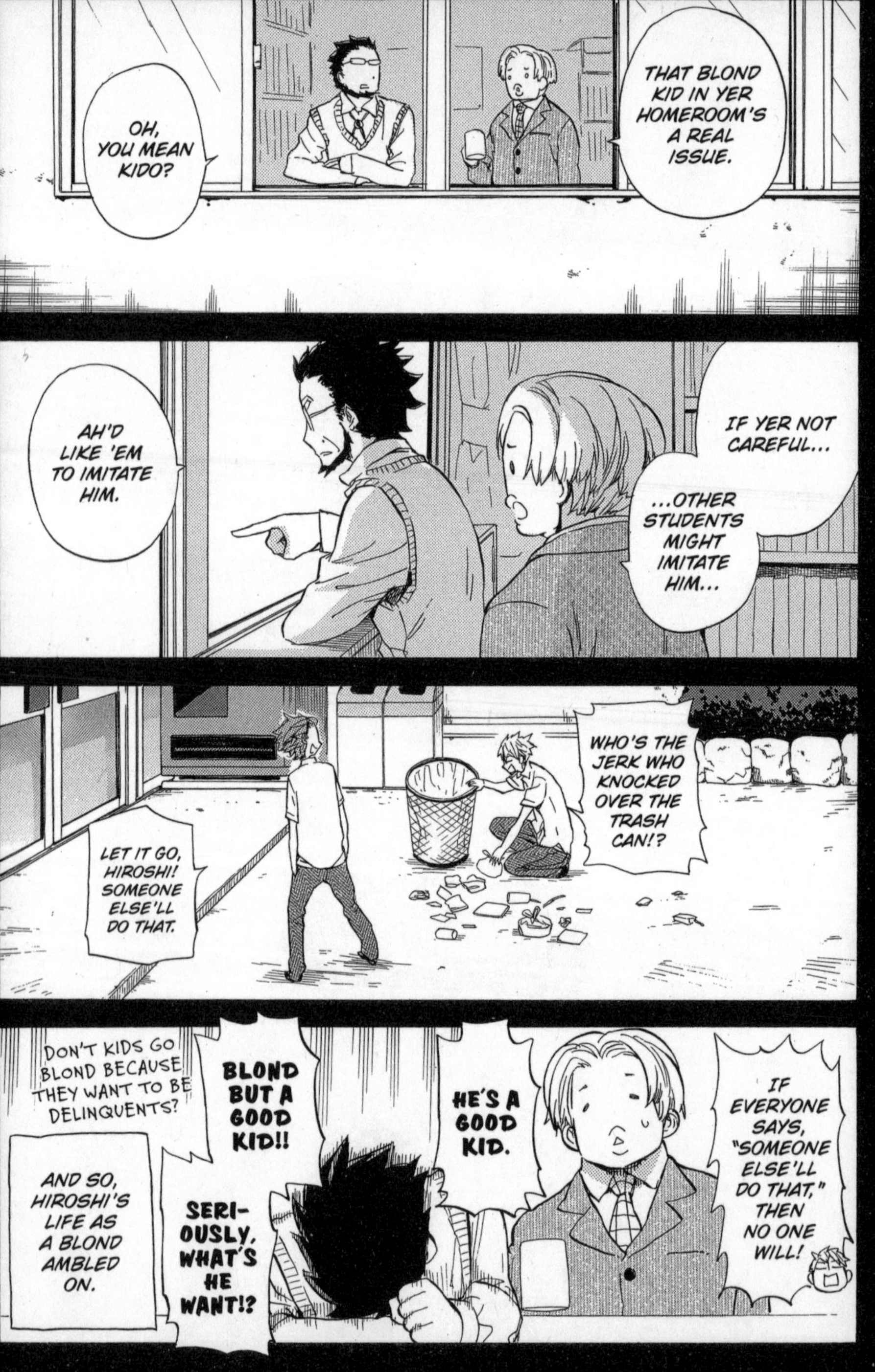
THAT BLOND KID IN YER HOMEROOM'S A REAL ISSUE.
OH, YOU MEAN KIDO?
IF YER NOT CAREFUL...
...OTHER STUDENTS MIGHT IMITATE HIM...
AH'D LIKE 'EM TO IMITATE HIM.
WHO'S THE JERK WHO KNOCKED OVER THE TRASH CAN!?
LET IT GO, HIROSHI! SOMEONE ELSE'LL DO THAT.
IF EVERYONE SAYS, "SOMEONE ELSE'LL DO THAT," THEN NO ONE WILL!
HE'S A GOOD KID.
BLOND BUT A GOOD KID!!
SERI-OUSLY, WHAT'S HE WANT!?
DON'T KIDS GO BLOND BECAUSE THEY WANT TO BE DELINQUENTS?
AND SO, HIROSHI'S LIFE AS A BLOND AMBLED ON.

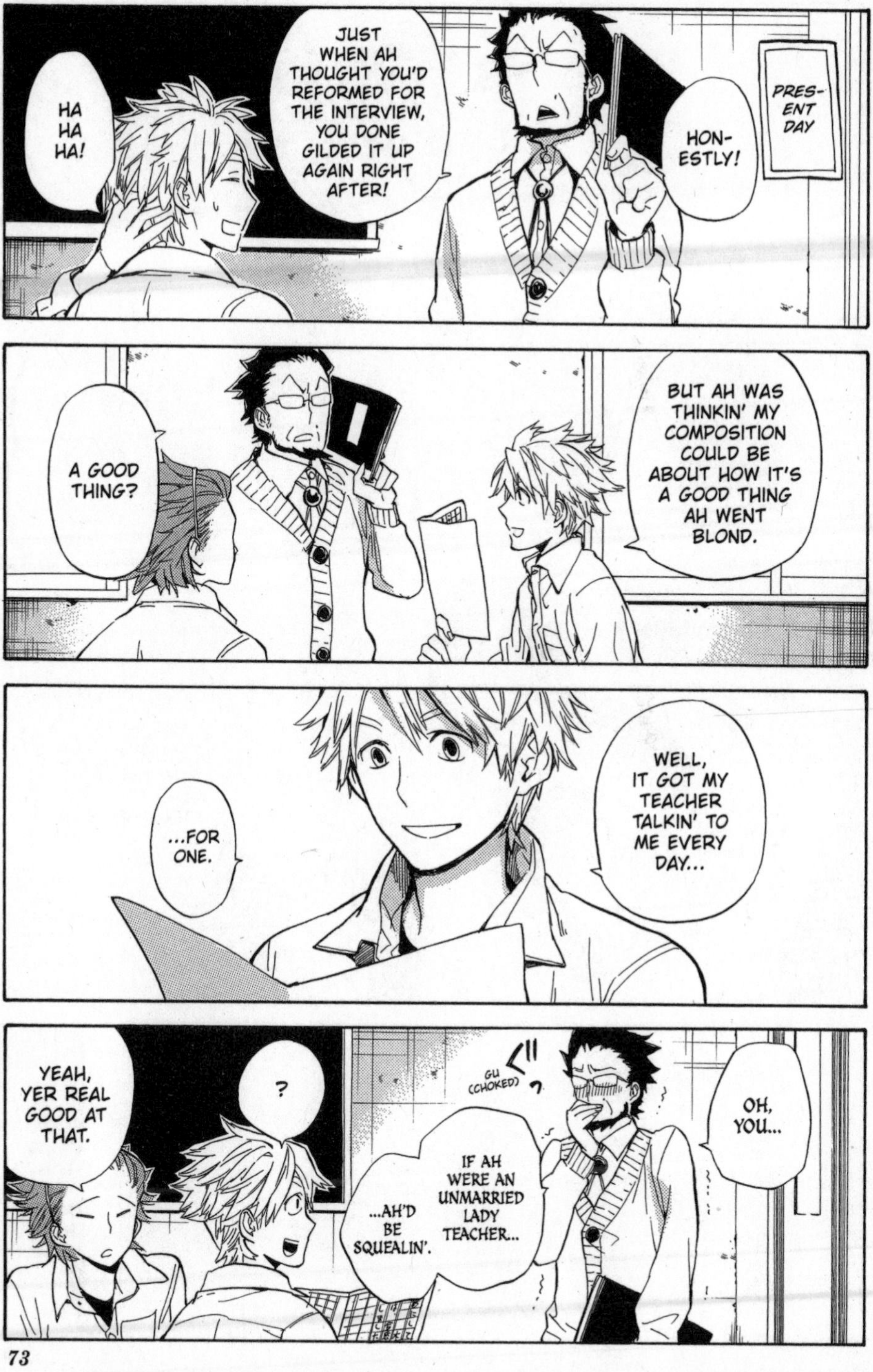
PRES-ENT DAY
HON-ESTLY!
JUST WHEN AH THOUGHT YOU'D REFORMED FOR THE INTERVIEW, YOU DONE GILDED IT UP AGAIN RIGHT AFTER!
HA HA HA!
BUT AH WAS THINKIN' MY COMPOSITION COULD BE ABOUT HOW IT'S A GOOD THING AH WENT BLOND.
A GOOD THING?
WELL, IT GOT MY TEACHER TALKIN' TO ME EVERY DAY...
...FOR ONE.
OH, YOU...
GU (CHOKED)
IF AH WERE AN UNMARRIED LADY TEACHER...
...AH'D BE SQUEALIN'.
?
YEAH, YER REAL GOOD AT THAT.

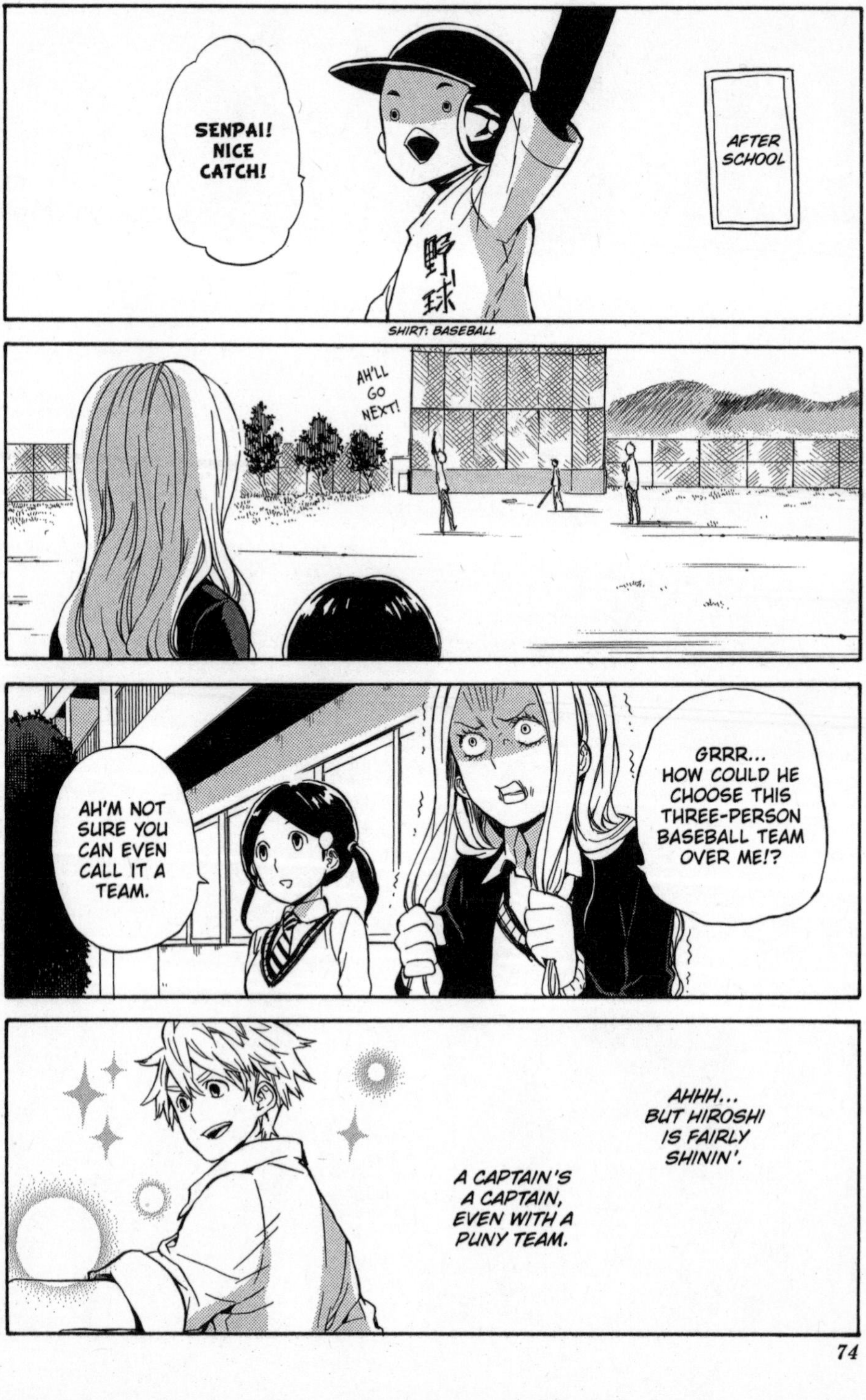
AFTER SCHOOL
SENPAI! NICE CATCH!
SHIRT: BASEBALL
AH'LL GO NEXT!
GRRR... HOW COULD HE CHOOSE THIS THREE-PERSON BASEBALL TEAM OVER ME!?
AH'M NOT SURE YOU CAN EVEN CALL IT A TEAM.
AHHH... BUT HIROSHI IS FAIRLY SHININ'.
A CAPTAIN'S A CAPTAIN, EVEN WITH A PUNY TEAM.

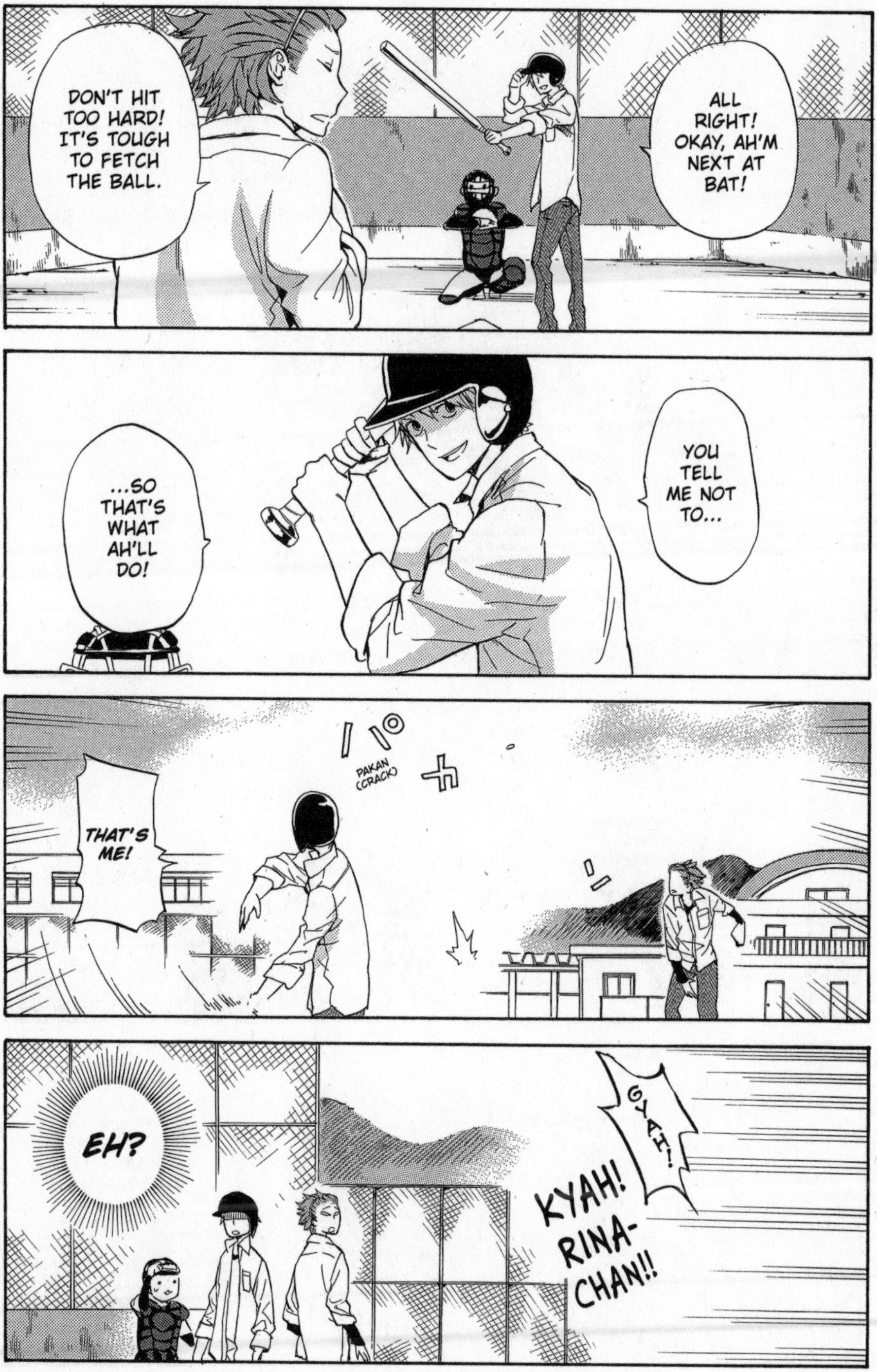
ALL RIGHT! OKAY, AH'M NEXT AT BAT!
DON'T HIT TOO HARD! IT'S TOUGH TO FETCH THE BALL.
YOU TELL ME NOT TO...
...SO THAT'S WHAT AH'LL DO!
PAKAN (CRACK)
THAT'S ME!
GYAH!
KYAH! RINA-CHAN!!
EH?

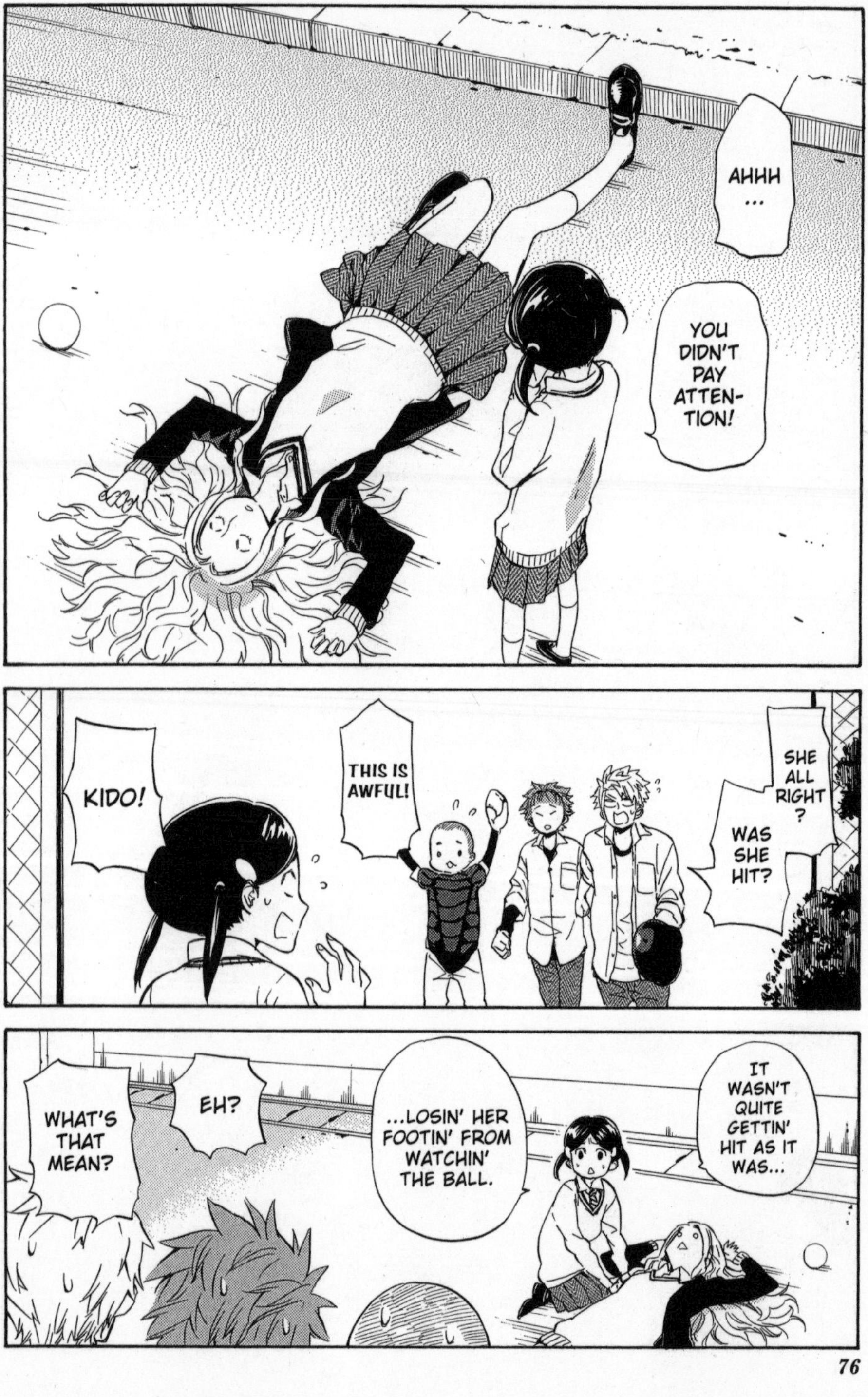
AHHH ...
YOU DIDN'T PAY ATTEN-TION!
SHE ALL RIGHT?
WAS SHE HIT?
THIS IS AWFUL!
KIDO!
IT WASN'T QUITE GETTIN' HIT AS IT WAS...
...LOSIN' HER FOOTIN' FROM WATCHIN' THE BALL.
EH?
WHAT'S THAT MEAN?

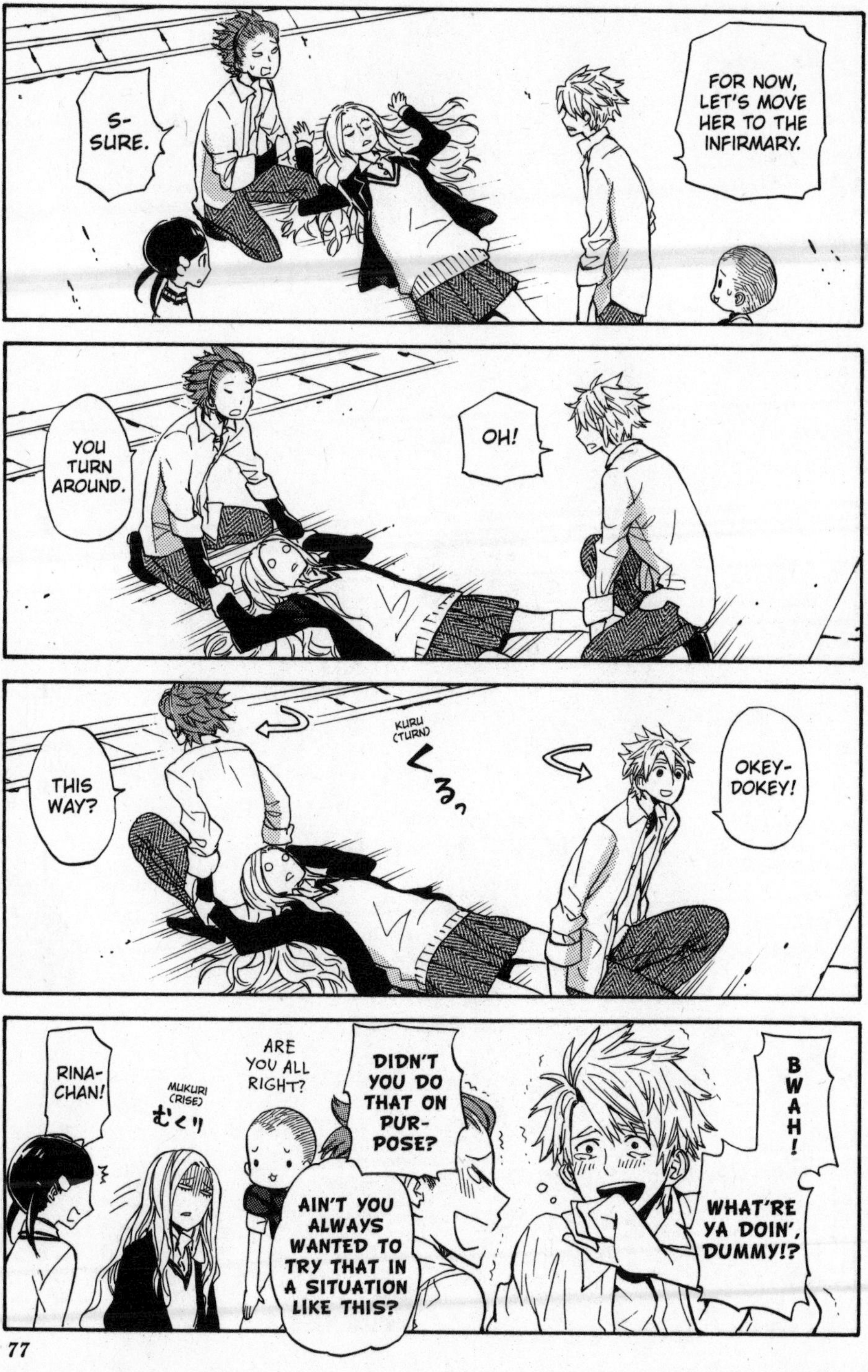
FOR NOW, LET'S MOVE HER TO THE INFIRMARY.
S-SURE.
OH!
YOU TURN AROUND.
OKEY-DOKEY!
KURU (TURN)
くるっ
THIS WAY?
BWAH!
WHAT'RE YA DOIN', DUMMY!?
DIDN'T YOU DO THAT ON PUR-POSE?
AIN'T YOU ALWAYS WANTED TO TRY THAT IN A SITUATION LIKE THIS?
ARE YOU ALL RIGHT?
MUKURI (RISE)
むくり
RINA-CHAN!

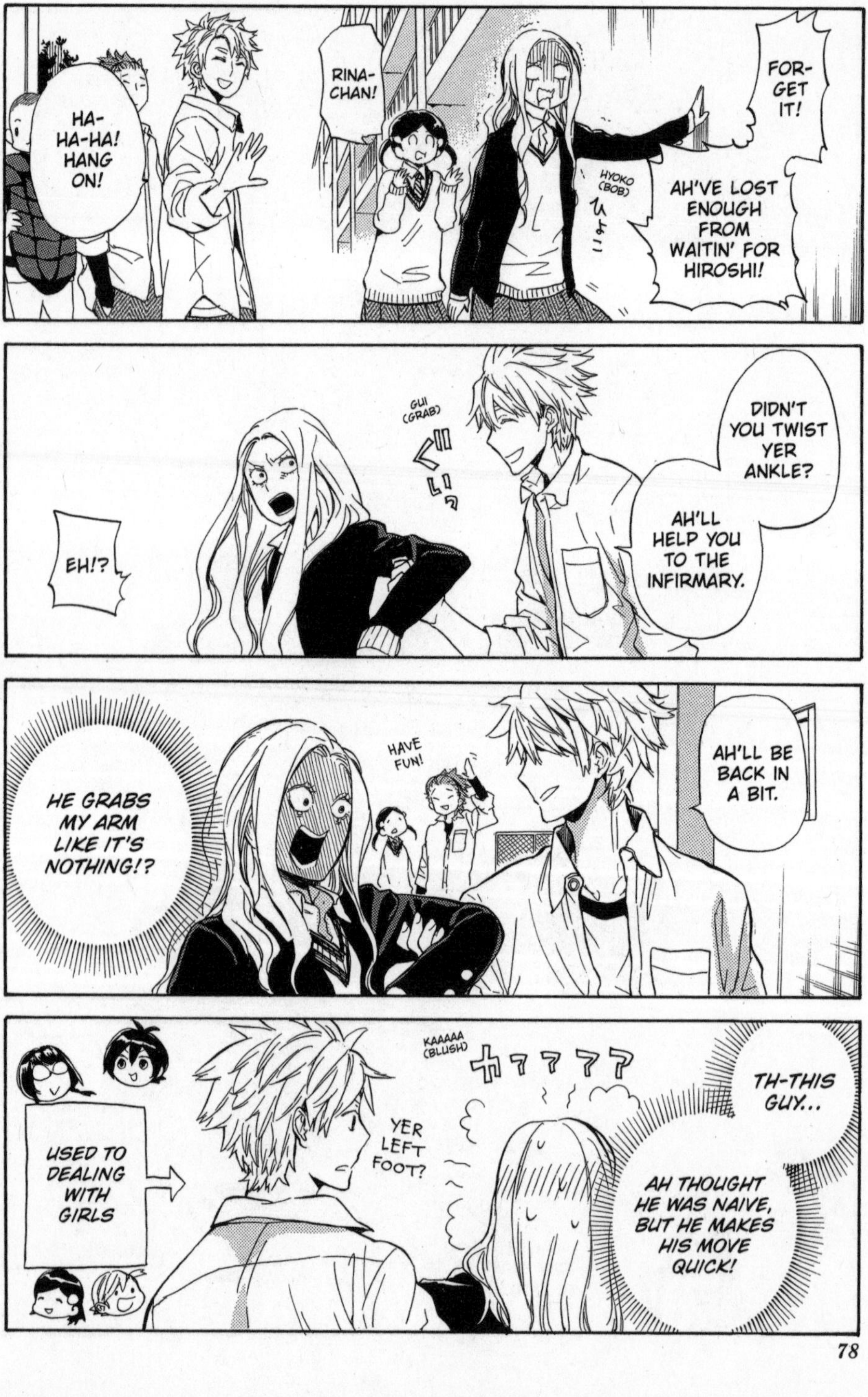
FOR-GET IT!
AH'VE LOST ENOUGH FROM WAITIN' FOR HIROSHI!
HYOKO (BOB)
ひょこ
RINA-CHAN!
HA-HA-HA! HANG ON!
DIDN'T YOU TWIST YER ANKLE?
AH'LL HELP YOU TO THE INFIRMARY.
GUI (GRAB)
ぐいっ
EH!?
AH'LL BE BACK IN A BIT.
HAVE FUN!
HE GRABS MY ARM LIKE IT'S NOTHING!?
TH-THIS GUY...
KAAAAA (BLUSH)
カァァァァ
AH THOUGHT HE WAS NAIVE, BUT HE MAKES HIS MOVE QUICK!
YER LEFT FOOT?
USED TO DEALING WITH GIRLS

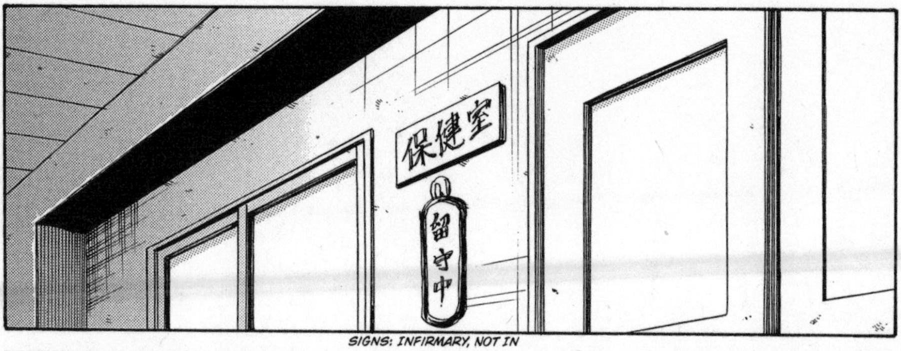
保健室
留守中

SIGNS: INFIRMARY, NOT IN

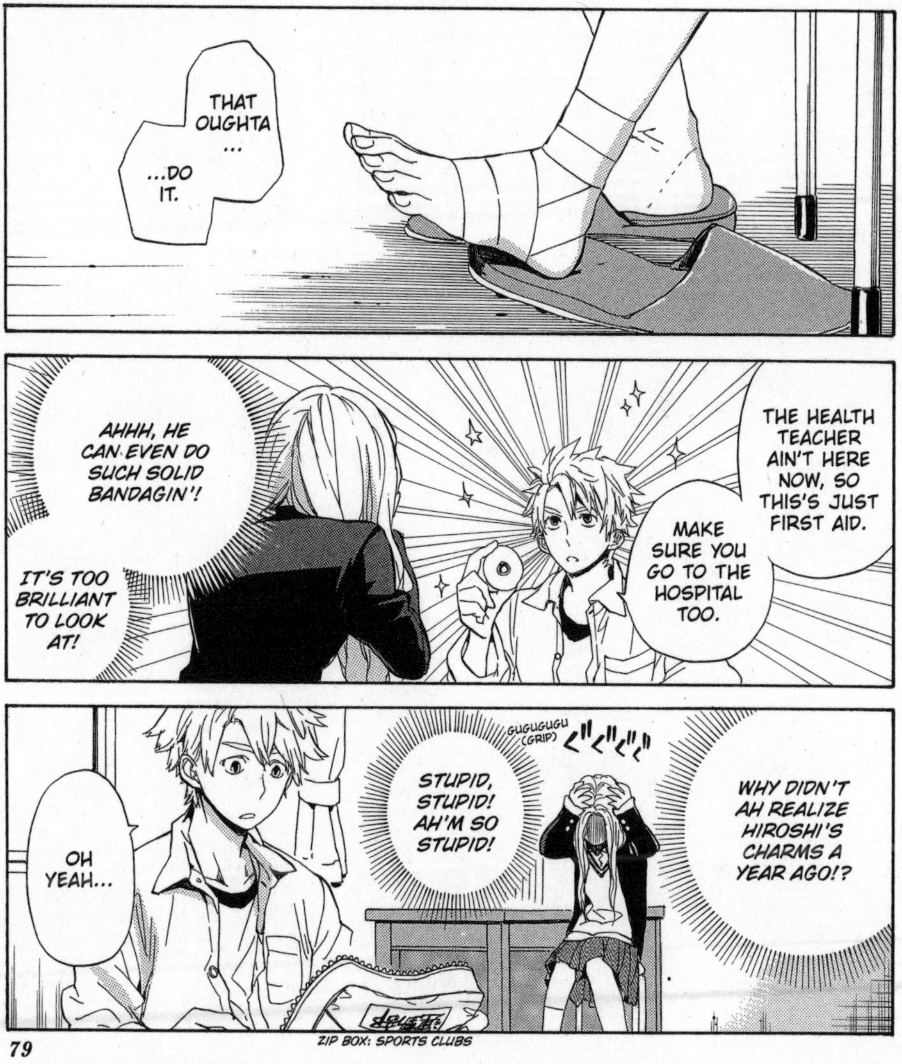
THAT OUGHTA ...
...DO IT.
THE HEALTH TEACHER AIN'T HERE NOW, SO THIS'S JUST FIRST AID.
MAKE SURE YOU GO TO THE HOSPITAL TOO.
AHHH, HE CAN EVEN DO SUCH SOLID BANDAGIN'!
IT'S TOO BRILLIANT TO LOOK AT!
WHY DIDN'T AH REALIZE HIROSHI'S CHARMS A YEAR AGO!?
GUGUGUGU (GRIP) ぐぐぐぐ
STUPID, STUPID! AH'M SO STUPID!
OH YEAH...

ZIP BOX: SPORTS CLUBS

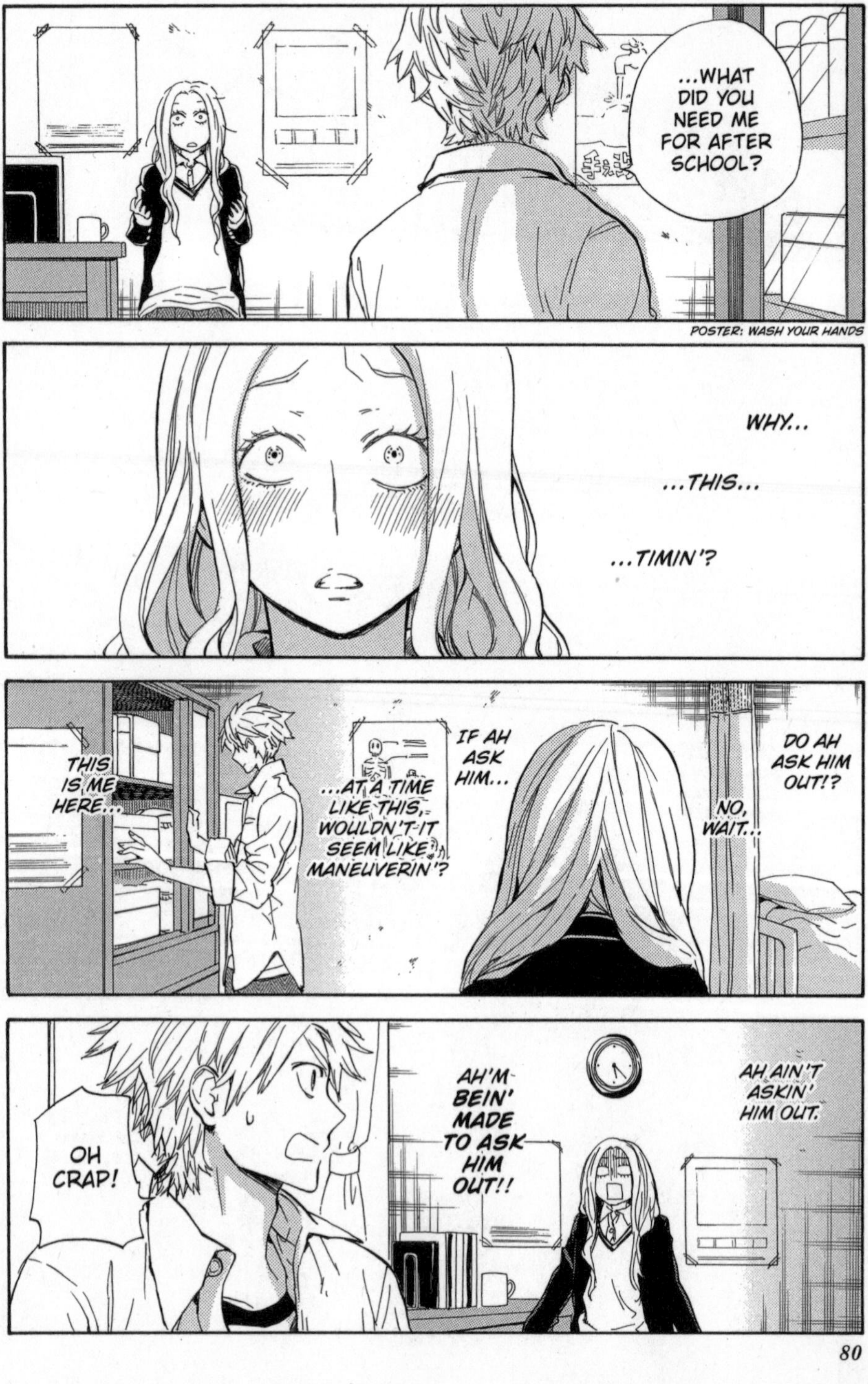
...WHAT DID YOU NEED ME FOR AFTER SCHOOL?
POSTER: WASH YOUR HANDS
WHY...
...THIS...
...TIMIN'?
DO AH ASK HIM OUT!?
NO, WAIT...
IF AH ASK HIM...
...AT A TIME LIKE THIS, WOULDN'T IT SEEM LIKE MANEUVERIN'?
THIS IS ME HERE...
AH AIN'T ASKIN' HIM OUT.
AH'M BEIN' MADE TO ASK HIM OUT!!
OH CRAP!

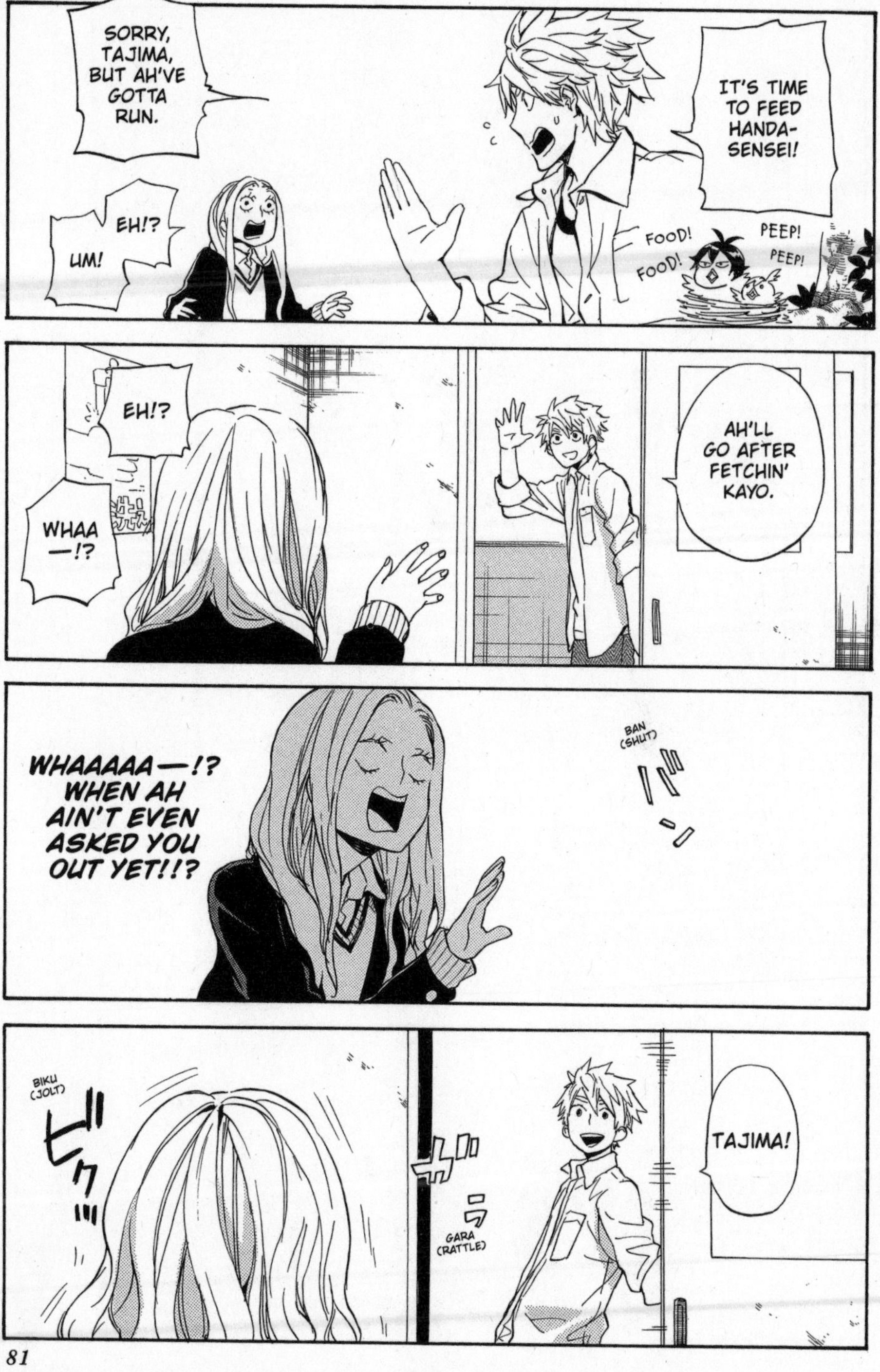
SORRY, TAJIMA, BUT AH'VE GOTTA RUN.
IT'S TIME TO FEED HANDA-SENSEI!
FOOD! FOOD!
PEEP! PEEP!
EH!?
UM!
AH'LL GO AFTER FETCHIN' KAYO.
EH!?
WHAA—!?
BAN (SHUT)
WHAAAAA—!? WHEN AH AIN'T EVEN ASKED YOU OUT YET!!?
TAJIMA!
GARA (RATTLE)
BIKU (JOLT)

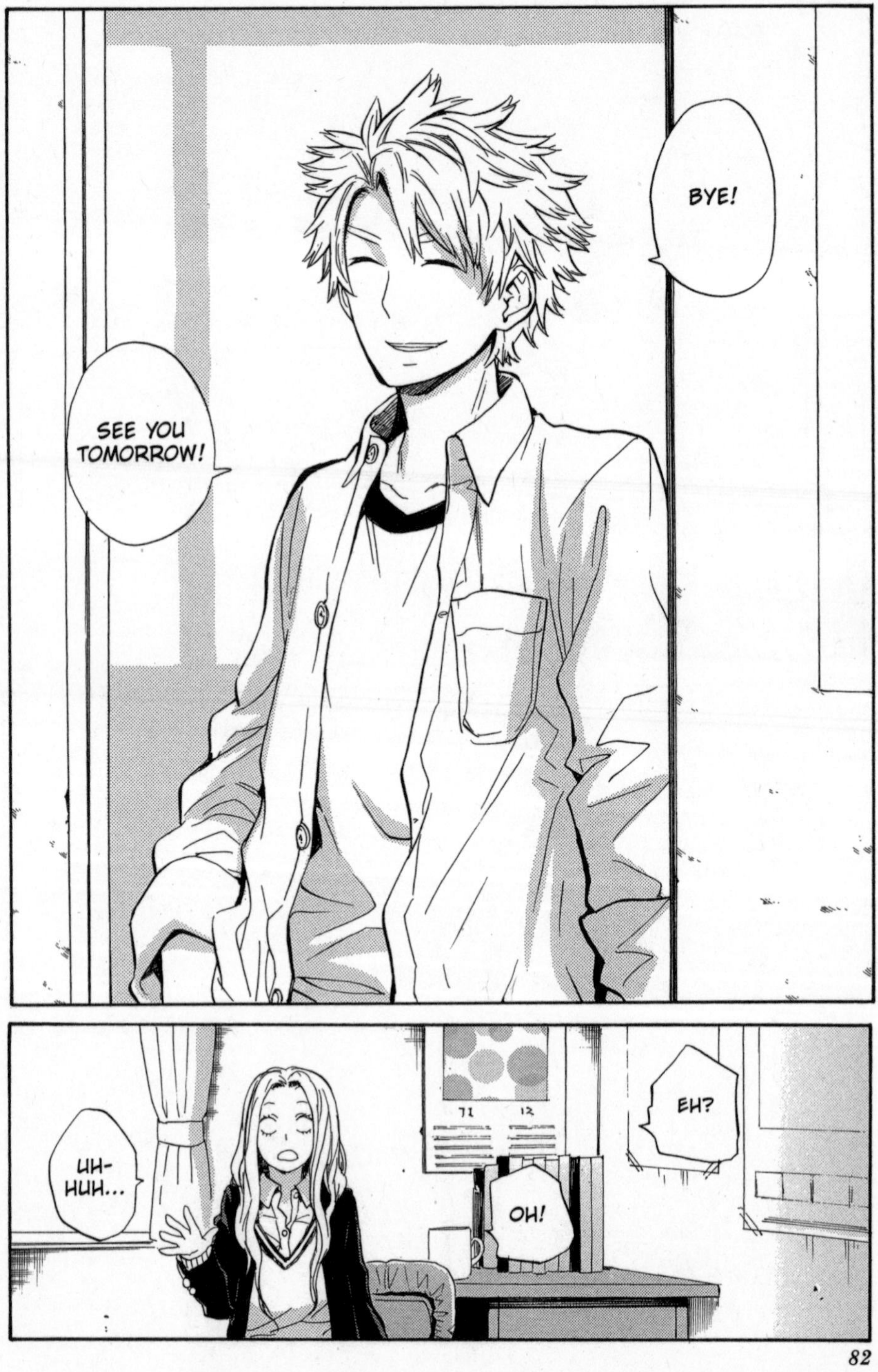
BYE!
SEE YOU TOMORROW!
EH?
OH!
UH-HUH...

SEE YOU TOMOR-ROW.

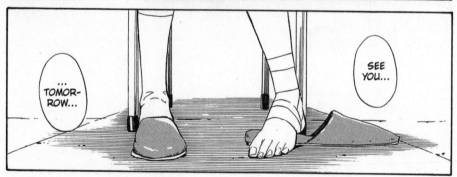

...TOMOR-ROW...

SEE YOU...

ACK!

YOU STARTLED ME!

BAN (BANG)

BIKU (JOLT)

RINA-CHAN!

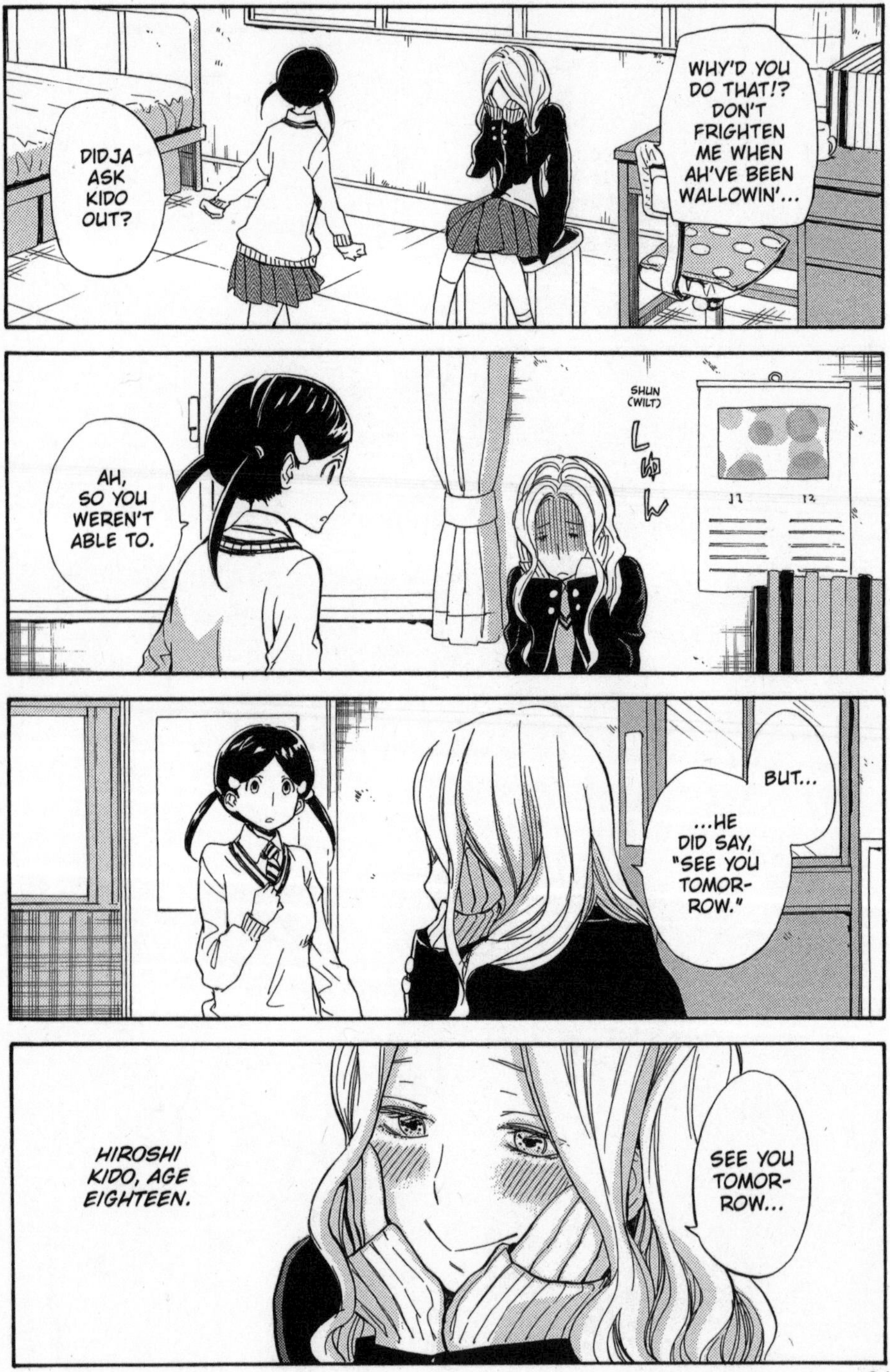
WHY'D YOU DO THAT!? DON'T FRIGHTEN ME WHEN AH'VE BEEN WALLOWIN'...
DIDJA ASK KIDO OUT?
SHUN (WILT)
しゅん
AH, SO YOU WEREN'T ABLE TO.
BUT...
...HE DID SAY, "SEE YOU TOMOR-ROW."
SEE YOU TOMOR-ROW...
HIROSHI KIDO, AGE EIGHTEEN.

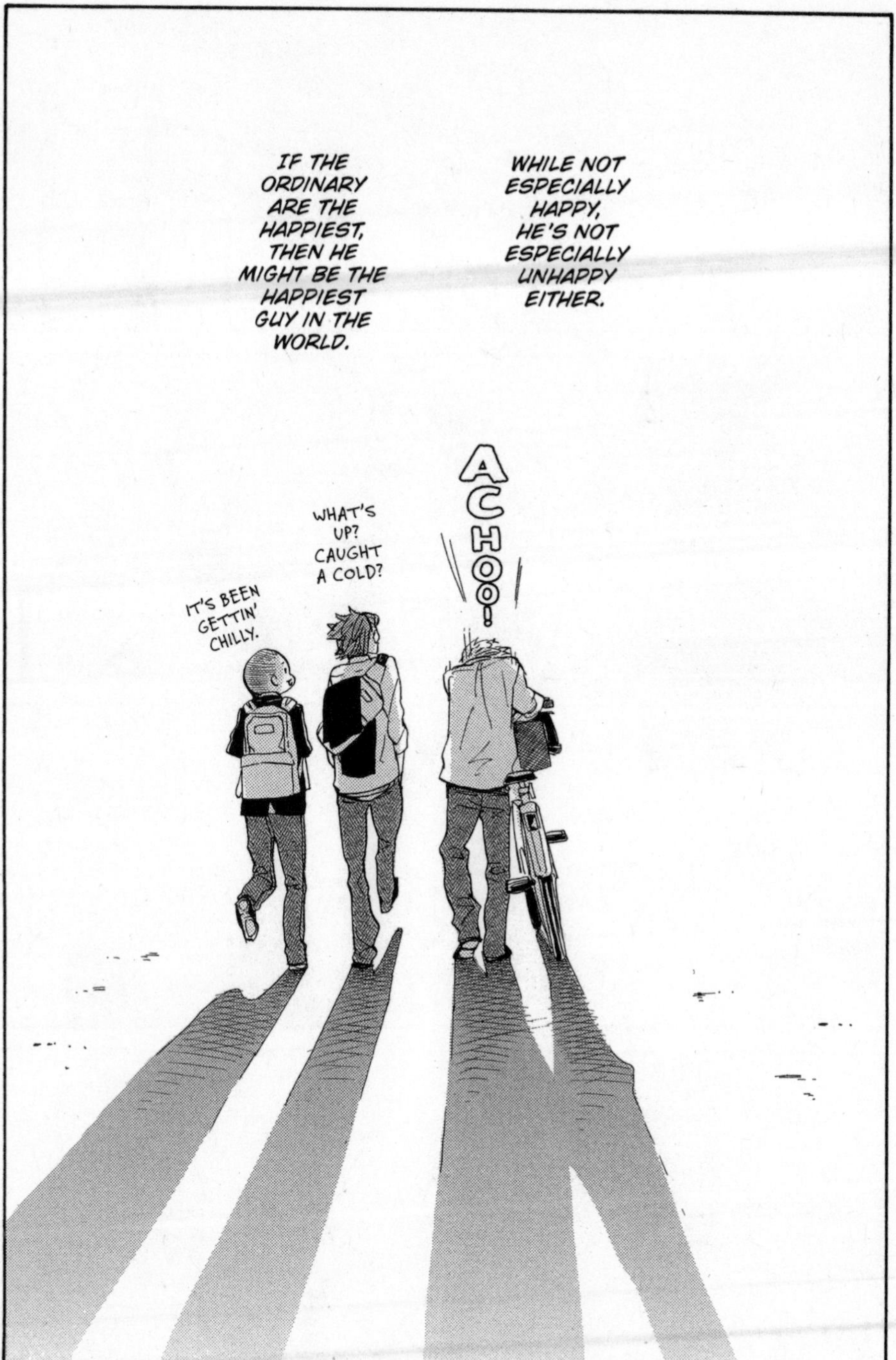
WHILE NOT ESPECIALLY HAPPY, HE'S NOT ESPECIALLY UNHAPPY EITHER.
IF THE ORDINARY ARE THE HAPPIEST, THEN HE MIGHT BE THE HAPPIEST GUY IN THE WORLD.
ACHOO!
WHAT'S UP? CAUGHT A COLD?
IT'S BEEN GETTIN' CHILLY.

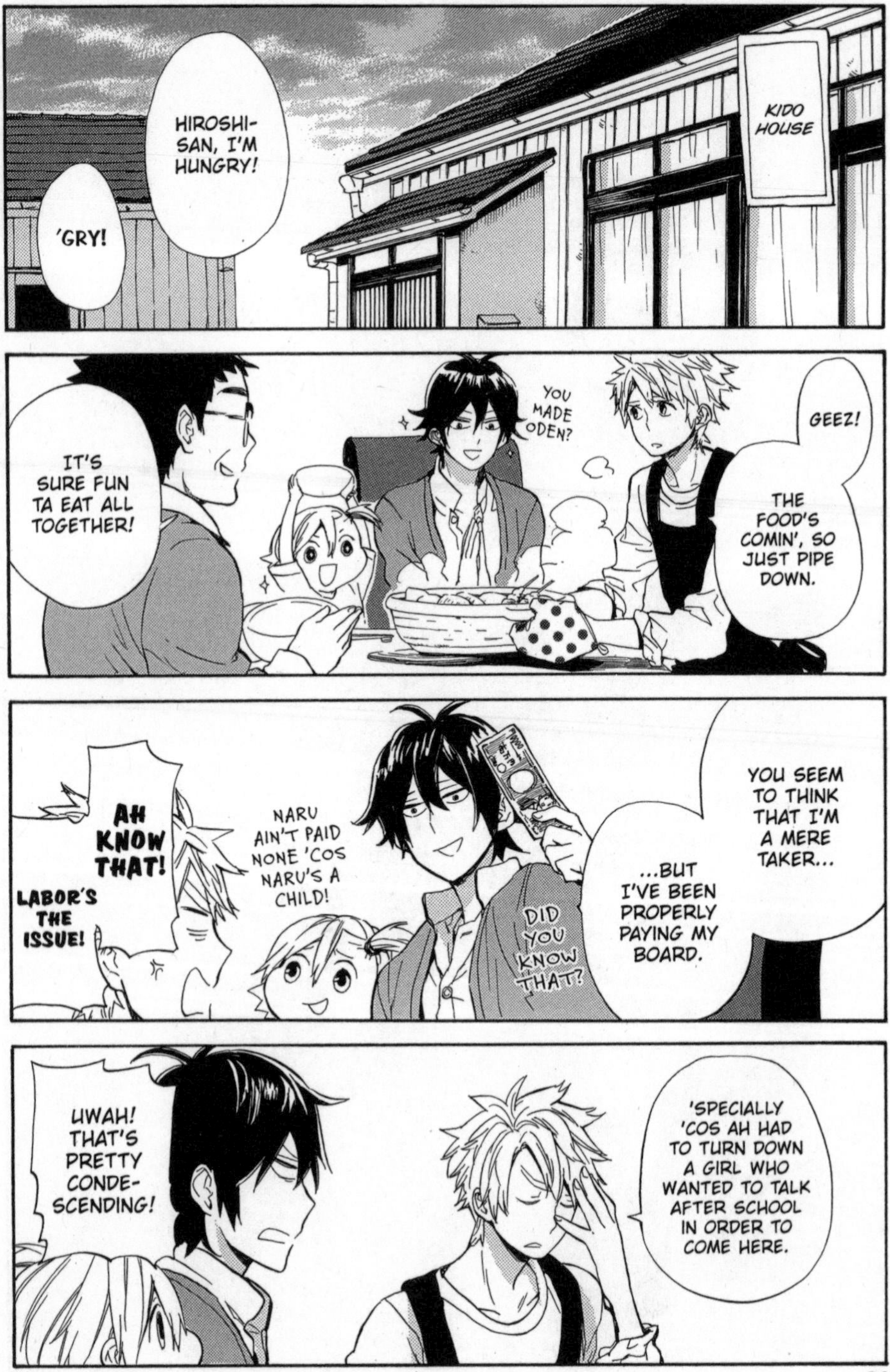
KIDO HOUSE
HIROSHI-SAN, I'M HUNGRY!
'GRY!
GEEZ!
THE FOOD'S COMIN', SO JUST PIPE DOWN.
YOU MADE ODEN?
IT'S SURE FUN TA EAT ALL TOGETHER!
YOU SEEM TO THINK THAT I'M A MERE TAKER...
...BUT I'VE BEEN PROPERLY PAYING MY BOARD.
DID YOU KNOW THAT?
NARU AIN'T PAID NONE 'COS NARU'S A CHILD!
AH KNOW THAT!
LABOR'S THE ISSUE!
'SPECIALLY 'COS AH HAD TO TURN DOWN A GIRL WHO WANTED TO TALK AFTER SCHOOL IN ORDER TO COME HERE.
UWAH! THAT'S PRETTY CONDE-SCENDING!

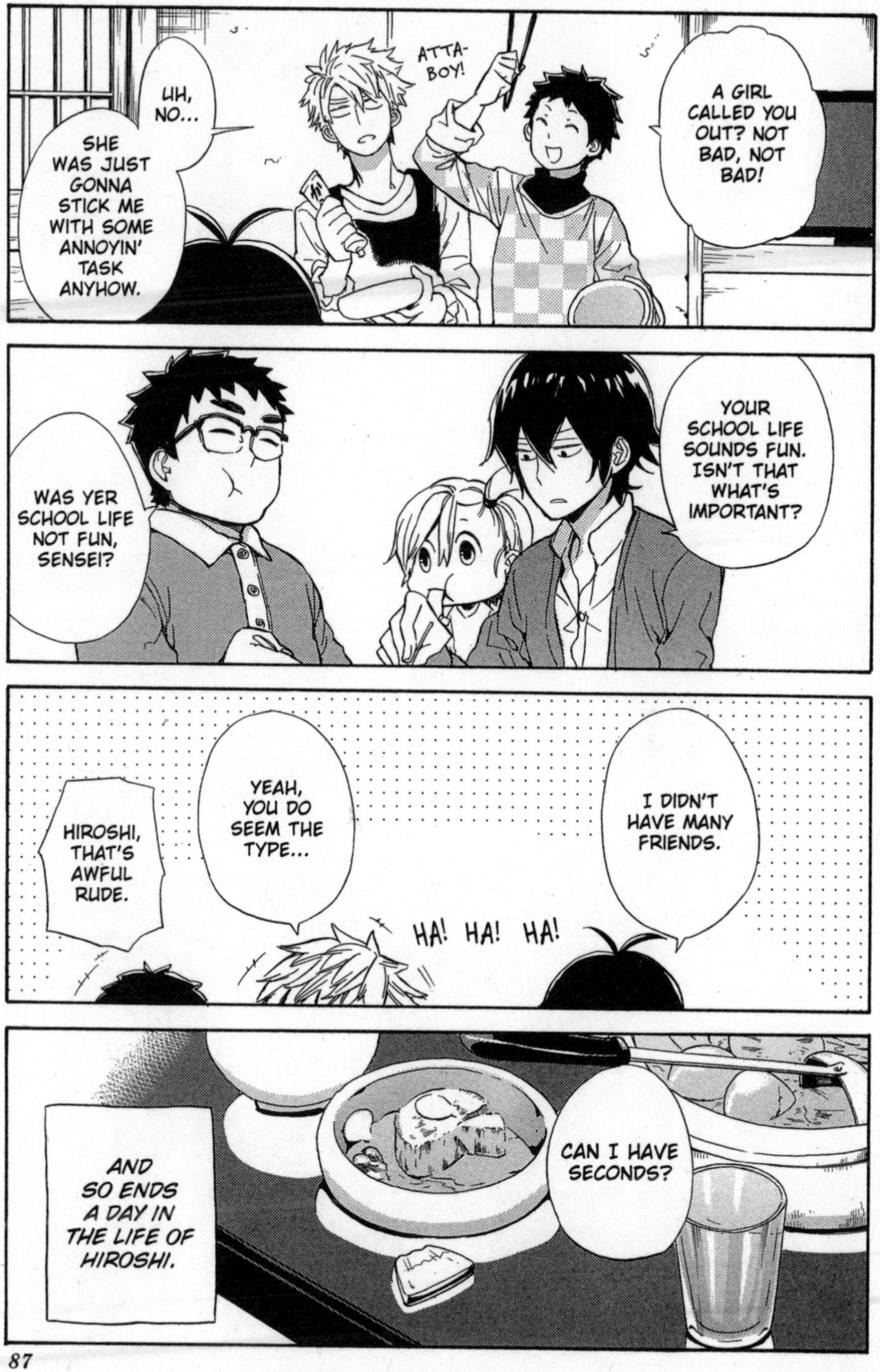
A GIRL CALLED YOU OUT? NOT BAD, NOT BAD!
ATTA-BOY!
UH, NO...
SHE WAS JUST GONNA STICK ME WITH SOME ANNOYIN' TASK ANYHOW.
YOUR SCHOOL LIFE SOUNDS FUN. ISN'T THAT WHAT'S IMPORTANT?
WAS YER SCHOOL LIFE NOT FUN, SENSEI?
I DIDN'T HAVE MANY FRIENDS.
HA! HA! HA!
YEAH, YOU DO SEEM THE TYPE...
HIROSHI, THAT'S AWFUL RUDE.
CAN I HAVE SECONDS?
AND SO ENDS A DAY IN THE LIFE OF HIROSHI.

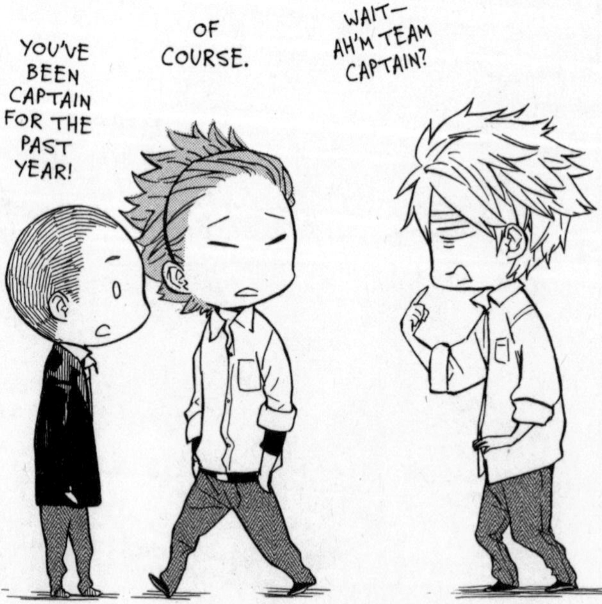
WAIT— AH'M TEAM CAPTAIN?
OF COURSE.
YOU'VE BEEN CAPTAIN FOR THE PAST YEAR!

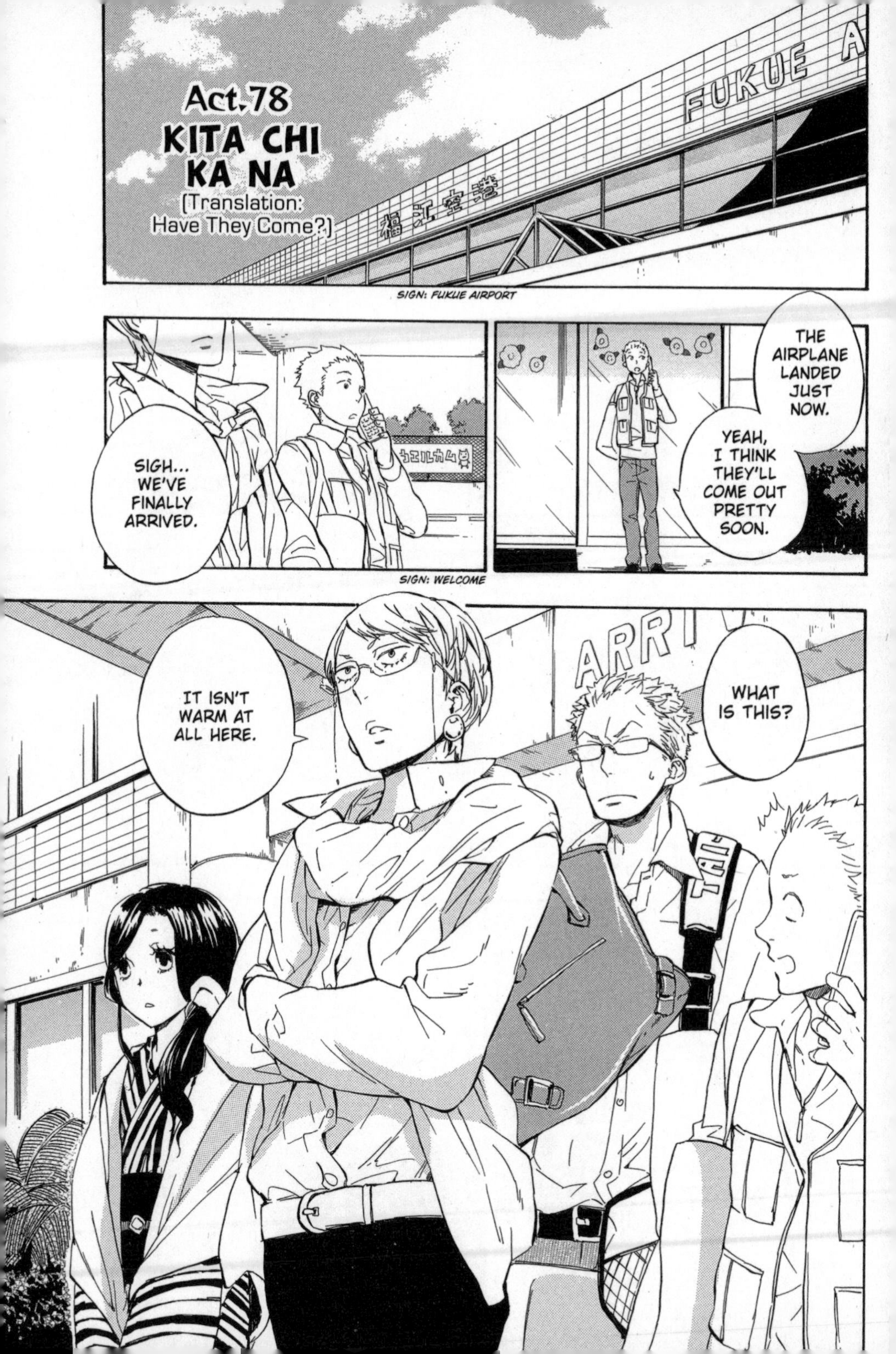
Act.78
KITA CHI KA NA
[Translation: Have They Come?]
SIGN: FUKUE AIRPORT
THE AIRPLANE LANDED JUST NOW.
YEAH, I THINK THEY'LL COME OUT PRETTY SOON.
SIGH... WE'VE FINALLY ARRIVED.
SIGN: WELCOME
WHAT IS THIS?
IT ISN'T WARM AT ALL HERE.

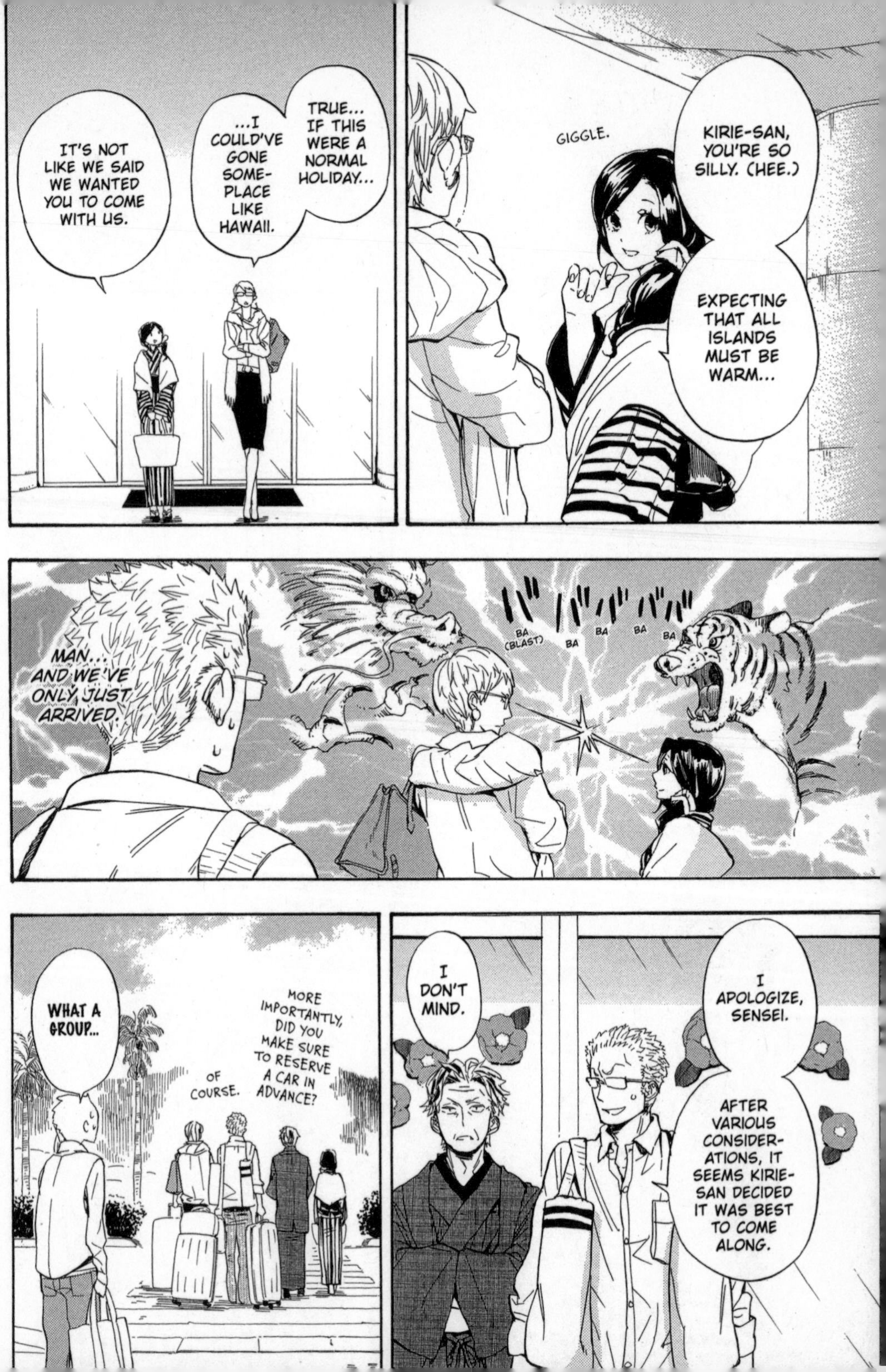
KIRIE-SAN, YOU'RE SO SILLY. (HEE.)
GIGGLE.
EXPECTING THAT ALL ISLANDS MUST BE WARM...
TRUE... IF THIS WERE A NORMAL HOLIDAY...
...I COULD'VE GONE SOME-PLACE LIKE HAWAII.
IT'S NOT LIKE WE SAID WE WANTED YOU TO COME WITH US.
バババババ
BA (BLAST) BA BA BA BA
MAN... AND WE'VE ONLY JUST ARRIVED.
I APOLOGIZE, SENSEI.
I DON'T MIND.
AFTER VARIOUS CONSIDER-ATIONS, IT SEEMS KIRIE-SAN DECIDED IT WAS BEST TO COME ALONG.
MORE IMPORTANTLY, DID YOU MAKE SURE TO RESERVE A CAR IN ADVANCE?
OF COURSE.
WHAT A GROUP...

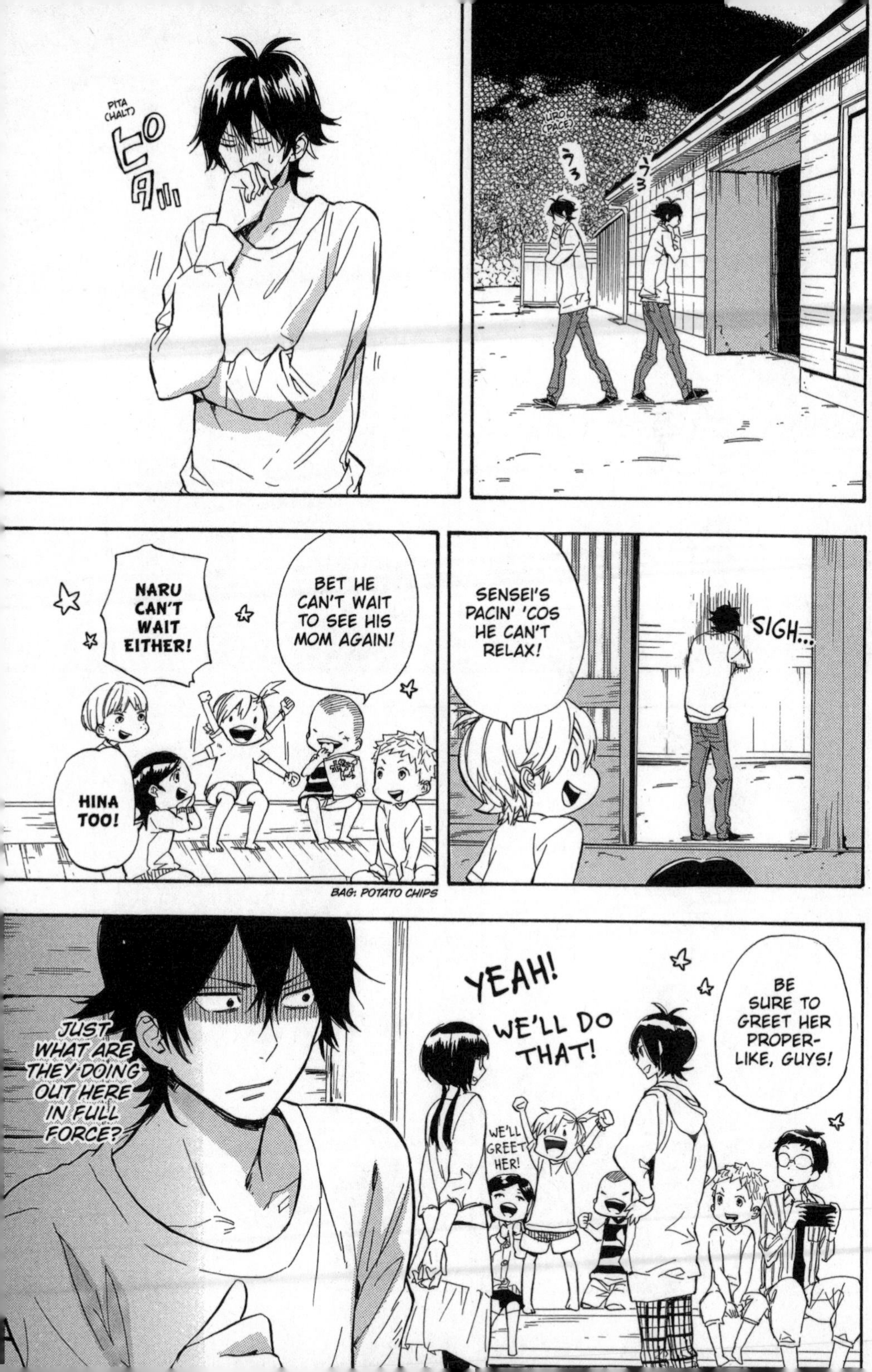

URO (PACE)
URO
PITA (HALT)
SENSEI'S PACIN' 'COS HE CAN'T RELAX!
SIGH...
BET HE CAN'T WAIT TO SEE HIS MOM AGAIN!
NARU CAN'T WAIT EITHER!
HINA TOO!
BAG: POTATO CHIPS
BE SURE TO GREET HER PROPER-LIKE, GUYS!
YEAH!
WE'LL DO THAT!
WE'LL GREET HER!
JUST WHAT ARE THEY DOING OUT HERE IN FULL FORCE?

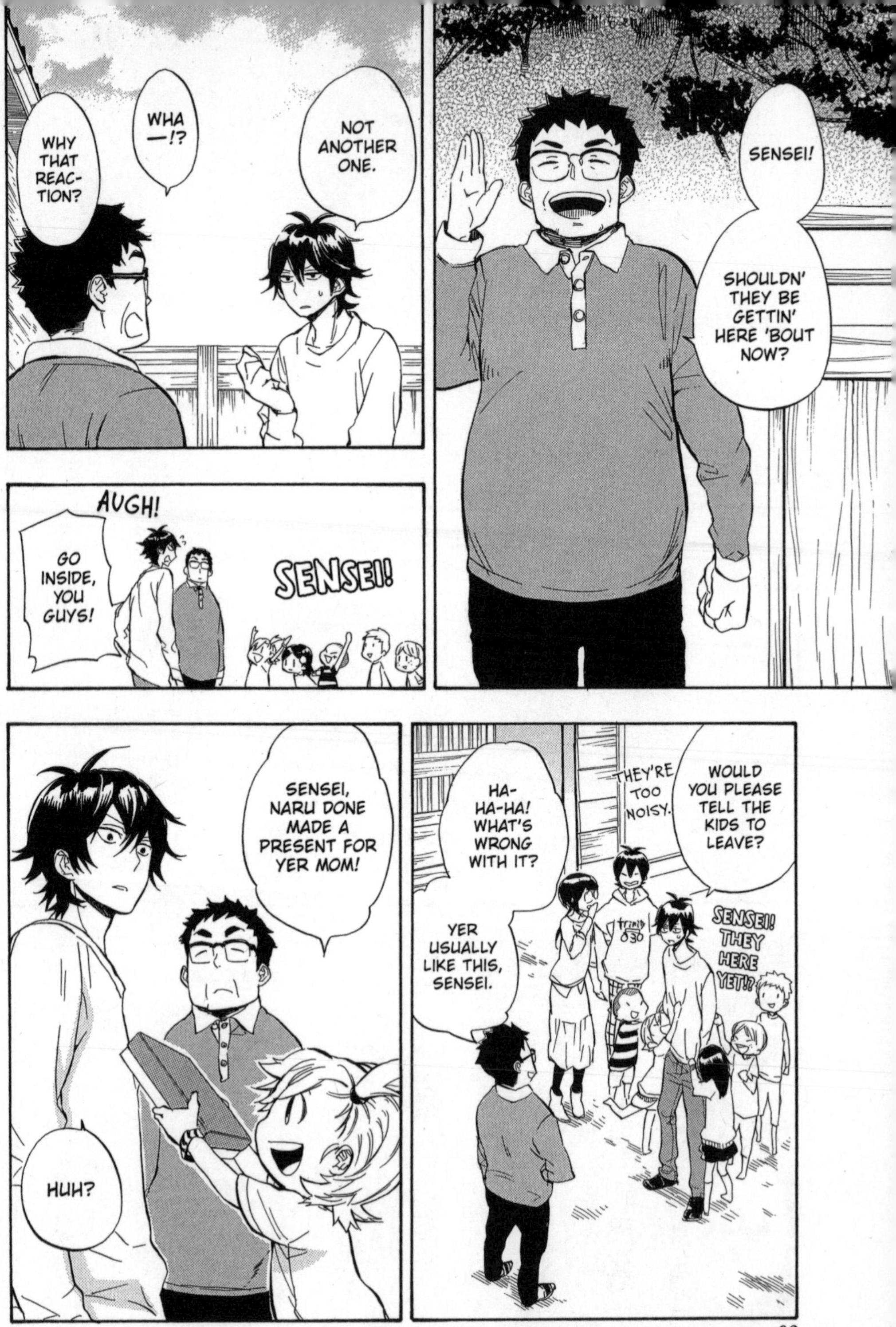
SENSEI!
SHOULDN' THEY BE GETTIN' HERE 'BOUT NOW?
NOT ANOTHER ONE.
WHA—!?
WHY THAT REACTION?
SENSEI!
AUGH!
GO INSIDE, YOU GUYS!
WOULD YOU PLEASE TELL THE KIDS TO LEAVE?
THEY'RE TOO NOISY.
SENSEI! THEY HERE YET!?
HA-HA-HA! WHAT'S WRONG WITH IT?
YER USUALLY LIKE THIS, SENSEI.
SENSEI, NARU DONE MADE A PRESENT FOR YER MOM!
HUH?

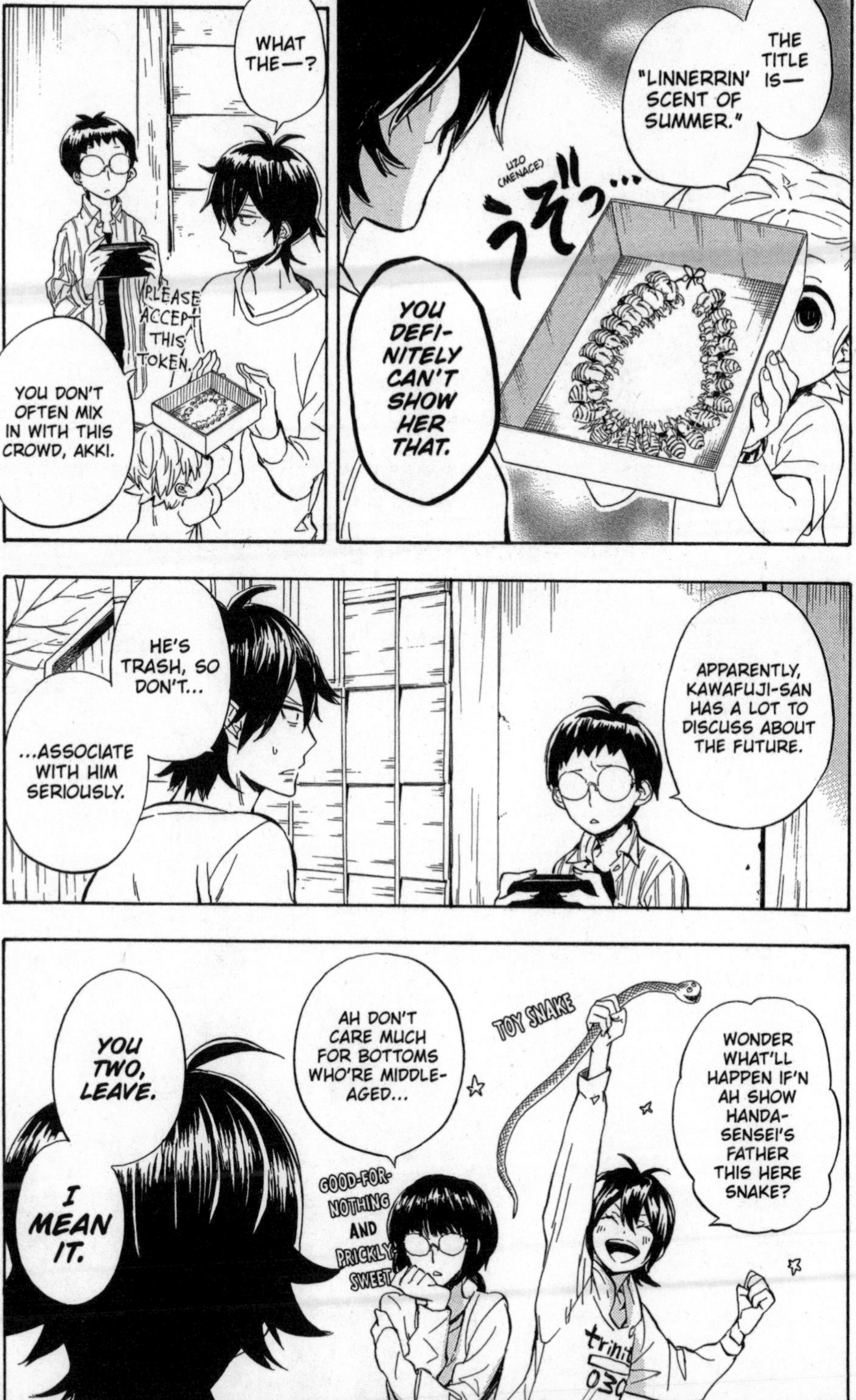

THE TITLE IS— "LINNERRIN' SCENT OF SUMMER."
UZO (MENACE)
うぞっ…
YOU DEFINITELY CAN'T SHOW HER THAT.
WHAT THE—?
PLEASE ACCEPT THIS TOKEN.
YOU DON'T OFTEN MIX IN WITH THIS CROWD, AKKI.
APPARENTLY, KAWAFUJI-SAN HAS A LOT TO DISCUSS ABOUT THE FUTURE.
HE'S TRASH, SO DON'T...
...ASSOCIATE WITH HIM SERIOUSLY.
WONDER WHAT'LL HAPPEN IF'N AH SHOW HANDA-SENSEI'S FATHER THIS HERE SNAKE?
TOY SNAKE
AH DON'T CARE MUCH FOR BOTTOMS WHO'RE MIDDLE-AGED...
GOOD-FOR-NOTHING AND PRICKLY SWEET
YOU TWO, LEAVE.
I MEAN IT.

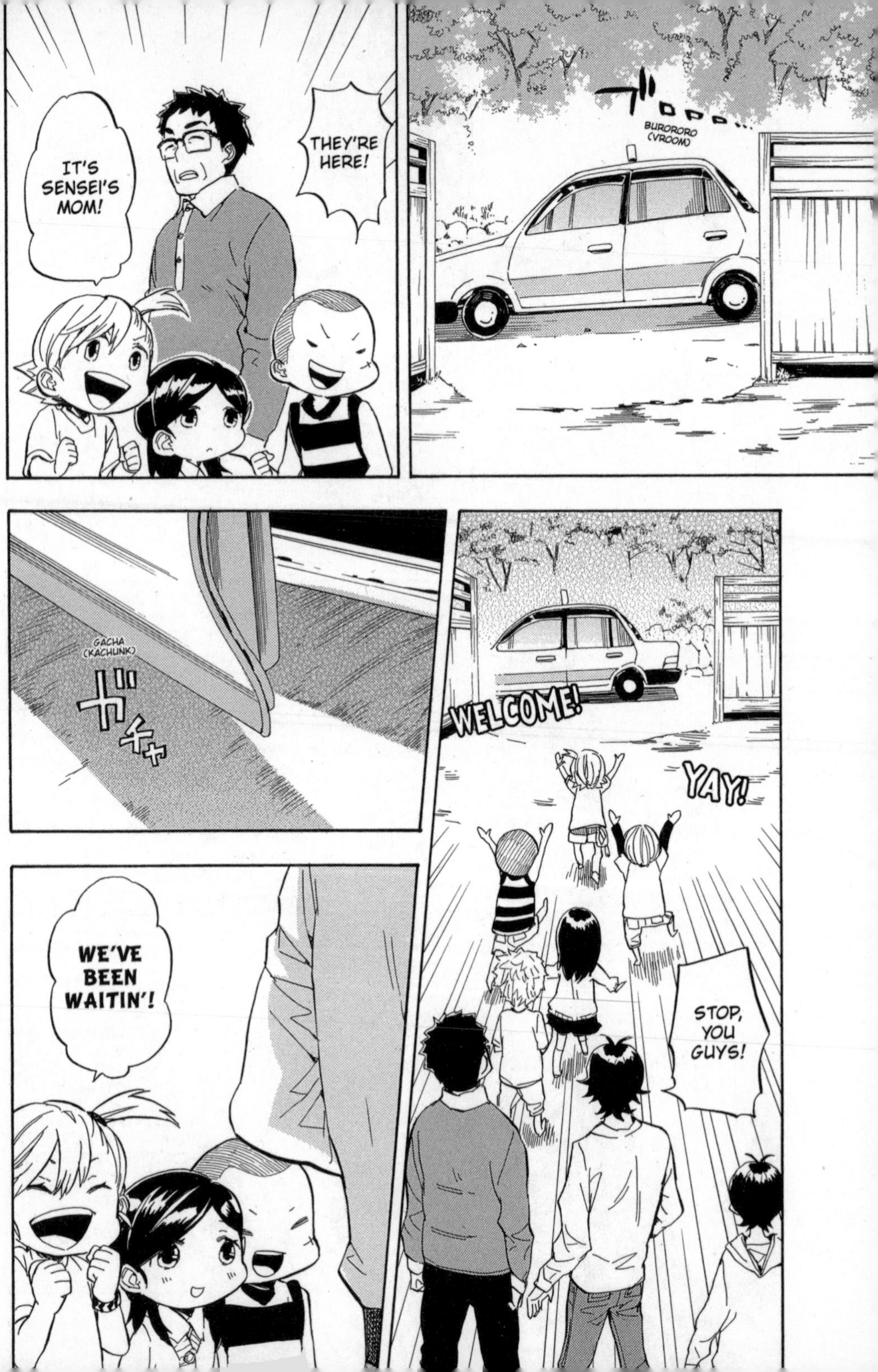

BURORORO (VROOM)
THEY'RE HERE!
IT'S SENSEI'S MOM!
WELCOME!
YAY!
STOP, YOU GUYS!
GACHA (KACHUNK)
WE'VE BEEN WAITIN'!

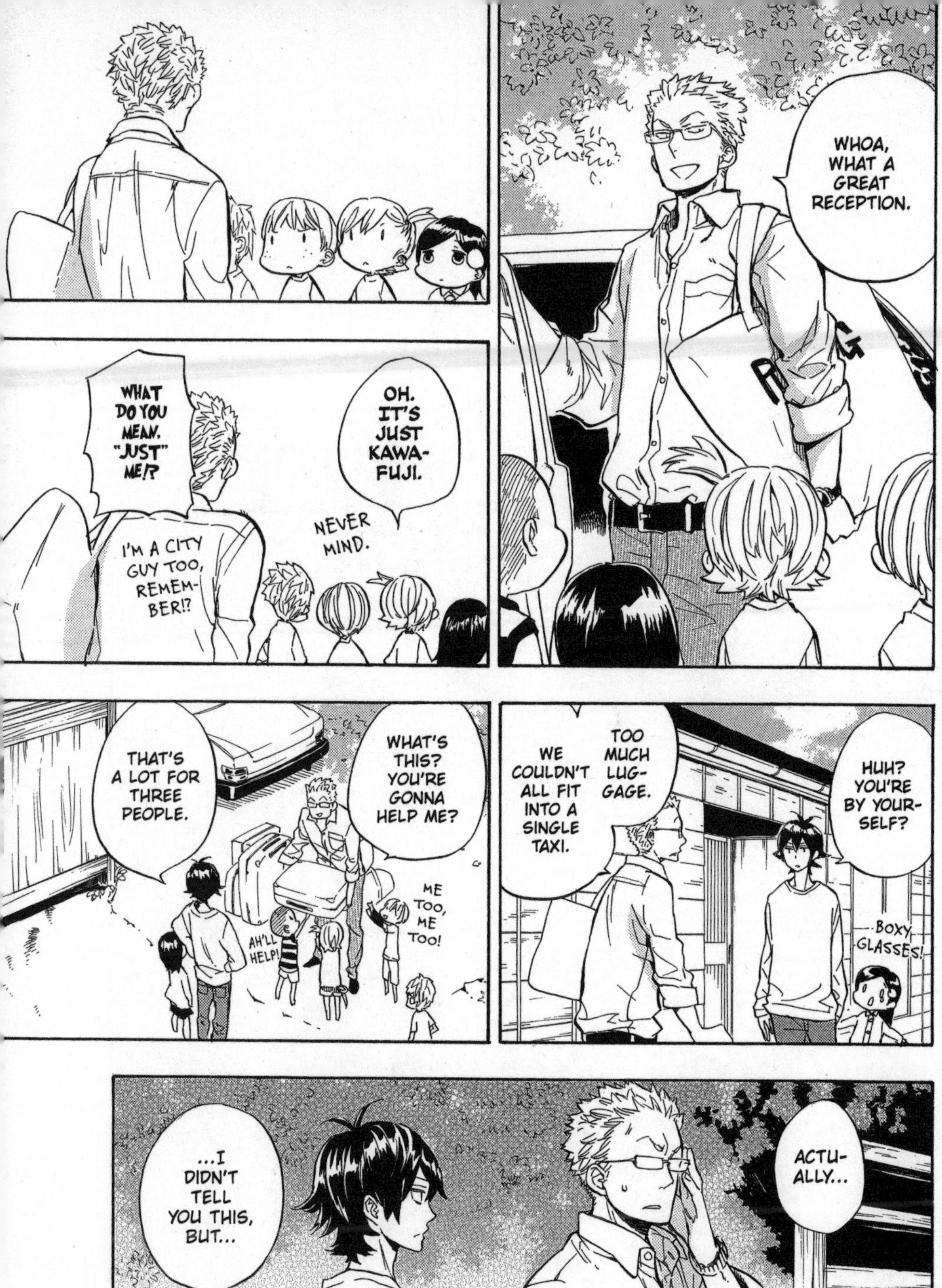
WHOA, WHAT A GREAT RECEPTION.
OH. IT'S JUST KAWA-FUJI.
WHAT DO YOU MEAN, "JUST" ME!?
NEVER MIND.
I'M A CITY GUY TOO, REMEMBER!?
HUH? YOU'RE BY YOURSELF?
TOO MUCH LUGGAGE.
WE COULDN'T ALL FIT INTO A SINGLE TAXI.
...BOXY GLASSES!
WHAT'S THIS? YOU'RE GONNA HELP ME?
THAT'S A LOT FOR THREE PEOPLE.
ME TOO, ME TOO!
AH'LL HELP!
ACTU-ALLY...
...I DIDN'T TELL YOU THIS, BUT...

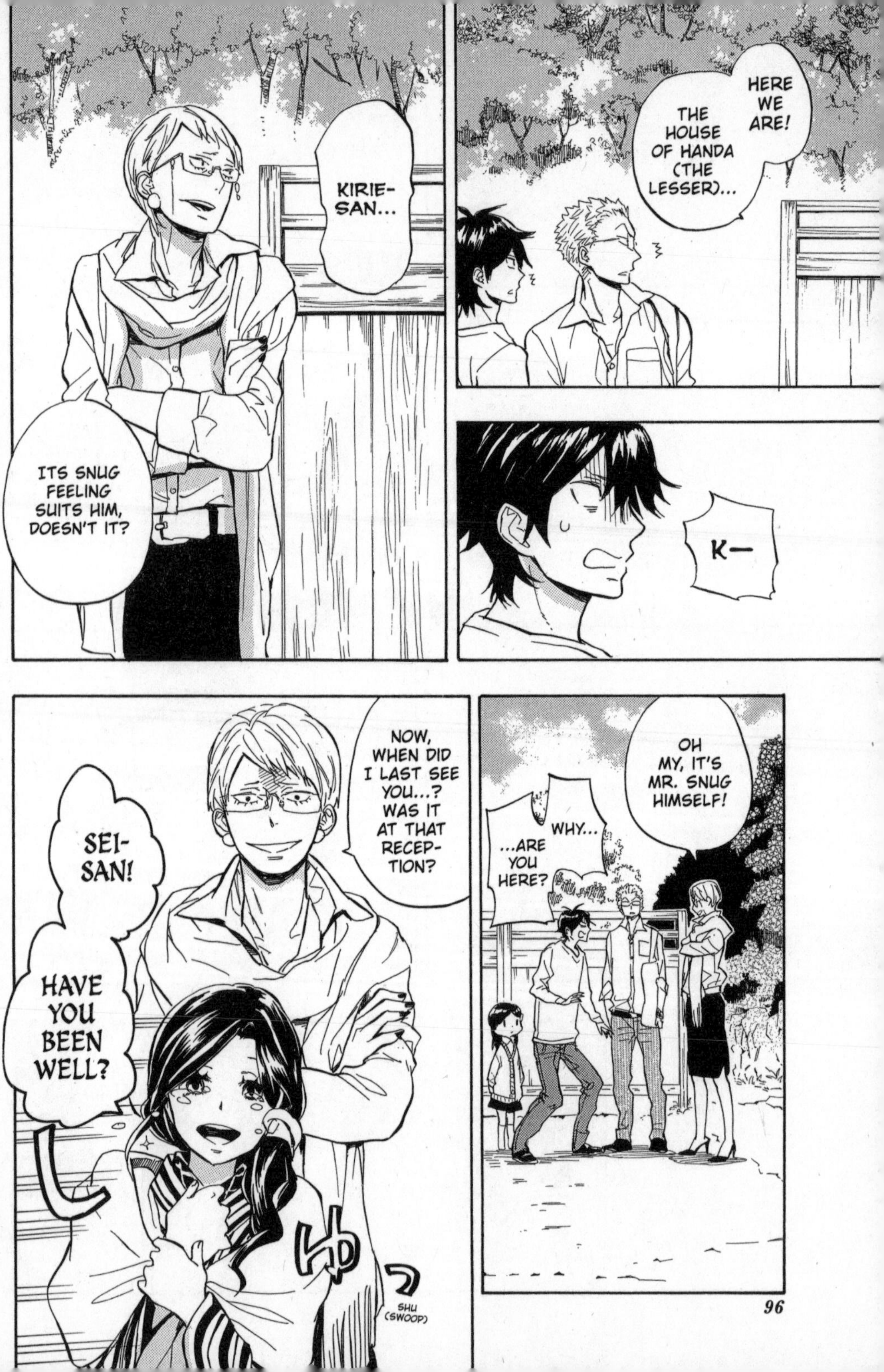

HERE WE ARE!
THE HOUSE OF HANDA (THE LESSER)...
K—
KIRIE-SAN...
ITS SNUG FEELING SUITS HIM, DOESN'T IT?
OH MY, IT'S MR. SNUG HIMSELF!
WHY...
...ARE YOU HERE?
NOW, WHEN DID I LAST SEE YOU...? WAS IT AT THAT RECEPTION?
SEI-SAN!
HAVE YOU BEEN WELL?
SHU (SWOOP)

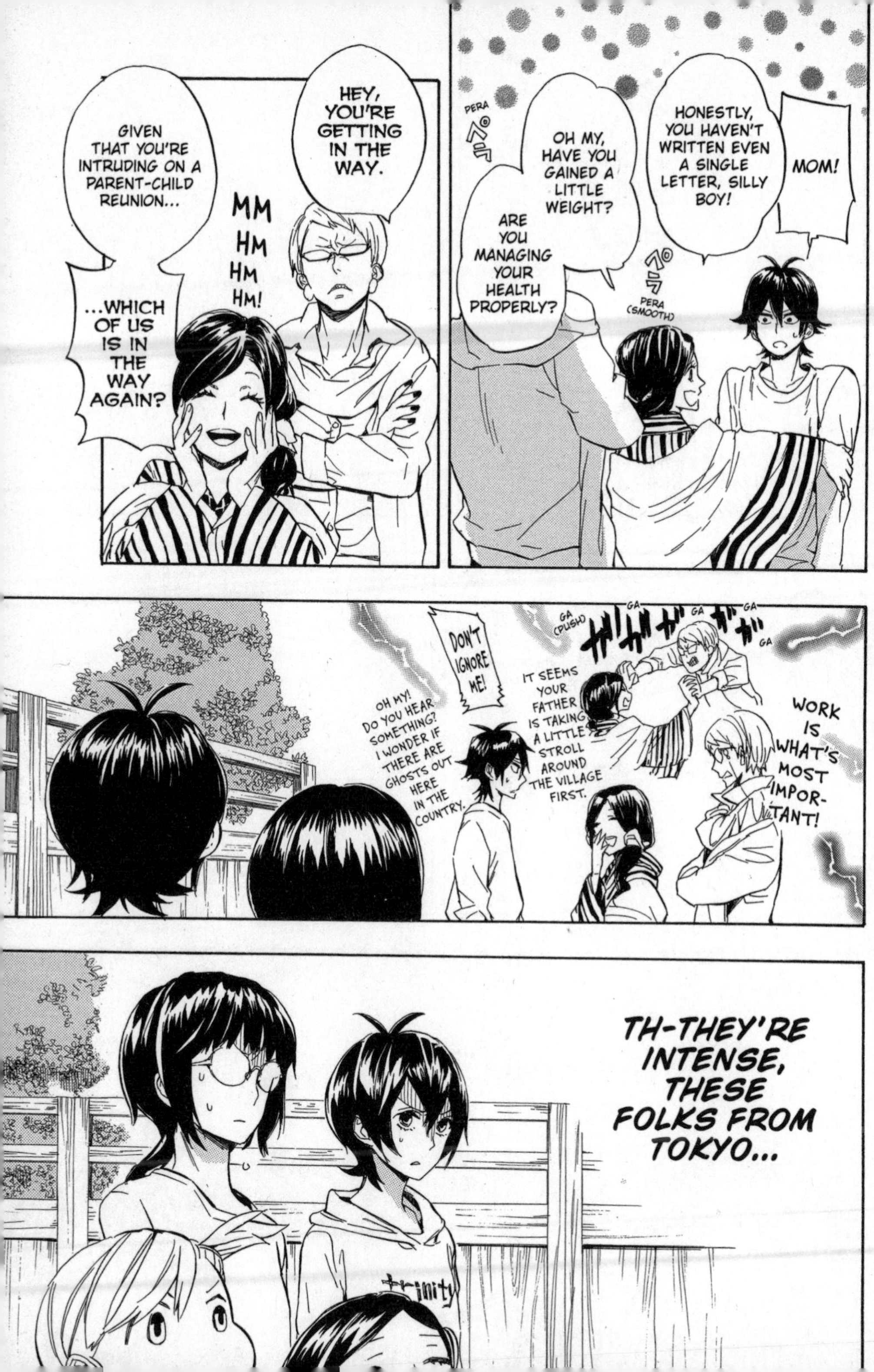
MOM!
HONESTLY, YOU HAVEN'T WRITTEN EVEN A SINGLE LETTER, SILLY BOY!
PERA
OH MY, HAVE YOU GAINED A LITTLE WEIGHT?
ARE YOU MANAGING YOUR HEALTH PROPERLY?
PERA (SMOOTH)
HEY, YOU'RE GETTING IN THE WAY.
GIVEN THAT YOU'RE INTRUDING ON A PARENT-CHILD REUNION...
MM HM HM HM!
...WHICH OF US IS IN THE WAY AGAIN?
WORK IS WHAT'S MOST IMPOR-TANT!
GA GA GA GA GA (PUSH)
DON'T IGNORE ME!
IT SEEMS YOUR FATHER IS TAKING A LITTLE STROLL AROUND THE VILLAGE FIRST.
OH MY! DO YOU HEAR SOMETHING? I WONDER IF THERE ARE GHOSTS OUT HERE IN THE COUNTRY.
TH-THEY'RE INTENSE, THESE FOLKS FROM TOKYO...

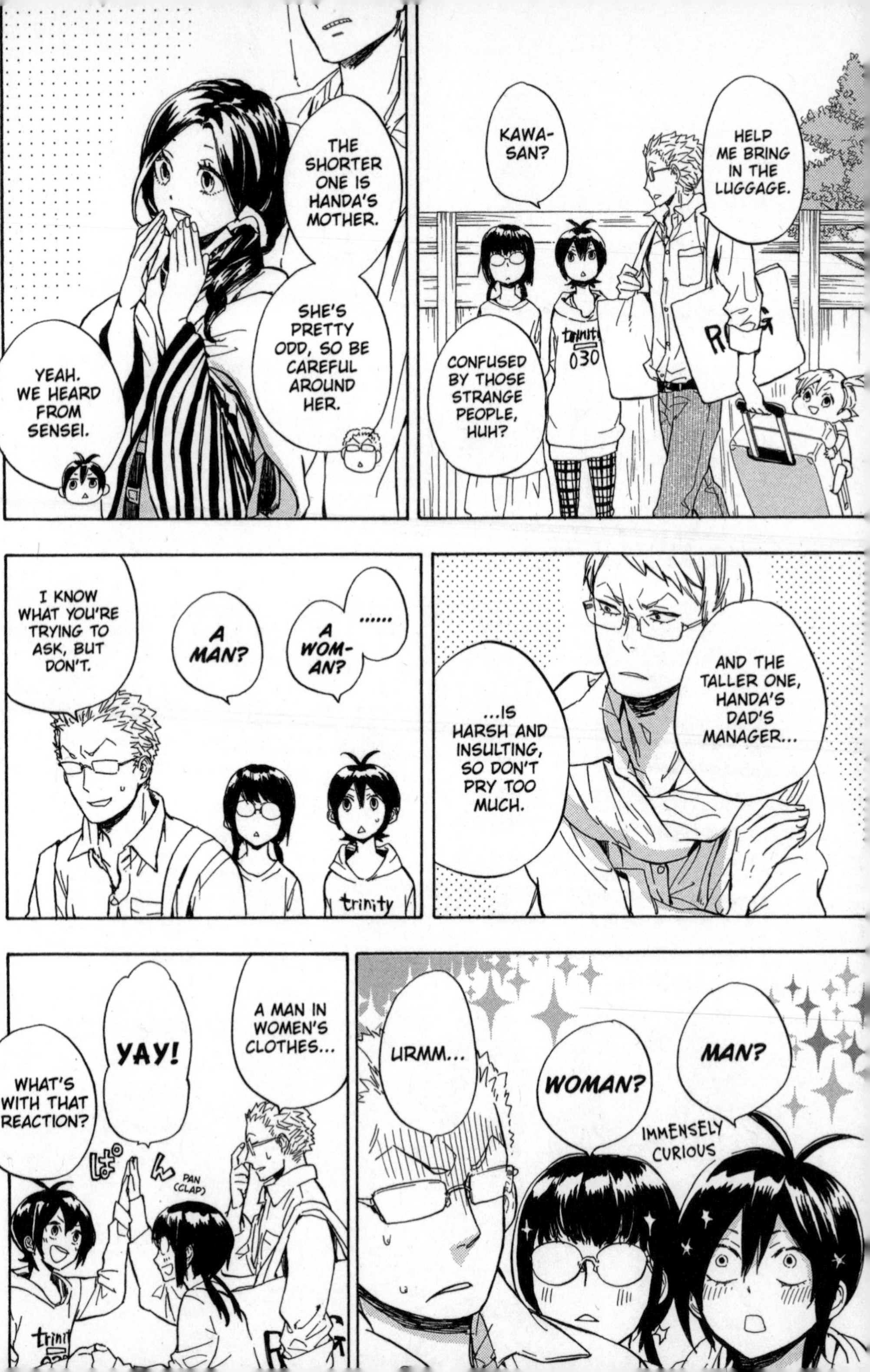
HELP ME BRING IN THE LUGGAGE.
KAWA-SAN?
CONFUSED BY THOSE STRANGE PEOPLE, HUH?
THE SHORTER ONE IS HANDA'S MOTHER.
SHE'S PRETTY ODD, SO BE CAREFUL AROUND HER.
YEAH. WE HEARD FROM SENSEI.
AND THE TALLER ONE, HANDA'S DAD'S MANAGER...
...IS HARSH AND INSULTING, SO DON'T PRY TOO MUCH.
......
A WOMAN?
A MAN?
I KNOW WHAT YOU'RE TRYING TO ASK, BUT DON'T.
MAN?
WOMAN?
IMMENSELY CURIOUS
URMM...
A MAN IN WOMEN'S CLOTHES...
YAY!
WHAT'S WITH THAT REACTION?
ぱん
PAN (CLAP)

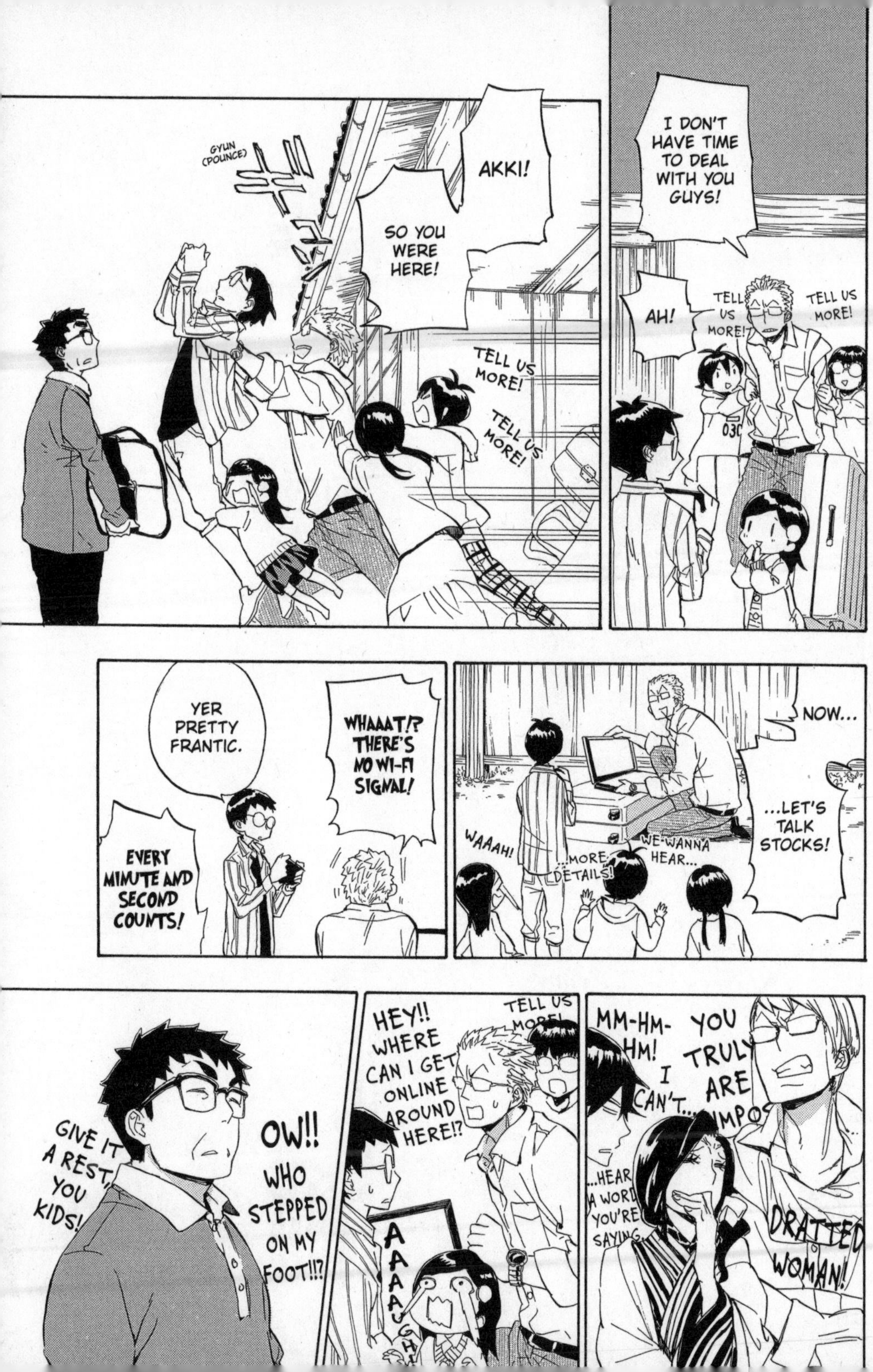
I DON'T HAVE TIME TO DEAL WITH YOU GUYS!
TELL US MORE!
TELL US MORE!
AH!
AKKI!
SO YOU WERE HERE!
GYUN (POUNCE)
TELL US MORE!
TELL US MORE!
NOW...
...LET'S TALK STOCKS!
WE WANNA HEAR...
...MORE DETAILS!
WAAAH!
WHAAAT!? THERE'S NO WI-FI SIGNAL!
YER PRETTY FRANTIC.
EVERY MINUTE AND SECOND COUNTS!
YOU TRULY ARE IMPOS
MM-HM-HM! I CAN'T...
...HEAR A WORD YOU'RE SAYING.
DRATTED WOMAN!
TELL US MORE!
HEY!! WHERE CAN I GET ONLINE AROUND HERE!?
AAAAAUGH!
OW!! WHO STEPPED ON MY FOOT!!?
GIVE IT A REST, YOU KIDS!

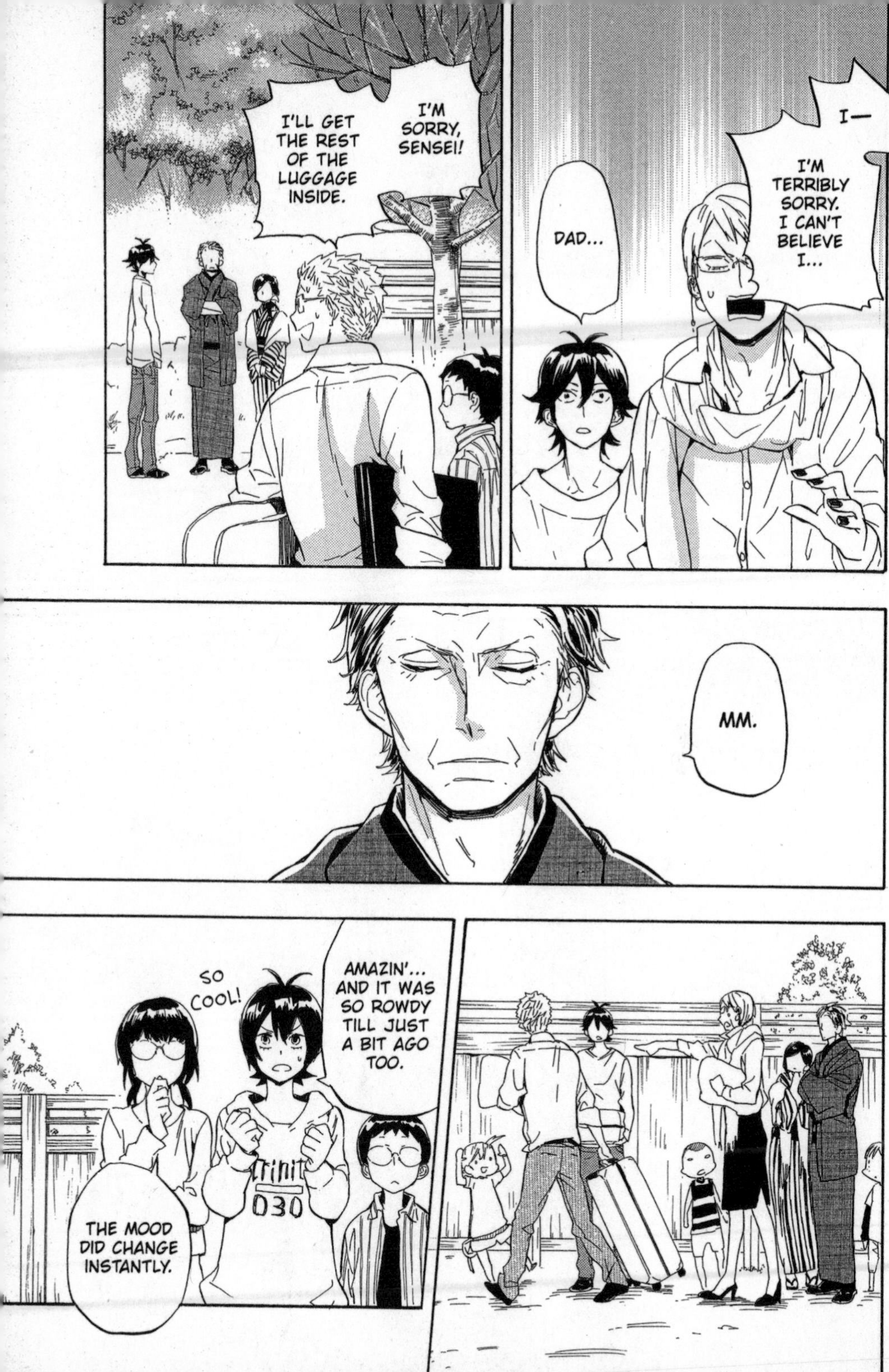
I—
I'M TERRIBLY SORRY. I CAN'T BELIEVE I...
DAD...
I'M SORRY, SENSEI!
I'LL GET THE REST OF THE LUGGAGE INSIDE.
MM.
AMAZIN'... AND IT WAS SO ROWDY TILL JUST A BIT AGO TOO.
SO COOL!
THE MOOD DID CHANGE INSTANTLY.
trinit
030

WAIT, VILLAGE CHIEF!

DO YA REMEMBER ME!?

LONG TIME NO SEE!

HANDA-SAAAN!

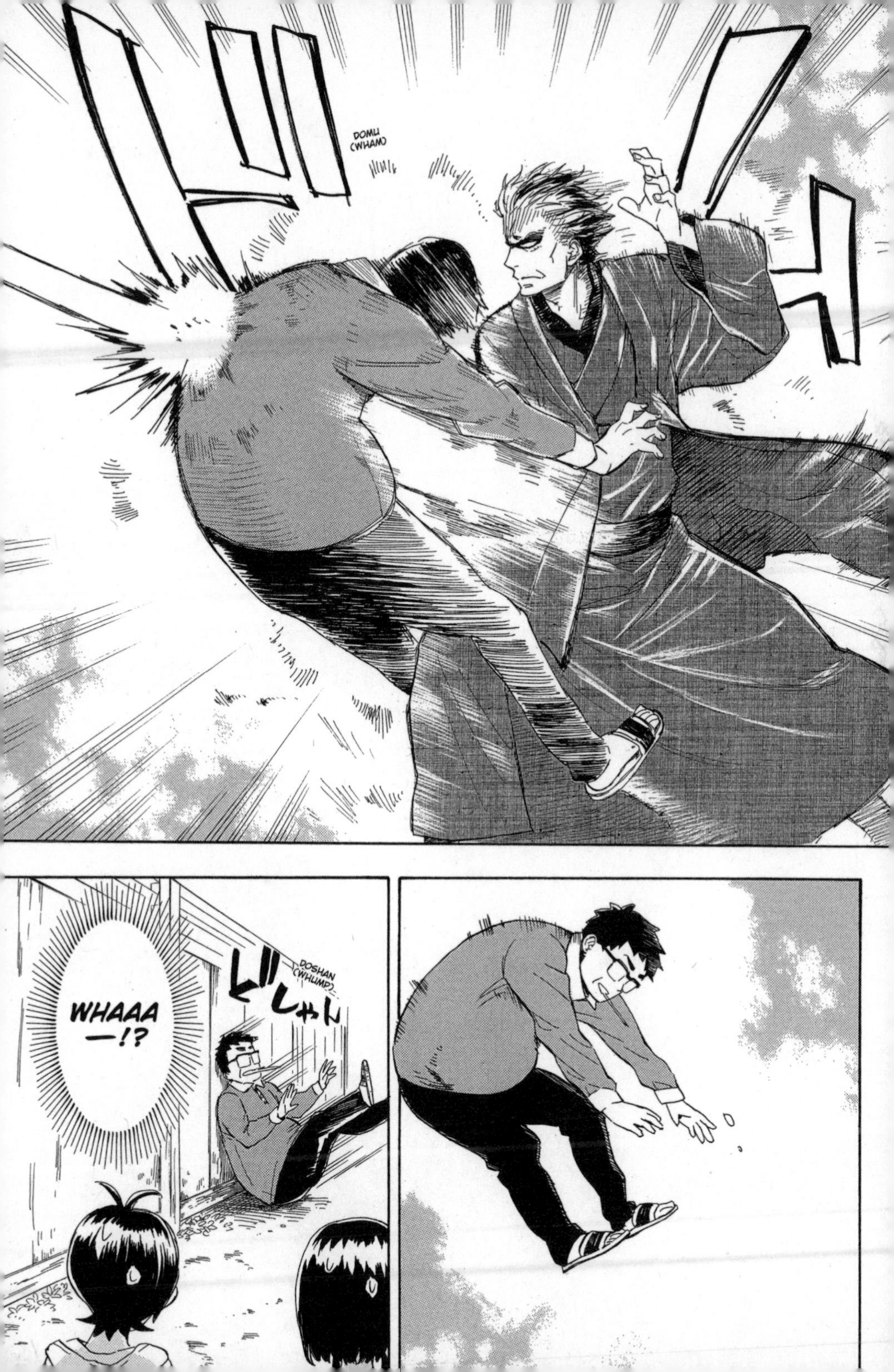
DOMU (WHAM)
DOSHAN (WHUMP)
WHAAA—!?

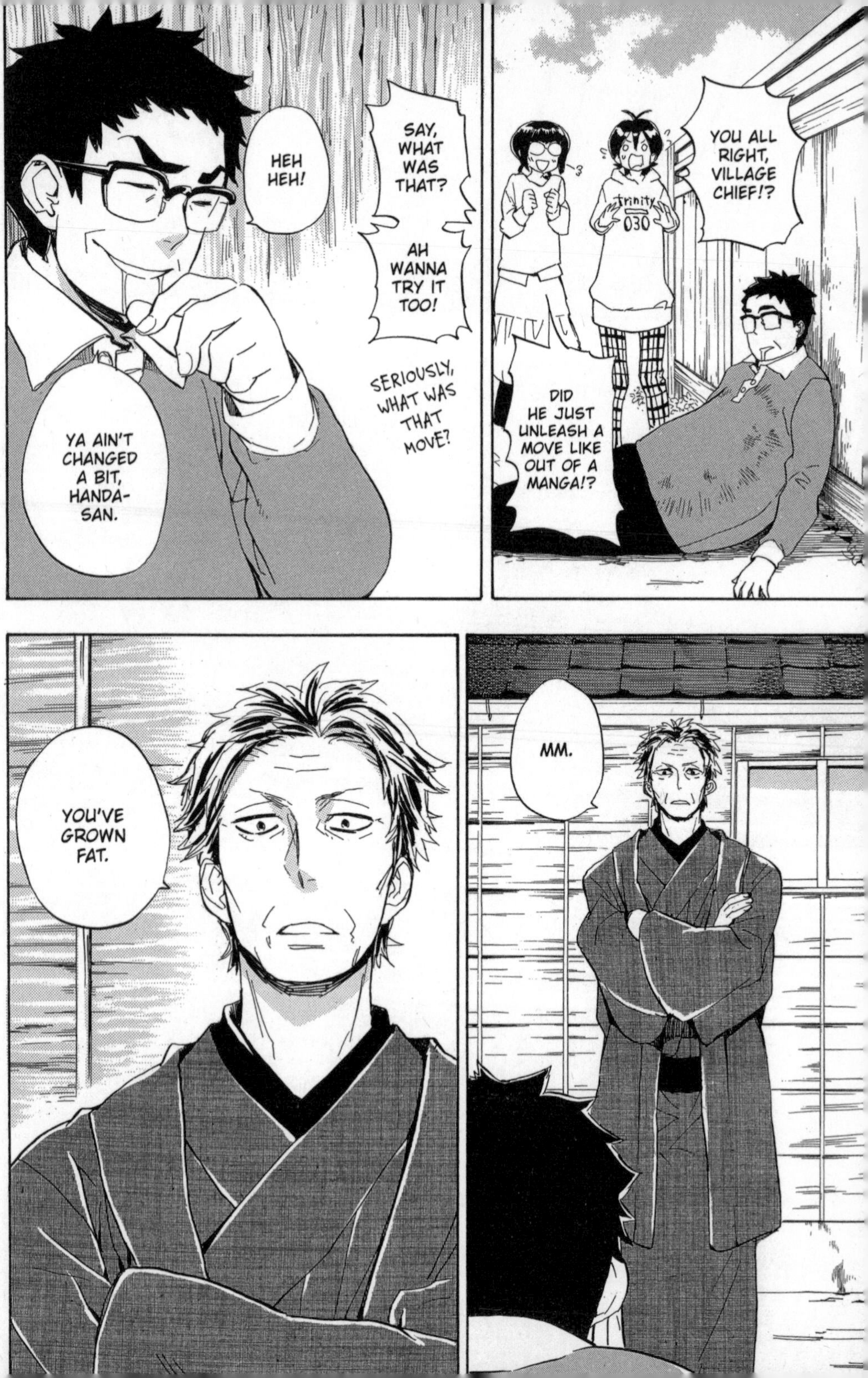
YOU ALL RIGHT, VILLAGE CHIEF!?
DID HE JUST UNLEASH A MOVE LIKE OUT OF A MANGA!?
SAY, WHAT WAS THAT?
HEH HEH!
AH WANNA TRY IT TOO!
SERIOUSLY, WHAT WAS THAT MOVE?
YA AIN'T CHANGED A BIT, HANDA-SAN.
MM.
YOU'VE GROWN FAT.

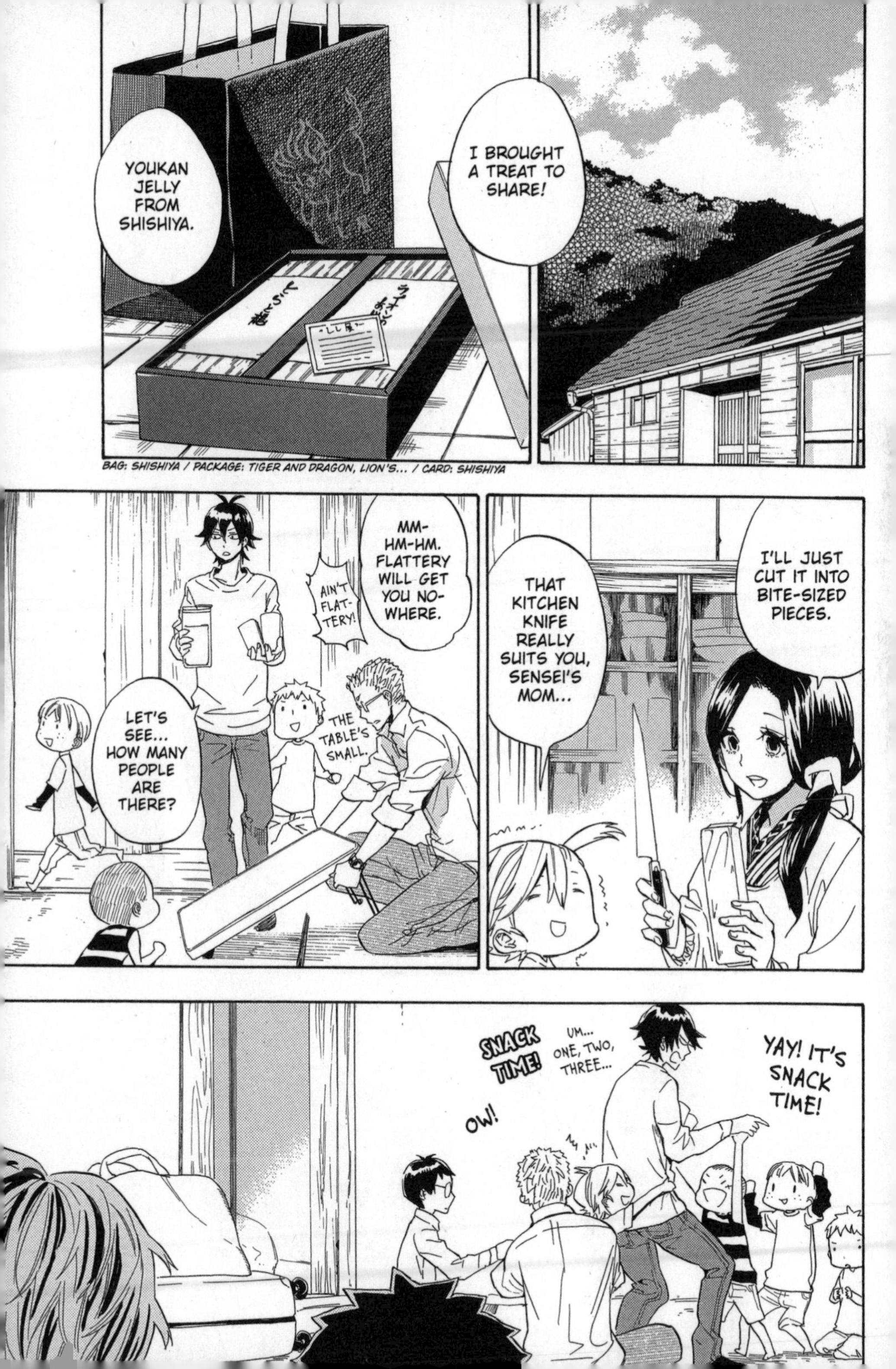
I BROUGHT A TREAT TO SHARE!
YOUKAN JELLY FROM SHISHIYA.
BAG: SHISHIYA / PACKAGE: TIGER AND DRAGON, LION'S... / CARD: SHISHIYA
I'LL JUST CUT IT INTO BITE-SIZED PIECES.
THAT KITCHEN KNIFE REALLY SUITS YOU, SENSEI'S MOM...
MM-HM-HM. FLATTERY WILL GET YOU NOWHERE.
AIN'T FLATTERY!
THE TABLE'S SMALL.
LET'S SEE... HOW MANY PEOPLE ARE THERE?
YAY! IT'S SNACK TIME!
UM... ONE, TWO, THREE...
SNACK TIME!
OW!

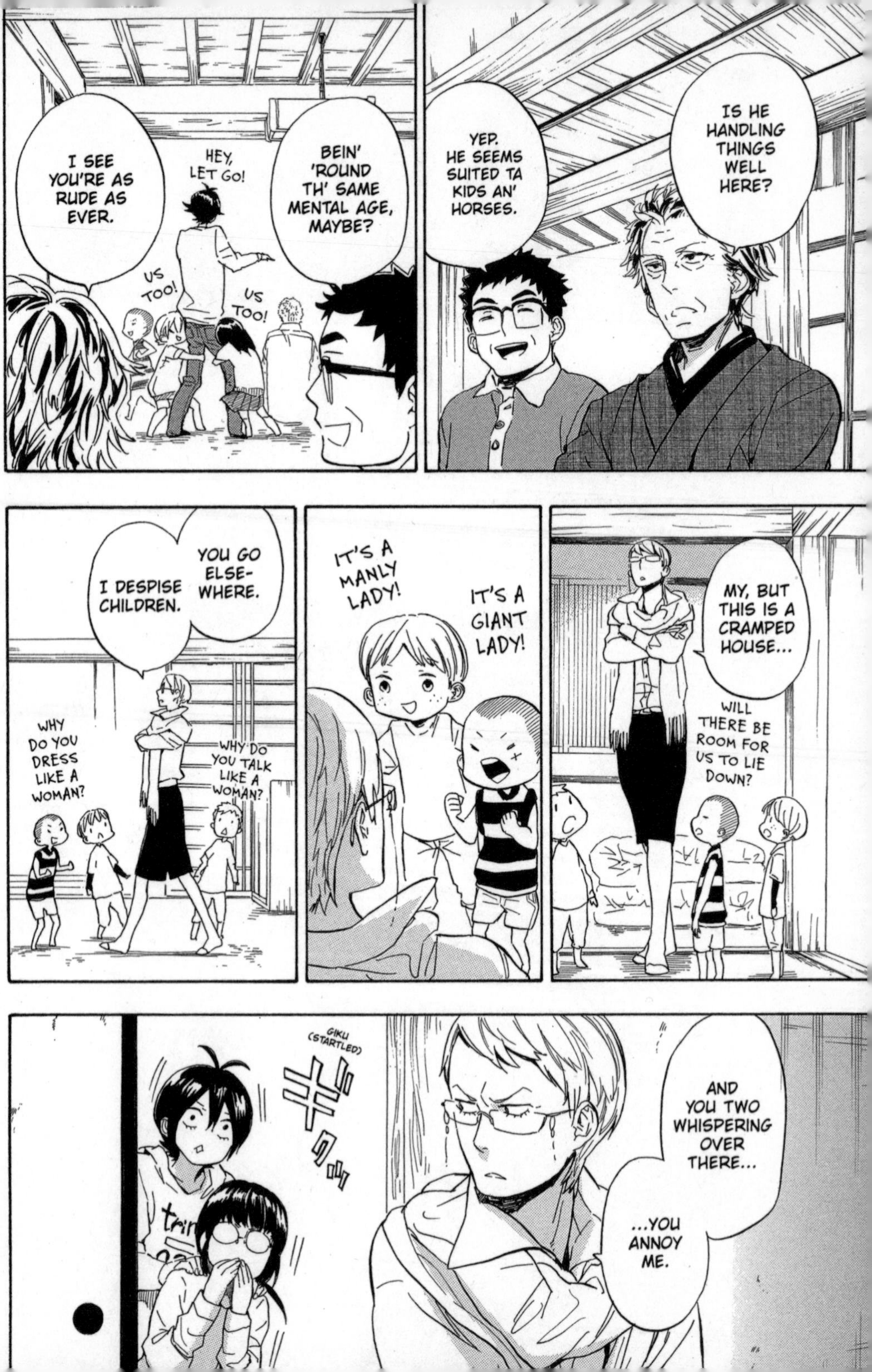
IS HE HANDLING THINGS WELL HERE?
YEP. HE SEEMS SUITED TA KIDS AN' HORSES.
BEIN' 'ROUND TH' SAME MENTAL AGE, MAYBE?
HEY, LET GO!
I SEE YOU'RE AS RUDE AS EVER.
US TOO!
US TOO!
MY, BUT THIS IS A CRAMPED HOUSE...
WILL THERE BE ROOM FOR US TO LIE DOWN?
IT'S A GIANT LADY!
IT'S A MANLY LADY!
YOU GO ELSE-WHERE.
I DESPISE CHILDREN.
WHY DO YOU TALK LIKE A WOMAN?
WHY DO YOU DRESS LIKE A WOMAN?
AND YOU TWO WHISPERING OVER THERE...
...YOU ANNOY ME.
GIKU (STARTLED)

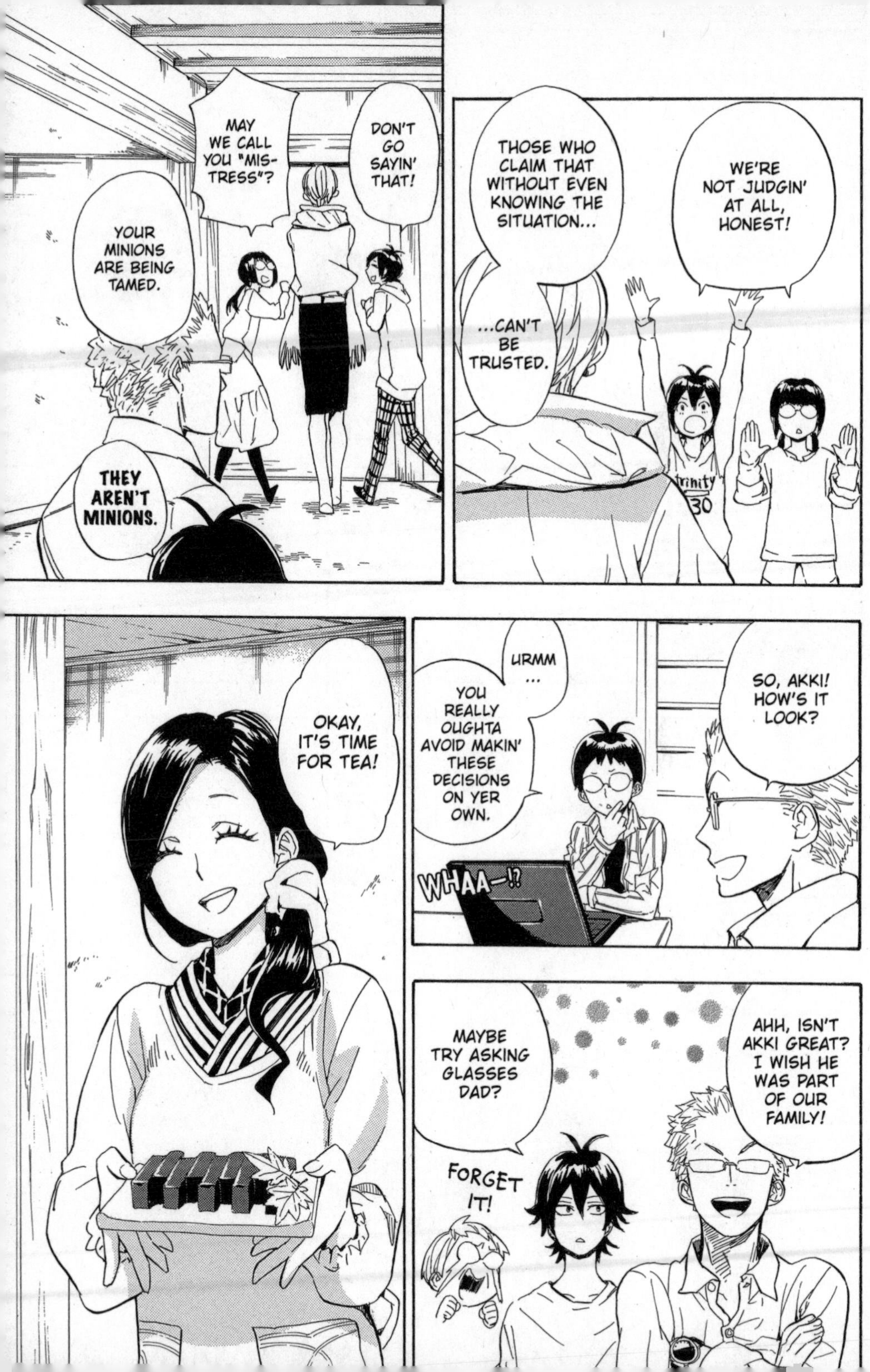
WE'RE NOT JUDGIN' AT ALL, HONEST!
THOSE WHO CLAIM THAT WITHOUT EVEN KNOWING THE SITUATION...
...CAN'T BE TRUSTED.
DON'T GO SAYIN' THAT!
MAY WE CALL YOU "MIS-TRESS"?
YOUR MINIONS ARE BEING TAMED.
THEY AREN'T MINIONS.
SO, AKKI! HOW'S IT LOOK?
URMM ...
YOU REALLY OUGHTA AVOID MAKIN' THESE DECISIONS ON YER OWN.
WHAA-!?
AHH, ISN'T AKKI GREAT? I WISH HE WAS PART OF OUR FAMILY!
MAYBE TRY ASKING GLASSES DAD?
FORGET IT!
OKAY, IT'S TIME FOR TEA!

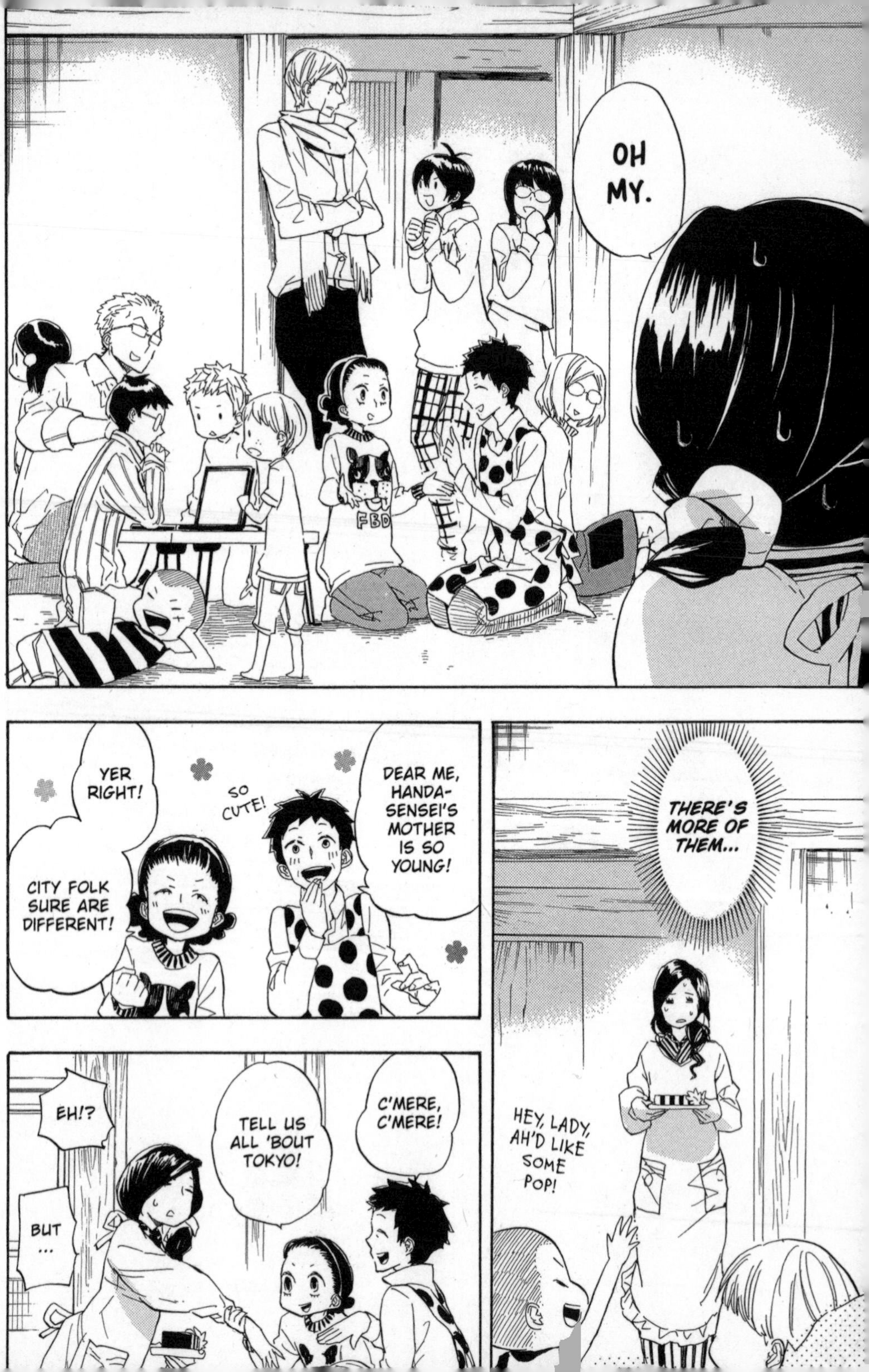
OH MY.
THERE'S MORE OF THEM...
HEY, LADY, AH'D LIKE SOME POP!
DEAR ME, HANDA-SENSEI'S MOTHER IS SO YOUNG!
SO CUTE!
YER RIGHT!
CITY FOLK SURE ARE DIFFERENT!
C'MERE, C'MERE!
TELL US ALL 'BOUT TOKYO!
EH!?
BUT ...

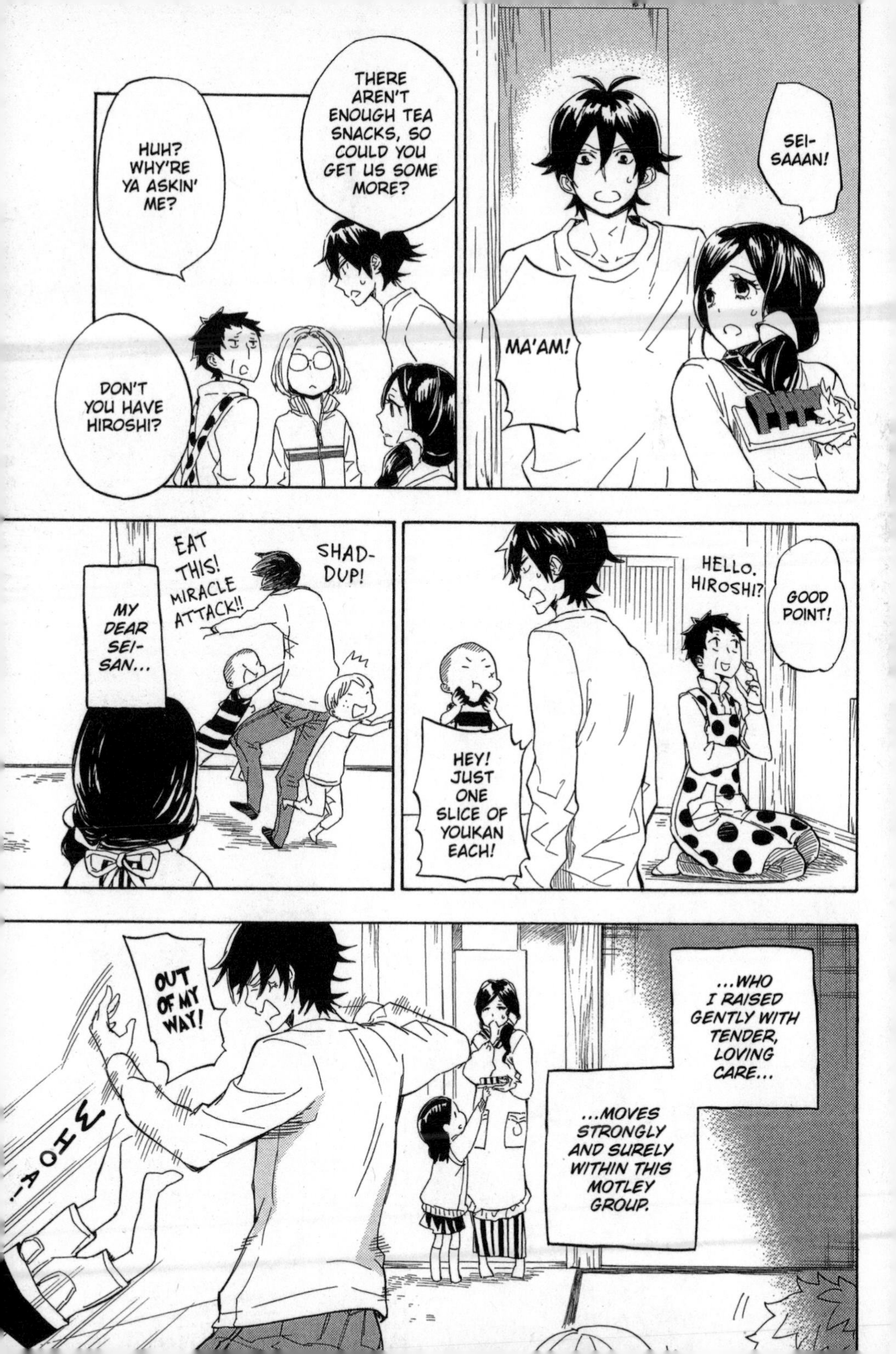
SEI-SAAAN!
MA'AM!
THERE AREN'T ENOUGH TEA SNACKS, SO COULD YOU GET US SOME MORE?
HUH? WHY'RE YA ASKIN' ME?
DON'T YOU HAVE HIROSHI?
HELLO. HIROSHI!?
GOOD POINT!
HEY! JUST ONE SLICE OF YOUKAN EACH!
SHAD-DUP!
EAT THIS! MIRACLE ATTACK!!
MY DEAR SEI-SAN...
...WHO I RAISED GENTLY WITH TENDER, LOVING CARE...
...MOVES STRONGLY AND SURELY WITHIN THIS MOTLEY GROUP.
OUT OF MY WAY!
WHOA-!

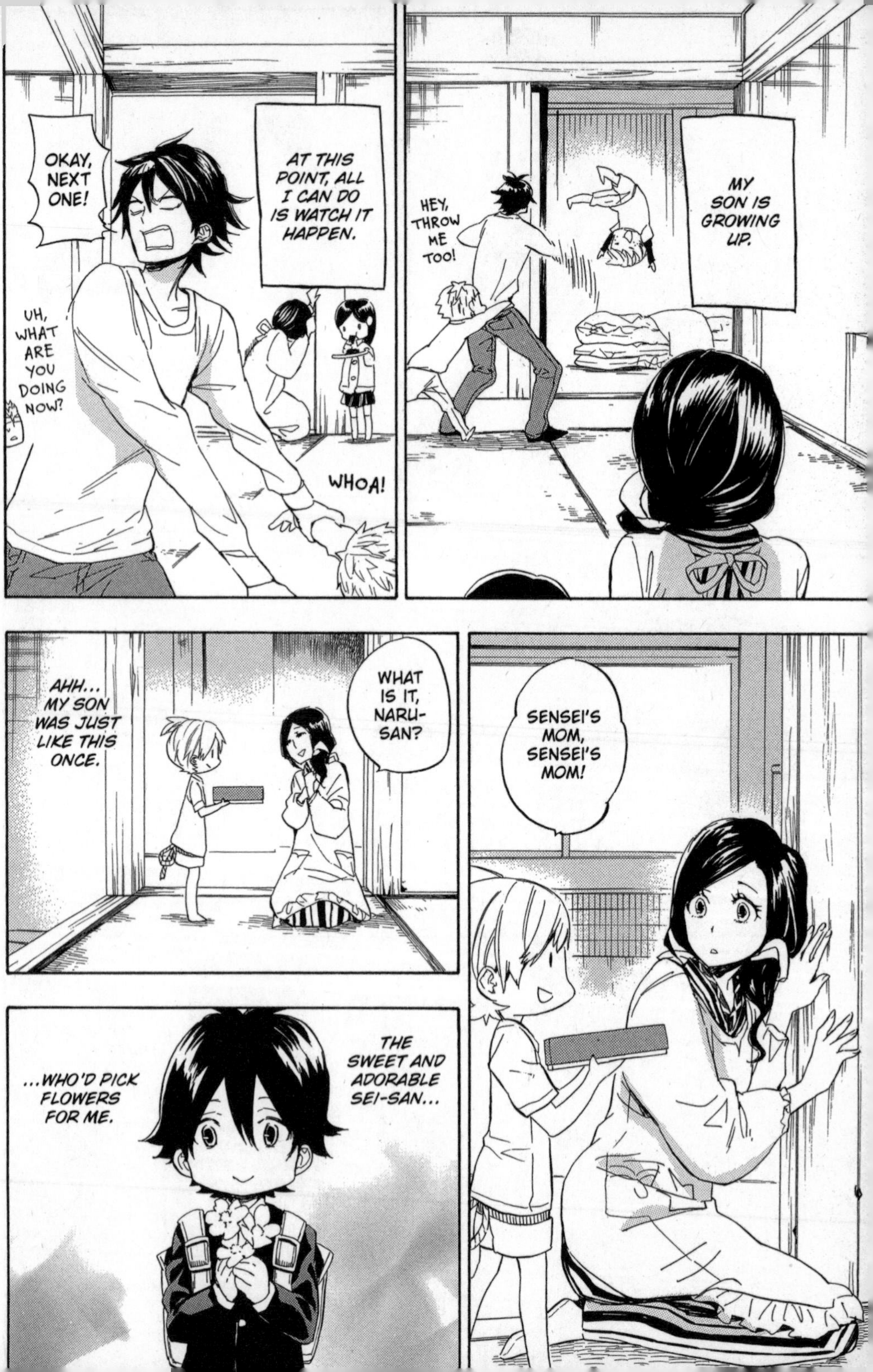
MY SON IS GROWING UP.
HEY, THROW ME TOO!
AT THIS POINT, ALL I CAN DO IS WATCH IT HAPPEN.
OKAY, NEXT ONE!
UH, WHAT ARE YOU DOING NOW?
WHOA!
SENSEI'S MOM, SENSEI'S MOM!
WHAT IS IT, NARU-SAN?
AHH... MY SON WAS JUST LIKE THIS ONCE.
THE SWEET AND ADORABLE SEI-SAN...
...WHO'D PICK FLOWERS FOR ME.

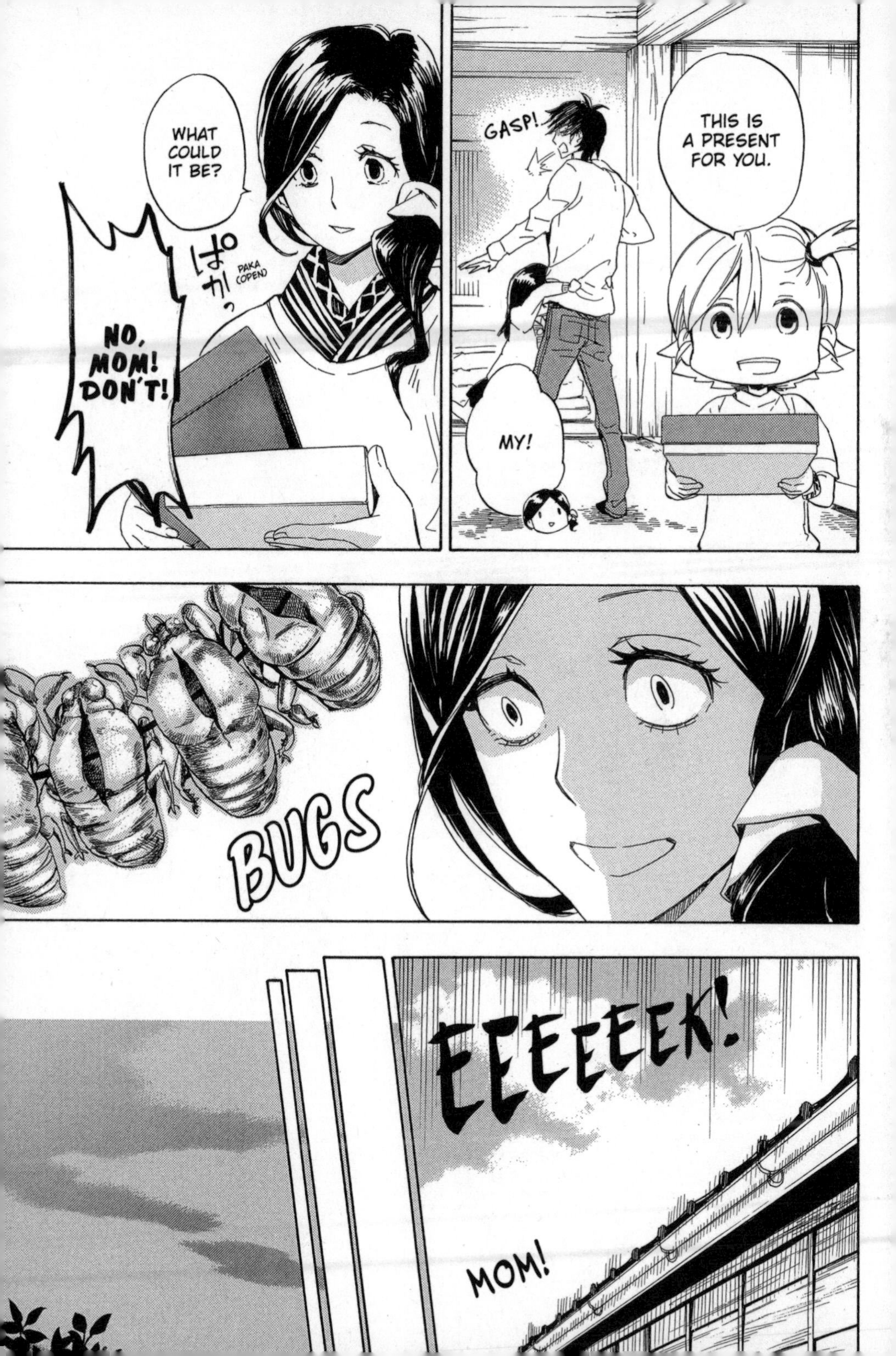
THIS IS A PRESENT FOR YOU.
GASP!
MY!
WHAT COULD IT BE?
ぱかっ
PAKA (OPEN)
NO, MOM! DON'T!
BUGS
EEEEEEK!
MOM!

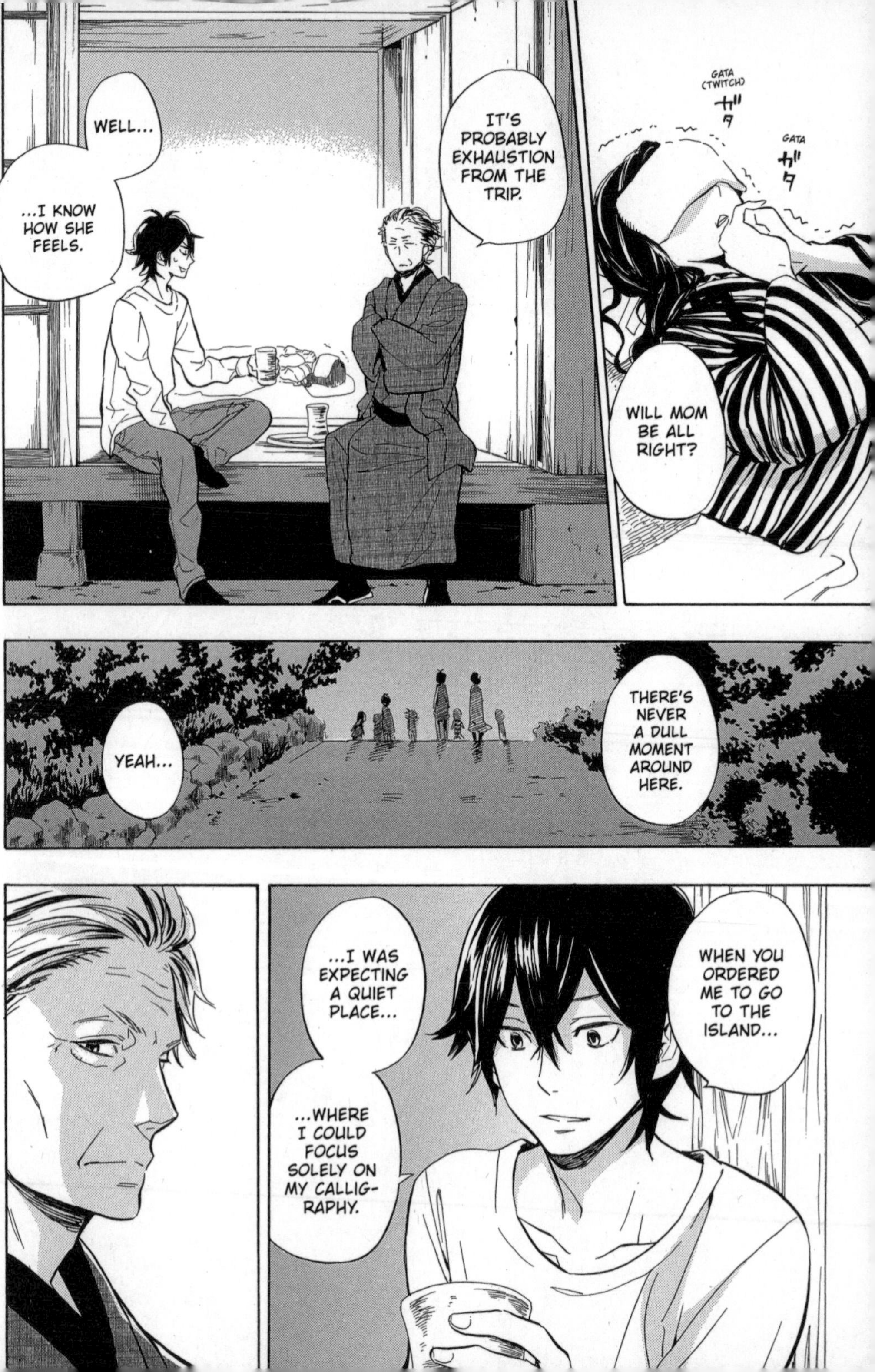
GATA (TWITCH)
ガタ
GATA
ガタ
WILL MOM BE ALL RIGHT?
IT'S PROBABLY EXHAUSTION FROM THE TRIP.
WELL...
...I KNOW HOW SHE FEELS.
THERE'S NEVER A DULL MOMENT AROUND HERE.
YEAH...
WHEN YOU ORDERED ME TO GO TO THE ISLAND...
...I WAS EXPECTING A QUIET PLACE...
...WHERE I COULD FOCUS SOLELY ON MY CALLIGRAPHY.

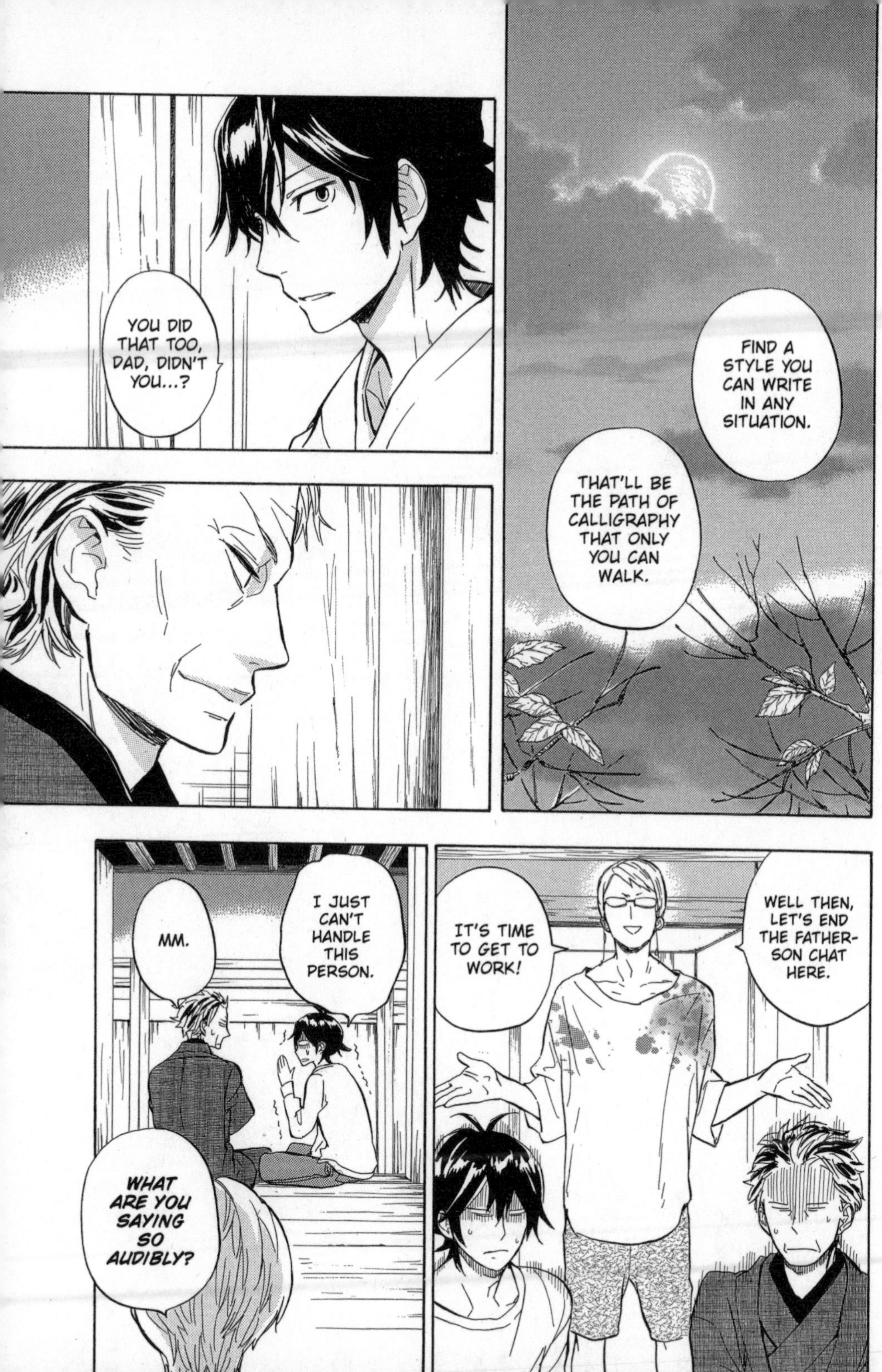
FIND A STYLE YOU CAN WRITE IN ANY SITUATION.
THAT'LL BE THE PATH OF CALLIGRAPHY THAT ONLY YOU CAN WALK.
YOU DID THAT TOO, DAD, DIDN'T YOU...?
WELL THEN, LET'S END THE FATHER-SON CHAT HERE.
IT'S TIME TO GET TO WORK!
I JUST CAN'T HANDLE THIS PERSON.
MM.
WHAT ARE YOU SAYING SO AUDIBLY?

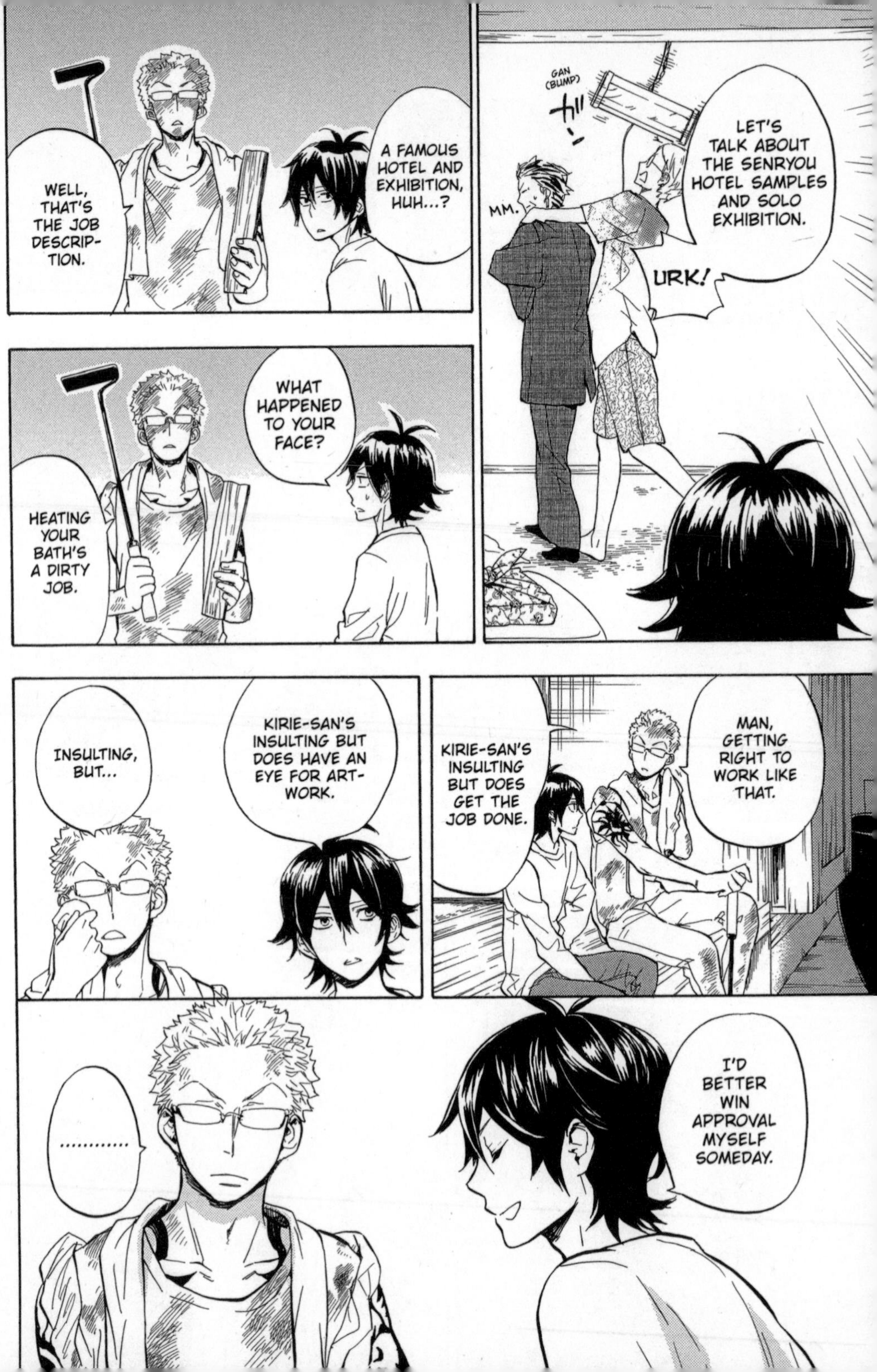
LET'S TALK ABOUT THE SENRYOU HOTEL SAMPLES AND SOLO EXHIBITION.
GAN (BUMP)
MM.
URK!
A FAMOUS HOTEL AND EXHIBITION, HUH...?
WELL, THAT'S THE JOB DESCRIPTION.
WHAT HAPPENED TO YOUR FACE?
HEATING YOUR BATH'S A DIRTY JOB.
MAN, GETTING RIGHT TO WORK LIKE THAT.
KIRIE-SAN'S INSULTING BUT DOES GET THE JOB DONE.
KIRIE-SAN'S INSULTING BUT DOES HAVE AN EYE FOR ART-WORK.
INSULTING, BUT...
I'D BETTER WIN APPROVAL MYSELF SOMEDAY.
....

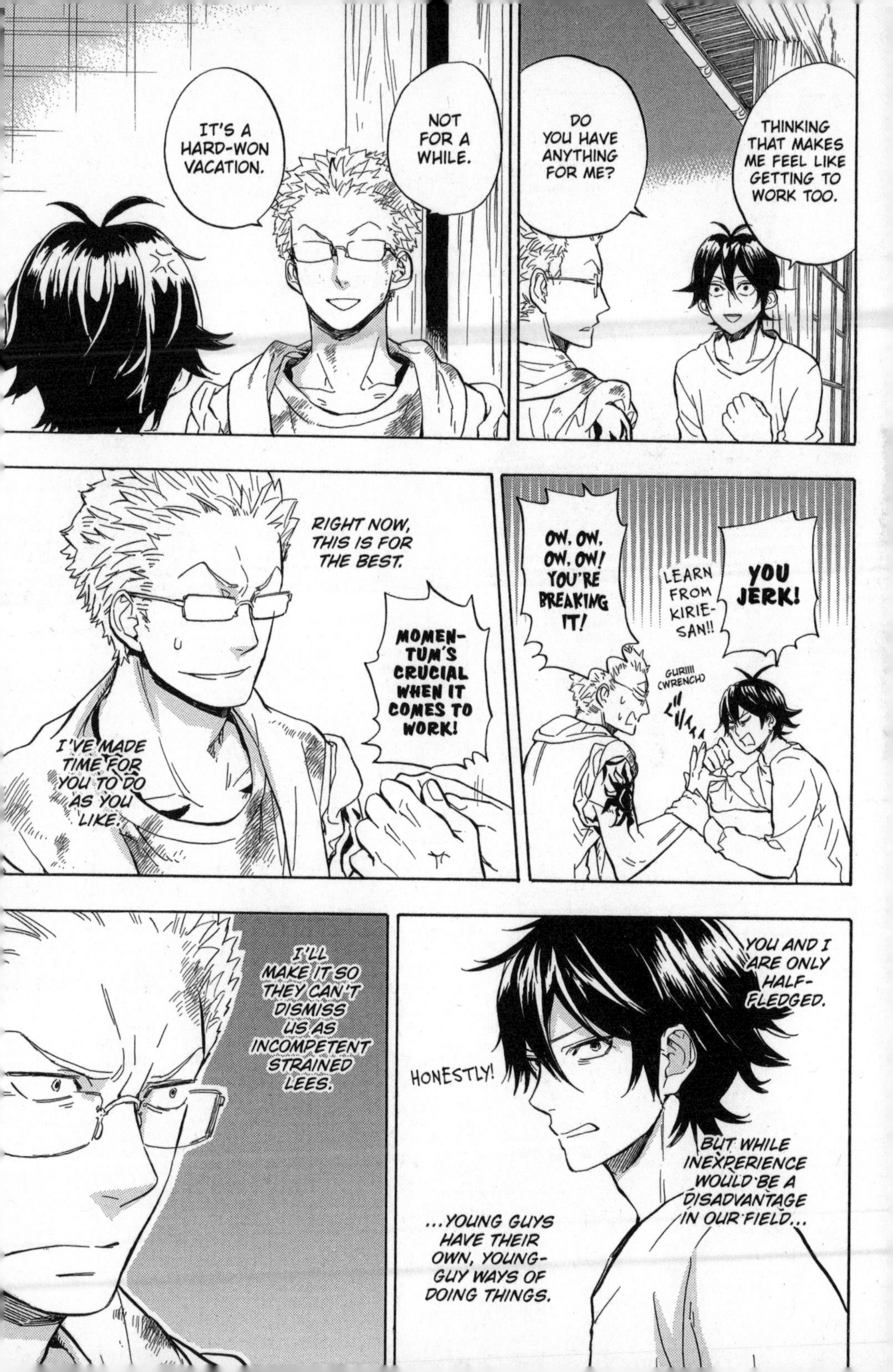
THINKING THAT MAKES ME FEEL LIKE GETTING TO WORK TOO.
DO YOU HAVE ANYTHING FOR ME?
NOT FOR A WHILE.
IT'S A HARD-WON VACATION.
YOU JERK!
LEARN FROM KIRIE-SAN!!
OW, OW, OW, OW! YOU'RE BREAKING IT!
GURIIII (WRENCH)
RIGHT NOW, THIS IS FOR THE BEST.
MOMENTUM'S CRUCIAL WHEN IT COMES TO WORK!
I'VE MADE TIME FOR YOU TO DO AS YOU LIKE.
YOU AND I ARE ONLY HALF-FLEDGED.
HONESTLY!
BUT WHILE INEXPERIENCE WOULD BE A DISADVANTAGE IN OUR FIELD...
...YOUNG GUYS HAVE THEIR OWN, YOUNG-GUY WAYS OF DOING THINGS.
I'LL MAKE IT SO THEY CAN'T DISMISS US AS INCOMPETENT STRAINED LEES.

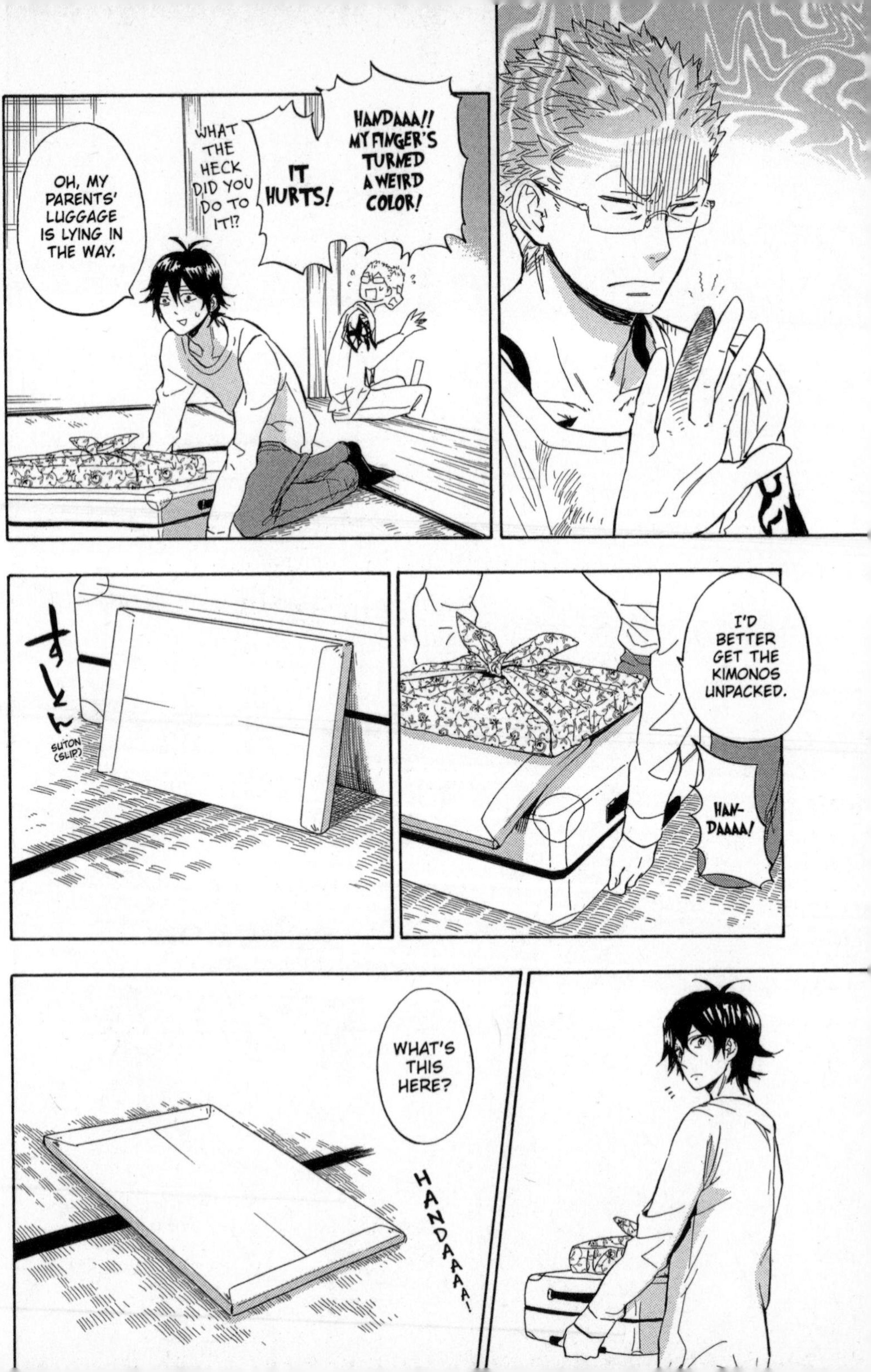
HANDAAA!! MY FINGER'S TURNED A WEIRD COLOR!
IT HURTS!
WHAT THE HECK DID YOU DO TO IT!?
OH, MY PARENTS' LUGGAGE IS LYING IN THE WAY.
I'D BETTER GET THE KIMONOS UNPACKED.
HAN-DAAAA!
すとん
SUTON (SLIP)
WHAT'S THIS HERE?
HANDAAAA!

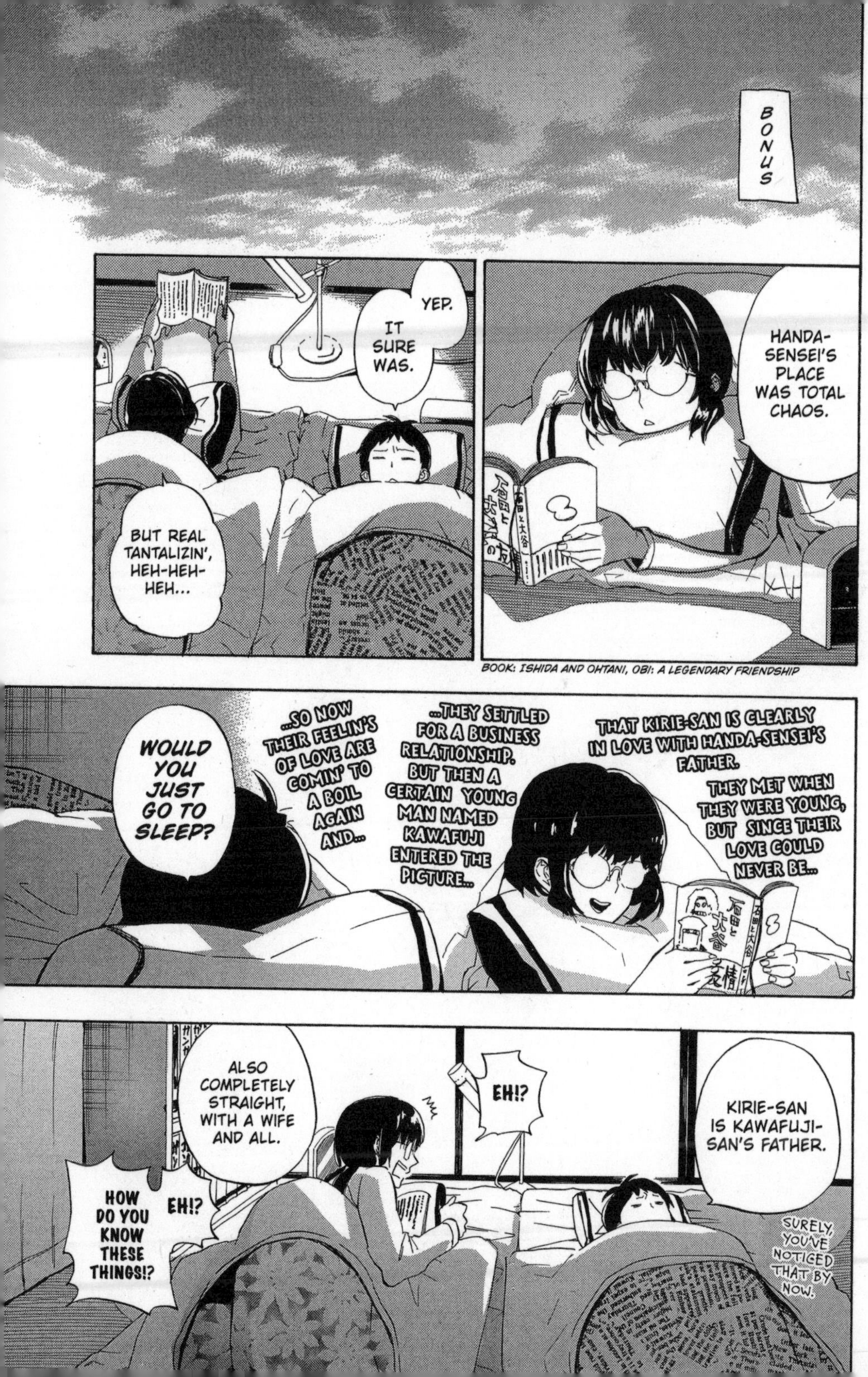
BONUS
HANDA-SENSEI'S PLACE WAS TOTAL CHAOS.
YEP. IT SURE WAS.
BUT REAL TANTALIZIN', HEH-HEH-HEH...
BOOK: ISHIDA AND OHTANI, OBI: A LEGENDARY FRIENDSHIP
THAT KIRIE-SAN IS CLEARLY IN LOVE WITH HANDA-SENSEI'S FATHER.
THEY MET WHEN THEY WERE YOUNG, BUT SINCE THEIR LOVE COULD NEVER BE...
...THEY SETTLED FOR A BUSINESS RELATIONSHIP. BUT THEN A CERTAIN YOUNG MAN NAMED KAWAFUJI ENTERED THE PICTURE...
...SO NOW THEIR FEELIN'S OF LOVE ARE COMIN' TO A BOIL AGAIN AND...
WOULD YOU JUST GO TO SLEEP?
KIRIE-SAN IS KAWAFUJI-SAN'S FATHER.
SURELY, YOU'VE NOTICED THAT BY NOW.
EH!?
ALSO COMPLETELY STRAIGHT, WITH A WIFE AND ALL.
EH!?
HOW DO YOU KNOW THESE THINGS!?

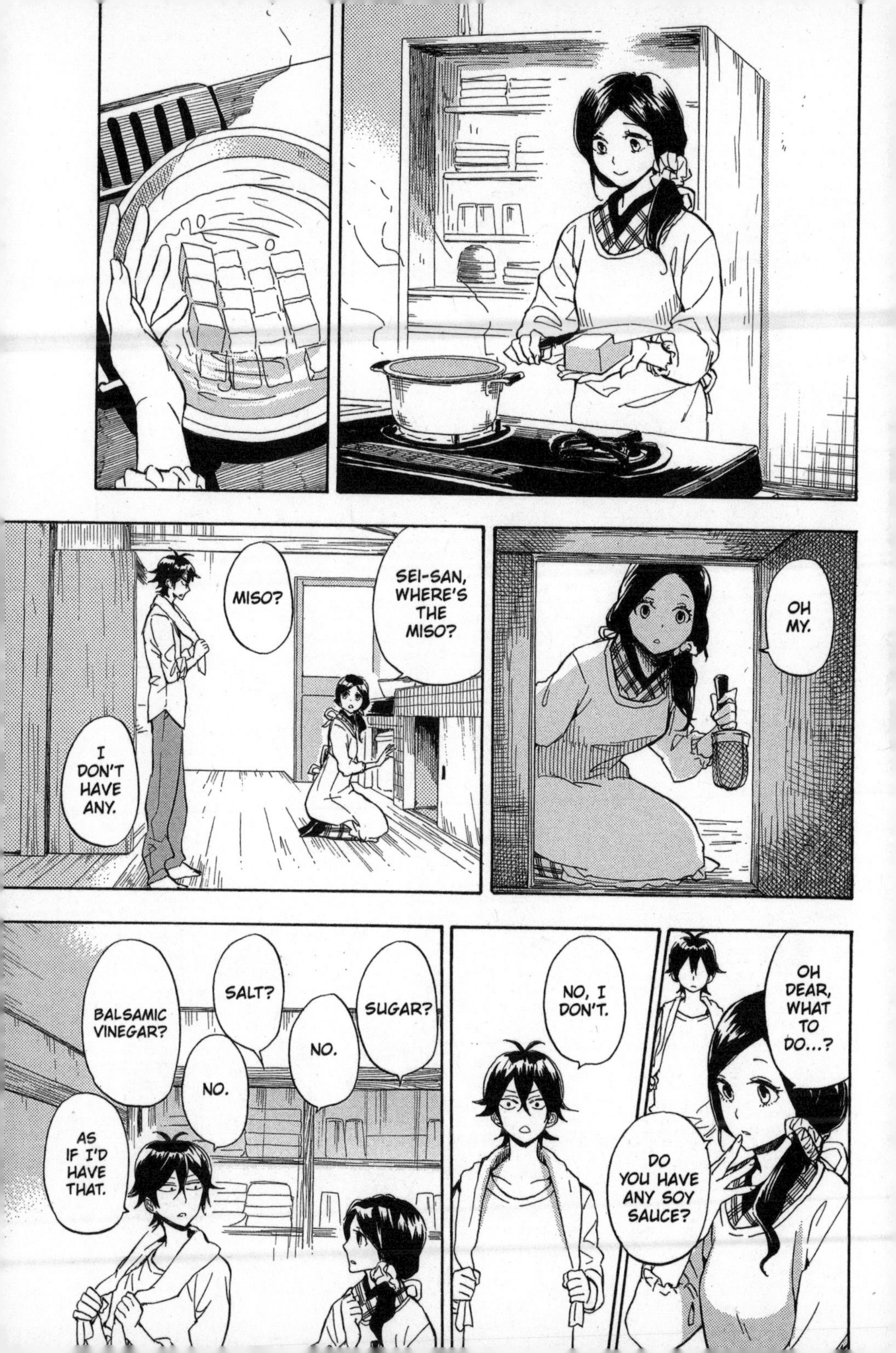
OH MY.
SEI-SAN, WHERE'S THE MISO?
MISO?
I DON'T HAVE ANY.
OH DEAR, WHAT TO DO...?
DO YOU HAVE ANY SOY SAUCE?
NO, I DON'T.
SUGAR?
NO.
SALT?
NO.
BALSAMIC VINEGAR?
AS IF I'D HAVE THAT.

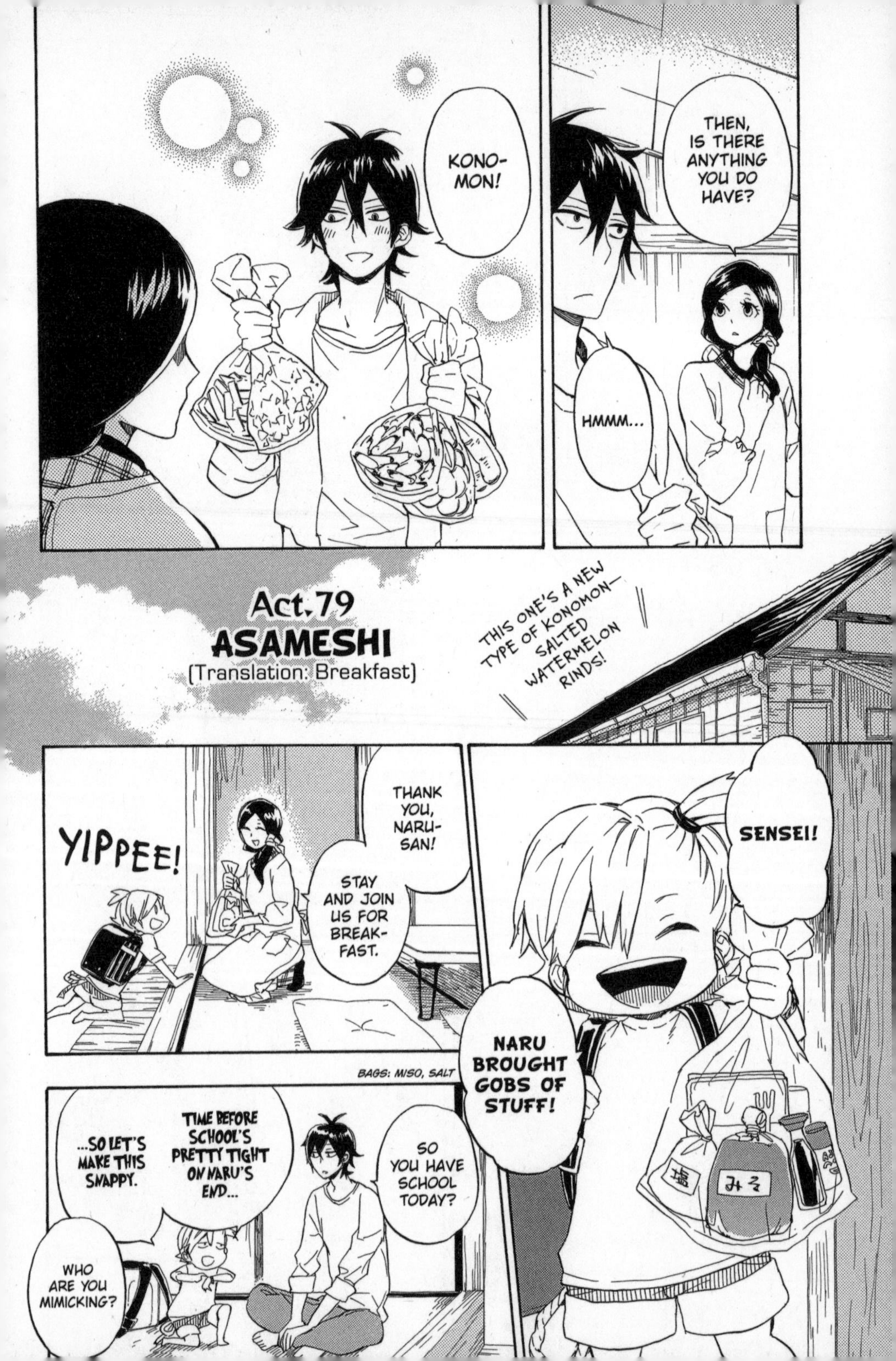
THEN, IS THERE ANYTHING YOU DO HAVE?
HMMM...
KONO-MON!
THIS ONE'S A NEW TYPE OF KONOMON—SALTED WATERMELON RINDS!
Act.79
ASAMESHI
[Translation: Breakfast]
SENSEI!
NARU BROUGHT GOBS OF STUFF!
THANK YOU, NARU-SAN!
STAY AND JOIN US FOR BREAK-FAST.
YIPPEE!
BAGS: MISO, SALT
SO YOU HAVE SCHOOL TODAY?
TIME BEFORE SCHOOL'S PRETTY TIGHT ON NARU'S END...
...SO LET'S MAKE THIS SNAPPY.
WHO ARE YOU MIMICKING?

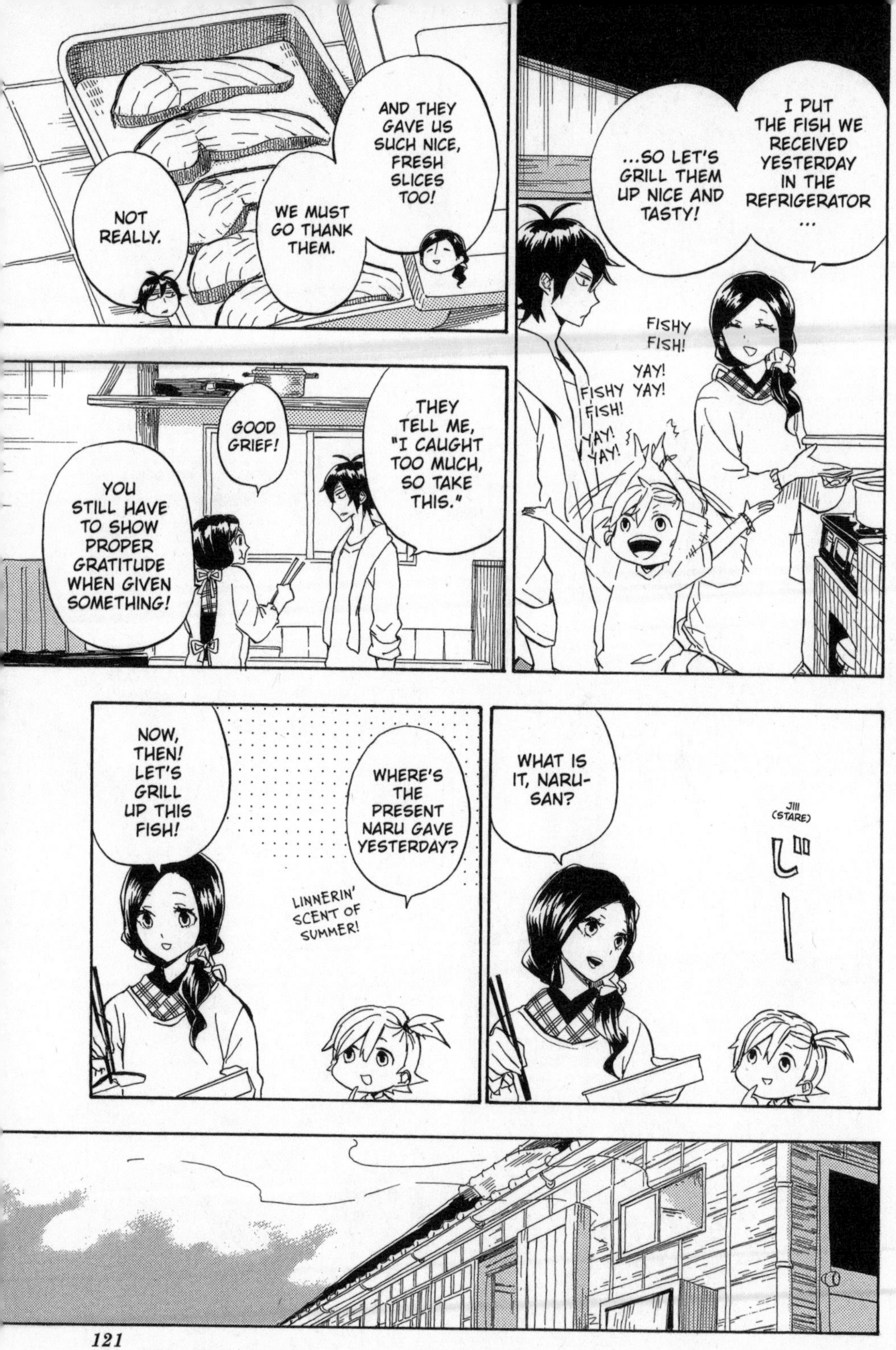
I PUT THE FISH WE RECEIVED YESTERDAY IN THE REFRIGERATOR ...
...SO LET'S GRILL THEM UP NICE AND TASTY!
FISHY FISH!
YAY! YAY!
FISHY FISH!
YAY! YAY!
AND THEY GAVE US SUCH NICE, FRESH SLICES TOO!
WE MUST GO THANK THEM.
NOT REALLY.
THEY TELL ME, "I CAUGHT TOO MUCH, SO TAKE THIS."
GOOD GRIEF!
YOU STILL HAVE TO SHOW PROPER GRATITUDE WHEN GIVEN SOMETHING!
WHAT IS IT, NARU-SAN?
JIII (STARE)
じー
NOW, THEN! LET'S GRILL UP THIS FISH!
WHERE'S THE PRESENT NARU GAVE YESTERDAY?
LINNERIN' SCENT OF SUMMER!

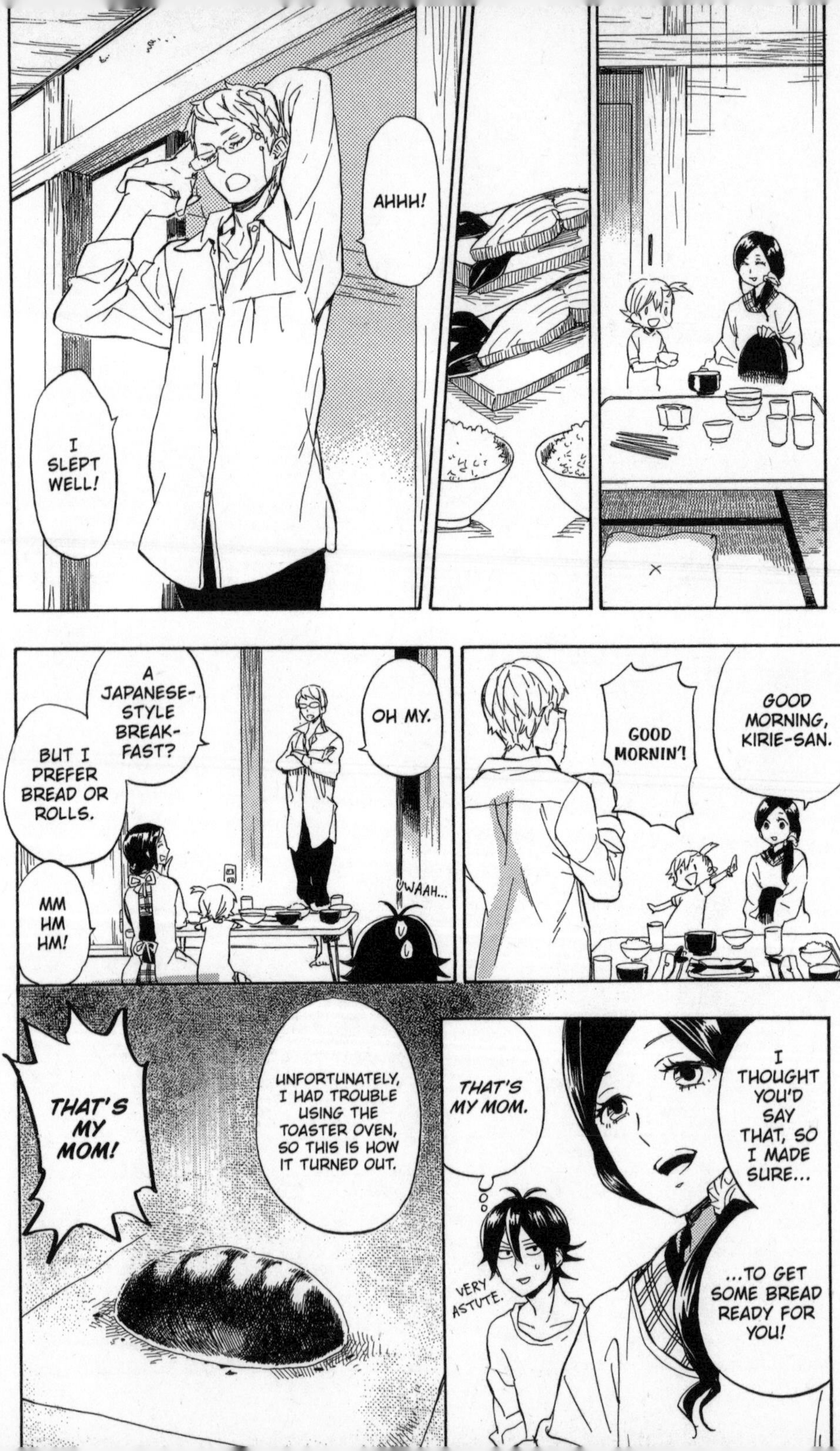
AHHH!
I SLEPT WELL!
GOOD MORNING, KIRIE-SAN.
GOOD MORNIN'!
OH MY.
A JAPANESE-STYLE BREAKFAST?
BUT I PREFER BREAD OR ROLLS.
MM HM HM!
UWAAH...
I THOUGHT YOU'D SAY THAT, SO I MADE SURE...
...TO GET SOME BREAD READY FOR YOU!
THAT'S MY MOM.
VERY ASTUTE.
UNFORTUNATELY, I HAD TROUBLE USING THE TOASTER OVEN, SO THIS IS HOW IT TURNED OUT.
THAT'S MY MOM!

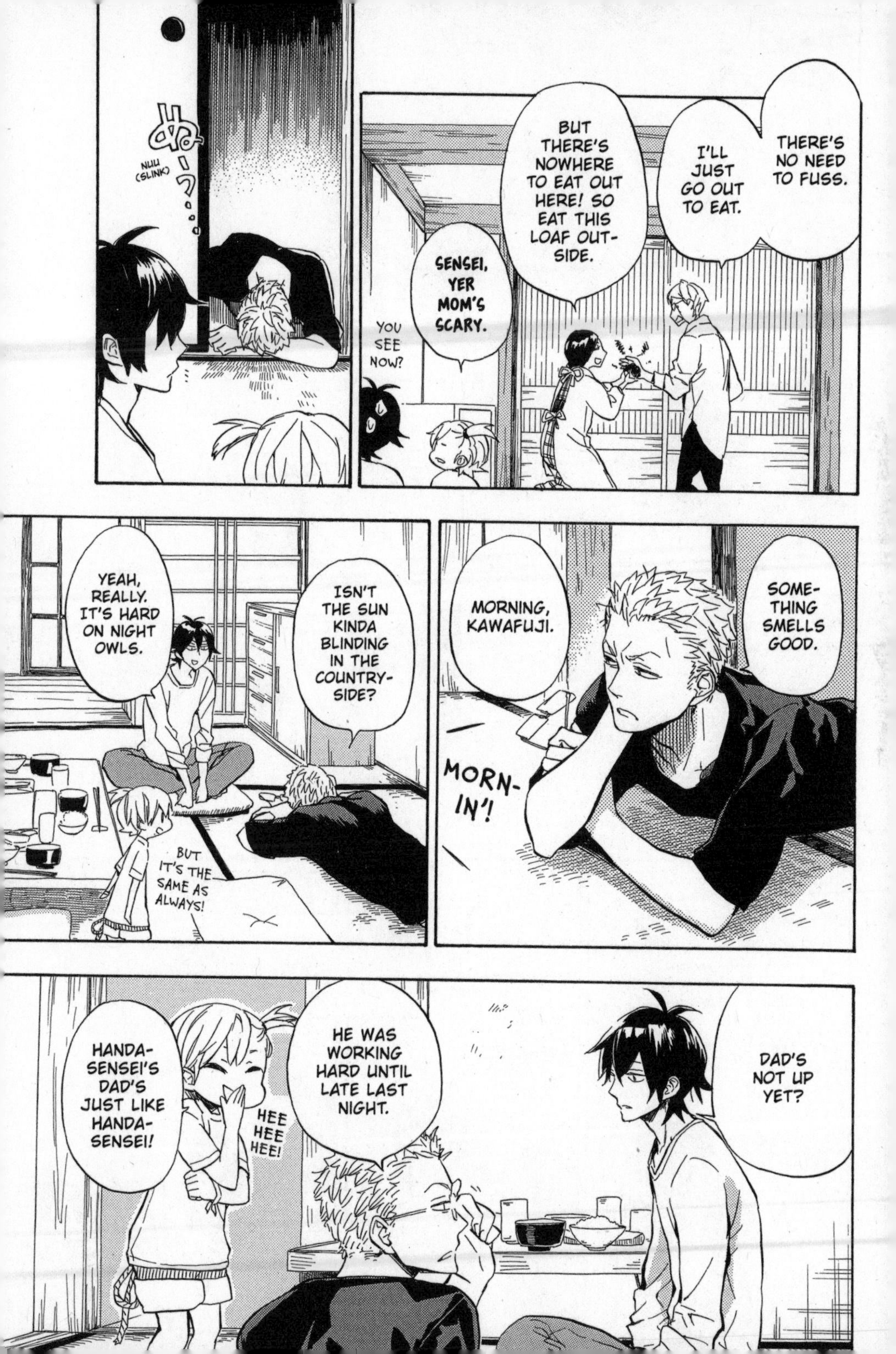
THERE'S NO NEED TO FUSS.
I'LL JUST GO OUT TO EAT.
BUT THERE'S NOWHERE TO EAT OUT HERE! SO EAT THIS LOAF OUT-SIDE.
SENSEI, YER MOM'S SCARY.
YOU SEE NOW?
ぬ〜っ
NUU (SLINK)
SOME-THING SMELLS GOOD.
MORNING, KAWAFUJI.
MORN-IN'!
ISN'T THE SUN KINDA BLINDING IN THE COUNTRY-SIDE?
YEAH, REALLY. IT'S HARD ON NIGHT OWLS.
BUT IT'S THE SAME AS ALWAYS!
DAD'S NOT UP YET?
HE WAS WORKING HARD UNTIL LATE LAST NIGHT.
HANDA-SENSEI'S DAD'S JUST LIKE HANDA-SENSEI!
HEE HEE HEE!

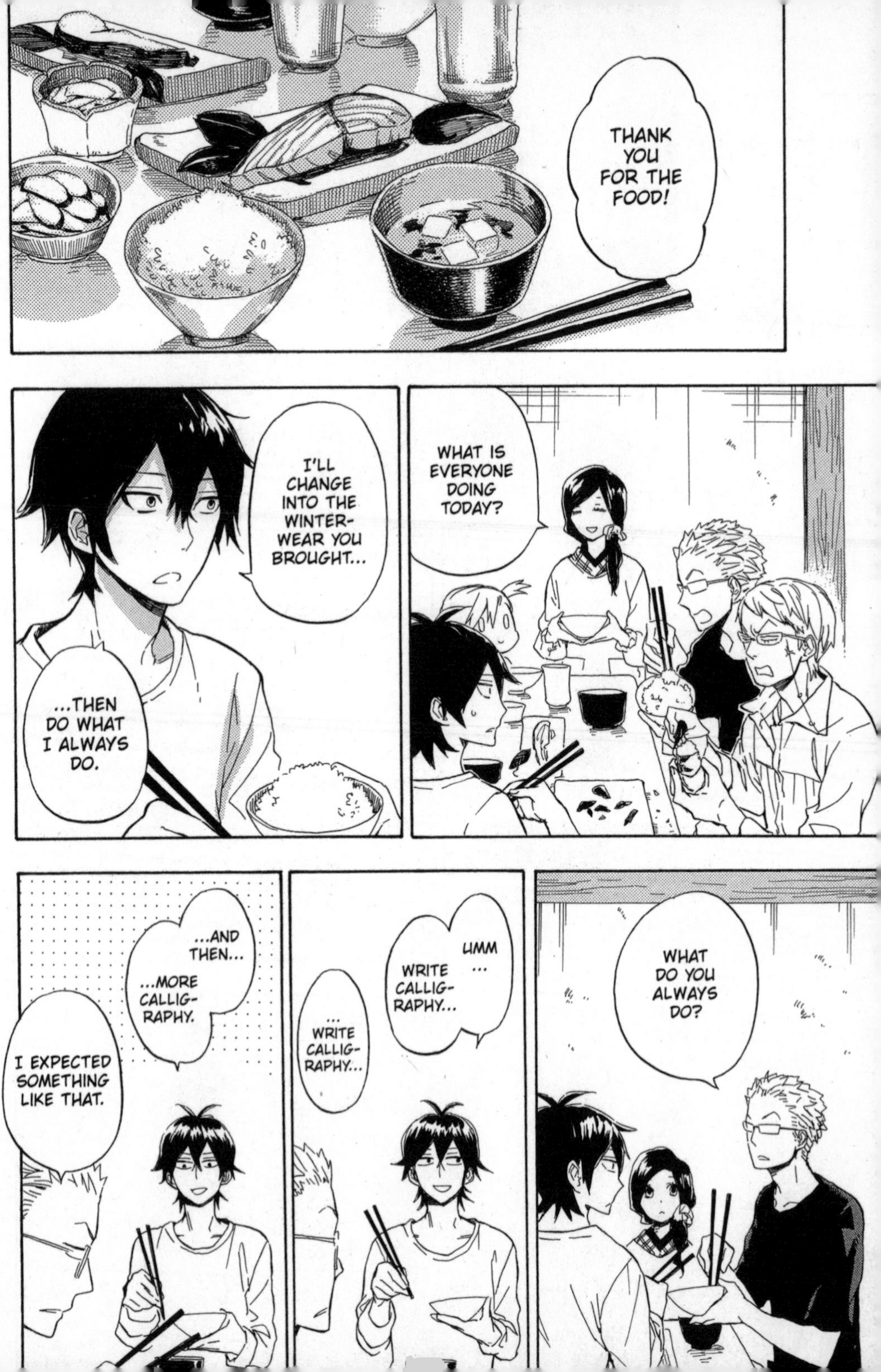
THANK YOU FOR THE FOOD!
WHAT IS EVERYONE DOING TODAY?
I'LL CHANGE INTO THE WINTER-WEAR YOU BROUGHT...
...THEN DO WHAT I ALWAYS DO.
WHAT DO YOU ALWAYS DO?
UMM...
WRITE CALLIGRAPHY...
...WRITE CALLIGRAPHY...
...AND THEN...
...MORE CALLIGRAPHY.
I EXPECTED SOMETHING LIKE THAT.

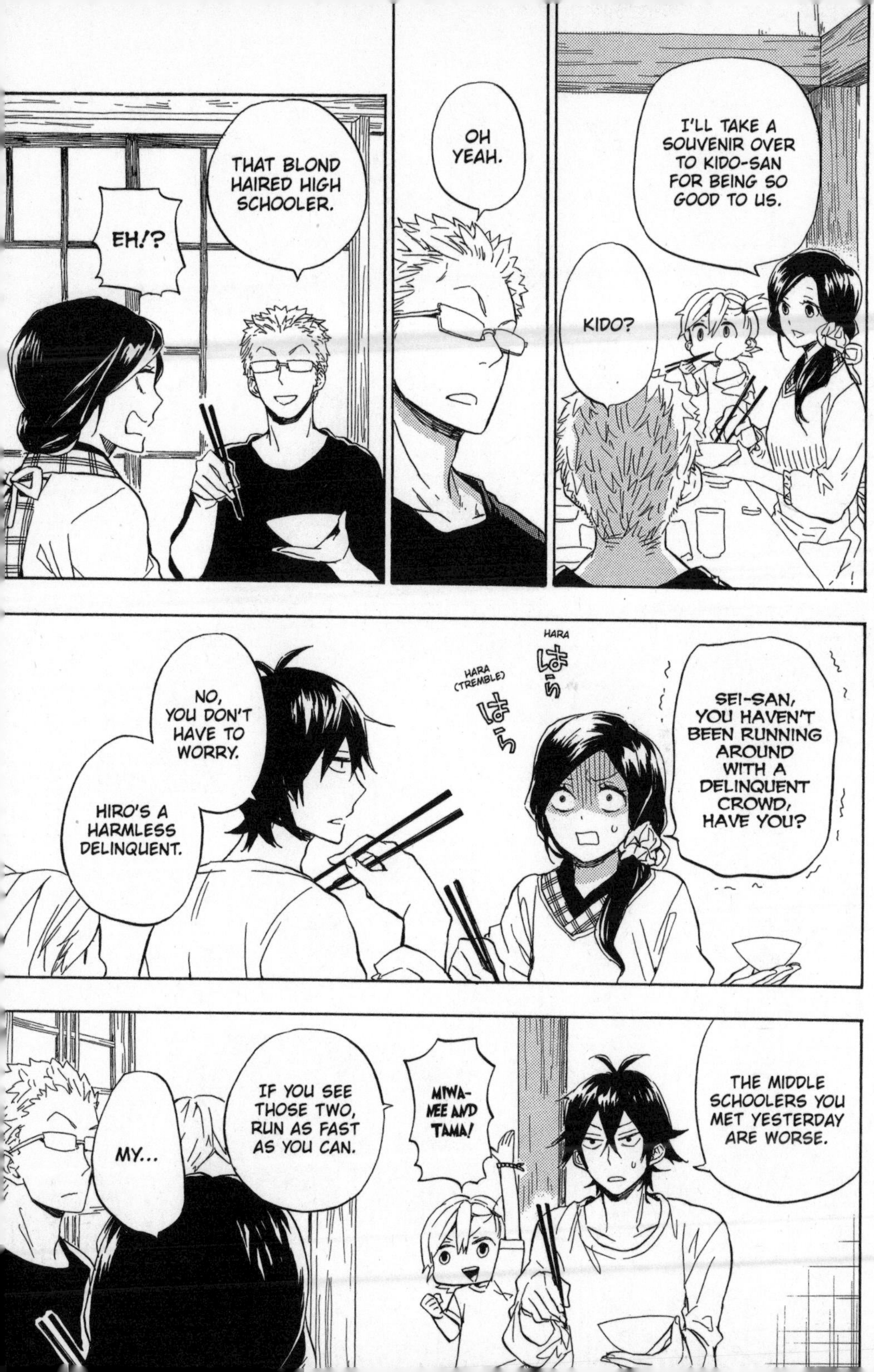
I'LL TAKE A SOUVENIR OVER TO KIDO-SAN FOR BEING SO GOOD TO US.
KIDO?
OH YEAH.
THAT BLOND HAIRED HIGH SCHOOLER.
EH!?
SEI-SAN, YOU HAVEN'T BEEN RUNNING AROUND WITH A DELINQUENT CROWD, HAVE YOU?
はら HARA
はら HARA (TREMBLE)
NO, YOU DON'T HAVE TO WORRY.
HIRO'S A HARMLESS DELINQUENT.
THE MIDDLE SCHOOLERS YOU MET YESTERDAY ARE WORSE.
MIWA-NEE AND TAMA!
IF YOU SEE THOSE TWO, RUN AS FAST AS YOU CAN.
MY...

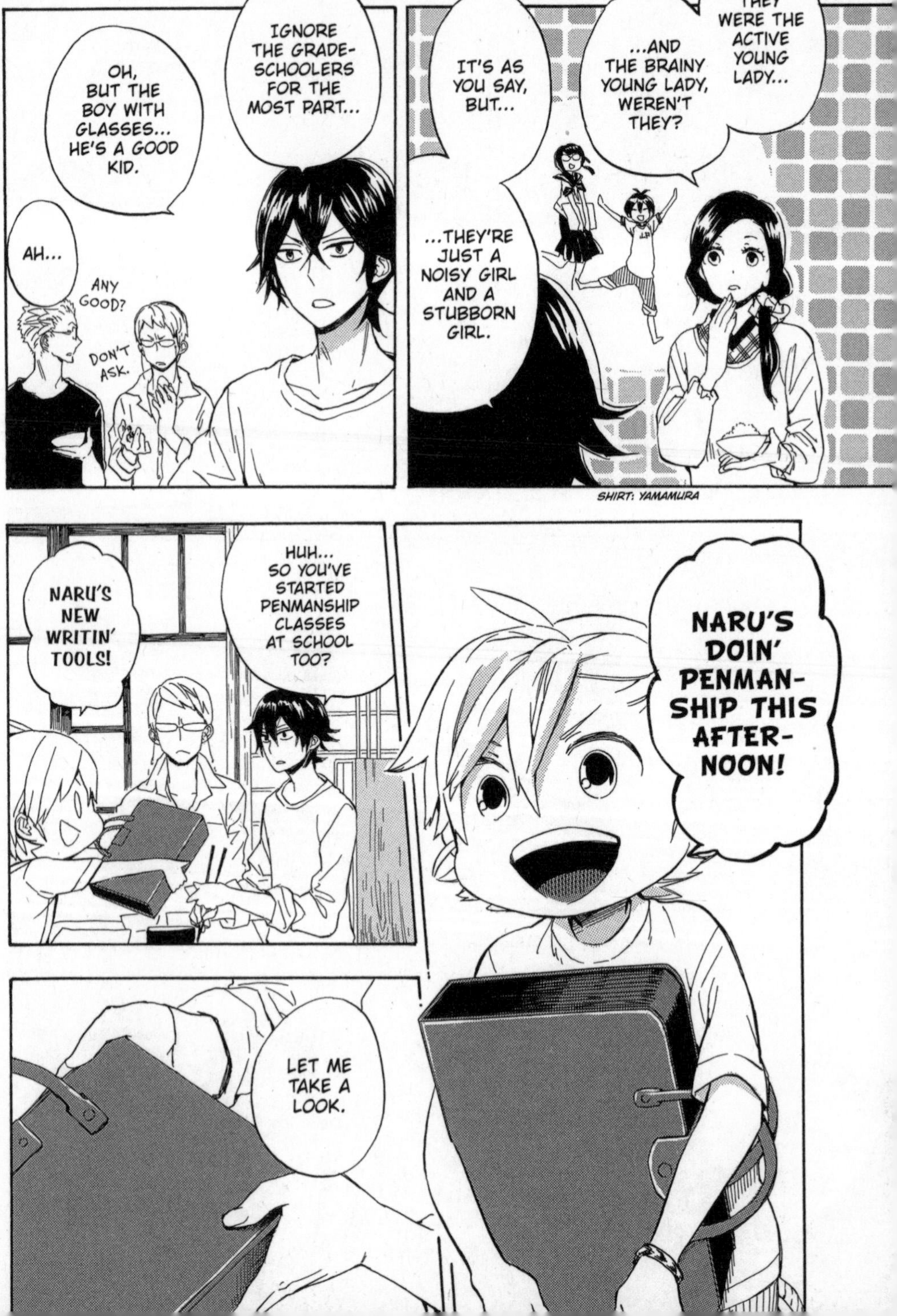
THEY WERE THE ACTIVE YOUNG LADY...
...AND THE BRAINY YOUNG LADY, WEREN'T THEY?
IT'S AS YOU SAY, BUT...
...THEY'RE JUST A NOISY GIRL AND A STUBBORN GIRL.
SHIRT: YAMAMURA
IGNORE THE GRADE-SCHOOLERS FOR THE MOST PART...
OH, BUT THE BOY WITH GLASSES... HE'S A GOOD KID.
AH...
ANY GOOD?
DON'T ASK.
NARU'S DOIN' PENMANSHIP THIS AFTERNOON!
HUH... SO YOU'VE STARTED PENMANSHIP CLASSES AT SCHOOL TOO?
NARU'S NEW WRITIN' TOOLS!
LET ME TAKE A LOOK.

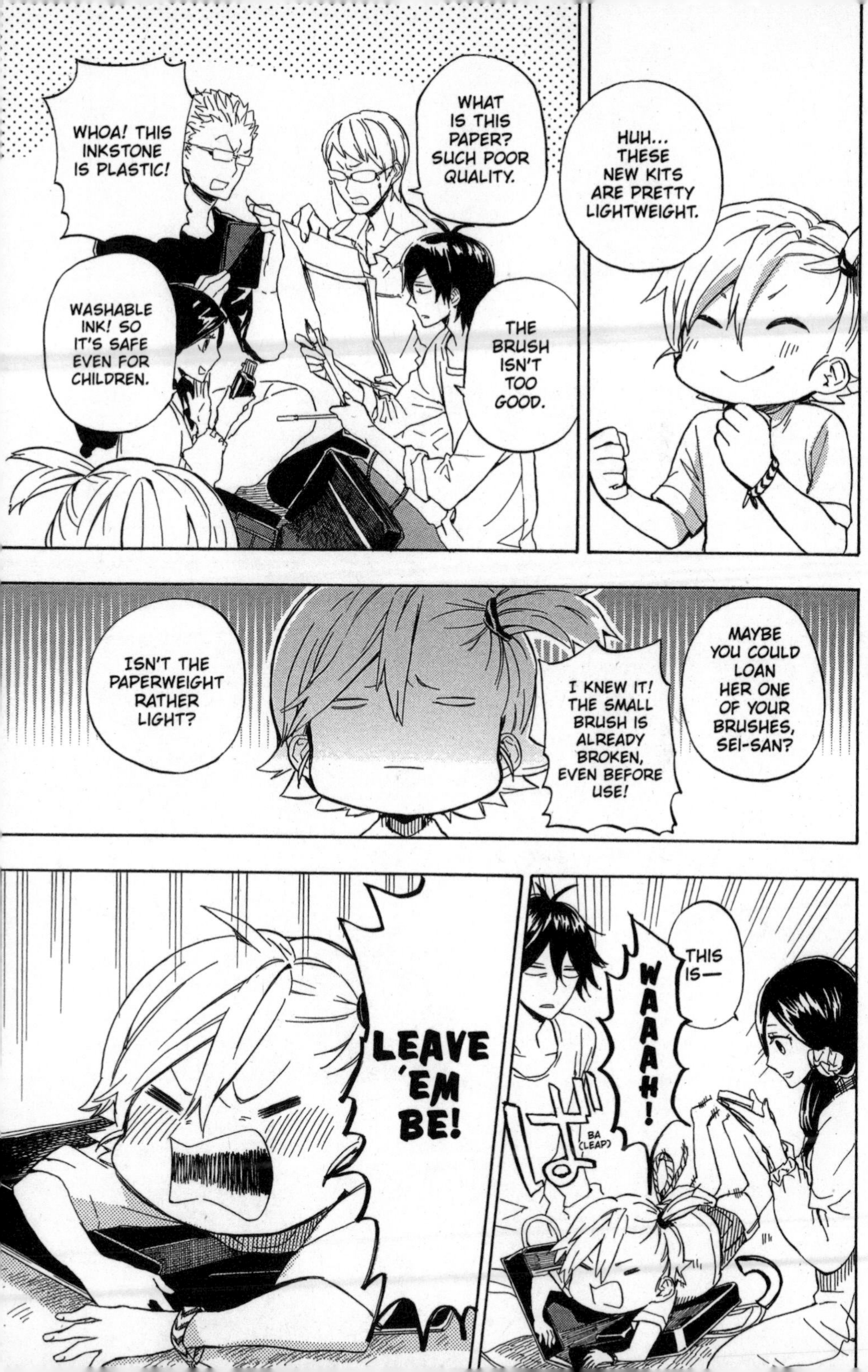

HUH... THESE NEW KITS ARE PRETTY LIGHTWEIGHT.
WHAT IS THIS PAPER? SUCH POOR QUALITY.
WHOA! THIS INKSTONE IS PLASTIC!
THE BRUSH ISN'T TOO GOOD.
WASHABLE INK! SO IT'S SAFE EVEN FOR CHILDREN.
MAYBE YOU COULD LOAN HER ONE OF YOUR BRUSHES, SEI-SAN?
I KNEW IT! THE SMALL BRUSH IS ALREADY BROKEN, EVEN BEFORE USE!
ISN'T THE PAPERWEIGHT RATHER LIGHT?
THIS IS—
WAAAAH!
BA (LEAP)
LEAVE 'EM BE!

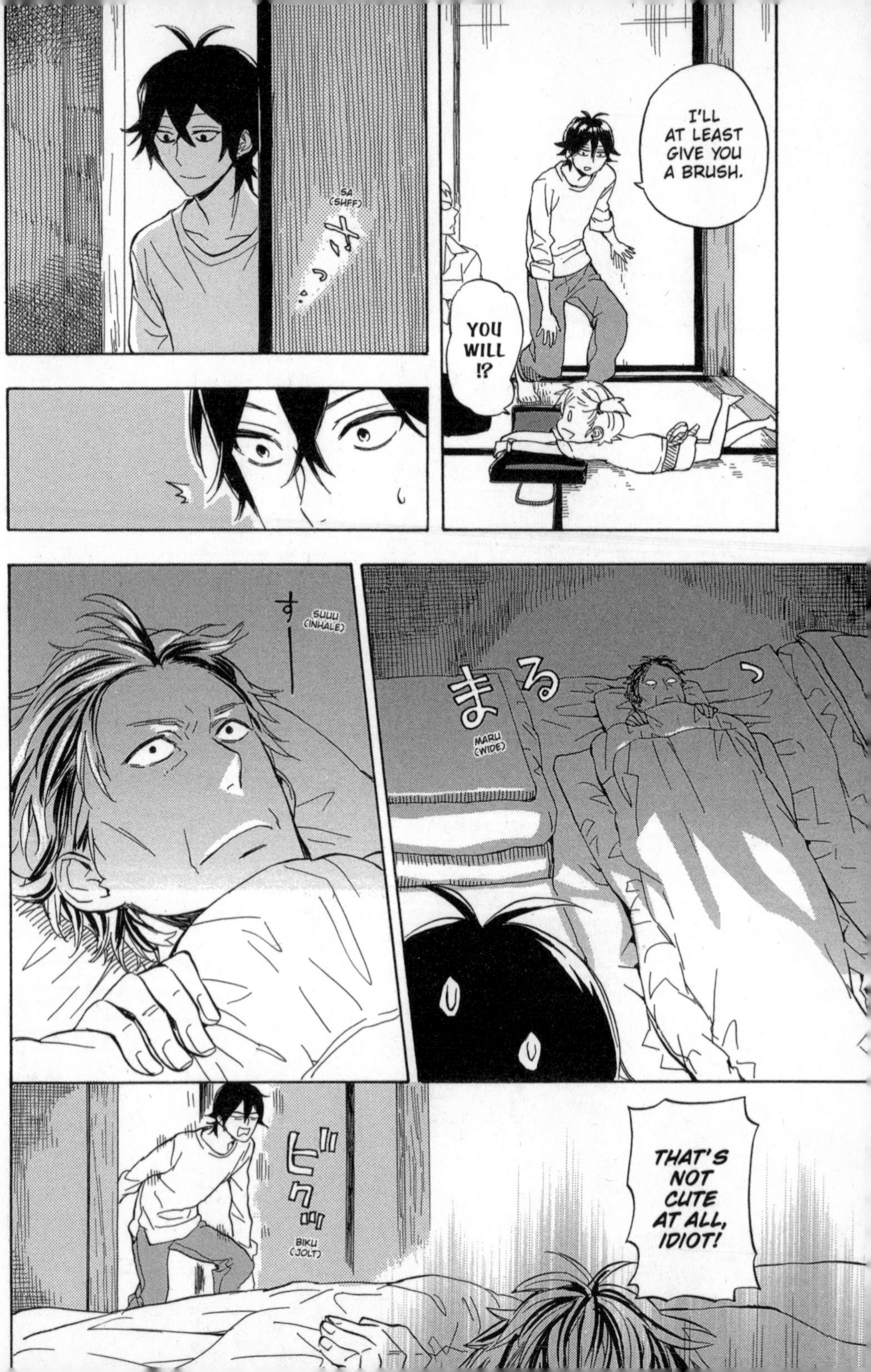
I'LL AT LEAST GIVE YOU A BRUSH.
YOU WILL!?
さっ
SA (SHFF)
まるっ
MARU (WIDE)
すー
SUUU (INHALE)
THAT'S NOT CUTE AT ALL, IDIOT!
ビクッ
BIKU (JOLT)

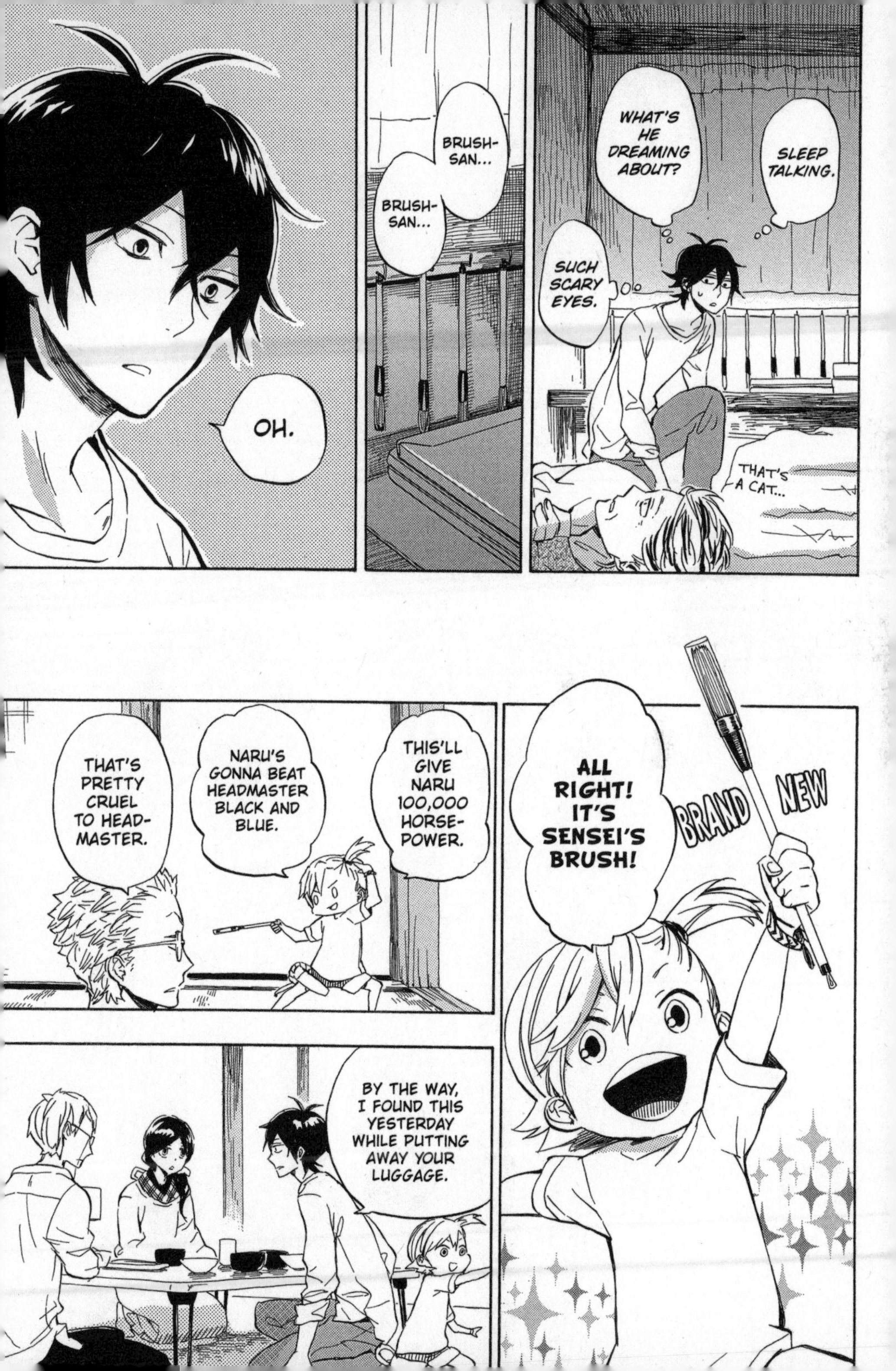
SLEEP TALKING.
WHAT'S HE DREAMING ABOUT?
SUCH SCARY EYES.
THAT'S A CAT...
BRUSH-SAN...
BRUSH-SAN...
OH.
BRAND NEW
ALL RIGHT! IT'S SENSEI'S BRUSH!
THIS'LL GIVE NARU 100,000 HORSE-POWER.
NARU'S GONNA BEAT HEADMASTER BLACK AND BLUE.
THAT'S PRETTY CRUEL TO HEAD-MASTER.
BY THE WAY, I FOUND THIS YESTERDAY WHILE PUTTING AWAY YOUR LUGGAGE.

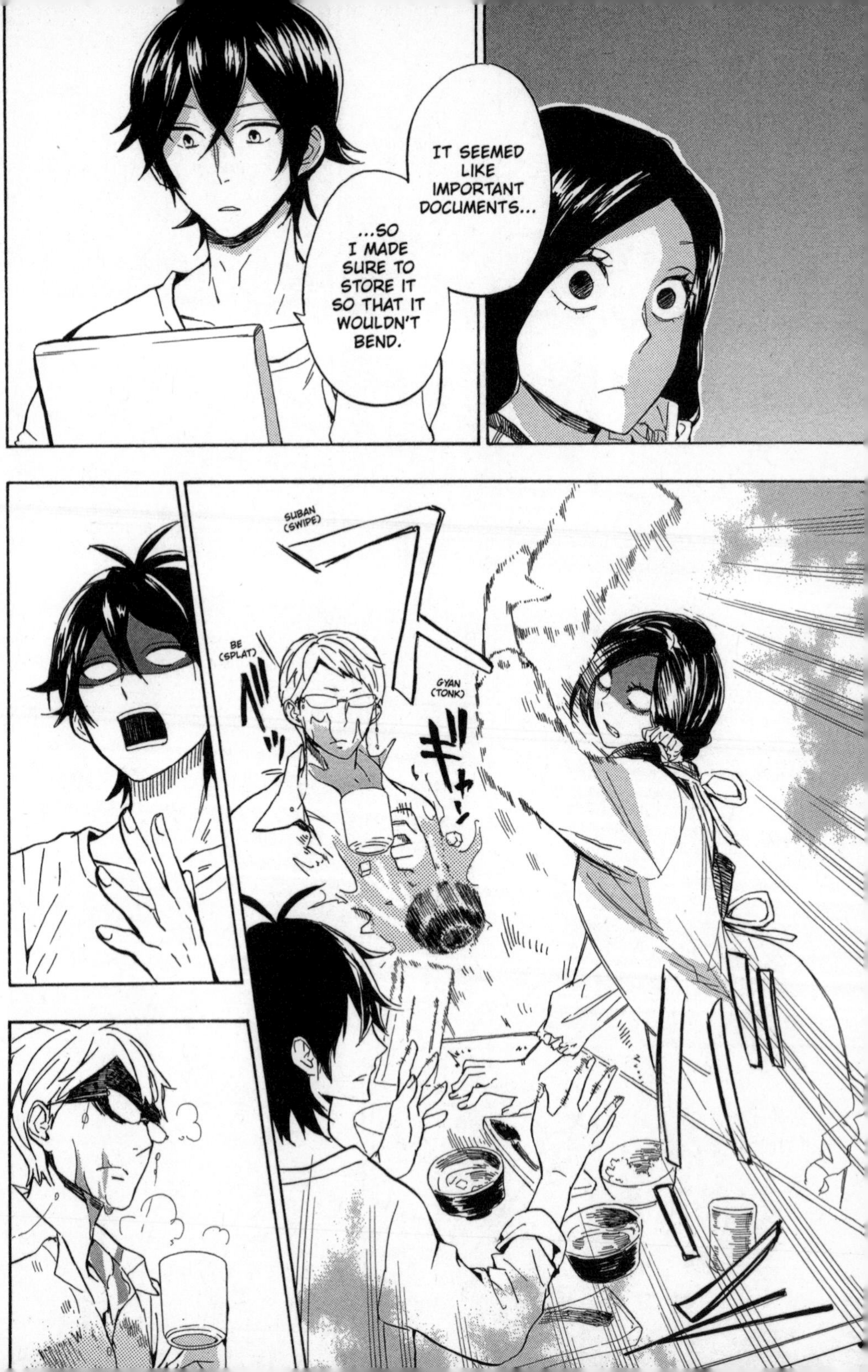
IT SEEMED LIKE IMPORTANT DOCUMENTS...
...SO I MADE SURE TO STORE IT SO THAT IT WOULDN'T BEND.
SUBAN (SWIPE)
GYAN (TONK)
BE (SPLAT)

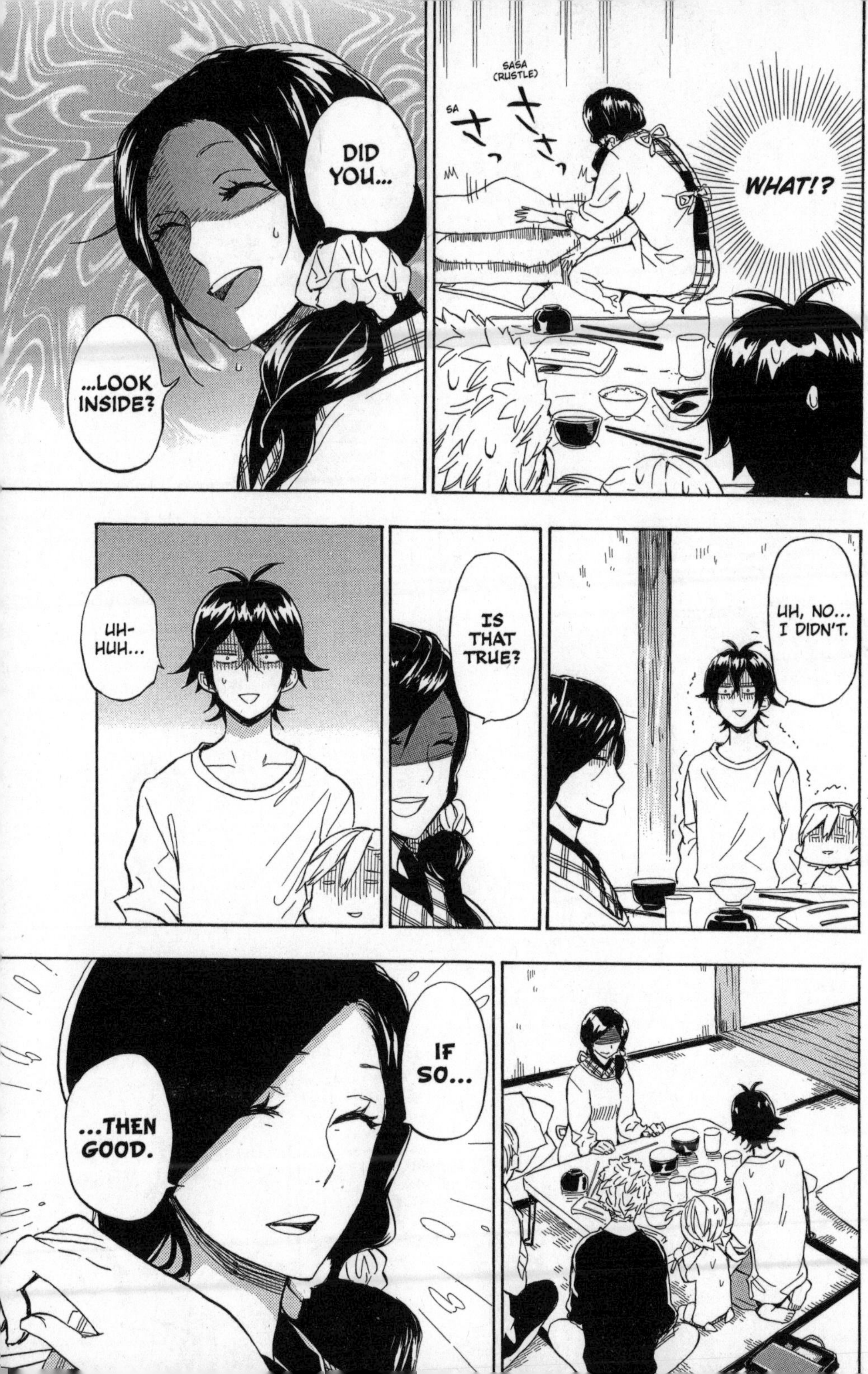

SASA (RUSTLE)
ささっ
SA
さっ
WHAT!?
DID YOU...
...LOOK INSIDE?
UH, NO... I DIDN'T.
IS THAT TRUE?
UH-HUH...
IF SO...
...THEN GOOD.

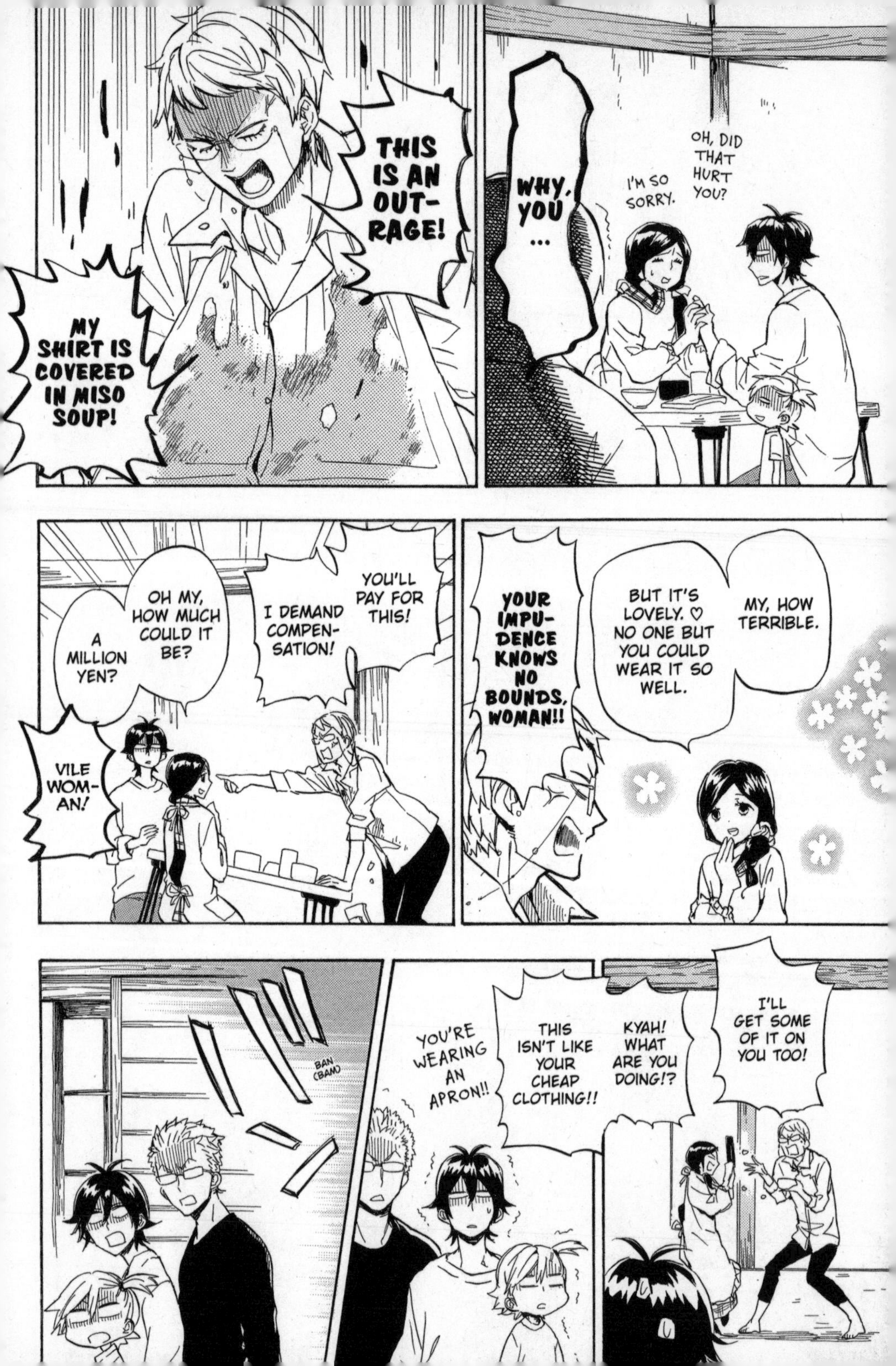

OH, DID THAT HURT YOU?
I'M SO SORRY.
WHY, YOU ...
THIS IS AN OUT-RAGE!
MY SHIRT IS COVERED IN MISO SOUP!
MY, HOW TERRIBLE.
BUT IT'S LOVELY. ♡ NO ONE BUT YOU COULD WEAR IT SO WELL.
YOUR IMPU-DENCE KNOWS NO BOUNDS, WOMAN!!
YOU'LL PAY FOR THIS!
I DEMAND COMPEN-SATION!
OH MY, HOW MUCH COULD IT BE?
A MILLION YEN?
VILE WOM-AN!
I'LL GET SOME OF IT ON YOU TOO!
KYAH! WHAT ARE YOU DOING!?
THIS ISN'T LIKE YOUR CHEAP CLOTHING!!
YOU'RE WEARING AN APRON!!
BAN (BAM)

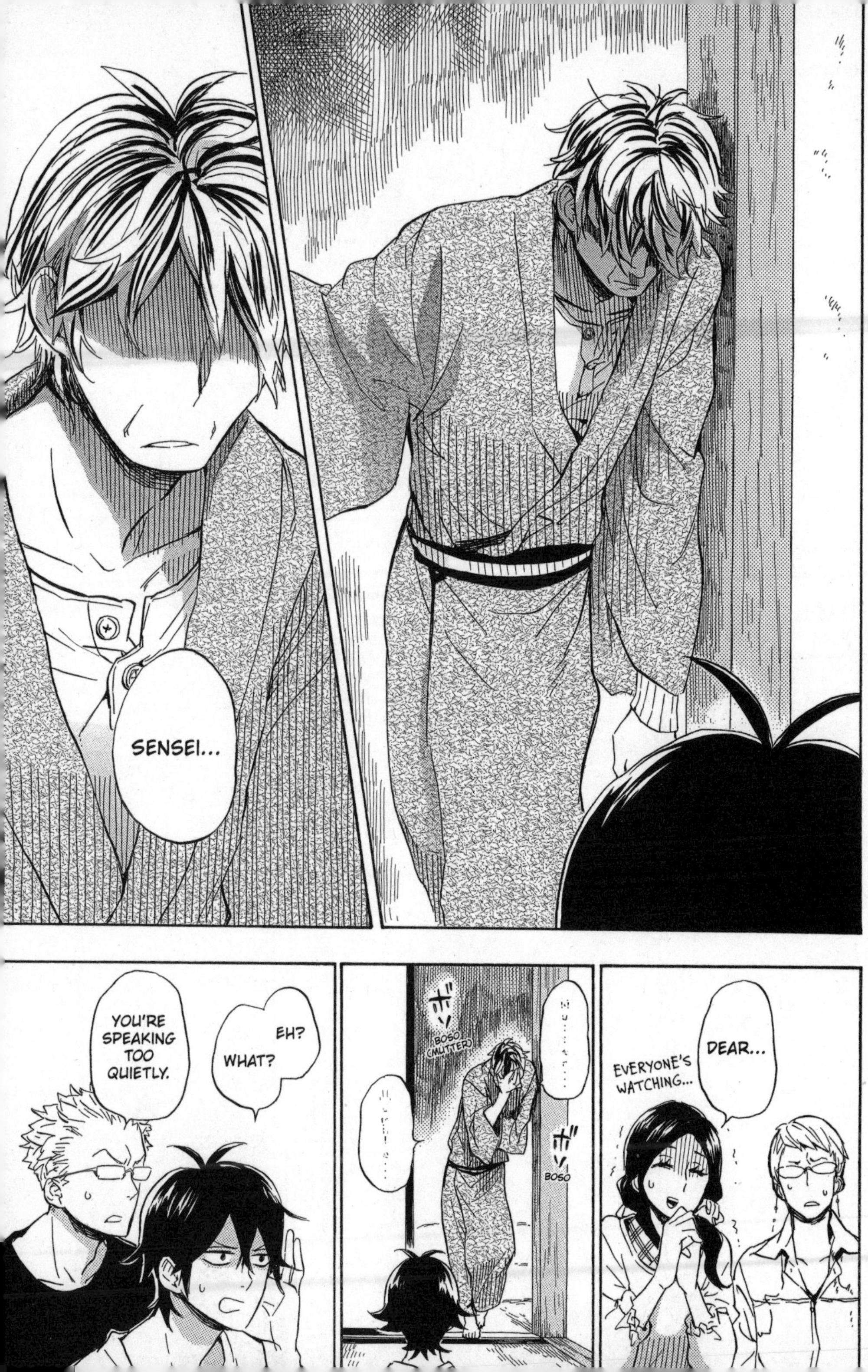
SENSEI...
DEAR...
EVERYONE'S WATCHING...
ボソ
BOSO (MUTTER)
ボソ
BOSO
EH? WHAT?
YOU'RE SPEAKING TOO QUIETLY.

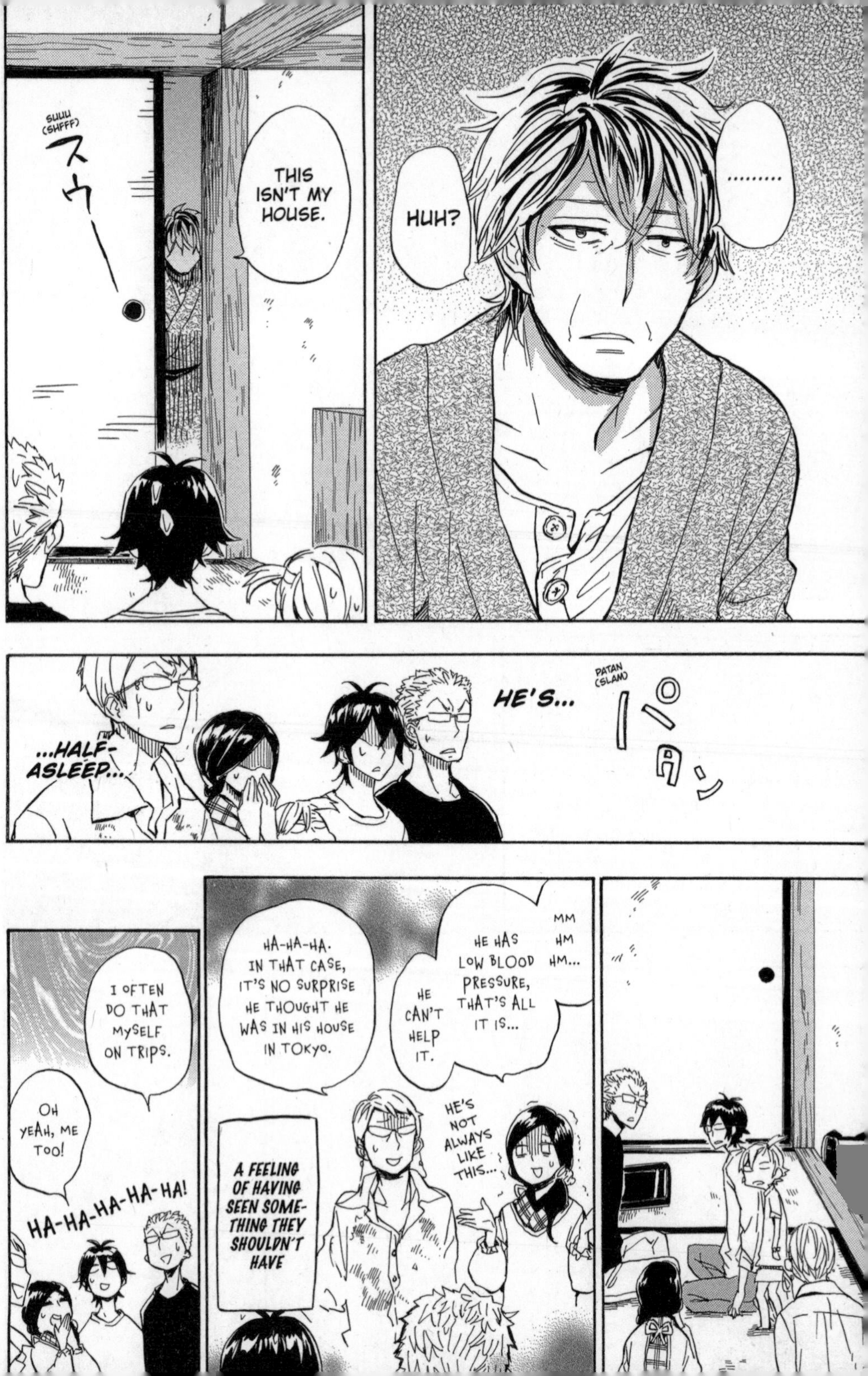

....
HUH?
THIS ISN'T MY HOUSE.
SUUU (SHFFF)
スウー
PATAN (SLAM)
パタン
HE'S...
...HALF-ASLEEP...
MM HM HM...
HE HAS LOW BLOOD PRESSURE, THAT'S ALL IT IS...
HE CAN'T HELP IT.
HE'S NOT ALWAYS LIKE THIS...
HA-HA-HA. IN THAT CASE, IT'S NO SURPRISE HE THOUGHT HE WAS IN HIS HOUSE IN TOKYO.
A FEELING OF HAVING SEEN SOMETHING THEY SHOULDN'T HAVE
I OFTEN DO THAT MYSELF ON TRIPS.
OH YEAH, ME TOO!
HA-HA-HA-HA-HA!

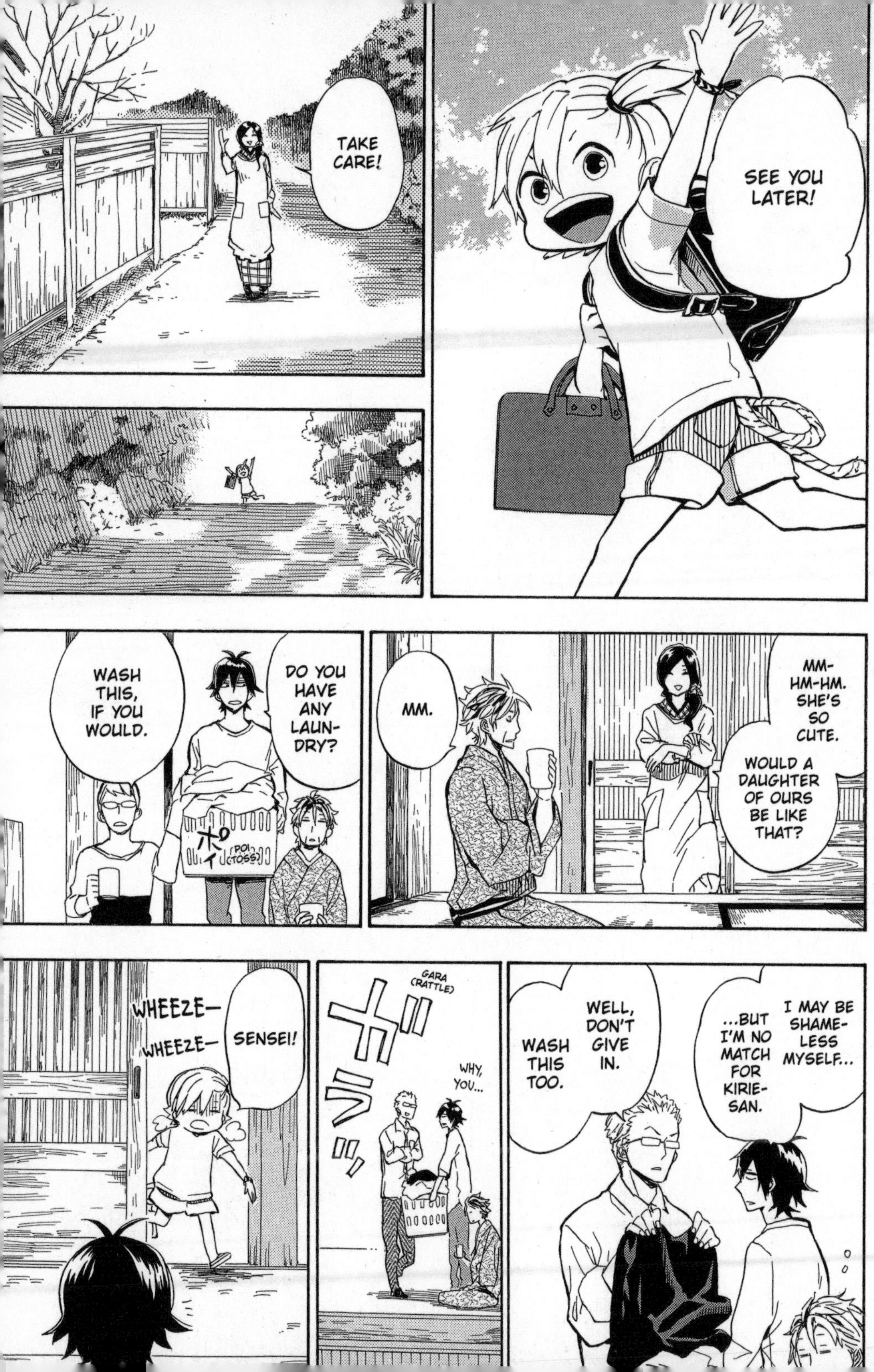
SEE YOU LATER!
TAKE CARE!
MM-HM-HM. SHE'S SO CUTE.
WOULD A DAUGHTER OF OURS BE LIKE THAT?
MM.
DO YOU HAVE ANY LAUNDRY?
WASH THIS, IF YOU WOULD.
ポイ POI (TOSS)
I MAY BE SHAME-LESS MYSELF...
...BUT I'M NO MATCH FOR KIRIE-SAN.
WELL, DON'T GIVE IN.
WASH THIS TOO.
ガラッ GARA (RATTLE)
WHY, YOU...
SENSEI!
WHEEZE—
WHEEZE—

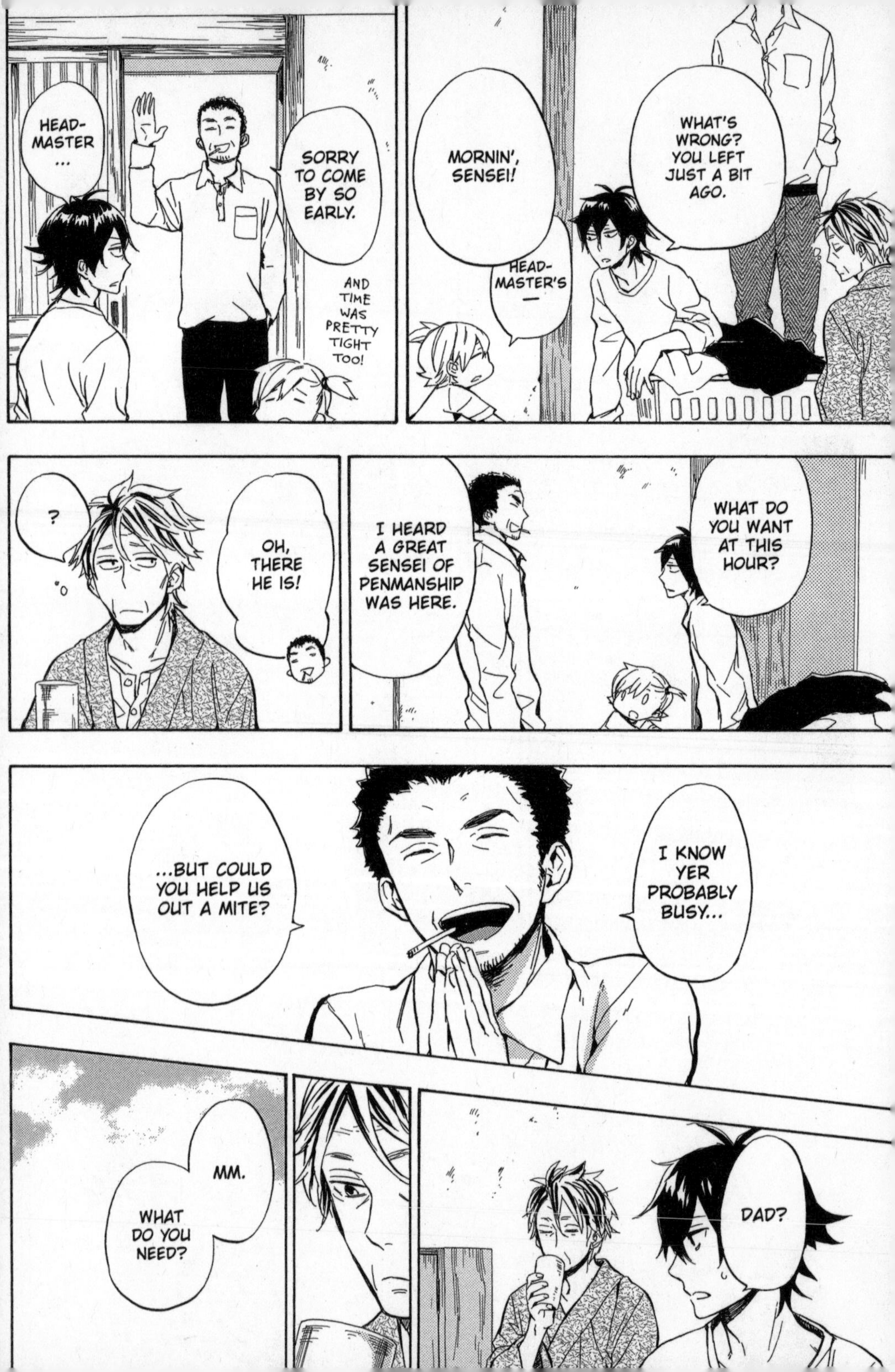
WHAT'S WRONG? YOU LEFT JUST A BIT AGO.
MORNIN', SENSEI!
HEAD-MASTER'S —
SORRY TO COME BY SO EARLY.
AND TIME WAS PRETTY TIGHT TOO!
HEAD-MASTER...
WHAT DO YOU WANT AT THIS HOUR?
I HEARD A GREAT SENSEI OF PENMANSHIP WAS HERE.
OH, THERE HE IS!
?
I KNOW YER PROBABLY BUSY...
...BUT COULD YOU HELP US OUT A MITE?
DAD?
MM.
WHAT DO YOU NEED?

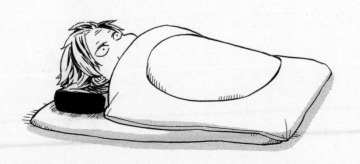

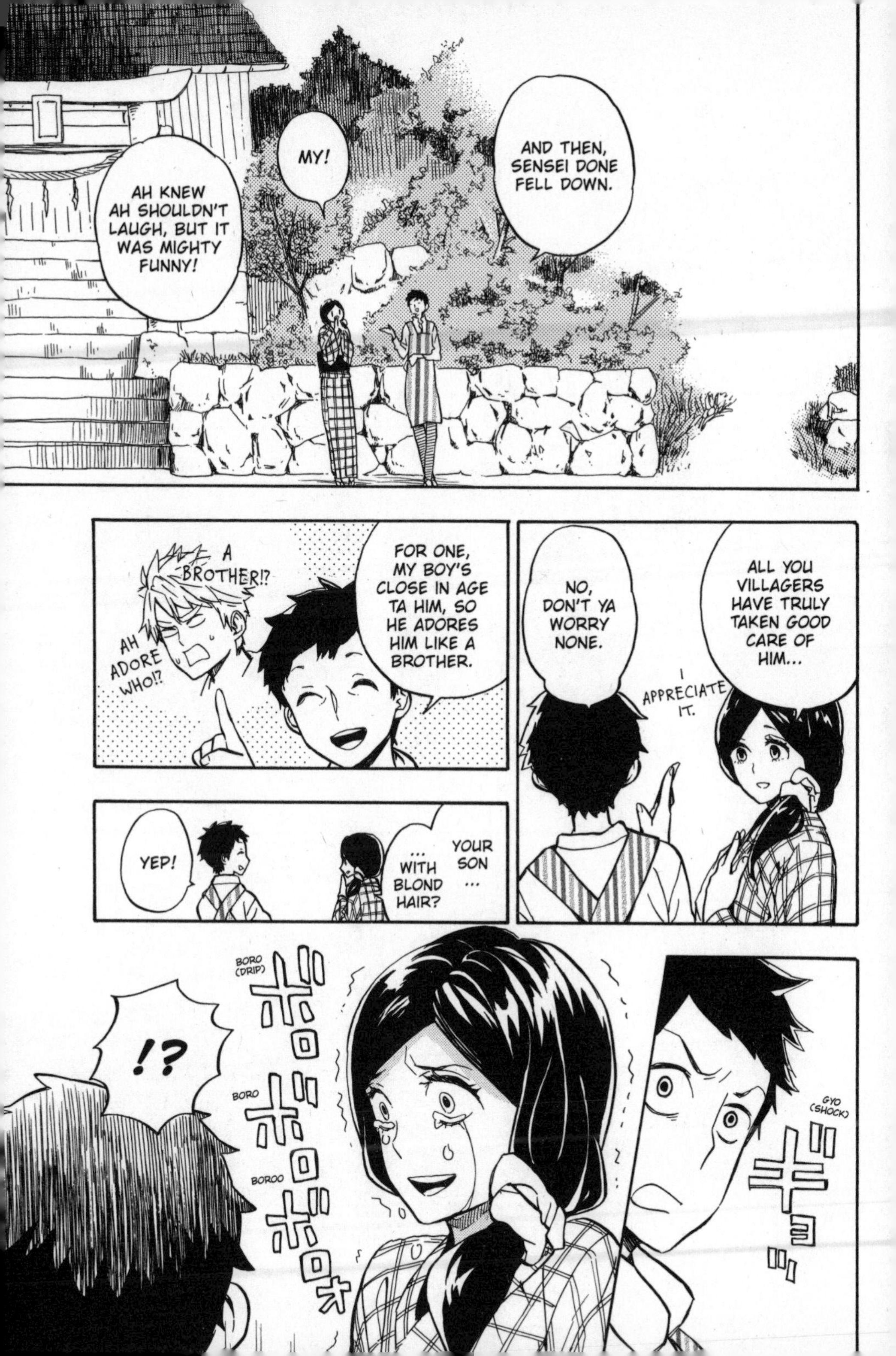

AND THEN, SENSEI DONE FELL DOWN.
MY!
AH KNEW AH SHOULDN'T LAUGH, BUT IT WAS MIGHTY FUNNY!
ALL YOU VILLAGERS HAVE TRULY TAKEN GOOD CARE OF HIM...
I APPRECIATE IT.
NO, DON'T YA WORRY NONE.
FOR ONE, MY BOY'S CLOSE IN AGE TA HIM, SO HE ADORES HIM LIKE A BROTHER.
A BROTHER!?
AH ADORE WHO!?
YOUR SON ...
... WITH BLOND HAIR?
YEP!
ギョッ
GYO (SHOCK)
ボロボロボロォ
BORO (DRIP)
BORO
BOROO
!?

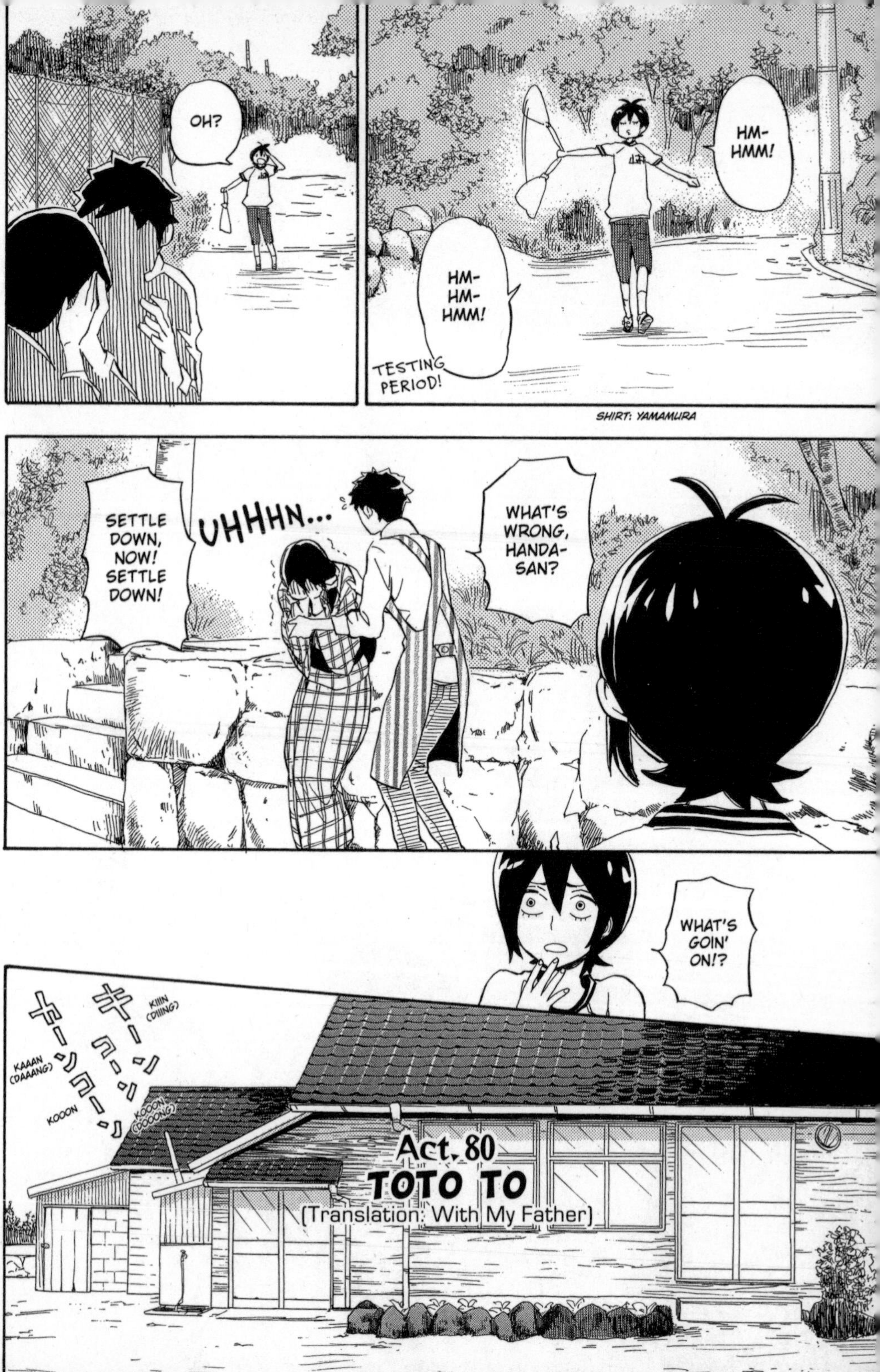
HM-HMM!
HM-HM-HMM!
TESTING PERIOD!
OH?
SHIRT: YAMAMURA
WHAT'S WRONG, HANDA-SAN?
UHHHN...
SETTLE DOWN, NOW! SETTLE DOWN!
WHAT'S GOIN' ON!?
キーン
KIIIN (DIIING)
カーン
KAAAN (DAAANG)
コーン
KOOON (DOOONG)
コーン
KOOON

Act. 80
TOTO TO
(Translation: With My Father)

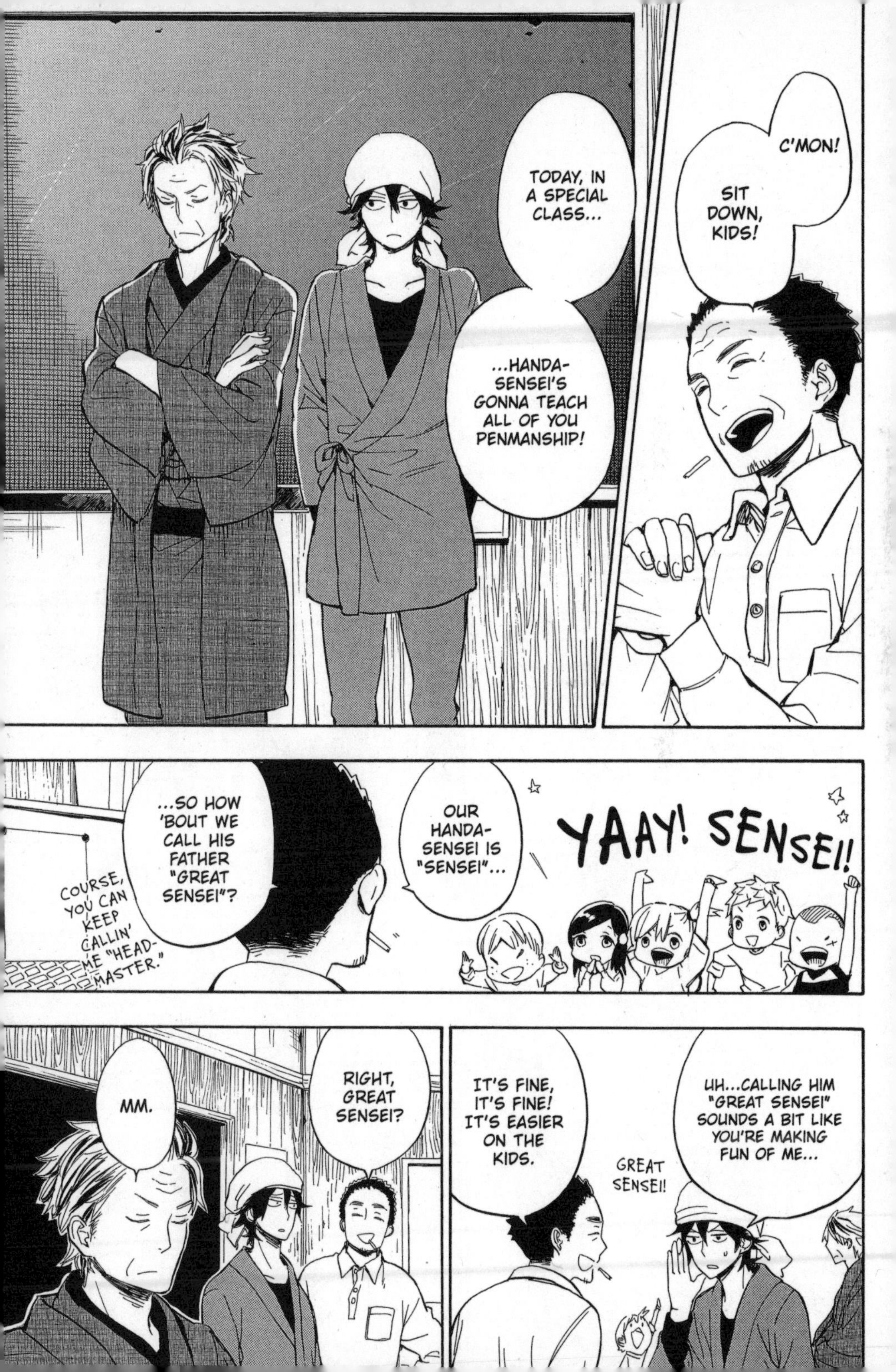
C'MON!
SIT DOWN, KIDS!
TODAY, IN A SPECIAL CLASS...
...HANDA-SENSEI'S GONNA TEACH ALL OF YOU PENMANSHIP!
YAAY! SENSEI!
OUR HANDA-SENSEI IS "SENSEI"...
...SO HOW 'BOUT WE CALL HIS FATHER "GREAT SENSEI"?
COURSE, YOU CAN KEEP CALLIN' ME "HEAD-MASTER."
UH...CALLING HIM "GREAT SENSEI" SOUNDS A BIT LIKE YOU'RE MAKING FUN OF ME...
GREAT SENSEI!
IT'S FINE, IT'S FINE! IT'S EASIER ON THE KIDS.
RIGHT, GREAT SENSEI?
MM.

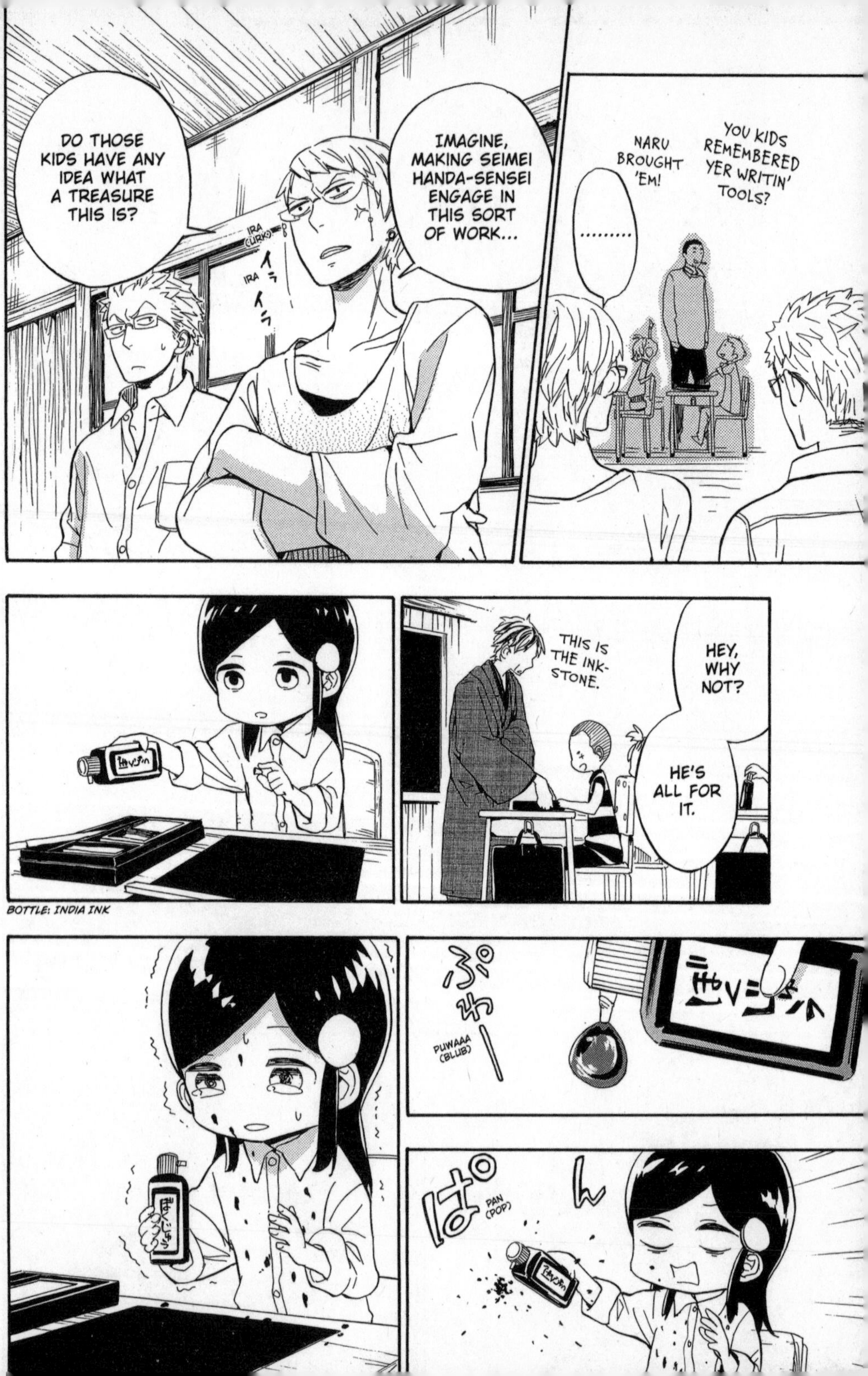
YOU KIDS REMEMBERED YER WRITIN' TOOLS?
NARU BROUGHT 'EM!
....
IMAGINE, MAKING SEIMEI HANDA-SENSEI ENGAGE IN THIS SORT OF WORK...
IRA (URK) IRA
DO THOSE KIDS HAVE ANY IDEA WHAT A TREASURE THIS IS?
HEY, WHY NOT?
HE'S ALL FOR IT.
THIS IS THE INK-STONE.
BOTTLE: INDIA INK
PUWAAA (BLUB)
PAN (POP)

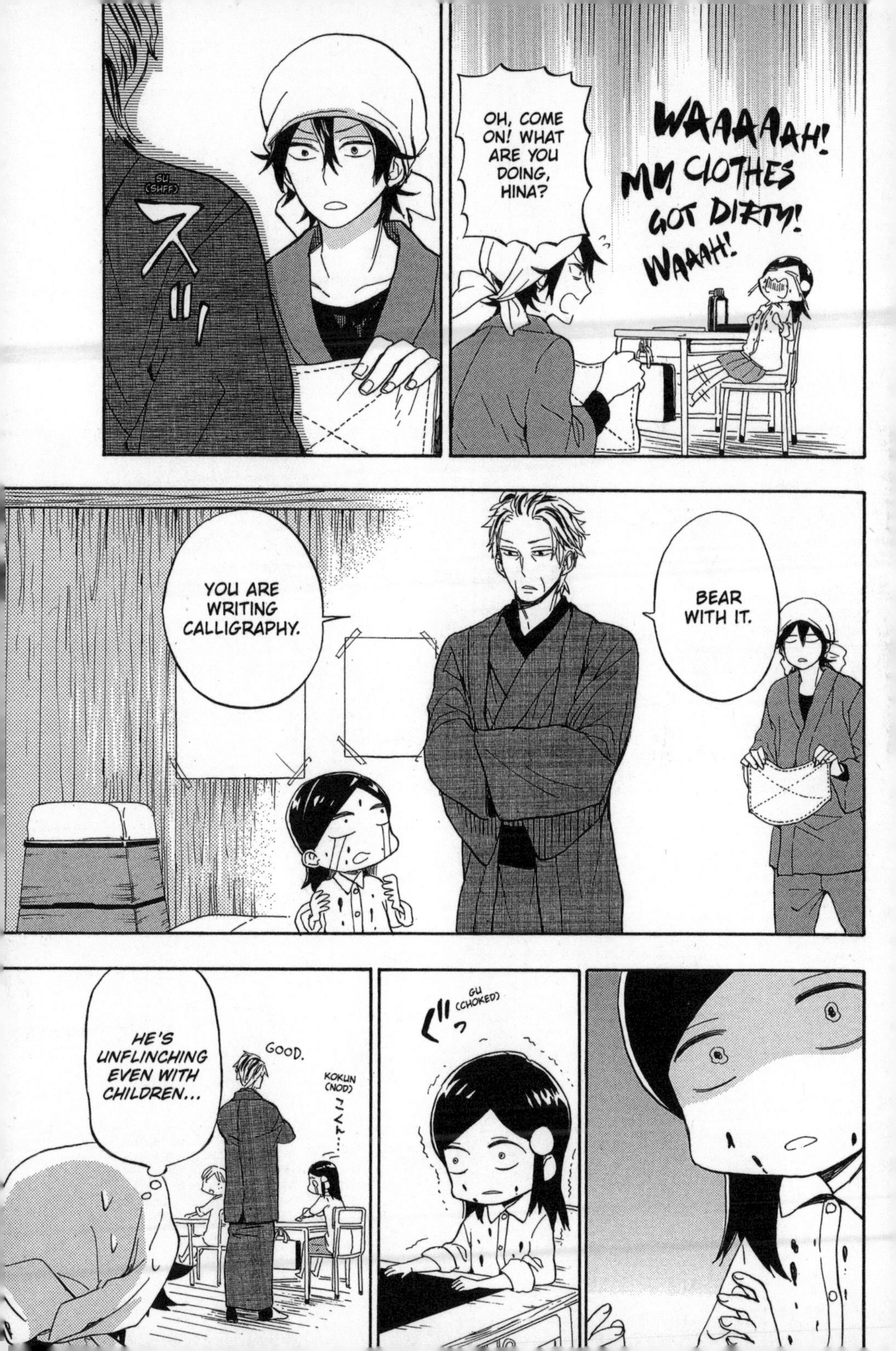
WAAAAAH! MY CLOTHES GOT DIRTY! WAAAH!
OH, COME ON! WHAT ARE YOU DOING, HINA?
SU (SHFF)
スッ
BEAR WITH IT.
YOU ARE WRITING CALLIGRAPHY.
GU (CHOKED)
KOKUN (NOD)
GOOD.
HE'S UNFLINCHING EVEN WITH CHILDREN...

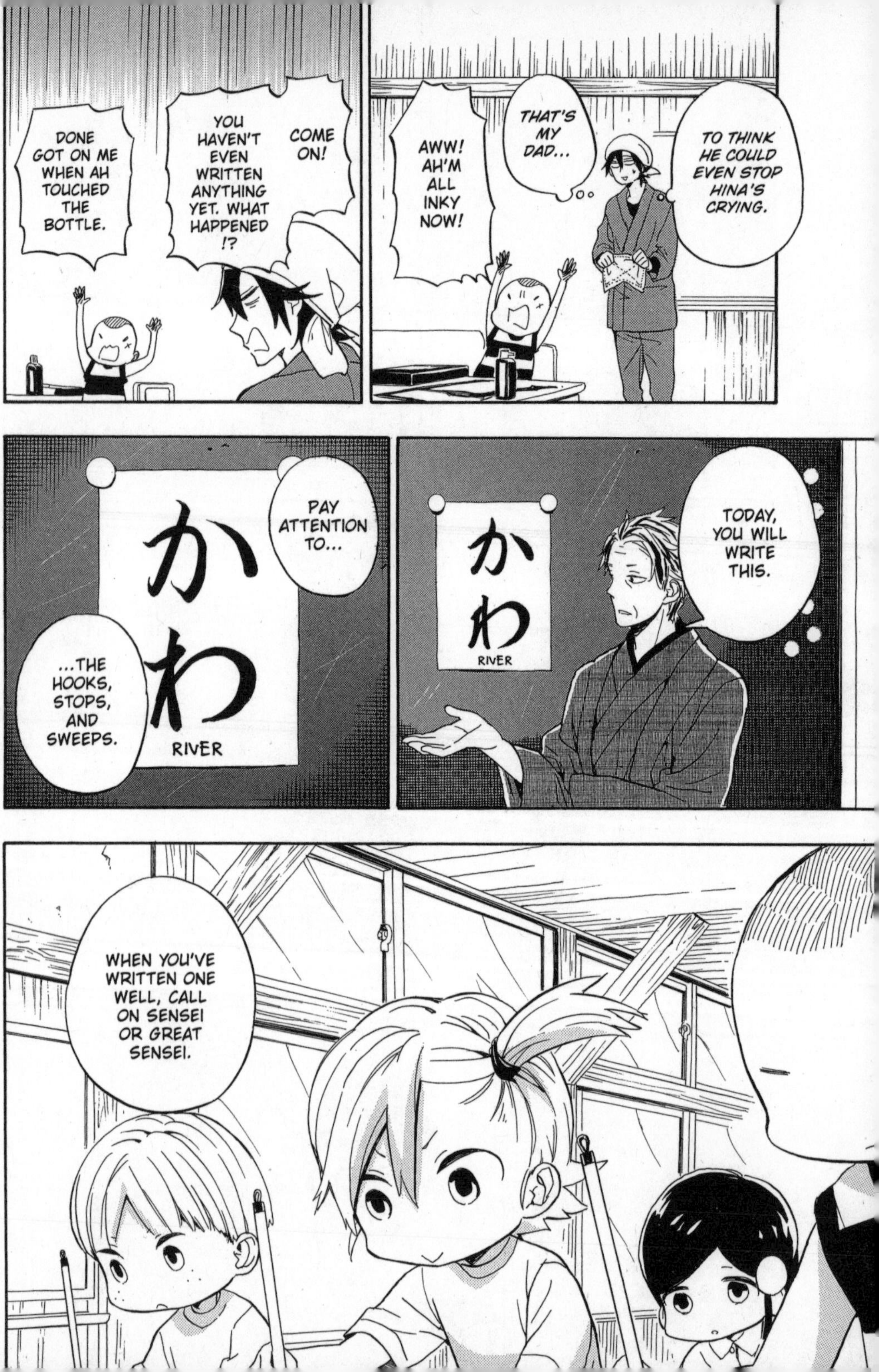
TO THINK HE COULD EVEN STOP HINA'S CRYING.
THAT'S MY DAD...
AWW! AH'M ALL INKY NOW!
COME ON!
YOU HAVEN'T EVEN WRITTEN ANYTHING YET. WHAT HAPPENED!?
DONE GOT ON ME WHEN AH TOUCHED THE BOTTLE.
TODAY, YOU WILL WRITE THIS.
かわ
RIVER
PAY ATTENTION TO...
かわ
RIVER
...THE HOOKS, STOPS, AND SWEEPS.
WHEN YOU'VE WRITTEN ONE WELL, CALL ON SENSEI OR GREAT SENSEI.

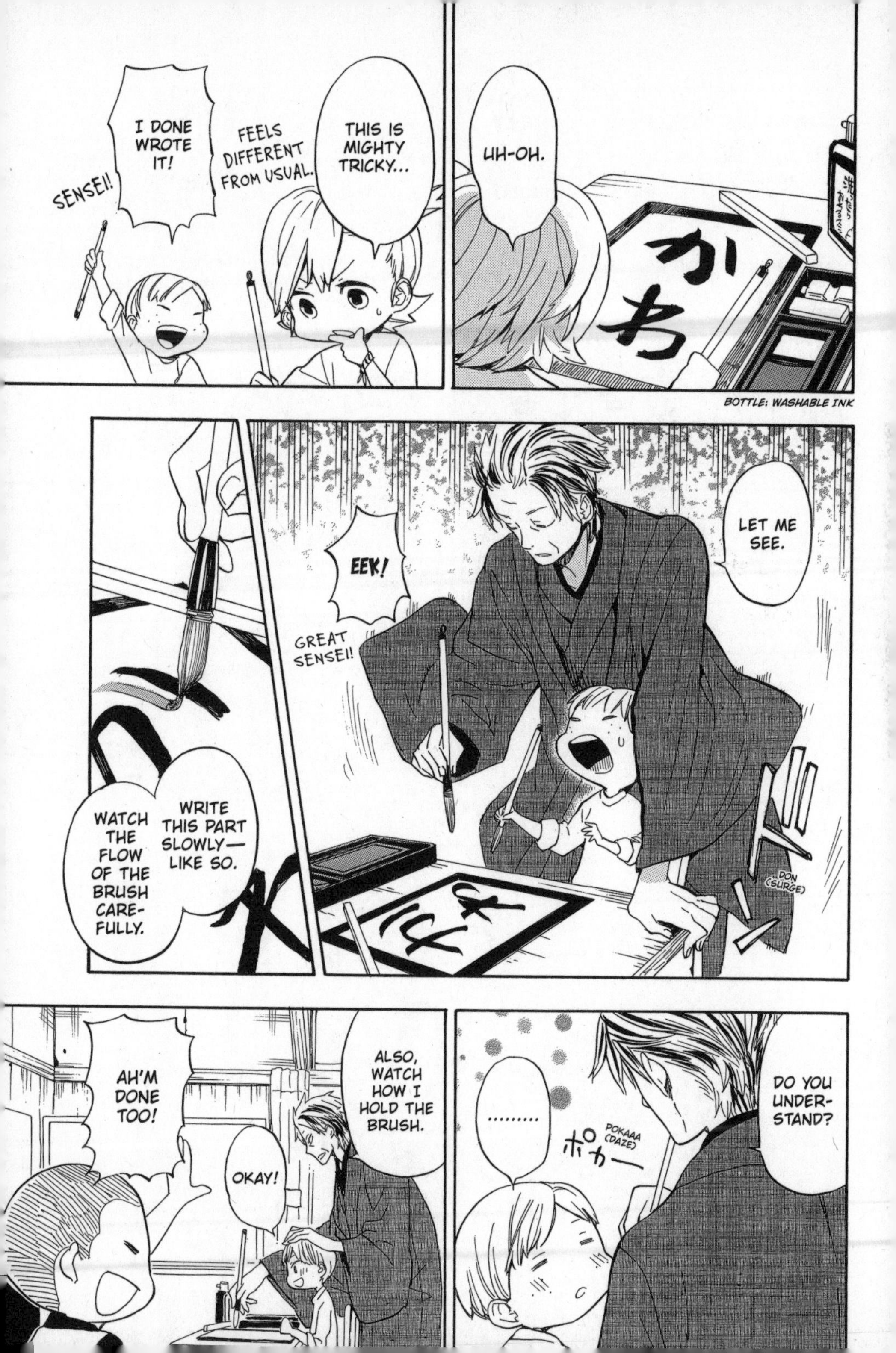
UH-OH.
THIS IS MIGHTY TRICKY...
FEELS DIFFERENT FROM USUAL.
I DONE WROTE IT!
SENSEI!
BOTTLE: WASHABLE INK
LET ME SEE.
EEK!
GREAT SENSEI!
DON (SURGE)
WRITE THIS PART SLOWLY—LIKE SO.
WATCH THE FLOW OF THE BRUSH CAREFULLY.
DO YOU UNDERSTAND?
POKAAA (DAZE)
....
ALSO, WATCH HOW I HOLD THE BRUSH.
OKAY!
AH'M DONE TOO!

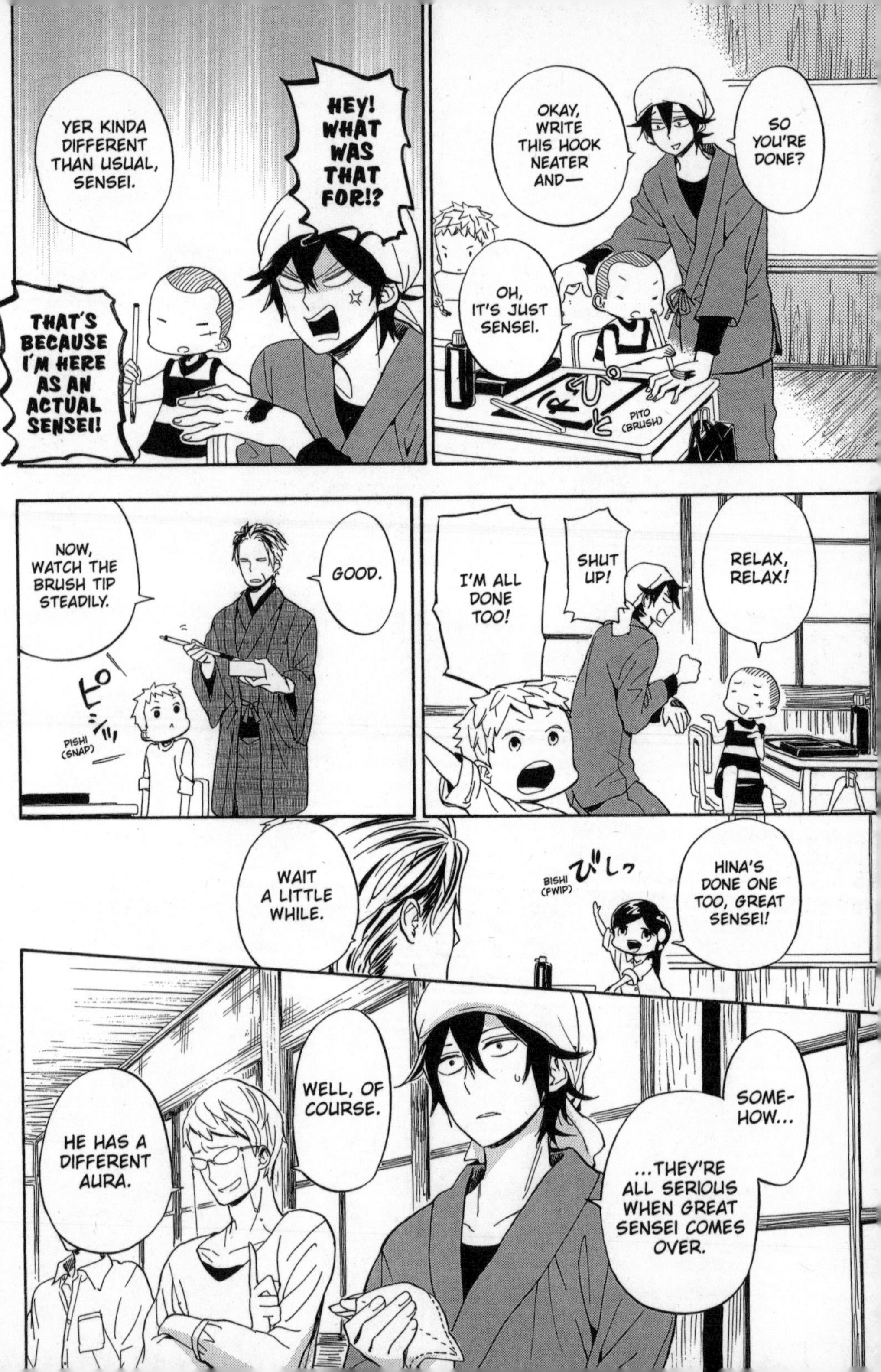
SO YOU'RE DONE?
OKAY, WRITE THIS HOOK NEATER AND—
OH, IT'S JUST SENSEI.
PITO (BRUSH)
HEY! WHAT WAS THAT FOR!?
YER KINDA DIFFERENT THAN USUAL, SENSEI.
THAT'S BECAUSE I'M HERE AS AN ACTUAL SENSEI!
RELAX, RELAX!
SHUT UP!
I'M ALL DONE TOO!
GOOD.
NOW, WATCH THE BRUSH TIP STEADILY.
ピシッ
PISHI (SNAP)
HINA'S DONE ONE TOO, GREAT SENSEI!
びしっ
BISHI (FWIP)
WAIT A LITTLE WHILE.
SOME-HOW...
...THEY'RE ALL SERIOUS WHEN GREAT SENSEI COMES OVER.
WELL, OF COURSE.
HE HAS A DIFFERENT AURA.

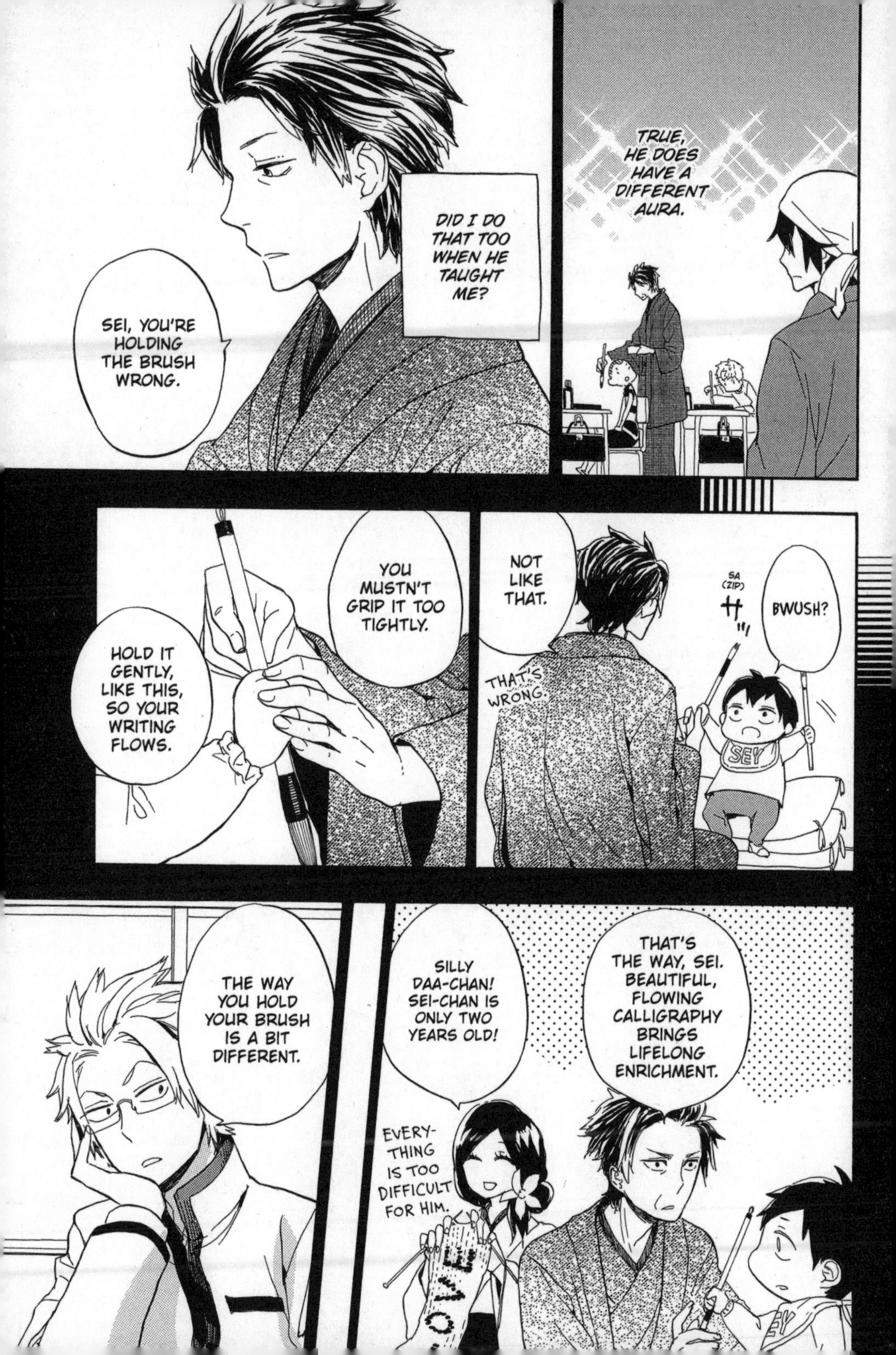
TRUE, HE DOES HAVE A DIFFERENT AURA.
DID I DO THAT TOO WHEN HE TAUGHT ME?
SEI, YOU'RE HOLDING THE BRUSH WRONG.
BWUSH?
SA (ZIP)
NOT LIKE THAT.
THAT'S WRONG.
YOU MUSTN'T GRIP IT TOO TIGHTLY.
HOLD IT GENTLY, LIKE THIS, SO YOUR WRITING FLOWS.
THAT'S THE WAY, SEI. BEAUTIFUL, FLOWING CALLIGRAPHY BRINGS LIFELONG ENRICHMENT.
SILLY DAA-CHAN! SEI-CHAN IS ONLY TWO YEARS OLD!
EVERY-THING IS TOO DIFFICULT FOR HIM.
THE WAY YOU HOLD YOUR BRUSH IS A BIT DIFFERENT.

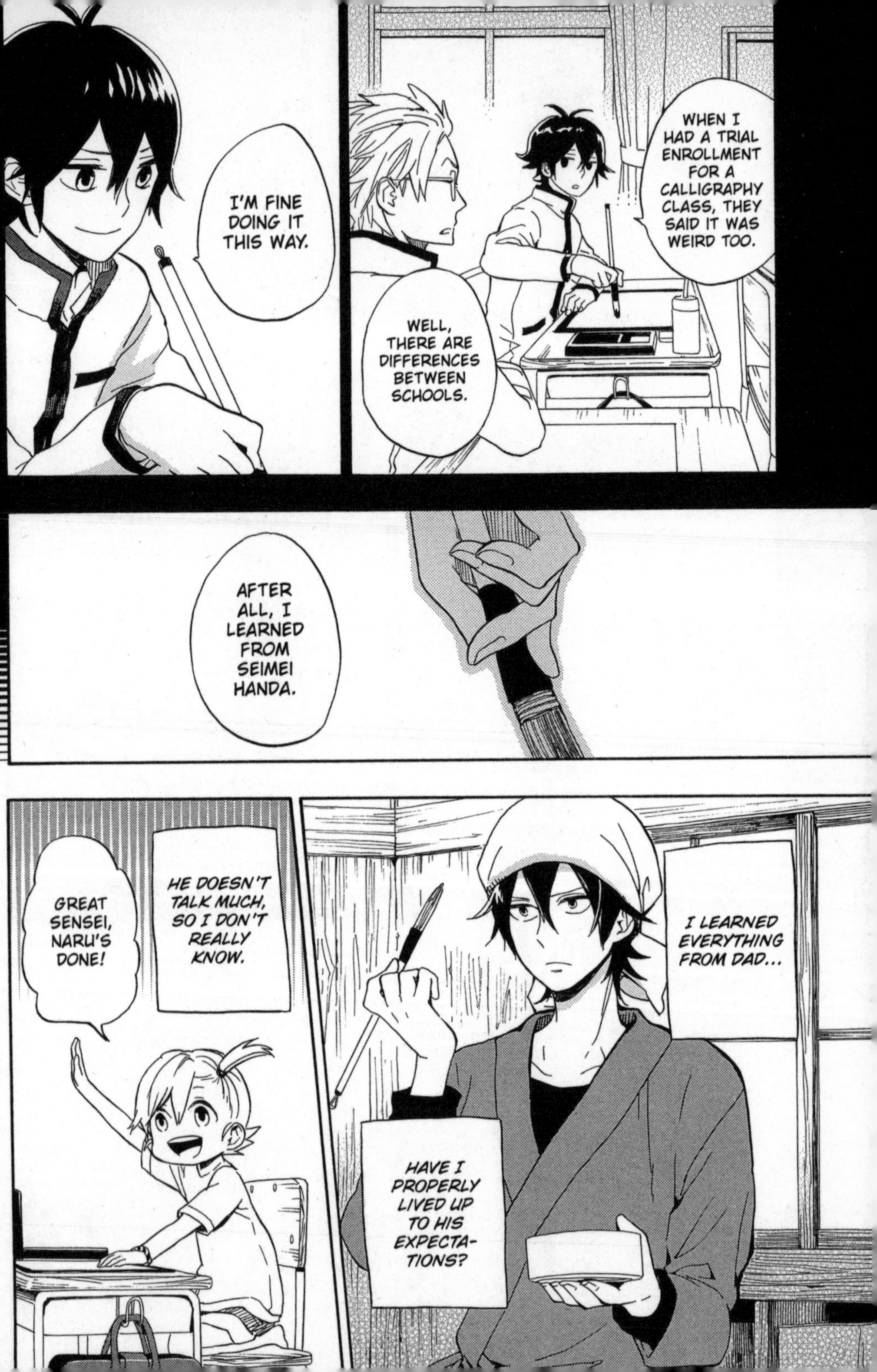
WHEN I HAD A TRIAL ENROLLMENT FOR A CALLIGRAPHY CLASS, THEY SAID IT WAS WEIRD TOO.
WELL, THERE ARE DIFFERENCES BETWEEN SCHOOLS.
I'M FINE DOING IT THIS WAY.
AFTER ALL, I LEARNED FROM SEIMEI HANDA.
I LEARNED EVERYTHING FROM DAD...
HAVE I PROPERLY LIVED UP TO HIS EXPECTATIONS?
HE DOESN'T TALK MUCH, SO I DON'T REALLY KNOW.
GREAT SENSEI, NARU'S DONE!

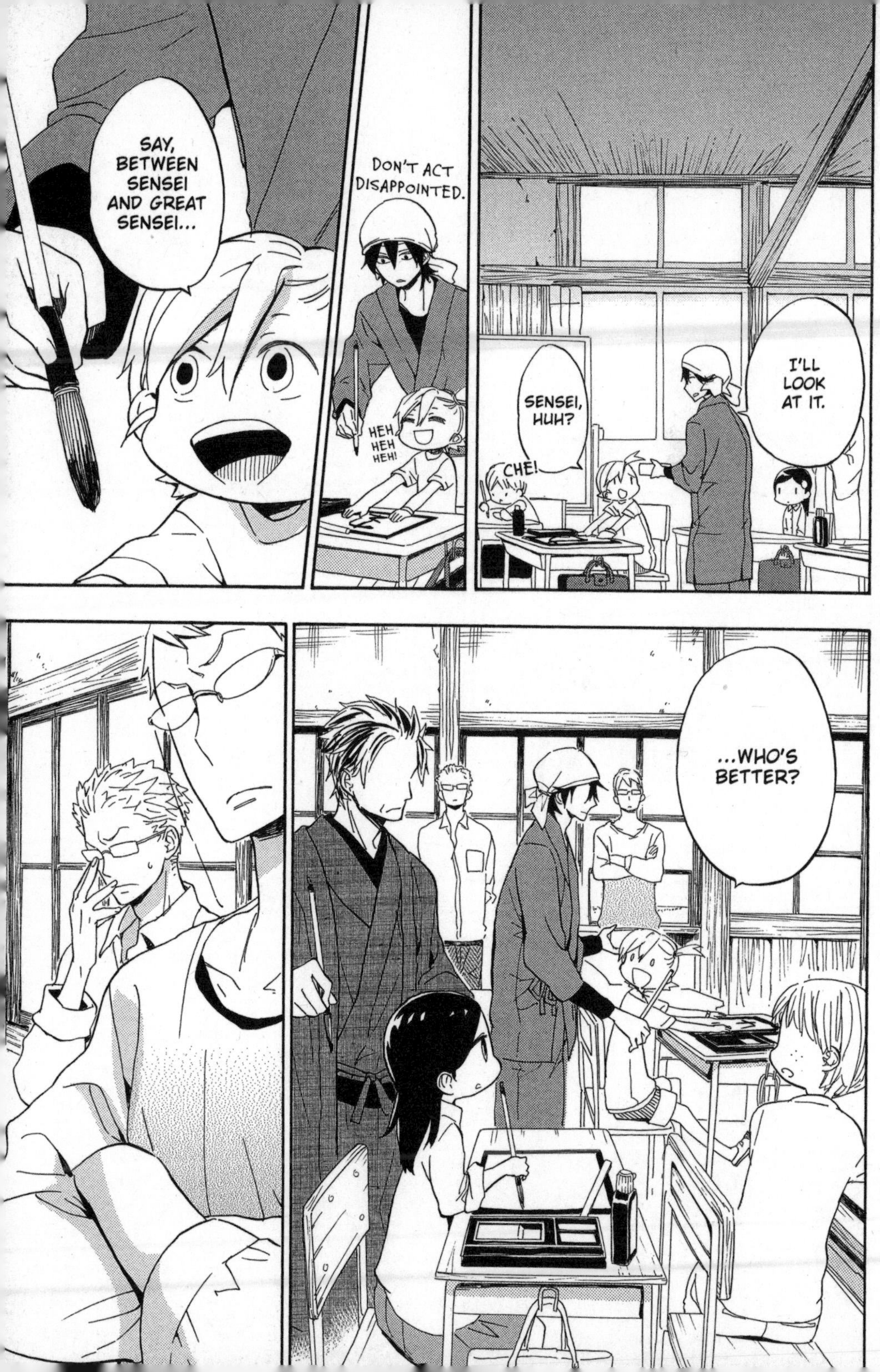
I'LL LOOK AT IT.
SENSEI, HUH?
CHE!
DON'T ACT DISAPPOINTED.
HEH HEH HEH!
SAY, BETWEEN SENSEI AND GREAT SENSEI...
...WHO'S BETTER?

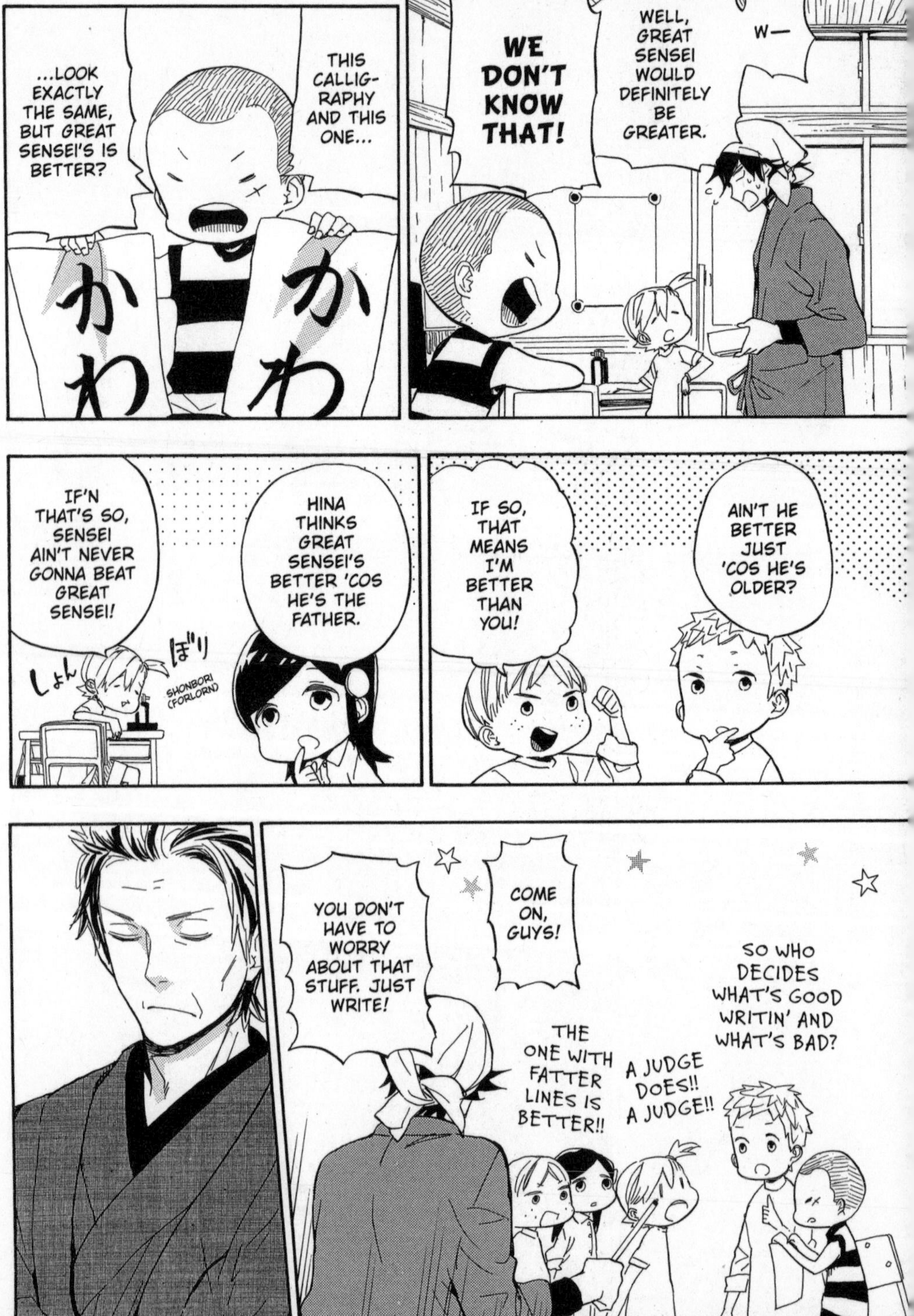
W—
WELL, GREAT SENSEI WOULD DEFINITELY BE GREATER.
WE DON'T KNOW THAT!
THIS CALLIGRAPHY AND THIS ONE...
...LOOK EXACTLY THE SAME, BUT GREAT SENSEI'S IS BETTER?
かわ
かわ
AIN'T HE BETTER JUST 'COS HE'S OLDER?
IF SO, THAT MEANS I'M BETTER THAN YOU!
HINA THINKS GREAT SENSEI'S BETTER 'COS HE'S THE FATHER.
IF'N THAT'S SO, SENSEI AIN'T NEVER GONNA BEAT GREAT SENSEI!
しょんぼり
SHONBORI (FORLORN)
SO WHO DECIDES WHAT'S GOOD WRITIN' AND WHAT'S BAD?
A JUDGE DOES!! A JUDGE!!
THE ONE WITH FATTER LINES IS BETTER!!
COME ON, GUYS!
YOU DON'T HAVE TO WORRY ABOUT THAT STUFF. JUST WRITE!

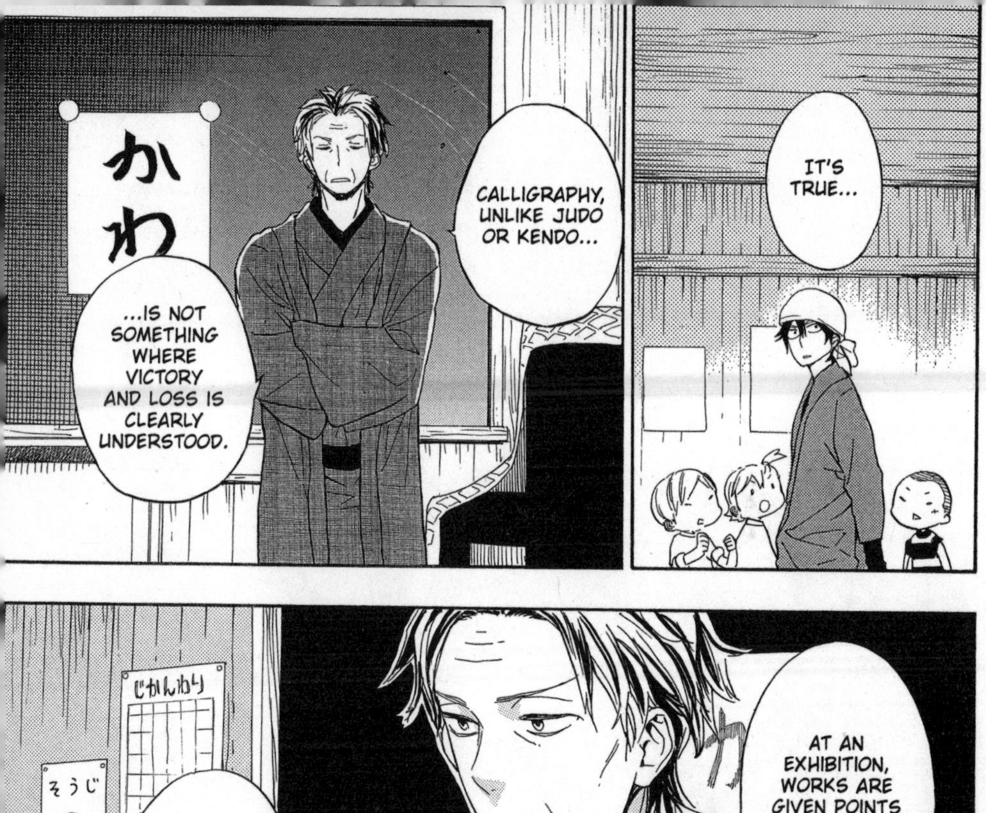
IT'S TRUE...
CALLIGRAPHY, UNLIKE JUDO OR KENDO...
かわ
...IS NOT SOMETHING WHERE VICTORY AND LOSS IS CLEARLY UNDERSTOOD.
AT AN EXHIBITION, WORKS ARE GIVEN POINTS AND RANKED...
じかんわり
そうじ
...BUT THOSE POINT VALUES VARY DEPENDING ON THE JUDGE.

SIGNS: SCHEDULE, CLEANING

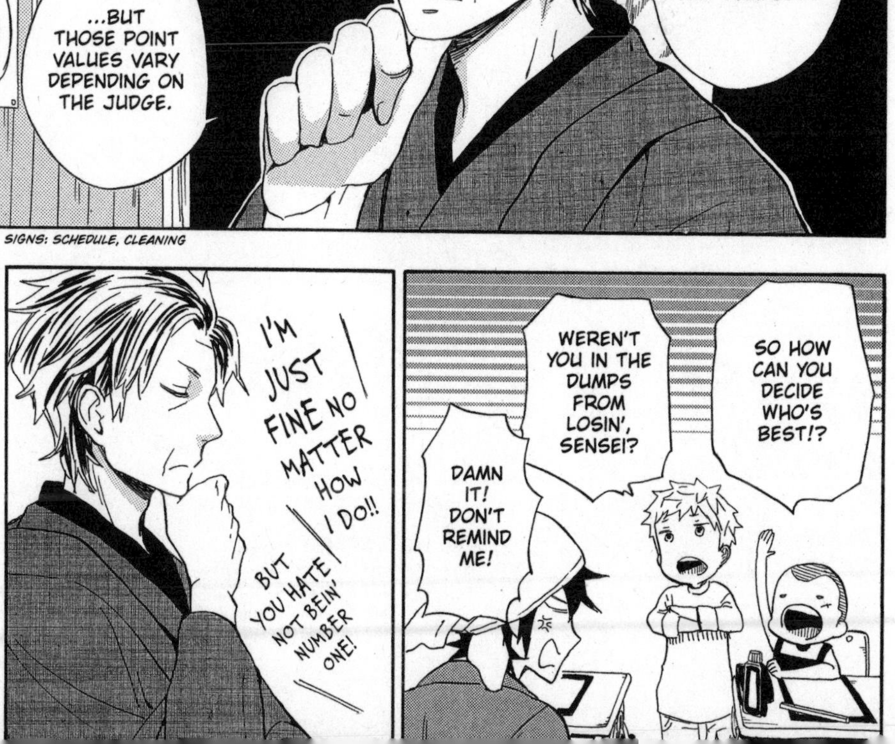
SO HOW CAN YOU DECIDE WHO'S BEST!?
WEREN'T YOU IN THE DUMPS FROM LOSIN', SENSEI?
DAMN IT! DON'T REMIND ME!
I'M JUST FINE NO MATTER HOW I DO!!
BUT YOU HATE NOT BEIN' NUMBER ONE!

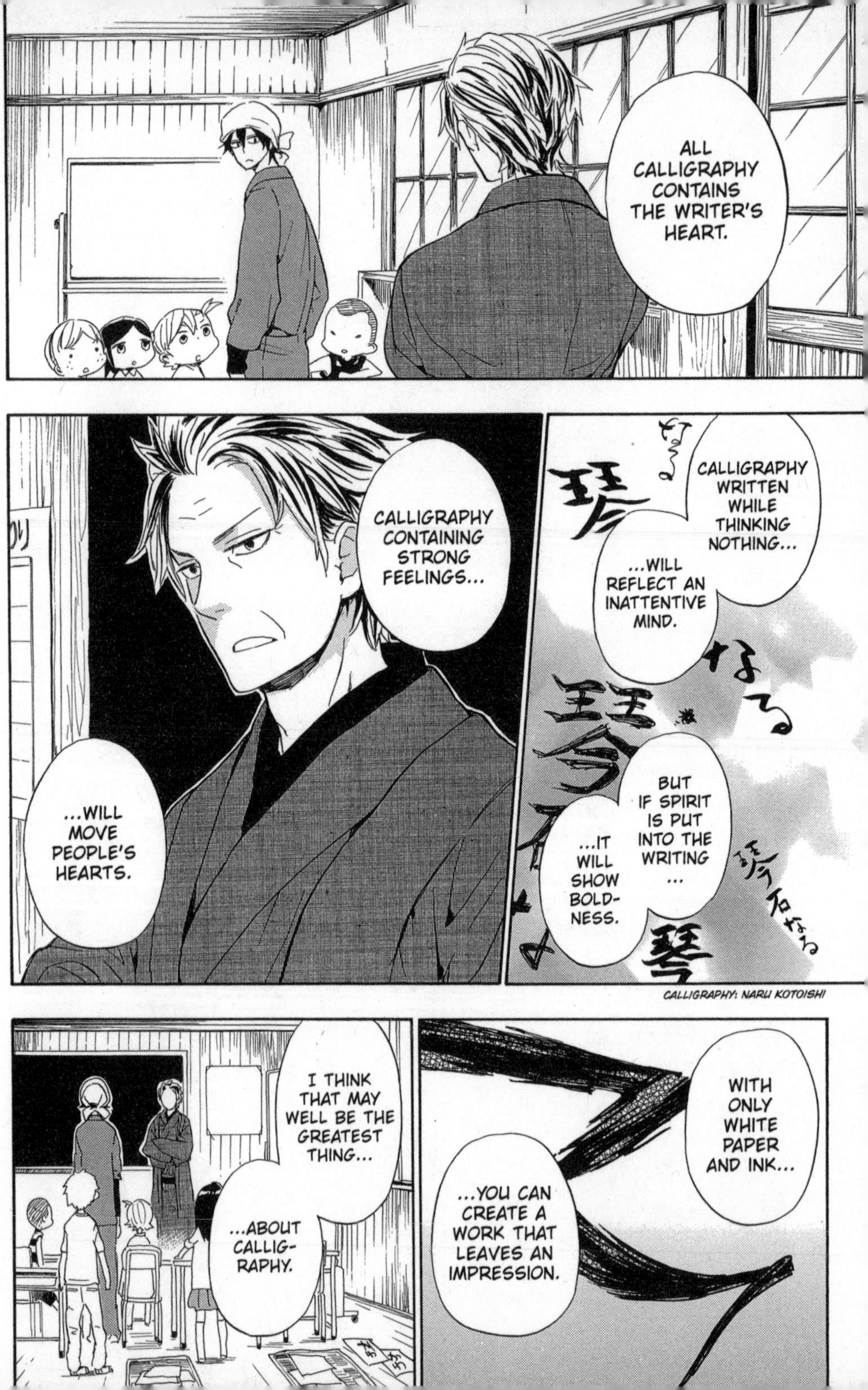
ALL CALLIGRAPHY CONTAINS THE WRITER'S HEART.
CALLIGRAPHY WRITTEN WHILE THINKING NOTHING...
...WILL REFLECT AN INATTENTIVE MIND.
BUT IF SPIRIT IS PUT INTO THE WRITING ...
...IT WILL SHOW BOLDNESS.
CALLIGRAPHY CONTAINING STRONG FEELINGS...
...WILL MOVE PEOPLE'S HEARTS.
CALLIGRAPHY: NARU KOTOISHI
WITH ONLY WHITE PAPER AND INK...
...YOU CAN CREATE A WORK THAT LEAVES AN IMPRESSION.
I THINK THAT MAY WELL BE THE GREATEST THING...
...ABOUT CALLIGRAPHY.

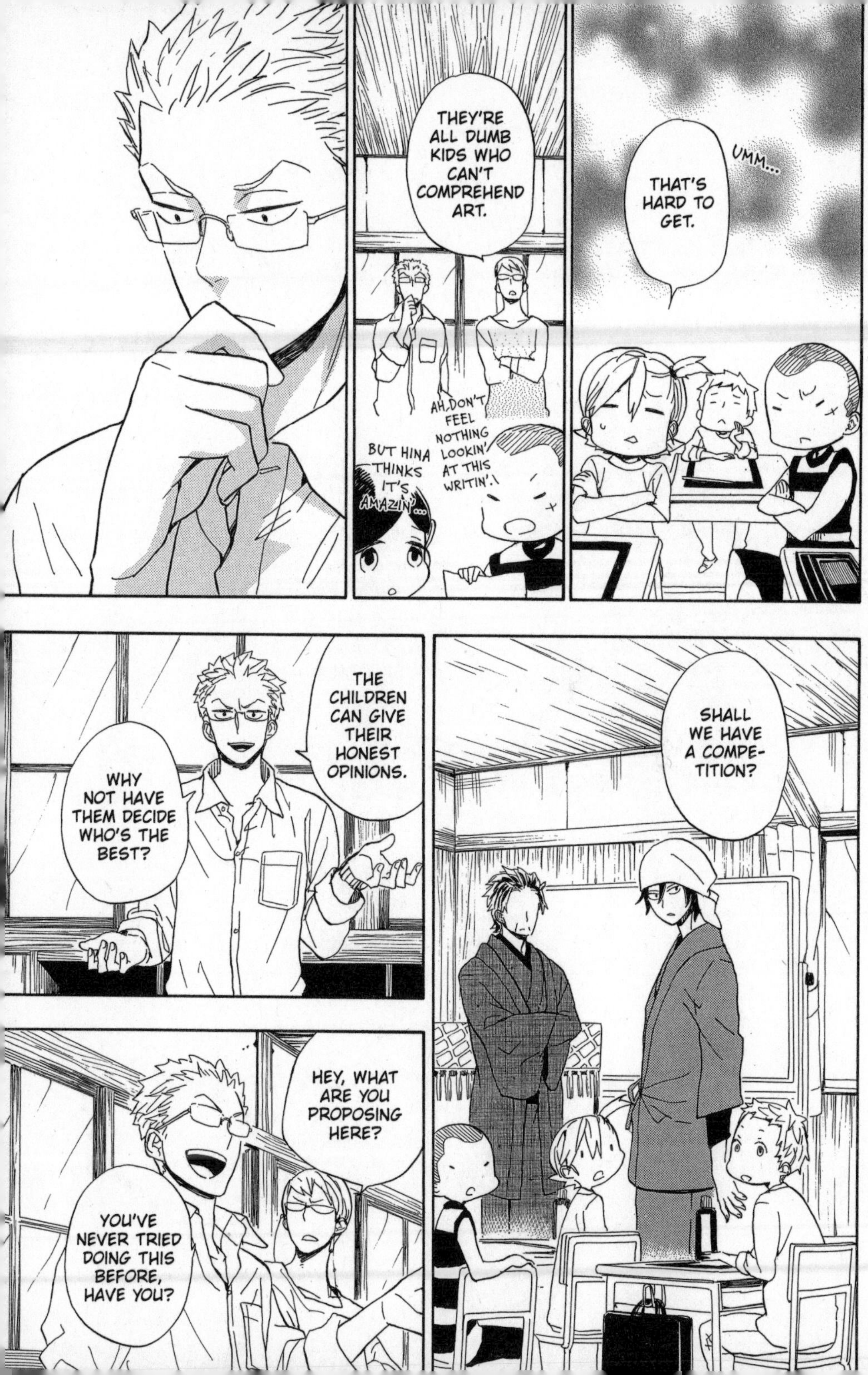
UMM...
THAT'S HARD TO GET.
THEY'RE ALL DUMB KIDS WHO CAN'T COMPREHEND ART.
AH, DON'T FEEL NOTHING LOOKIN' AT THIS WRITIN'.
BUT HINA THINKS IT'S AMAZIN'...
SHALL WE HAVE A COMPETITION?
THE CHILDREN CAN GIVE THEIR HONEST OPINIONS.
WHY NOT HAVE THEM DECIDE WHO'S THE BEST?
HEY, WHAT ARE YOU PROPOSING HERE?
YOU'VE NEVER TRIED DOING THIS BEFORE, HAVE YOU?

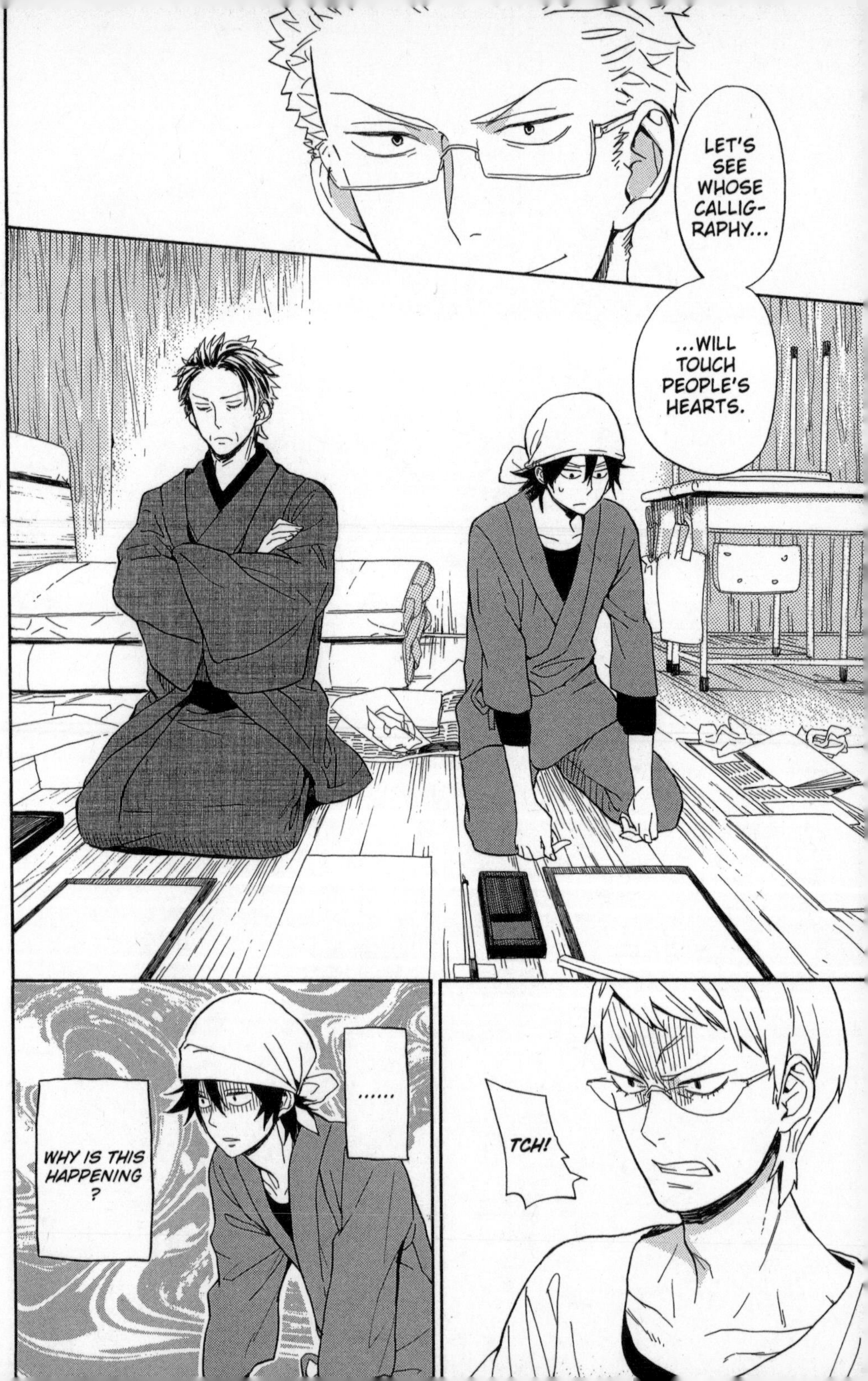
LET'S SEE WHOSE CALLIG-RAPHY...
...WILL TOUCH PEOPLE'S HEARTS.
TCH!
......
WHY IS THIS HAPPENING ?

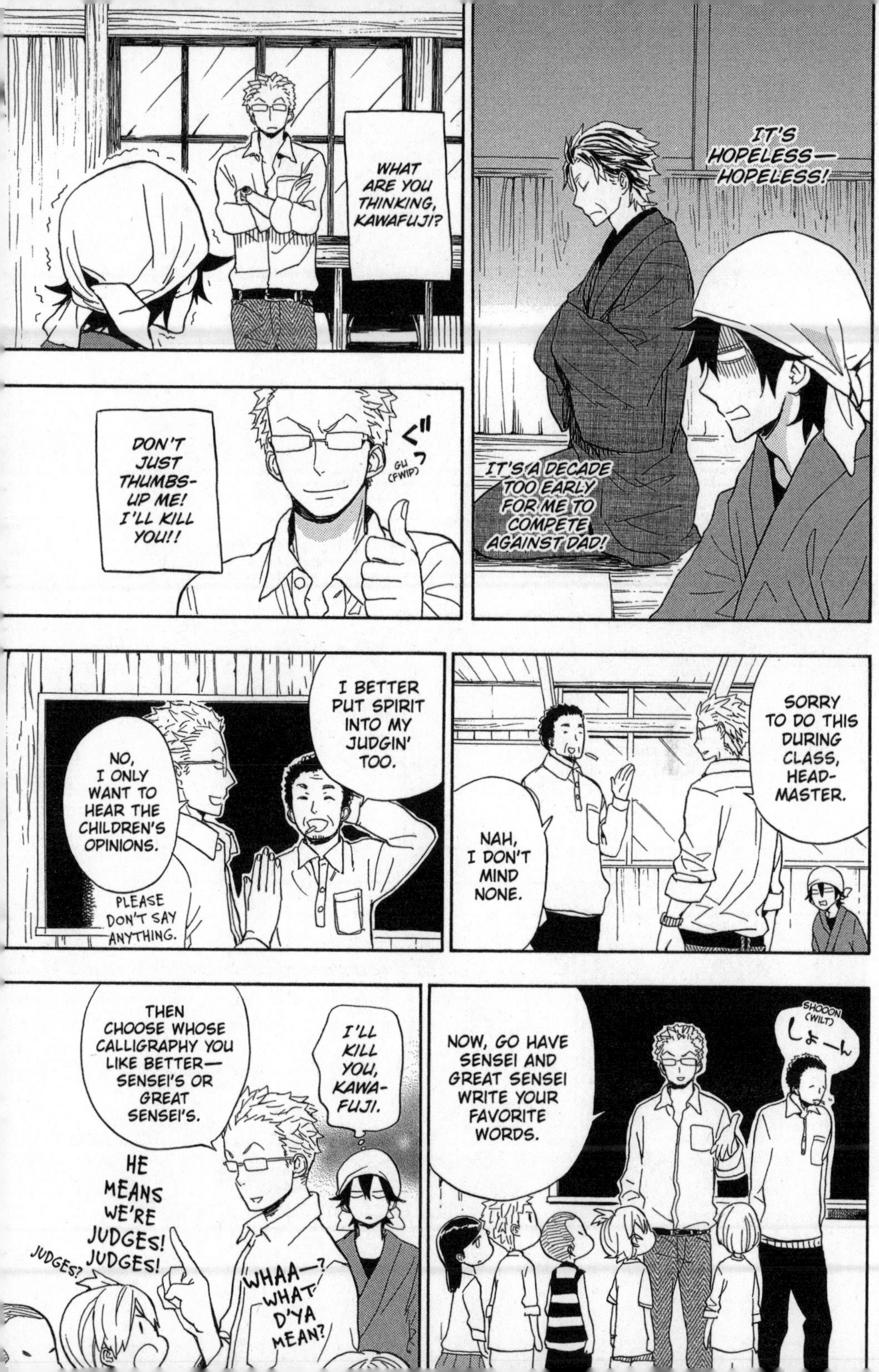
IT'S HOPELESS—HOPELESS!
IT'S A DECADE TOO EARLY FOR ME TO COMPETE AGAINST DAD!
WHAT ARE YOU THINKING, KAWAFUJI?
ぐっ
GU (FWIP)
DON'T JUST THUMBS-UP ME! I'LL KILL YOU!!
SORRY TO DO THIS DURING CLASS, HEAD-MASTER.
NAH, I DON'T MIND NONE.
I BETTER PUT SPIRIT INTO MY JUDGIN' TOO.
NO, I ONLY WANT TO HEAR THE CHILDREN'S OPINIONS.
PLEASE DON'T SAY ANYTHING.
SHOOON (WILT)
しょーん
NOW, GO HAVE SENSEI AND GREAT SENSEI WRITE YOUR FAVORITE WORDS.
THEN CHOOSE WHOSE CALLIGRAPHY YOU LIKE BETTER—SENSEI'S OR GREAT SENSEI'S.
I'LL KILL YOU, KAWA-FUJI.
HE MEANS WE'RE JUDGES! JUDGES!
JUDGES?
WHAA—? WHAT D'YA MEAN?

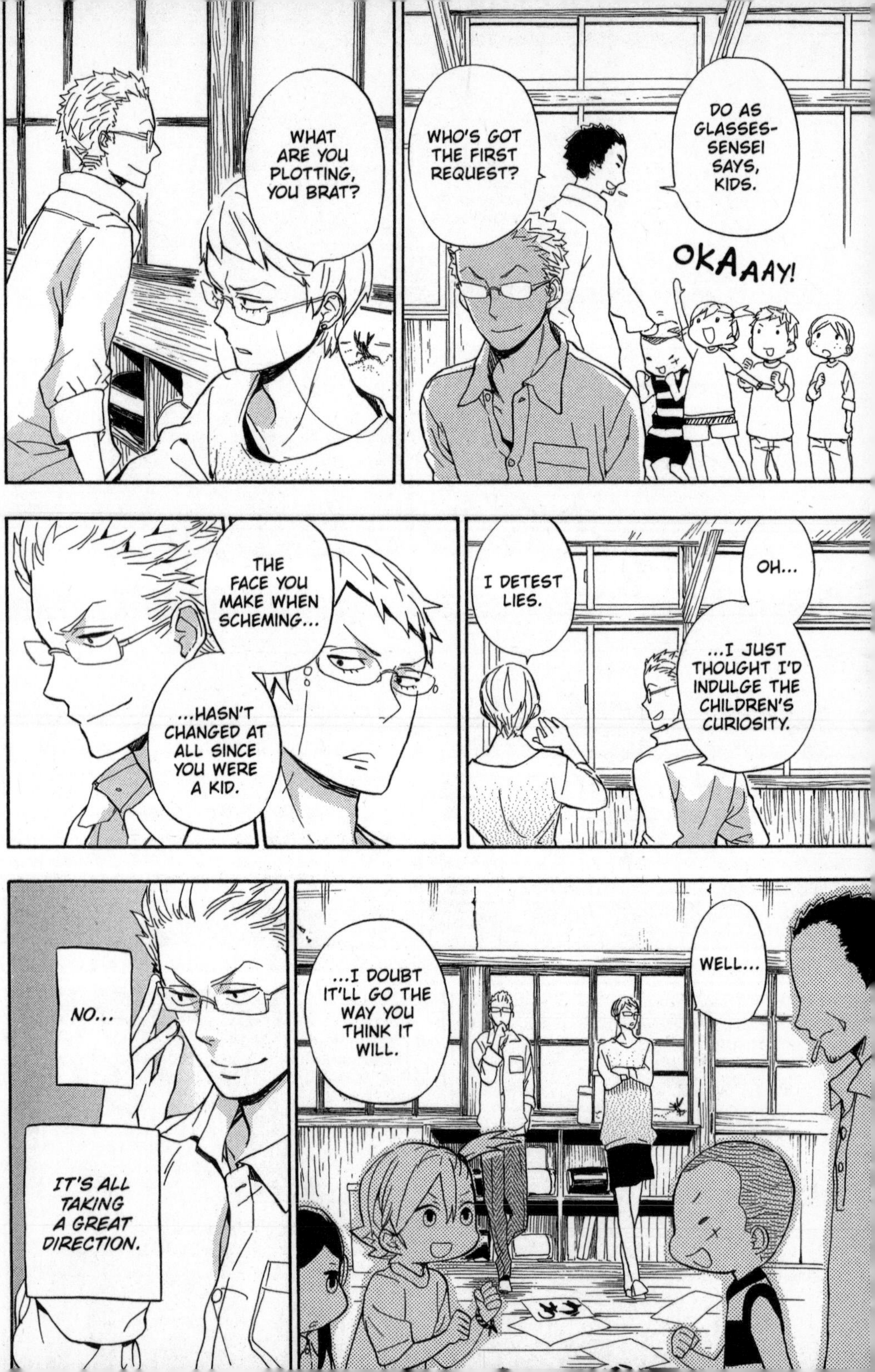

DO AS GLASSES-SENSEI SAYS, KIDS.
WHO'S GOT THE FIRST REQUEST?
OKAAAAY!
WHAT ARE YOU PLOTTING, YOU BRAT?
OH...
...I JUST THOUGHT I'D INDULGE THE CHILDREN'S CURIOSITY.
I DETEST LIES.
THE FACE YOU MAKE WHEN SCHEMING...
...HASN'T CHANGED AT ALL SINCE YOU WERE A KID.
WELL...
...I DOUBT IT'LL GO THE WAY YOU THINK IT WILL.
NO...
IT'S ALL TAKING A GREAT DIRECTION.

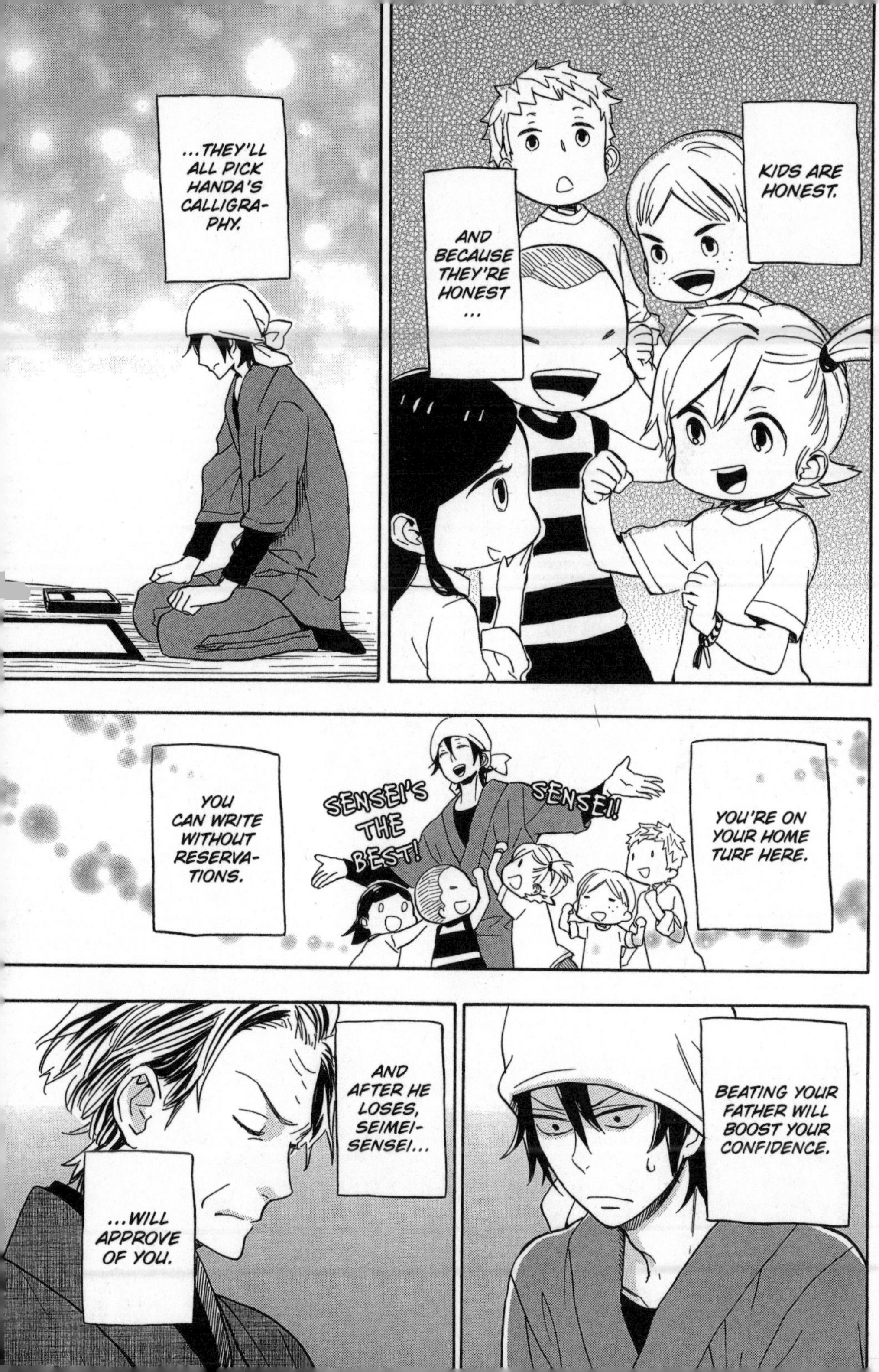
KIDS ARE HONEST.
AND BECAUSE THEY'RE HONEST ...
...THEY'LL ALL PICK HANDA'S CALLIGRA-PHY.
YOU'RE ON YOUR HOME TURF HERE.
SENSEI!!
SENSEI'S THE BEST!
YOU CAN WRITE WITHOUT RESERVA-TIONS.
BEATING YOUR FATHER WILL BOOST YOUR CONFIDENCE.
AND AFTER HE LOSES, SEIMEI-SENSEI...
...WILL APPROVE OF YOU.

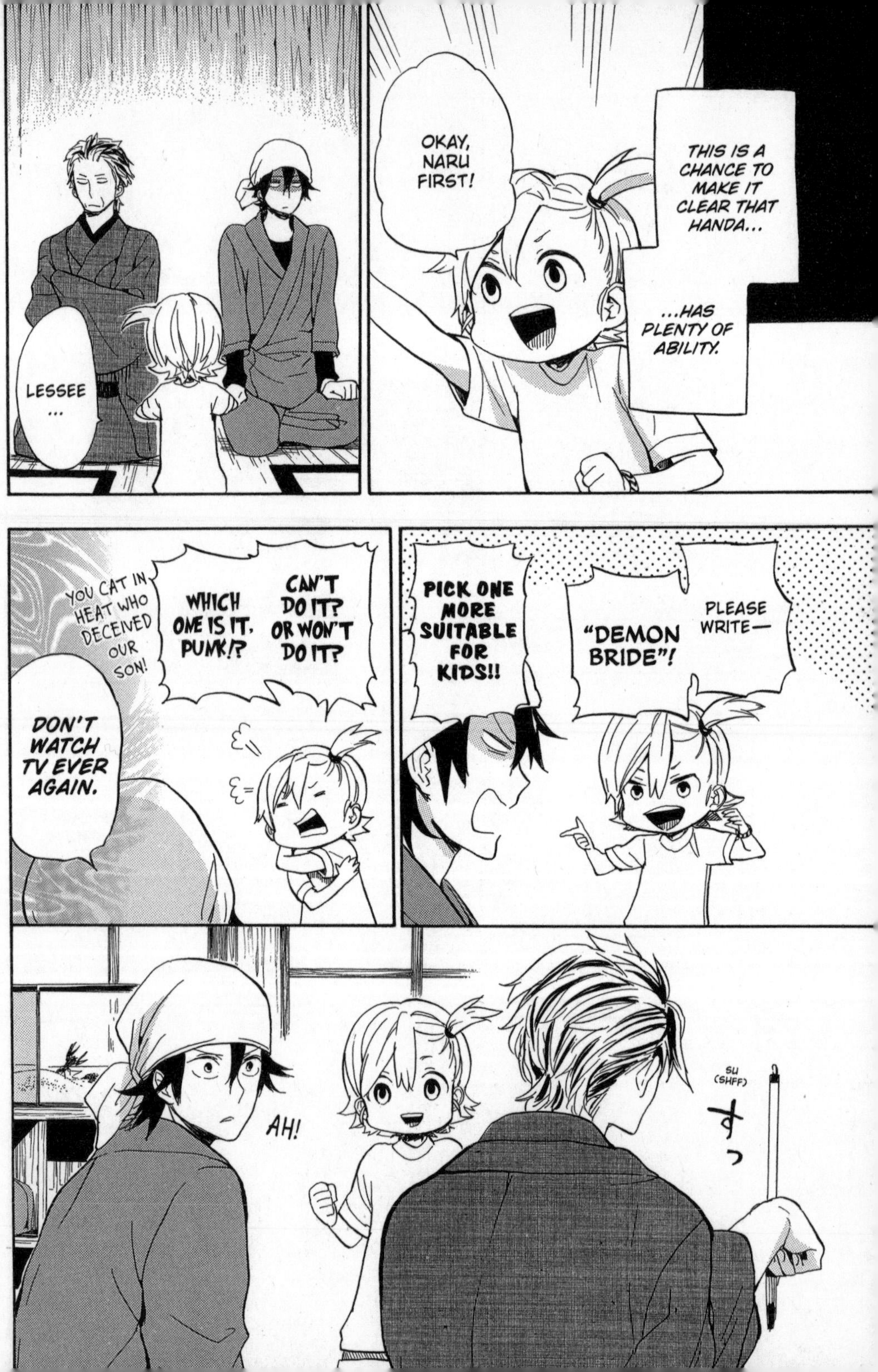
OKAY, NARU FIRST!
THIS IS A CHANCE TO MAKE IT CLEAR THAT HANDA...
...HAS PLENTY OF ABILITY.
LESSEE...
PLEASE WRITE—
"DEMON BRIDE"!
PICK ONE MORE SUITABLE FOR KIDS!!
CAN'T DO IT? OR WON'T DO IT?
WHICH ONE IS IT, PUNK!?
YOU CAT IN HEAT WHO DECEIVED OUR SON!
DON'T WATCH TV EVER AGAIN.
SU (SHFF)
すっ
AH!

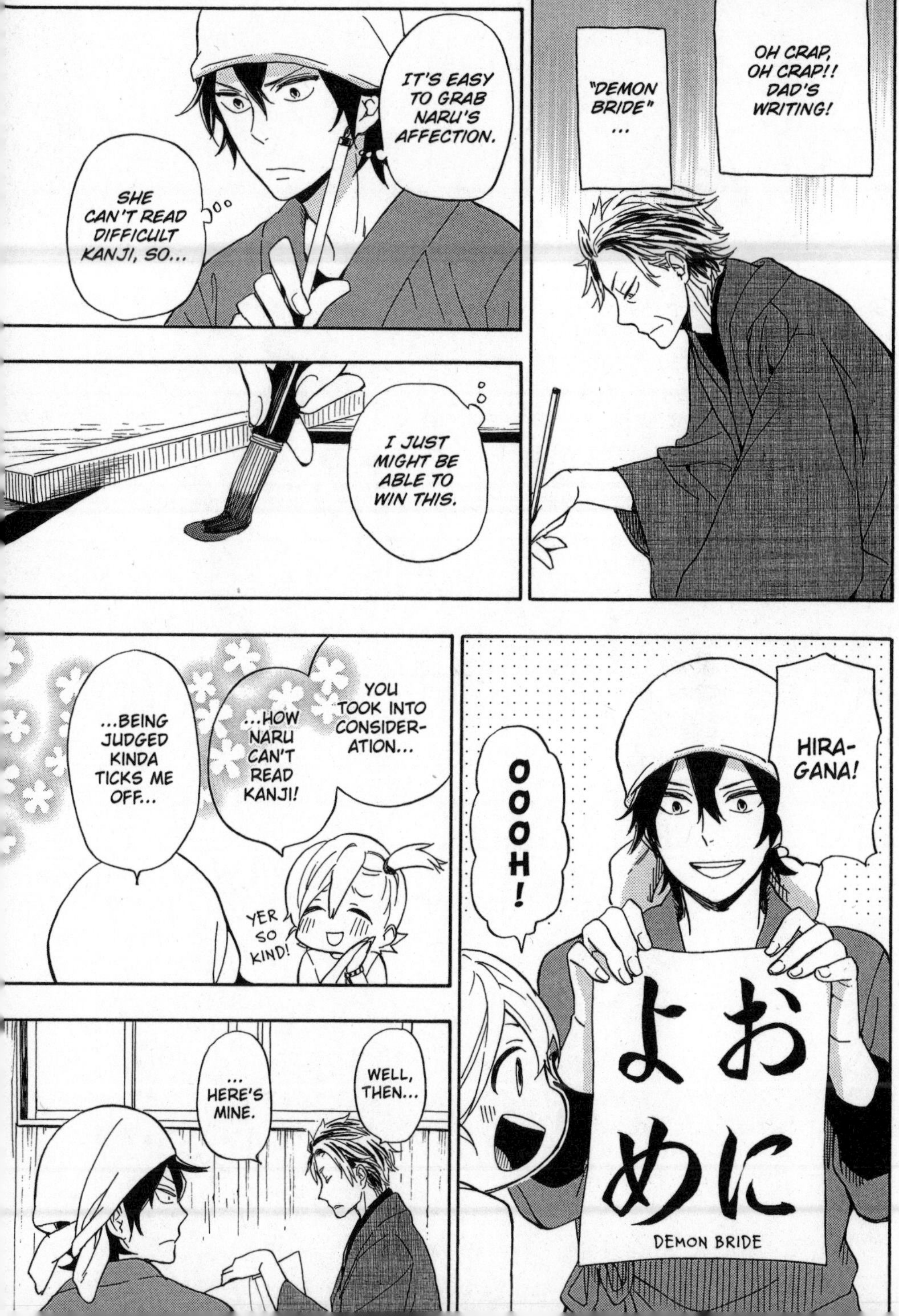
OH CRAP, OH CRAP!! DAD'S WRITING!
"DEMON BRIDE" ...
IT'S EASY TO GRAB NARU'S AFFECTION.
SHE CAN'T READ DIFFICULT KANJI, SO...
I JUST MIGHT BE ABLE TO WIN THIS.
HIRA-GANA!
OOOH!
おによめ
DEMON BRIDE
YOU TOOK INTO CONSIDER-ATION...
...HOW NARU CAN'T READ KANJI!
...BEING JUDGED KINDA TICKS ME OFF...
YER SO KIND!
WELL, THEN...
... HERE'S MINE.

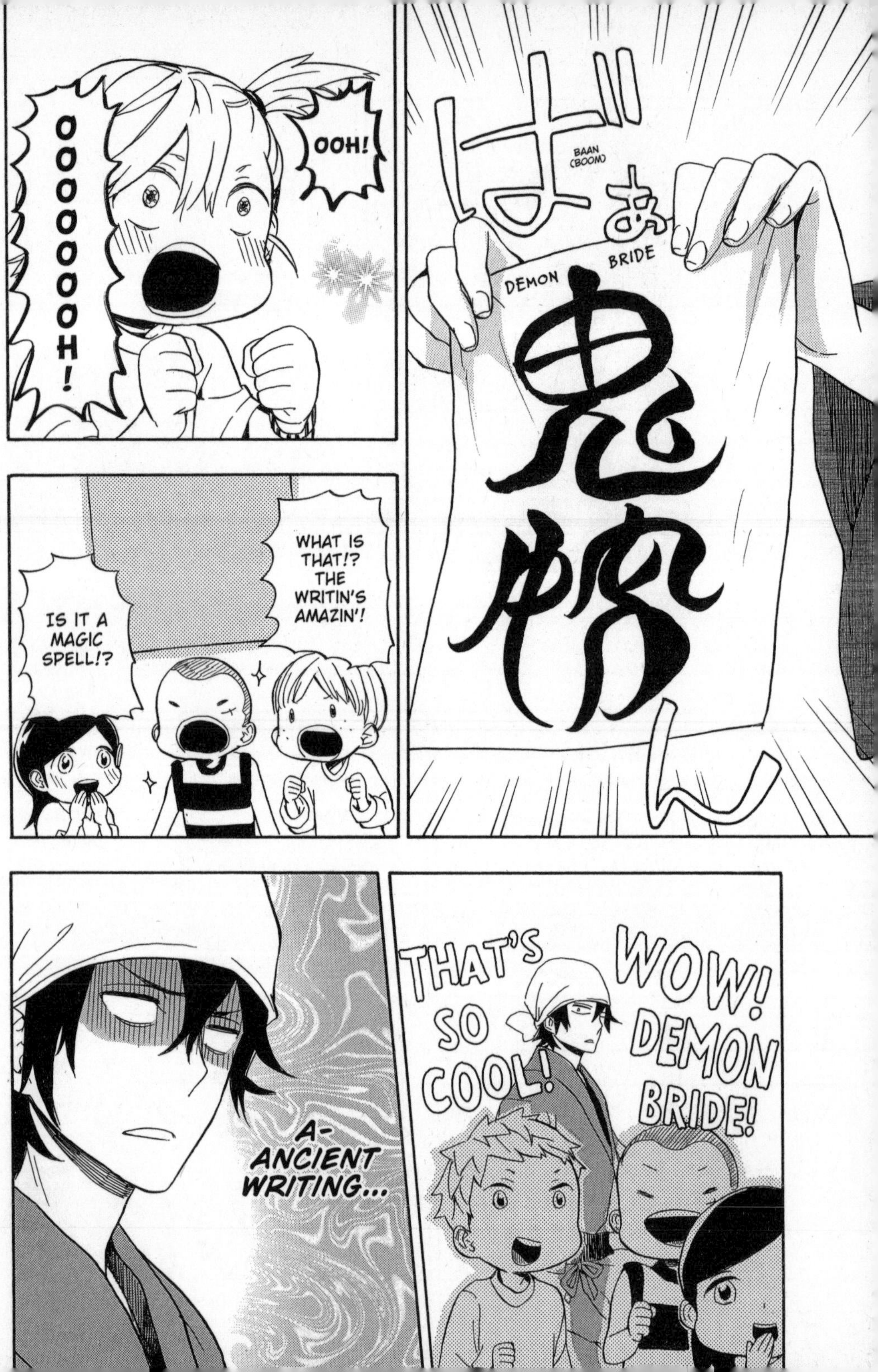
ばぁん
BAAN (BOOM)
DEMON BRIDE
鬼嫁
OOH!
OOOOOOOOOH!
WHAT IS THAT!? THE WRITIN'S AMAZIN'!
IS IT A MAGIC SPELL!?
WOW! DEMON BRIDE!
THAT'S SO COOL!
A-ANCIENT WRITING...

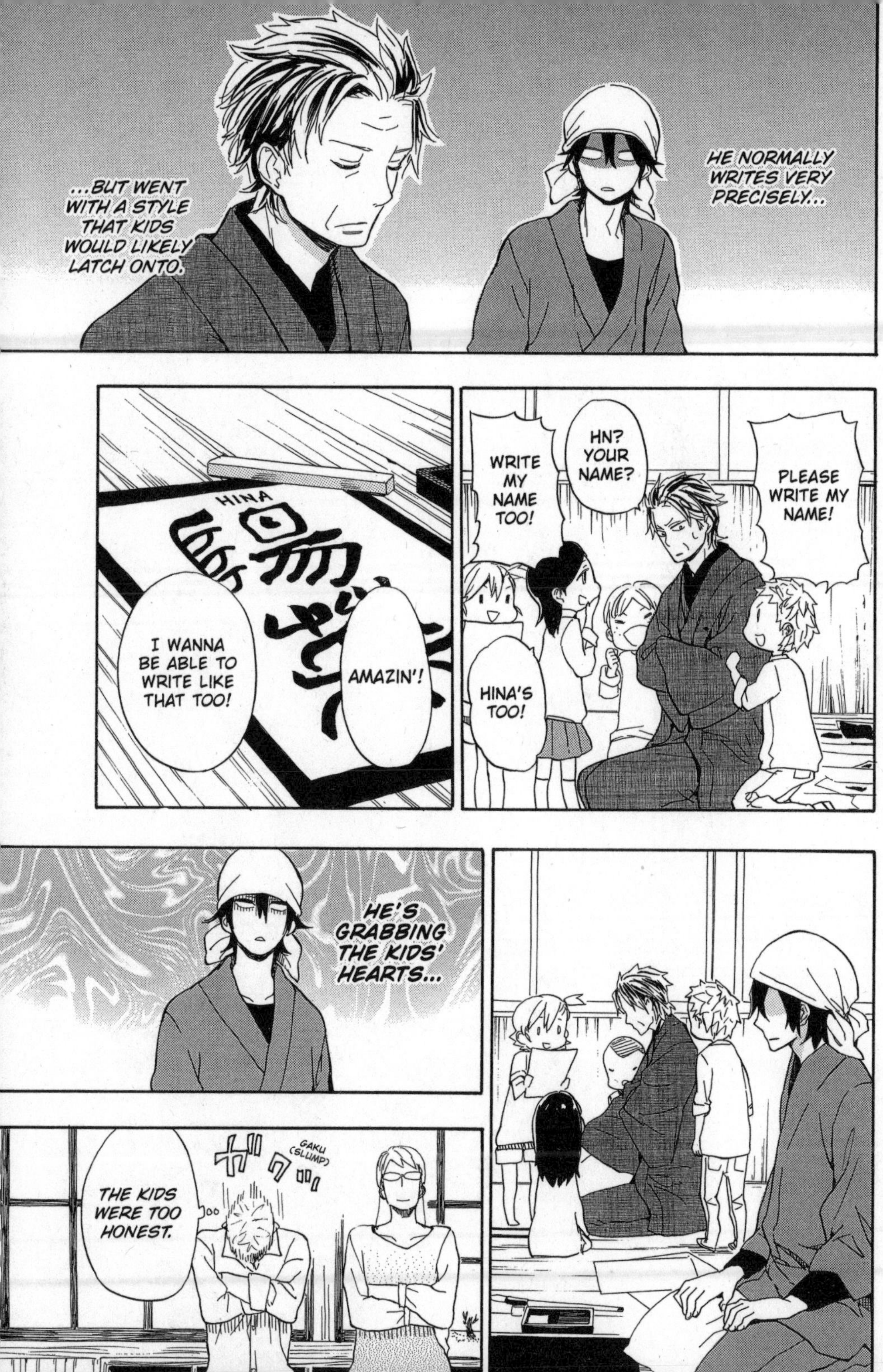
HE NORMALLY WRITES VERY PRECISELY...
...BUT WENT WITH A STYLE THAT KIDS WOULD LIKELY LATCH ONTO.
PLEASE WRITE MY NAME!
HN? YOUR NAME?
WRITE MY NAME TOO!
HINA'S TOO!
HINA
AMAZIN'!
I WANNA BE ABLE TO WRITE LIKE THAT TOO!
HE'S GRABBING THE KIDS' HEARTS...
GAKU (SLUMP)
THE KIDS WERE TOO HONEST.

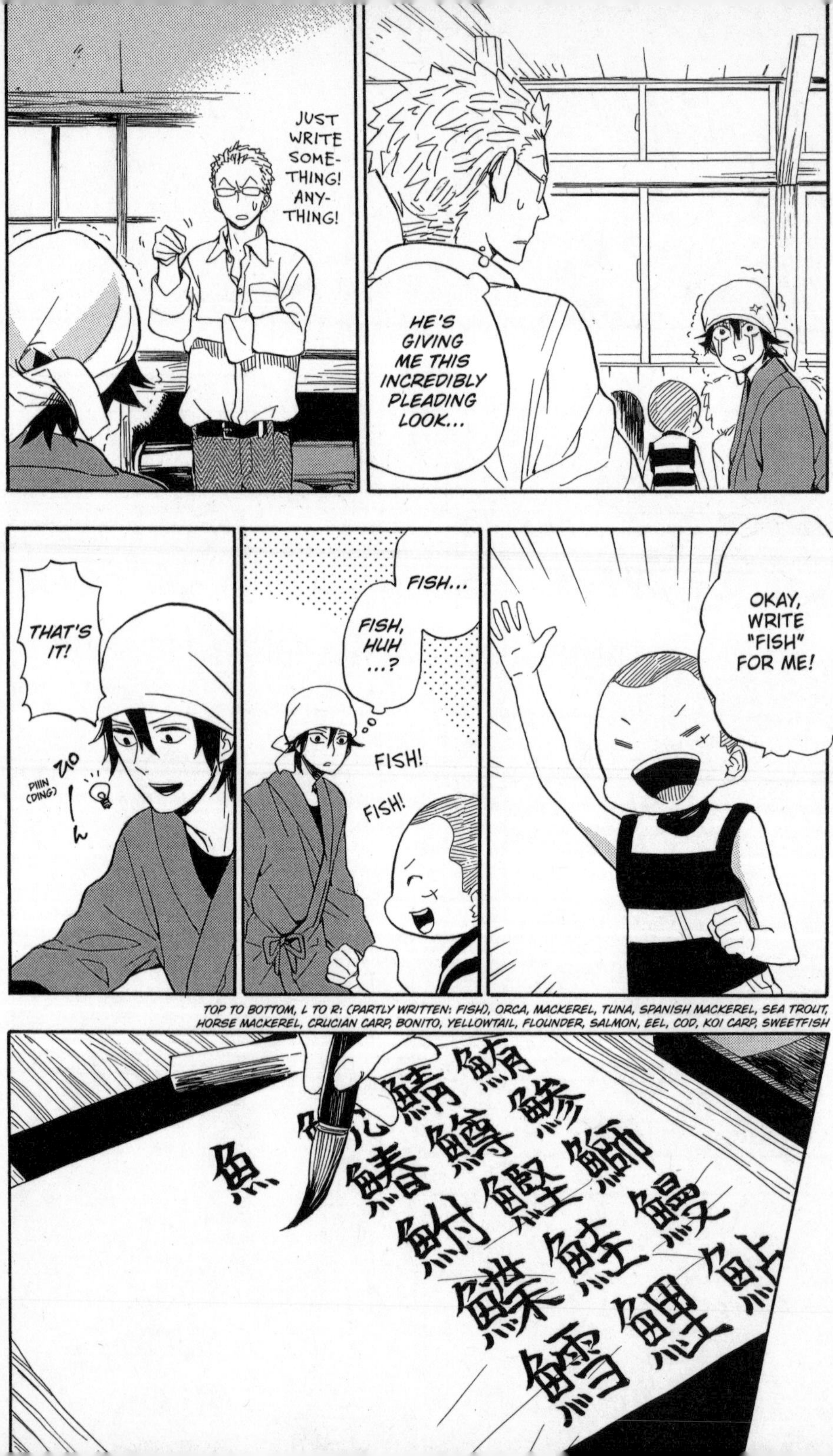
HE'S GIVING ME THIS INCREDIBLY PLEADING LOOK...
JUST WRITE SOME-THING! ANY-THING!
OKAY, WRITE "FISH" FOR ME!
FISH...
FISH, HUH ...?
FISH!
FISH!
THAT'S IT!
PIIIN (DING)
TOP TO BOTTOM, L TO R: (PARTLY WRITTEN: FISH), ORCA, MACKEREL, TUNA, SPANISH MACKEREL, SEA TROUT, HORSE MACKEREL, CRUCIAN CARP, BONITO, YELLOWTAIL, FLOUNDER, SALMON, EEL, COD, KOI CARP, SWEETFISH
魚 鯖 鮪 鰆 鱒 鯵 鮒 鰹 鰤 鰈 鮭 鰻 鱈 鯉 鮎

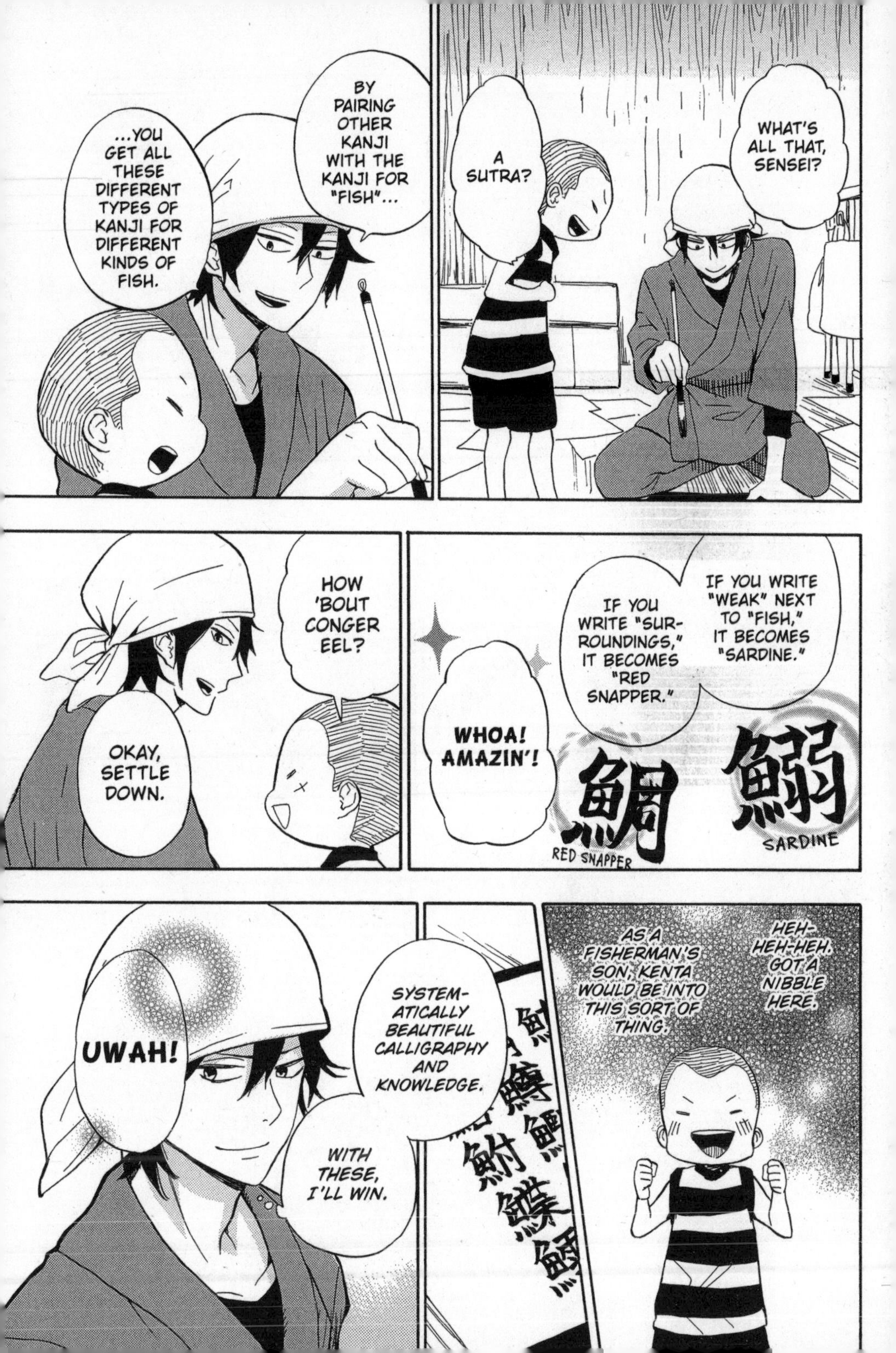
WHAT'S ALL THAT, SENSEI?
A SUTRA?
BY PAIRING OTHER KANJI WITH THE KANJI FOR "FISH"...
...YOU GET ALL THESE DIFFERENT TYPES OF KANJI FOR DIFFERENT KINDS OF FISH.
IF YOU WRITE "WEAK" NEXT TO "FISH," IT BECOMES "SARDINE."
IF YOU WRITE "SUR-ROUNDINGS," IT BECOMES "RED SNAPPER."
鰯
SARDINE
鯛
RED SNAPPER
WHOA! AMAZIN'!
HOW 'BOUT CONGER EEL?
OKAY, SETTLE DOWN.
HEH-HEH-HEH. GOT A NIBBLE HERE.
AS A FISHERMAN'S SON, KENTA WOULD BE INTO THIS SORT OF THING.
SYSTEM-ATICALLY BEAUTIFUL CALLIGRAPHY AND KNOWLEDGE.
WITH THESE, I'LL WIN.
UWAH!

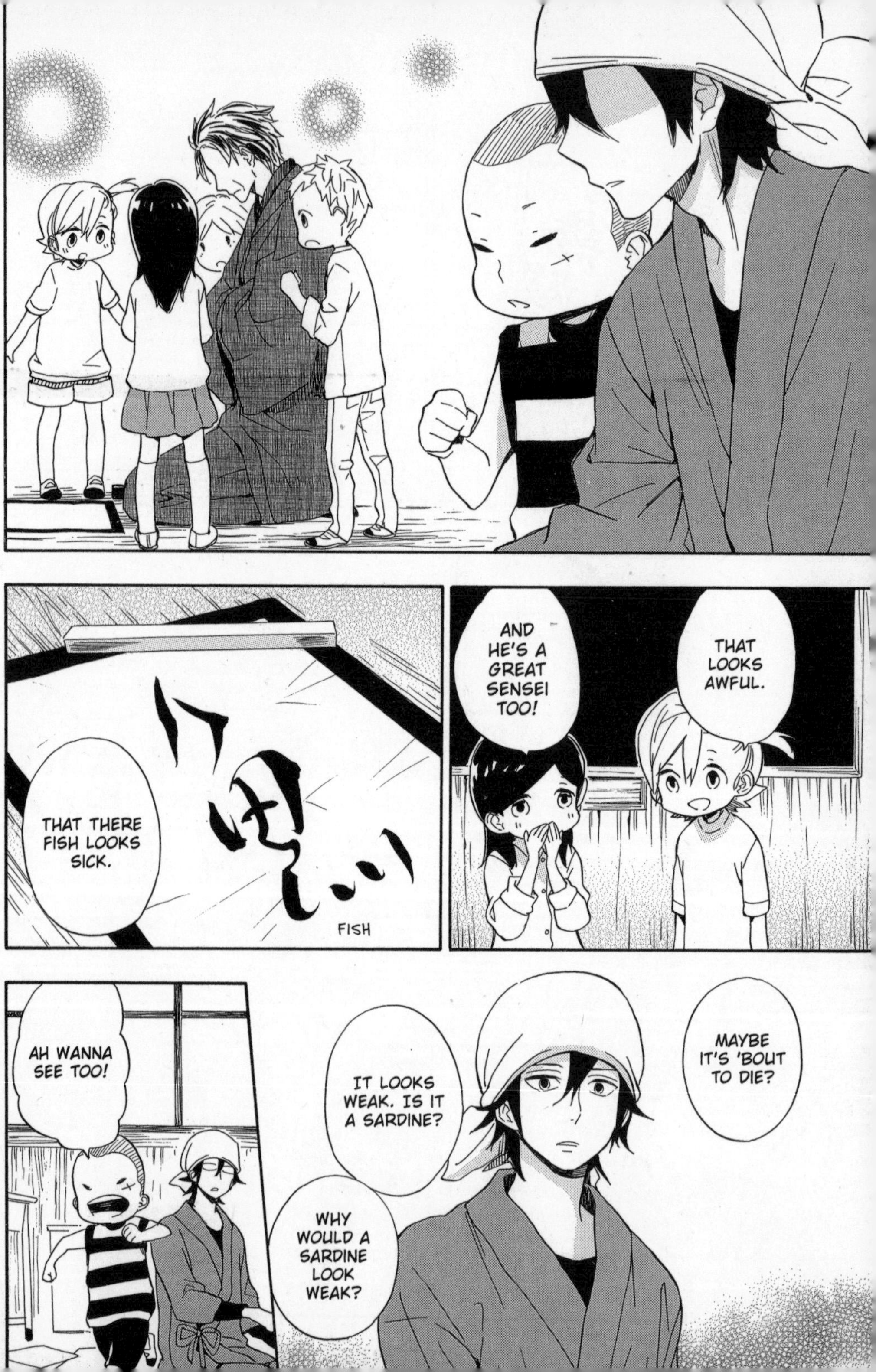
THAT LOOKS AWFUL.
AND HE'S A GREAT SENSEI TOO!
THAT THERE FISH LOOKS SICK.
FISH
MAYBE IT'S 'BOUT TO DIE?
IT LOOKS WEAK. IS IT A SARDINE?
WHY WOULD A SARDINE LOOK WEAK?
AH WANNA SEE TOO!

鯨鯖鮪
鯖鱚鮸
鮴鰹鰊
鰈鮭鮭
鱈

BOX: CRAWDADS

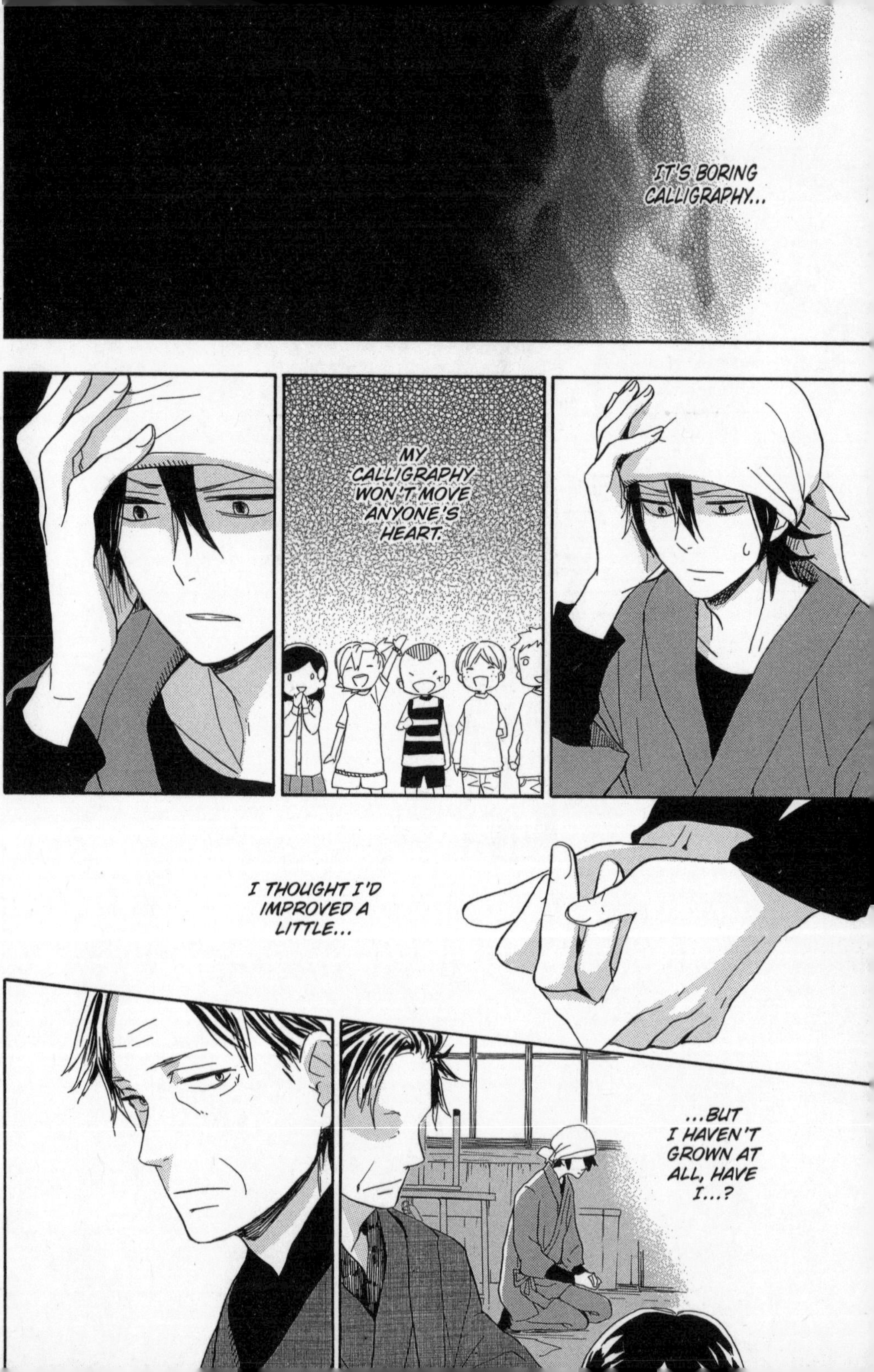
IT'S BORING CALLIGRAPHY...
MY CALLIGRAPHY WON'T MOVE ANYONE'S HEART.
I THOUGHT I'D IMPROVED A LITTLE...
...BUT I HAVEN'T GROWN AT ALL, HAVE I...?

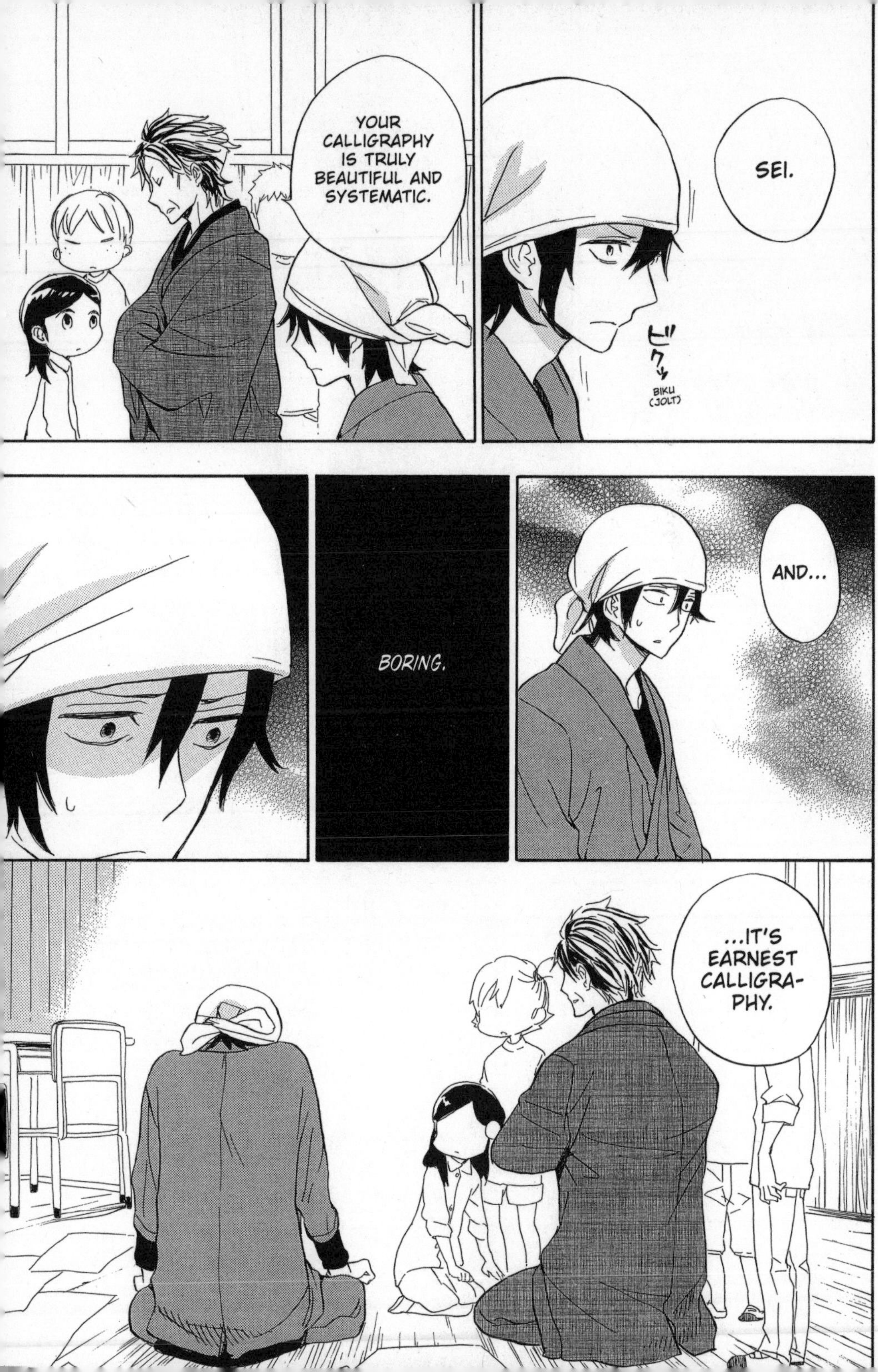
SEI.
ビクッ
BIKU (JOLT)
YOUR CALLIGRAPHY IS TRULY BEAUTIFUL AND SYSTEMATIC.
AND...
BORING.
...IT'S EARNEST CALLIGRA-PHY.

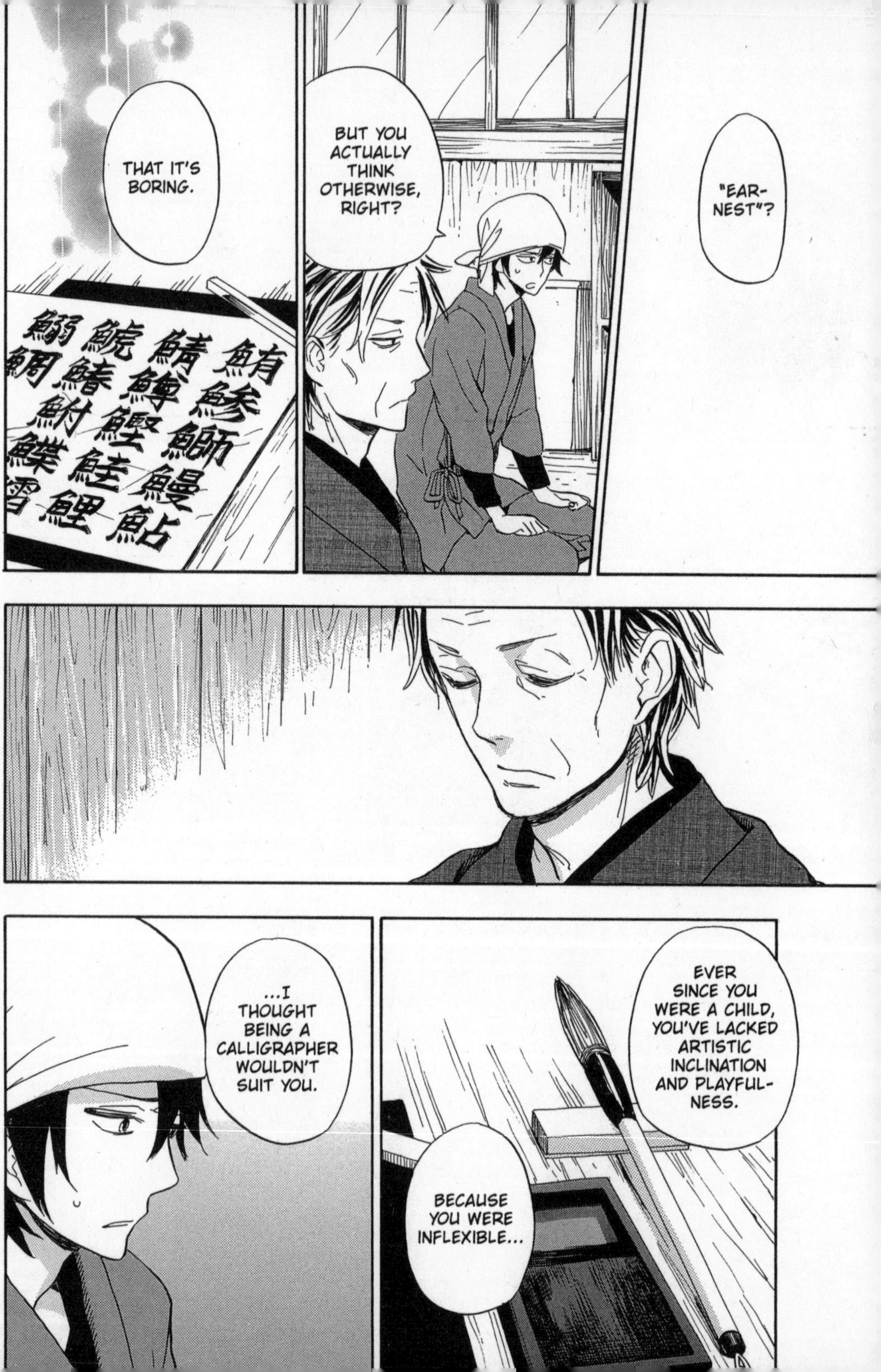
"EAR-NEST"?
BUT YOU ACTUALLY THINK OTHERWISE, RIGHT?
THAT IT'S BORING.
EVER SINCE YOU WERE A CHILD, YOU'VE LACKED ARTISTIC INCLINATION AND PLAYFUL-NESS.
BECAUSE YOU WERE INFLEXIBLE...
...I THOUGHT BEING A CALLIGRAPHER WOULDN'T SUIT YOU.

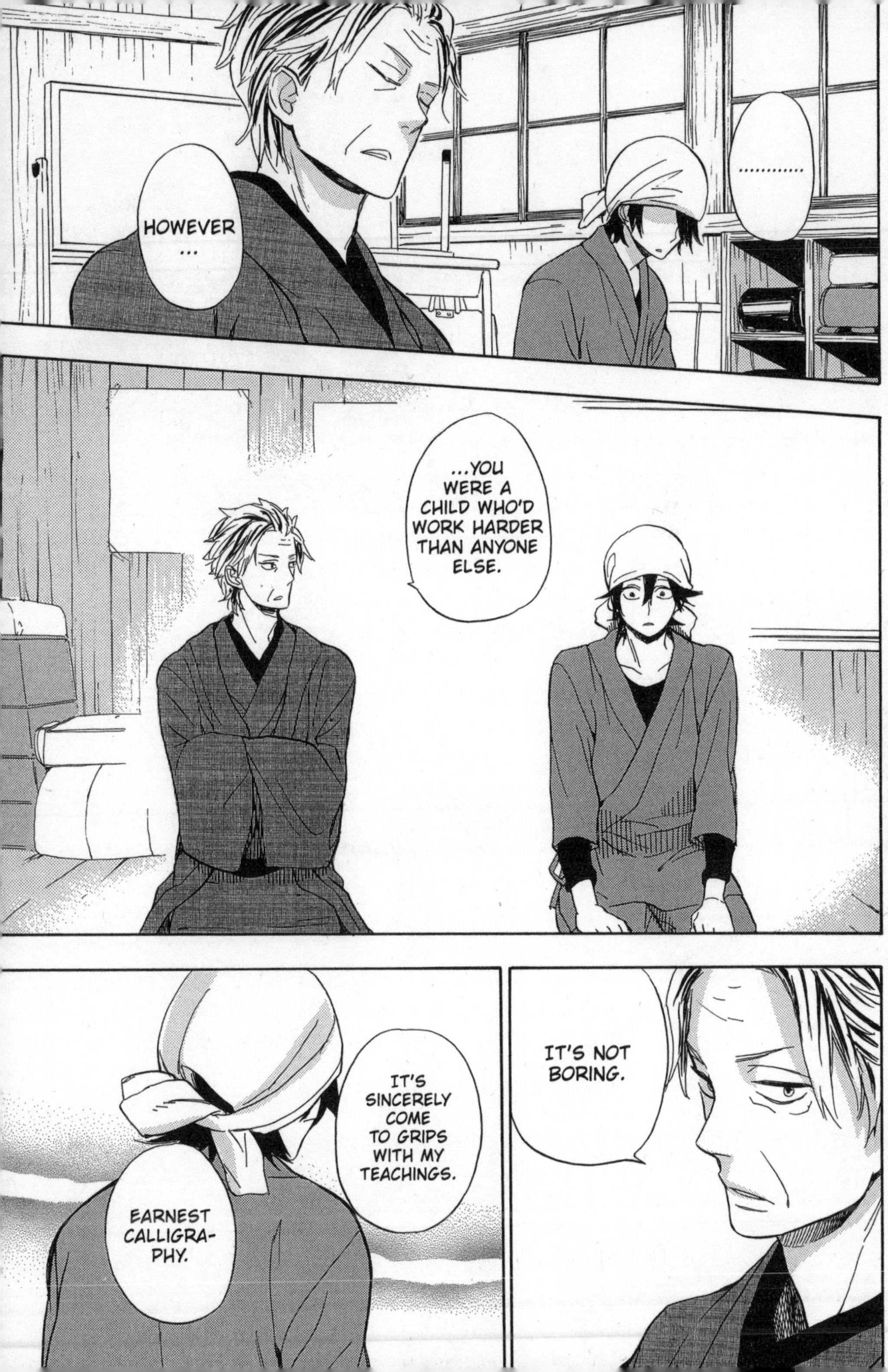
....
HOWEVER ...
...YOU WERE A CHILD WHO'D WORK HARDER THAN ANYONE ELSE.
IT'S NOT BORING.
IT'S SINCERELY COME TO GRIPS WITH MY TEACHINGS.
EARNEST CALLIGRA-PHY.

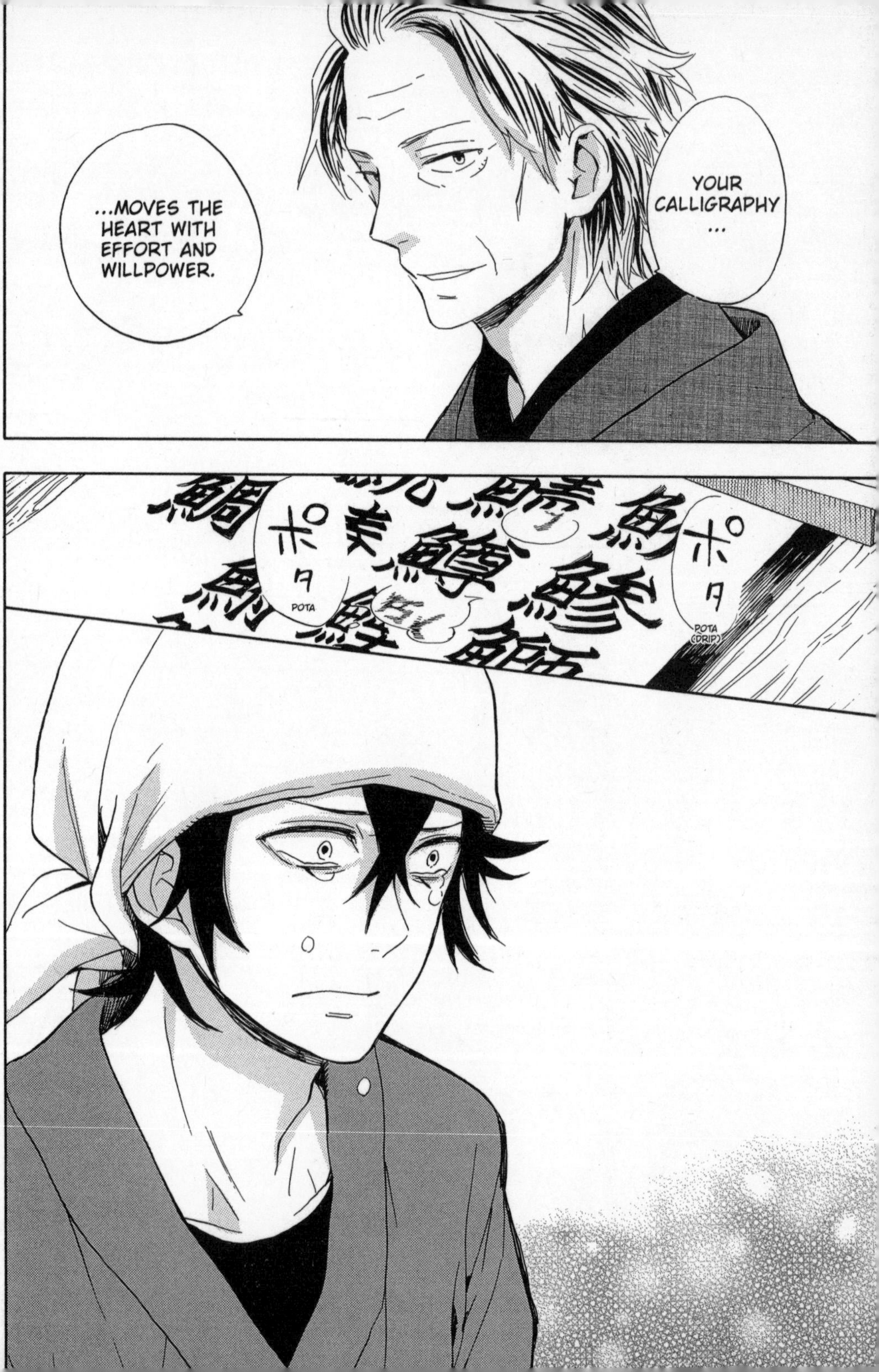
YOUR CALLIGRAPHY ...
...MOVES THE HEART WITH EFFORT AND WILLPOWER.
ポタ
POTA (DRIP)
ポタ
POTA

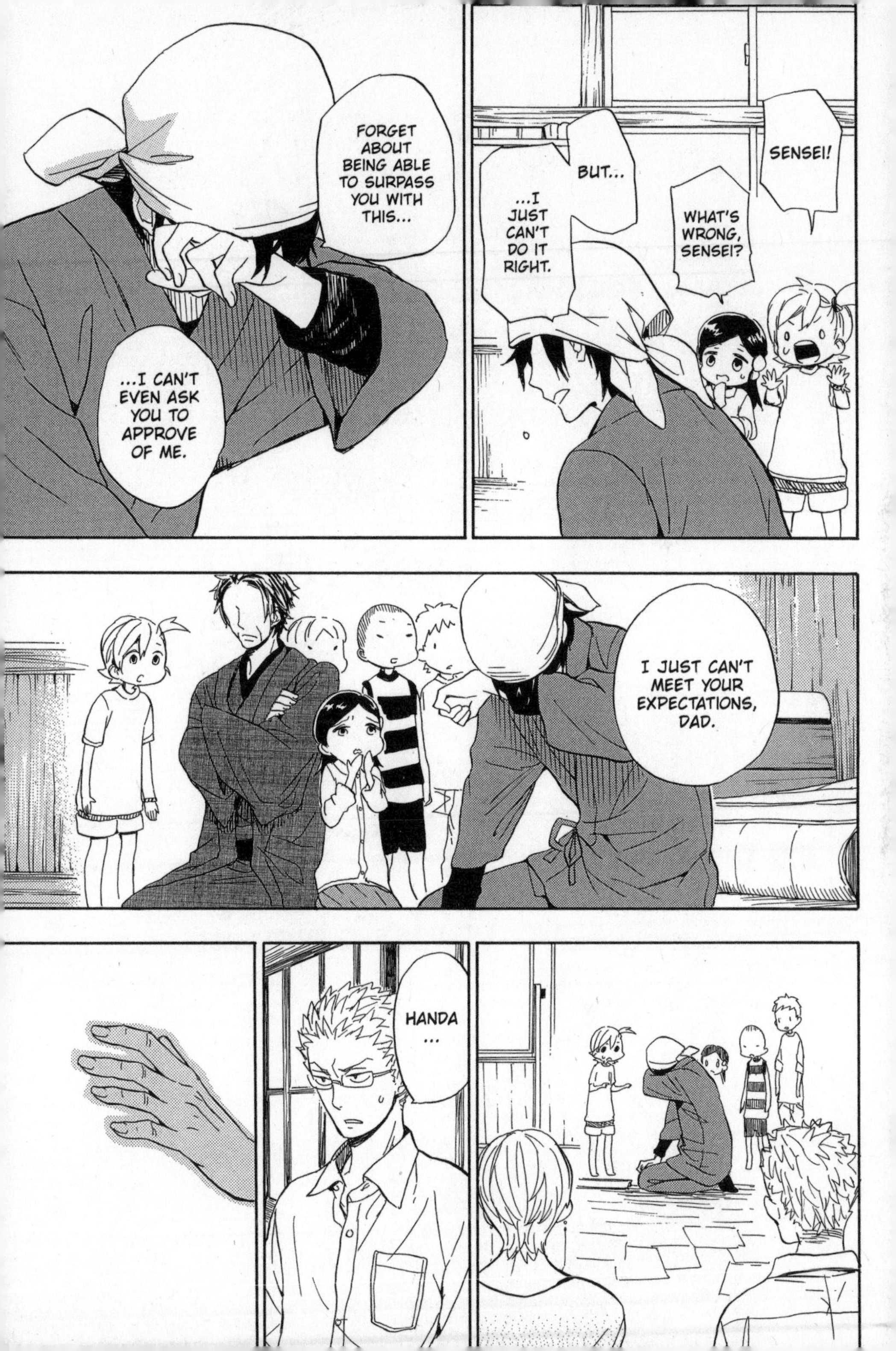
SENSEI!
WHAT'S WRONG, SENSEI?
BUT...
...I JUST CAN'T DO IT RIGHT.
FORGET ABOUT BEING ABLE TO SURPASS YOU WITH THIS...
...I CAN'T EVEN ASK YOU TO APPROVE OF ME.
I JUST CAN'T MEET YOUR EXPECTATIONS, DAD.
HANDA ...

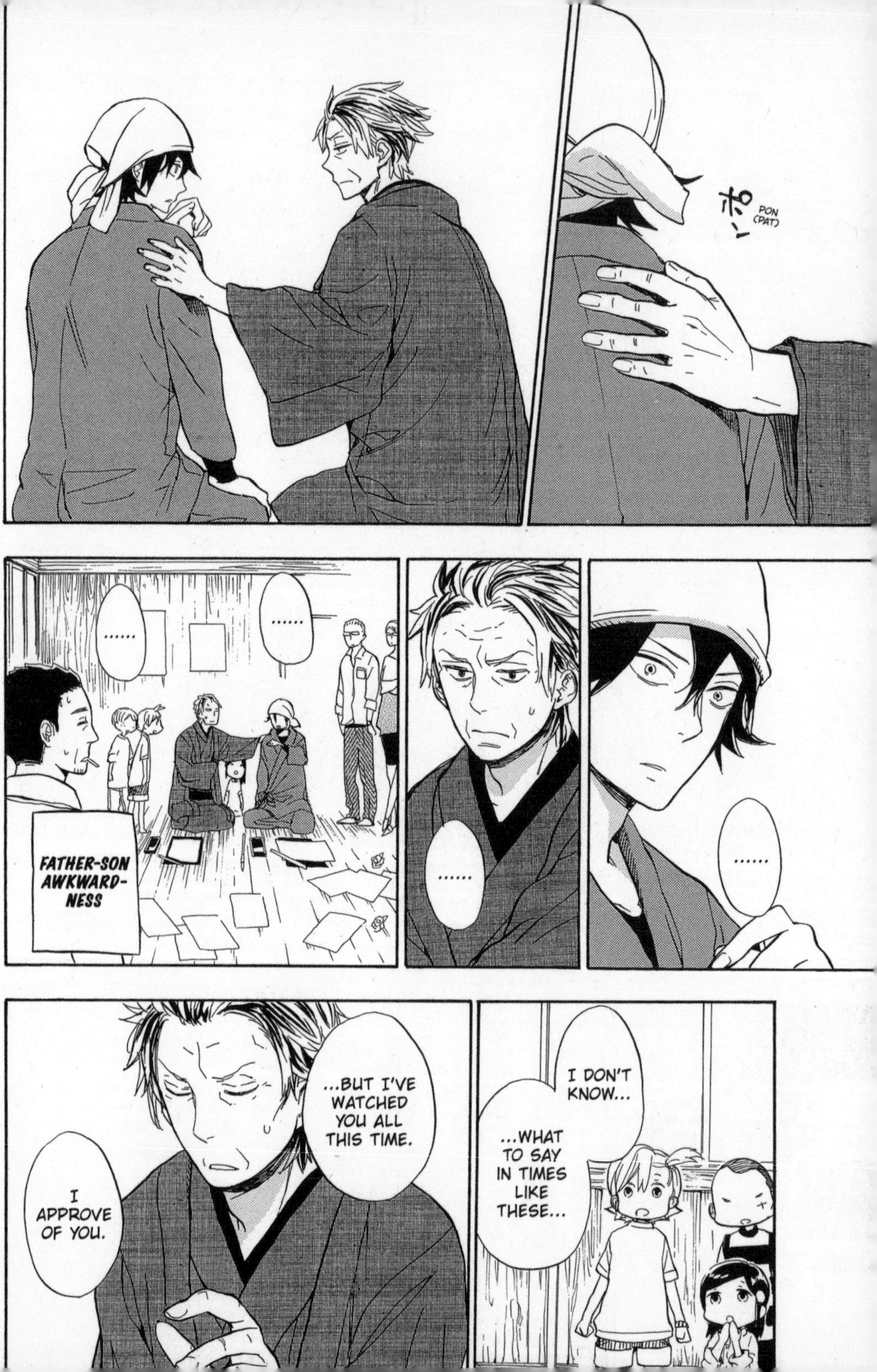

PON (PAT)
......
......
......
......
FATHER-SON AWKWARDNESS
I DON'T KNOW...
...WHAT TO SAY IN TIMES LIKE THESE...
...BUT I'VE WATCHED YOU ALL THIS TIME.
I APPROVE OF YOU.

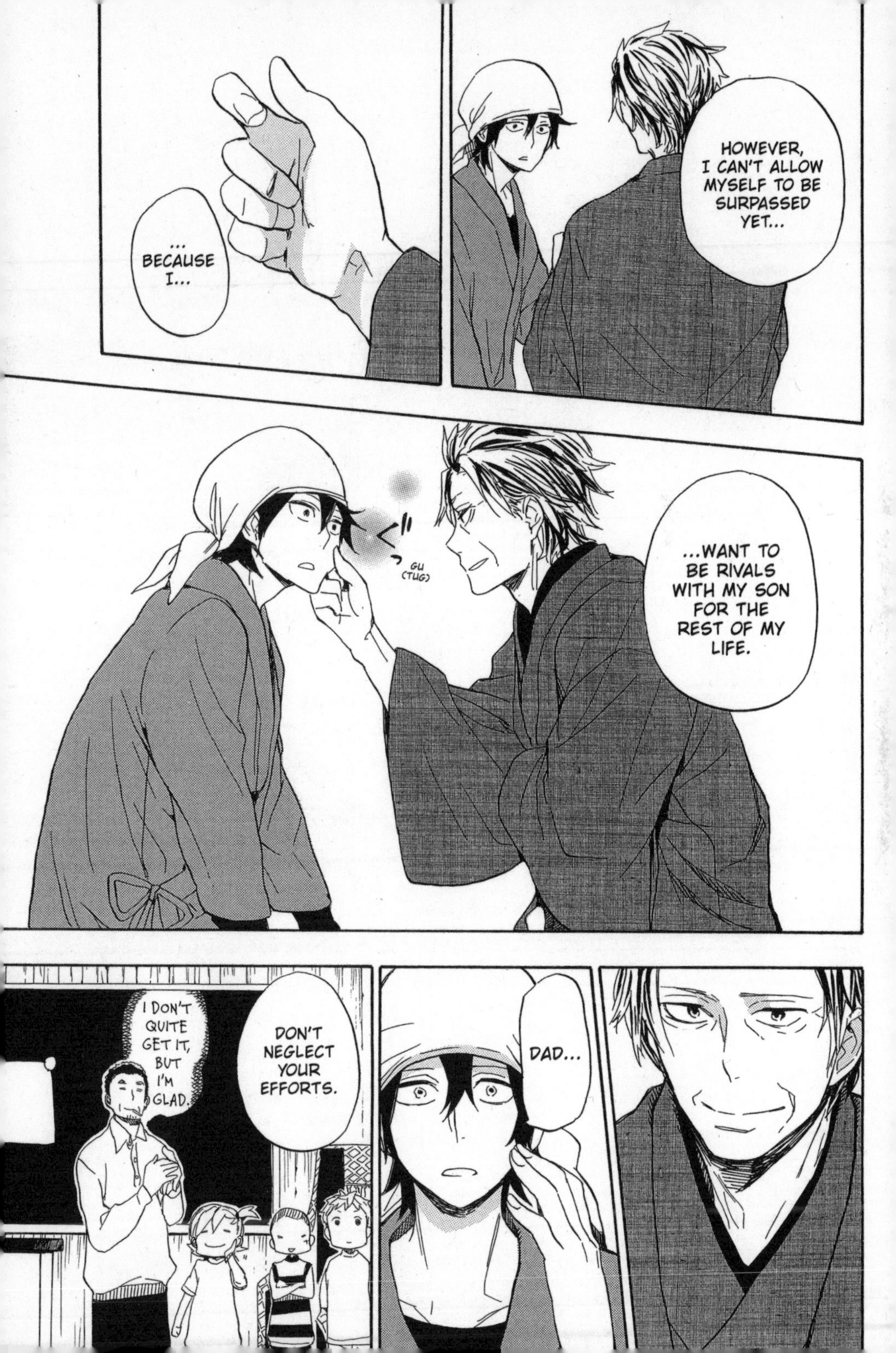
HOWEVER, I CAN'T ALLOW MYSELF TO BE SURPASSED YET...
...BECAUSE I...
...WANT TO BE RIVALS WITH MY SON FOR THE REST OF MY LIFE.
GU (TUG)
DAD...
DON'T NEGLECT YOUR EFFORTS.
I DON'T QUITE GET IT, BUT I'M GLAD.

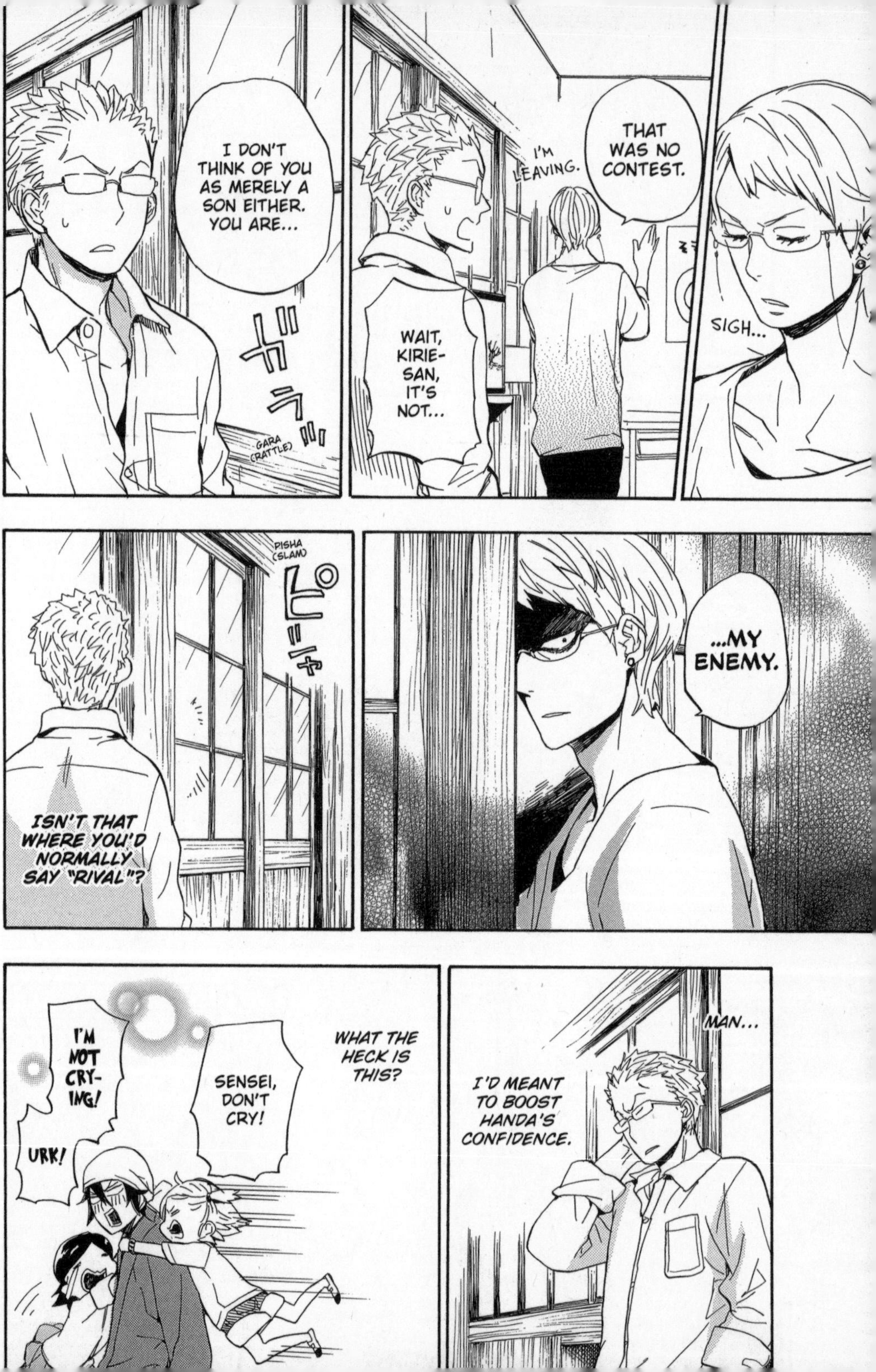
SIGH...
THAT WAS NO CONTEST.
I'M LEAVING.
WAIT, KIRIE-SAN, IT'S NOT...
I DON'T THINK OF YOU AS MERELY A SON EITHER. YOU ARE...
GARA (RATTLE)
...MY ENEMY.
PISHA (SLAM)
ISN'T THAT WHERE YOU'D NORMALLY SAY "RIVAL"?
MAN...
I'D MEANT TO BOOST HANDA'S CONFIDENCE.
WHAT THE HECK IS THIS?
SENSEI, DON'T CRY!
I'M NOT CRY-ING!
URK!

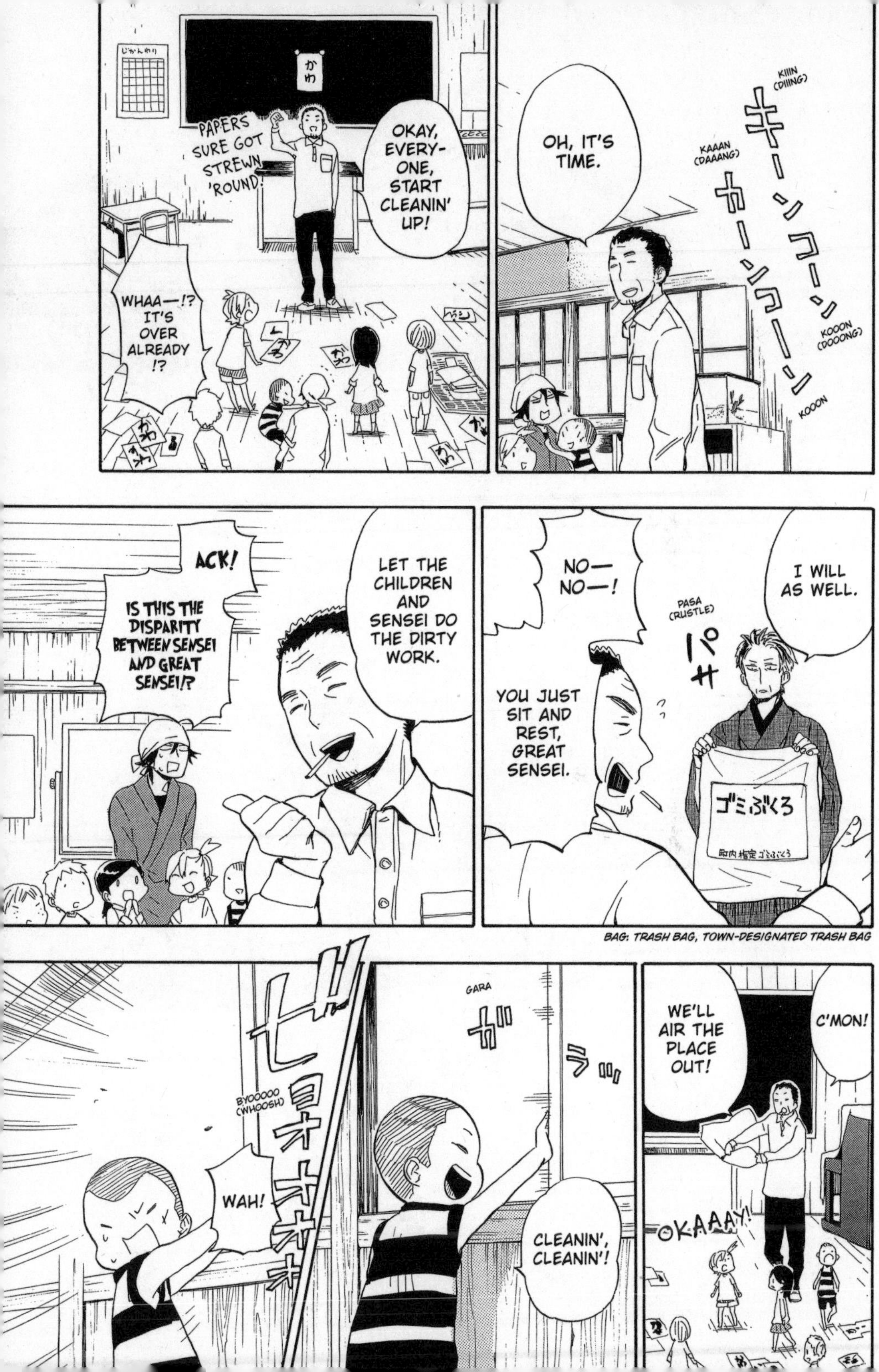
KIIN (DIIING)
KAAAN (DAAANG)
KOOON (DOOONG)
KOOON
OH, IT'S TIME.
OKAY, EVERY-ONE, START CLEANIN' UP!
PAPERS SURE GOT STREWN 'ROUND!
WHAA—!? IT'S OVER ALREADY!?
I WILL AS WELL.
PASA (RUSTLE)
ゴミぶくろ
NO— NO—!
YOU JUST SIT AND REST, GREAT SENSEI.
LET THE CHILDREN AND SENSEI DO THE DIRTY WORK.
ACK!
IS THIS THE DISPARITY BETWEEN SENSEI AND GREAT SENSEI!?
C'MON!
WE'LL AIR THE PLACE OUT!
OKAAAY!
GARA
CLEANIN', CLEANIN'!
BYOOOOO (WHOOSH)
WAH!

BAG: TRASH BAG, TOWN-DESIGNATED TRASH BAG

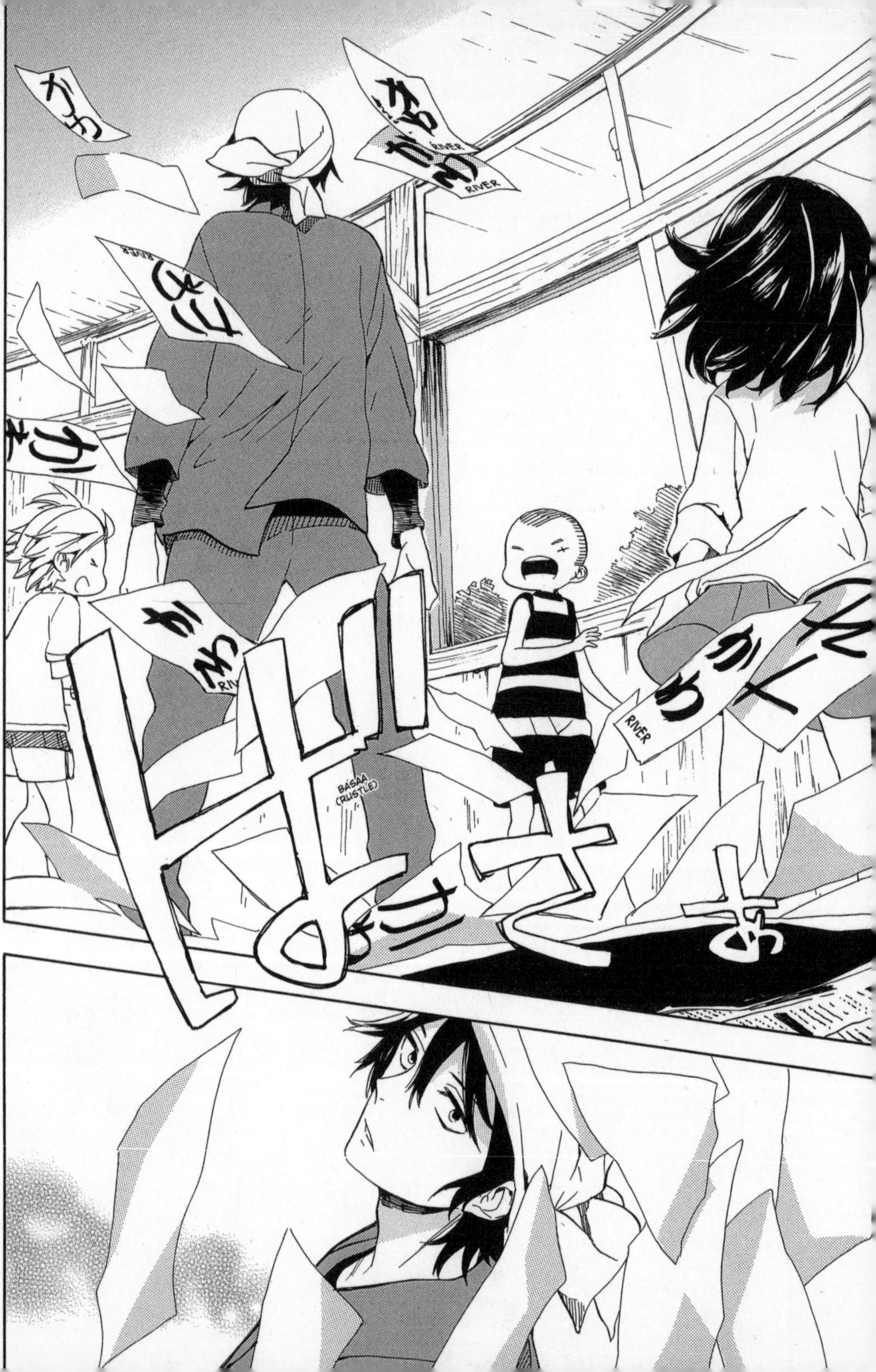
RIVER
RIVER
RIVER
RIVER
RIVER
BÁSAA (RUSTLE)

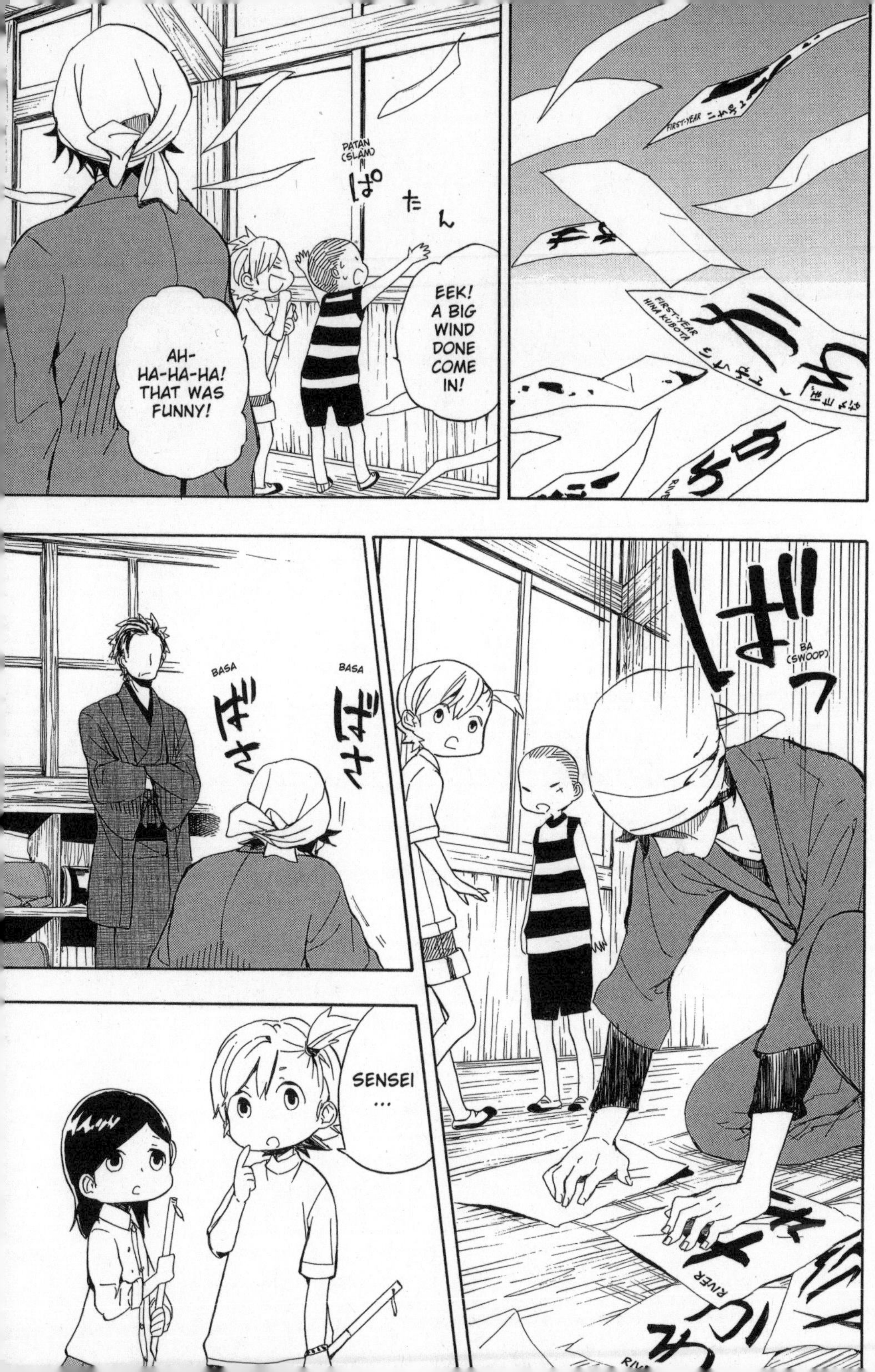
FIRST-YEAR
FIRST-YEAR HINA KUBOTA
RIVER
PATAN (SLAM)
ぱたん
EEK! A BIG WIND DONE COME IN!
AH-HA-HA-HA! THAT WAS FUNNY!
BA (SWOOP)
ばっ
RIVER
BASA
ばさ
BASA
ばさ
SENSEI …

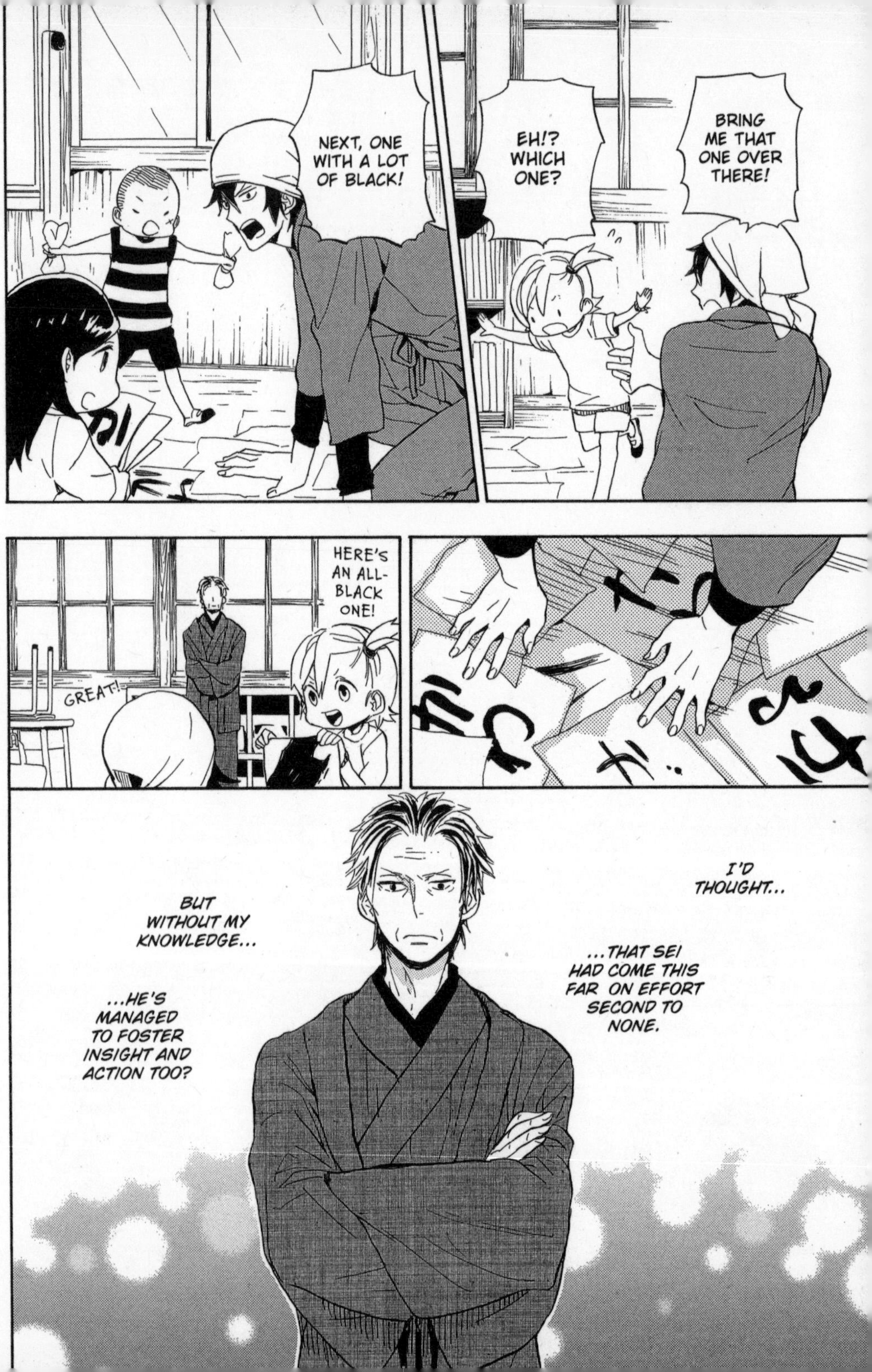
BRING ME THAT ONE OVER THERE!
EH!? WHICH ONE?
NEXT, ONE WITH A LOT OF BLACK!
HERE'S AN ALL-BLACK ONE!
GREAT!
I'D THOUGHT...
...THAT SEI HAD COME THIS FAR ON EFFORT SECOND TO NONE.
BUT WITHOUT MY KNOWLEDGE...
...HE'S MANAGED TO FOSTER INSIGHT AND ACTION TOO?

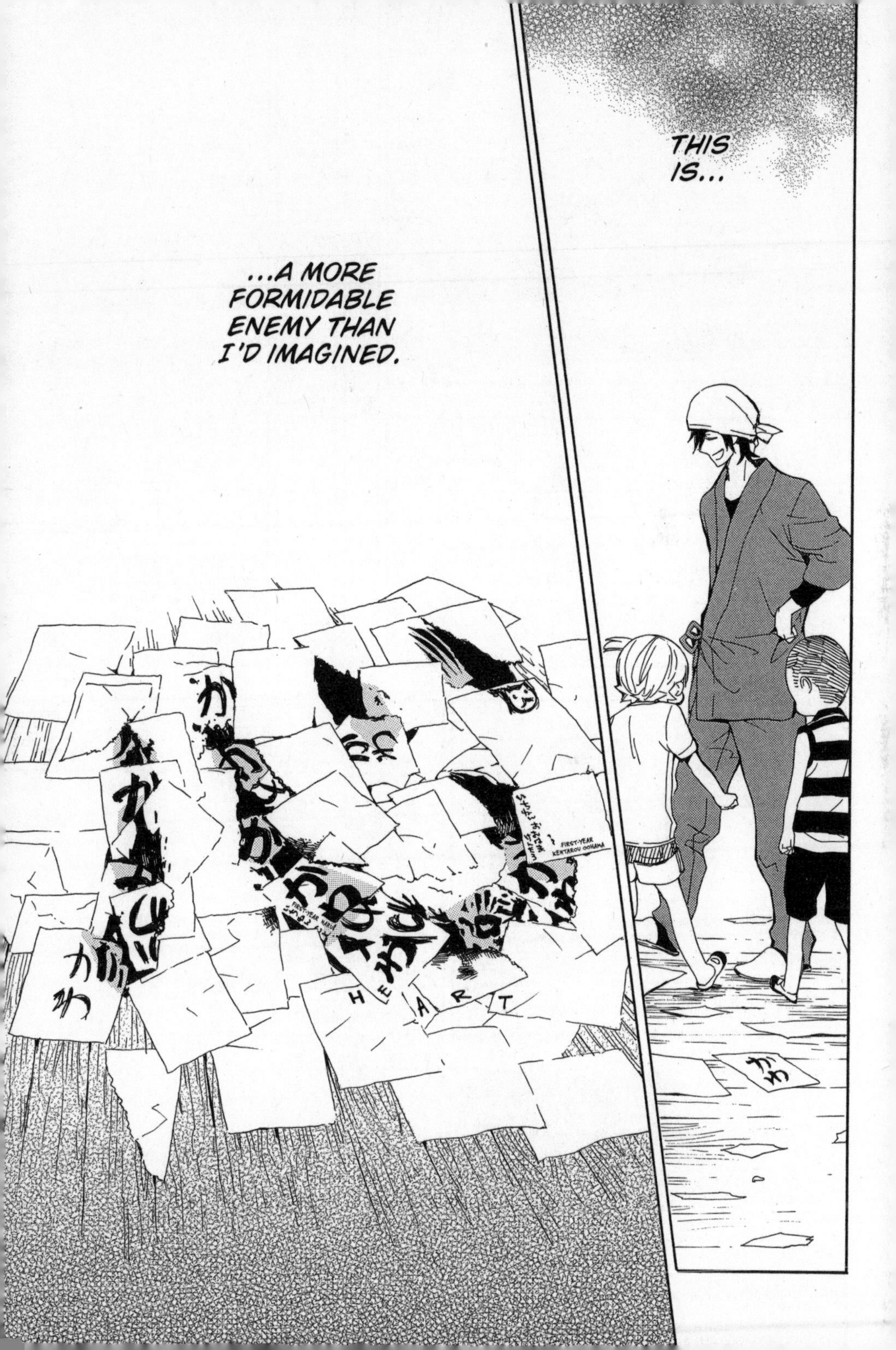
THIS IS...
FIRST-YEAR KENTAROU OOHAMA
...A MORE FORMIDABLE ENEMY THAN I'D IMAGINED.
HEART

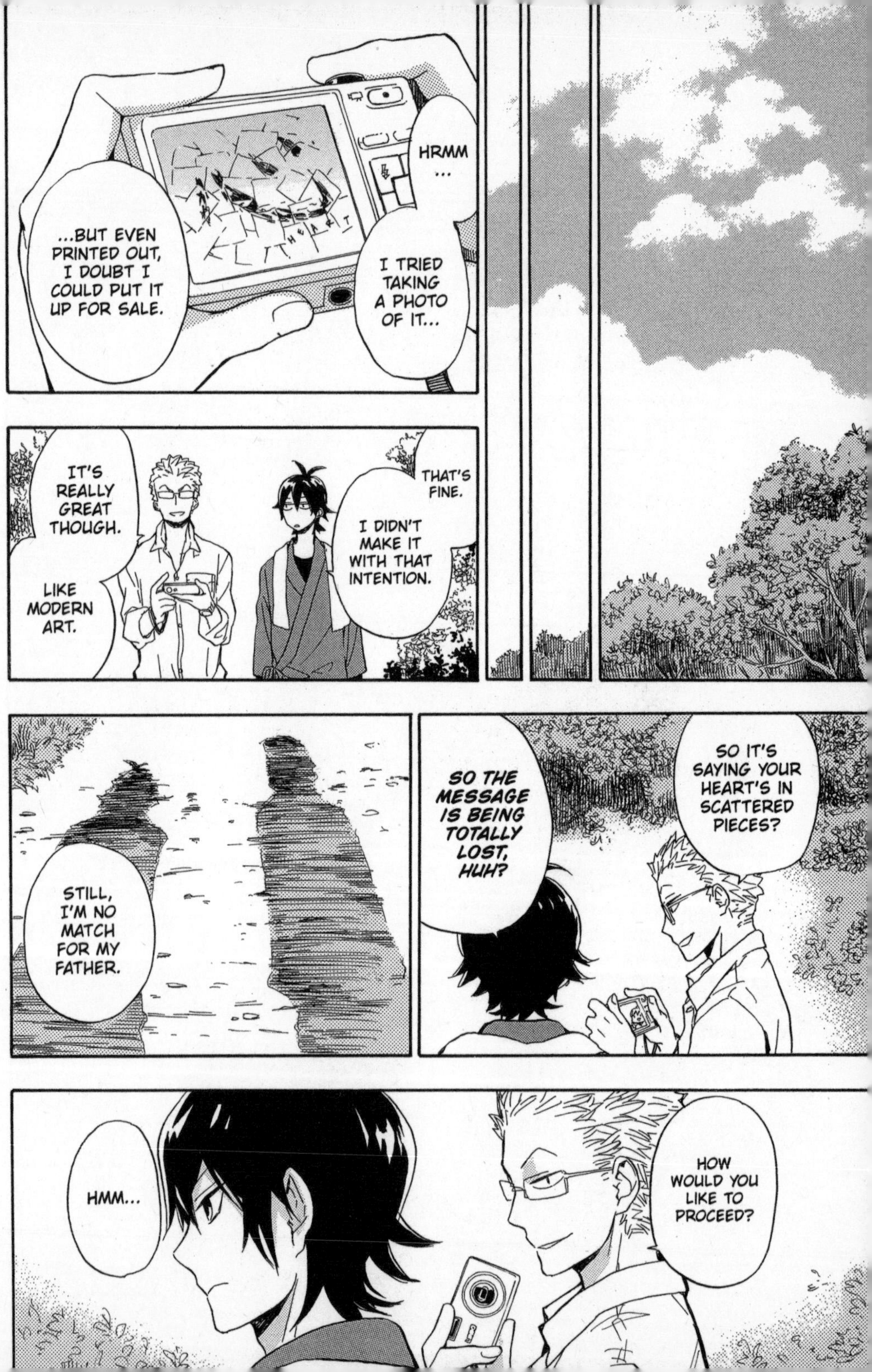
HRMM...
I TRIED TAKING A PHOTO OF IT...
...BUT EVEN PRINTED OUT, I DOUBT I COULD PUT IT UP FOR SALE.
THAT'S FINE.
I DIDN'T MAKE IT WITH THAT INTENTION.
IT'S REALLY GREAT THOUGH.
LIKE MODERN ART.
SO IT'S SAYING YOUR HEART'S IN SCATTERED PIECES?
SO THE MESSAGE IS BEING TOTALLY LOST, HUH?
STILL, I'M NO MATCH FOR MY FATHER.
HOW WOULD YOU LIKE TO PROCEED?
HMM...

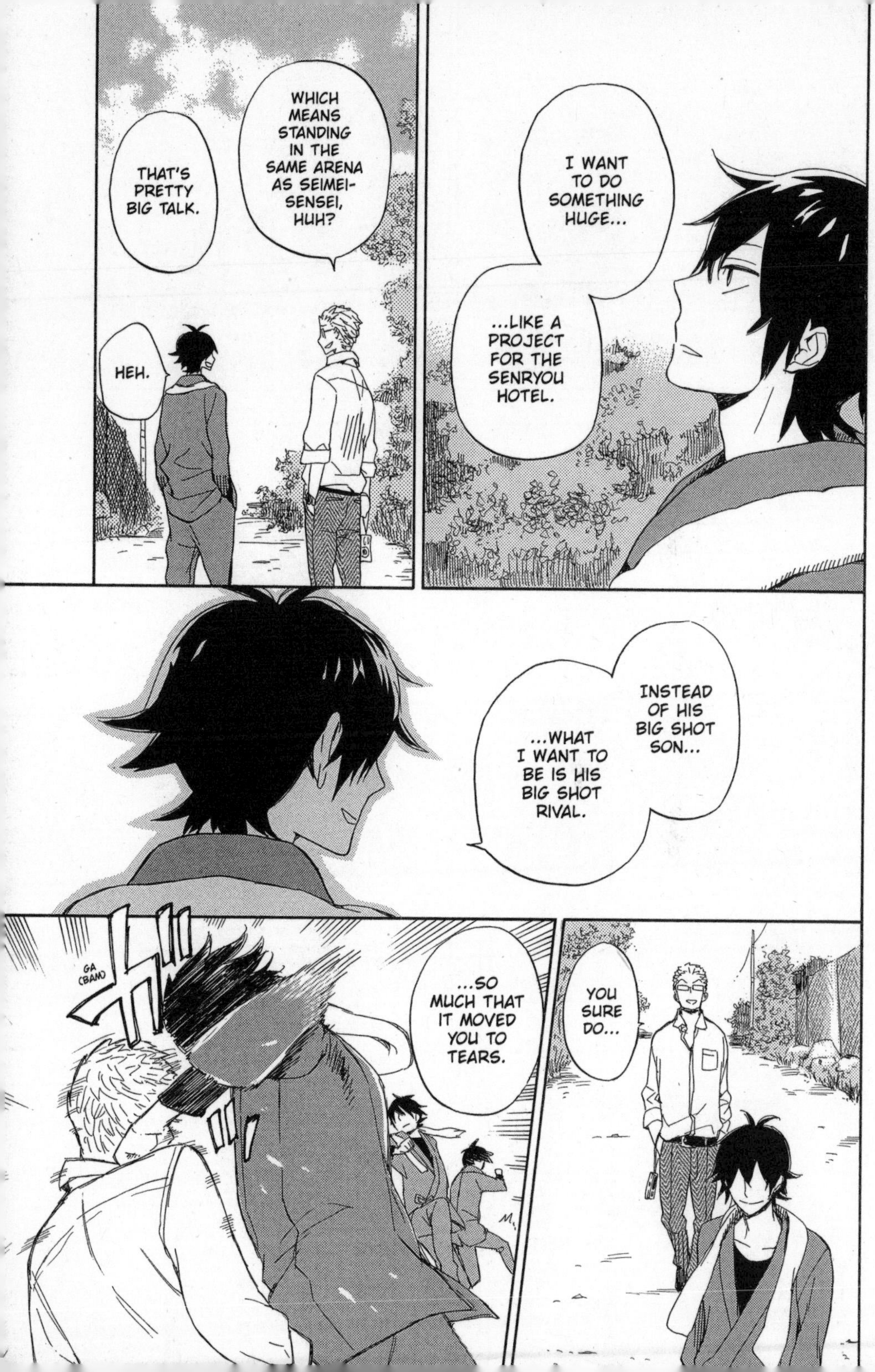
I WANT TO DO SOMETHING HUGE...
...LIKE A PROJECT FOR THE SENRYOU HOTEL.
WHICH MEANS STANDING IN THE SAME ARENA AS SEIMEI-SENSEI, HUH?
THAT'S PRETTY BIG TALK.
HEH.
INSTEAD OF HIS BIG SHOT SON...
...WHAT I WANT TO BE IS HIS BIG SHOT RIVAL.
YOU SURE DO...
...SO MUCH THAT IT MOVED YOU TO TEARS.
GA (BAM)

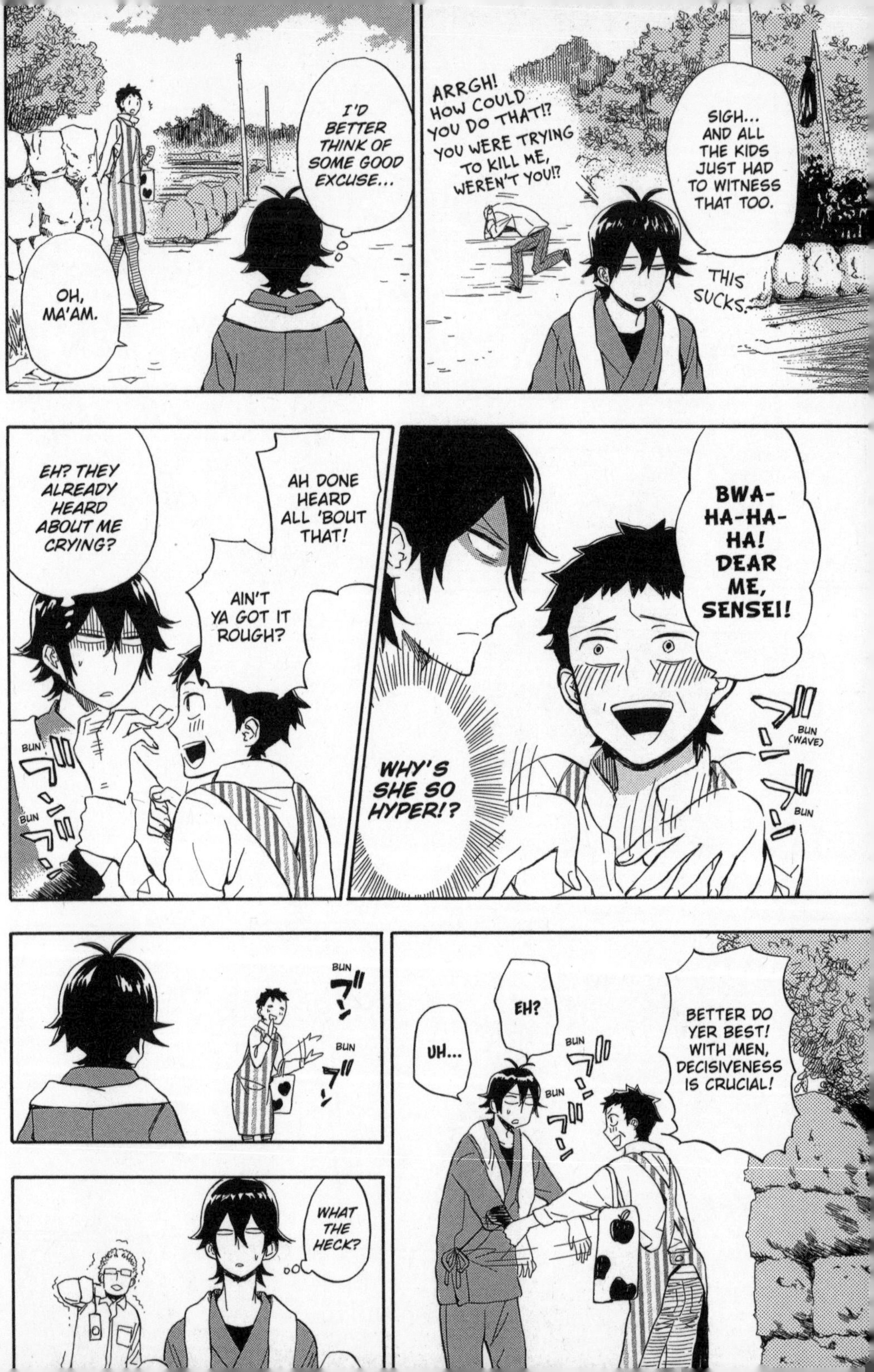
SIGH... AND ALL THE KIDS JUST HAD TO WITNESS THAT TOO.
ARRGH! HOW COULD YOU DO THAT!? YOU WERE TRYING TO KILL ME, WEREN'T YOU!?
THIS SUCKS.
I'D BETTER THINK OF SOME GOOD EXCUSE...
OH, MA'AM.
BWA-HA-HA-HA! DEAR ME, SENSEI!
BUN (WAVE)
BUN
WHY'S SHE SO HYPER!?
AH DONE HEARD ALL 'BOUT THAT!
EH? THEY ALREADY HEARD ABOUT ME CRYING?
AIN'T YA GOT IT ROUGH?
BUN
BUN
BETTER DO YER BEST! WITH MEN, DECISIVENESS IS CRUCIAL!
EH?
BUN
BUN
UH...
BUN
BUN
WHAT THE HECK?

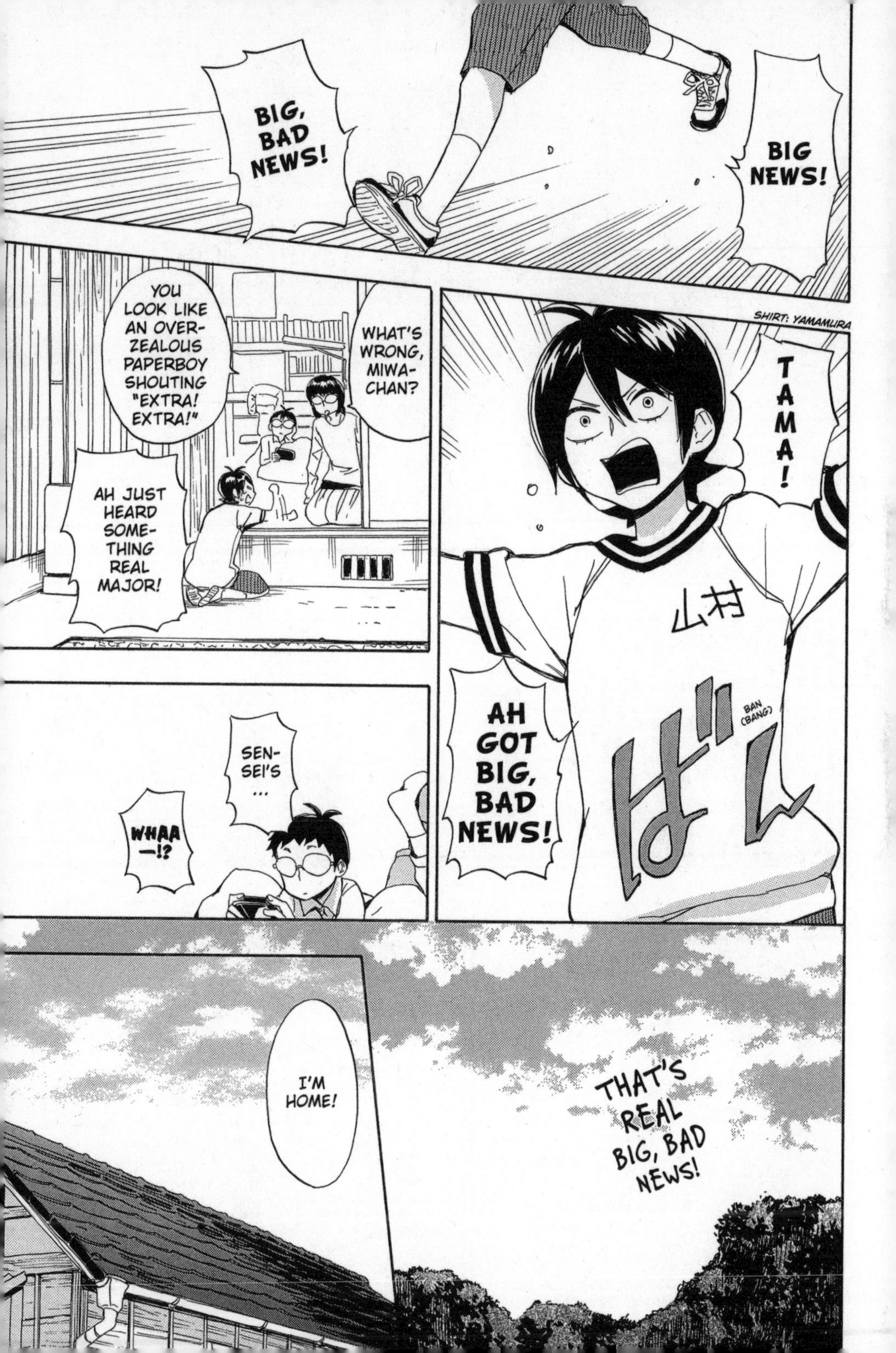
BIG NEWS!
BIG, BAD NEWS!
SHIRT: YAMAMURA
TAMA!
AH GOT BIG, BAD NEWS!
山村
BAN (BANG)
ばん
WHAT'S WRONG, MIWA-CHAN?
YOU LOOK LIKE AN OVER-ZEALOUS PAPERBOY SHOUTING "EXTRA! EXTRA!"
AH JUST HEARD SOME-THING REAL MAJOR!
SEN-SEI'S ...
WHAA—!?
THAT'S REAL BIG, BAD NEWS!
I'M HOME!

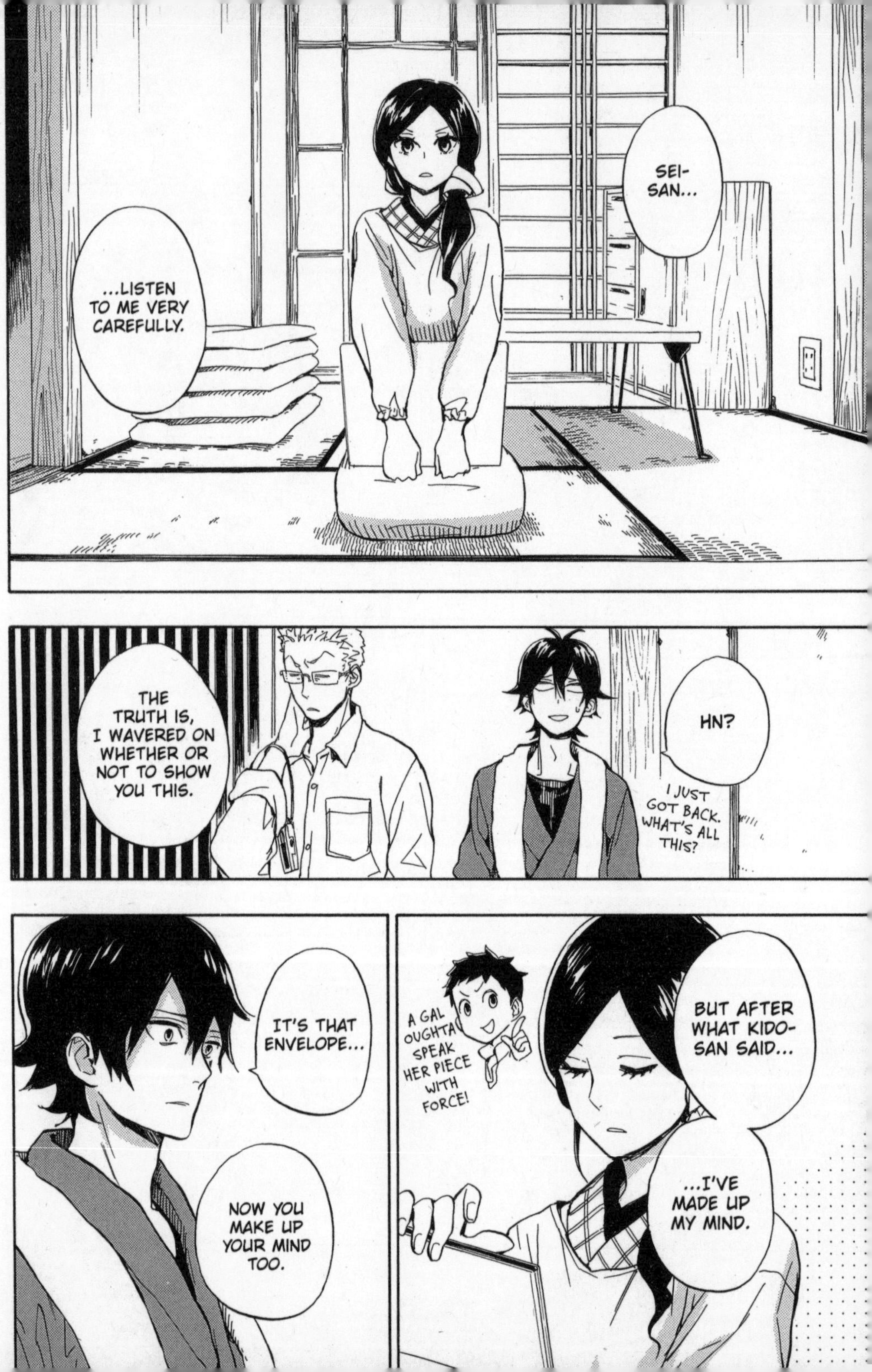
SEI-SAN...
...LISTEN TO ME VERY CAREFULLY.
HN?
I JUST GOT BACK. WHAT'S ALL THIS?
THE TRUTH IS, I WAVERED ON WHETHER OR NOT TO SHOW YOU THIS.
BUT AFTER WHAT KIDO-SAN SAID...
A GAL OUGHTA SPEAK HER PIECE WITH FORCE!
...I'VE MADE UP MY MIND.
IT'S THAT ENVELOPE...
NOW YOU MAKE UP YOUR MIND TOO.

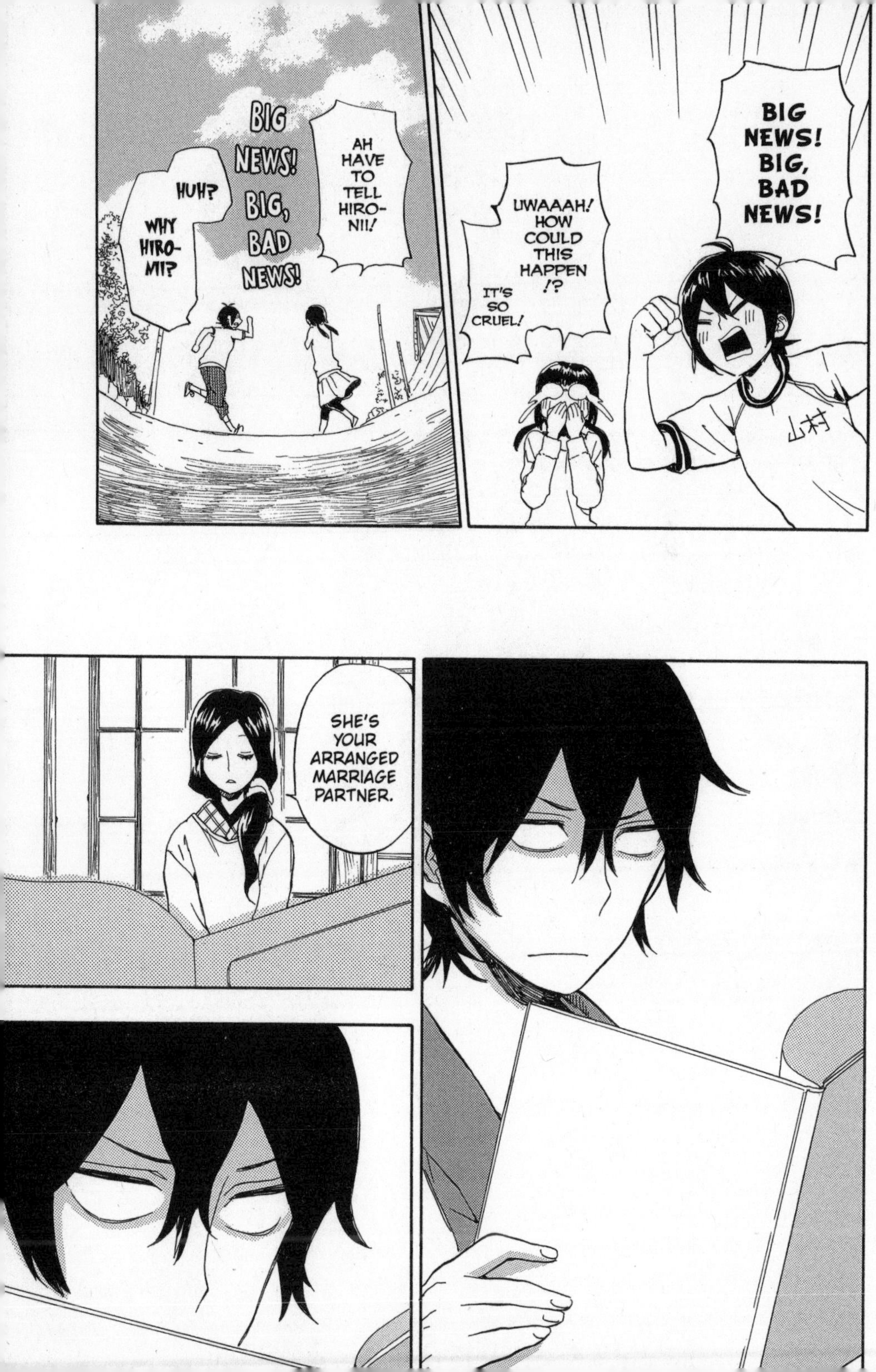
BIG NEWS! BIG, BAD NEWS!
UWAAAH! HOW COULD THIS HAPPEN!?
IT'S SO CRUEL!
山村
AH HAVE TO TELL HIRO-NI!!
BIG NEWS! BIG, BAD NEWS!
HUH?
WHY HIRO-MI?
SHE'S YOUR ARRANGED MARRIAGE PARTNER.

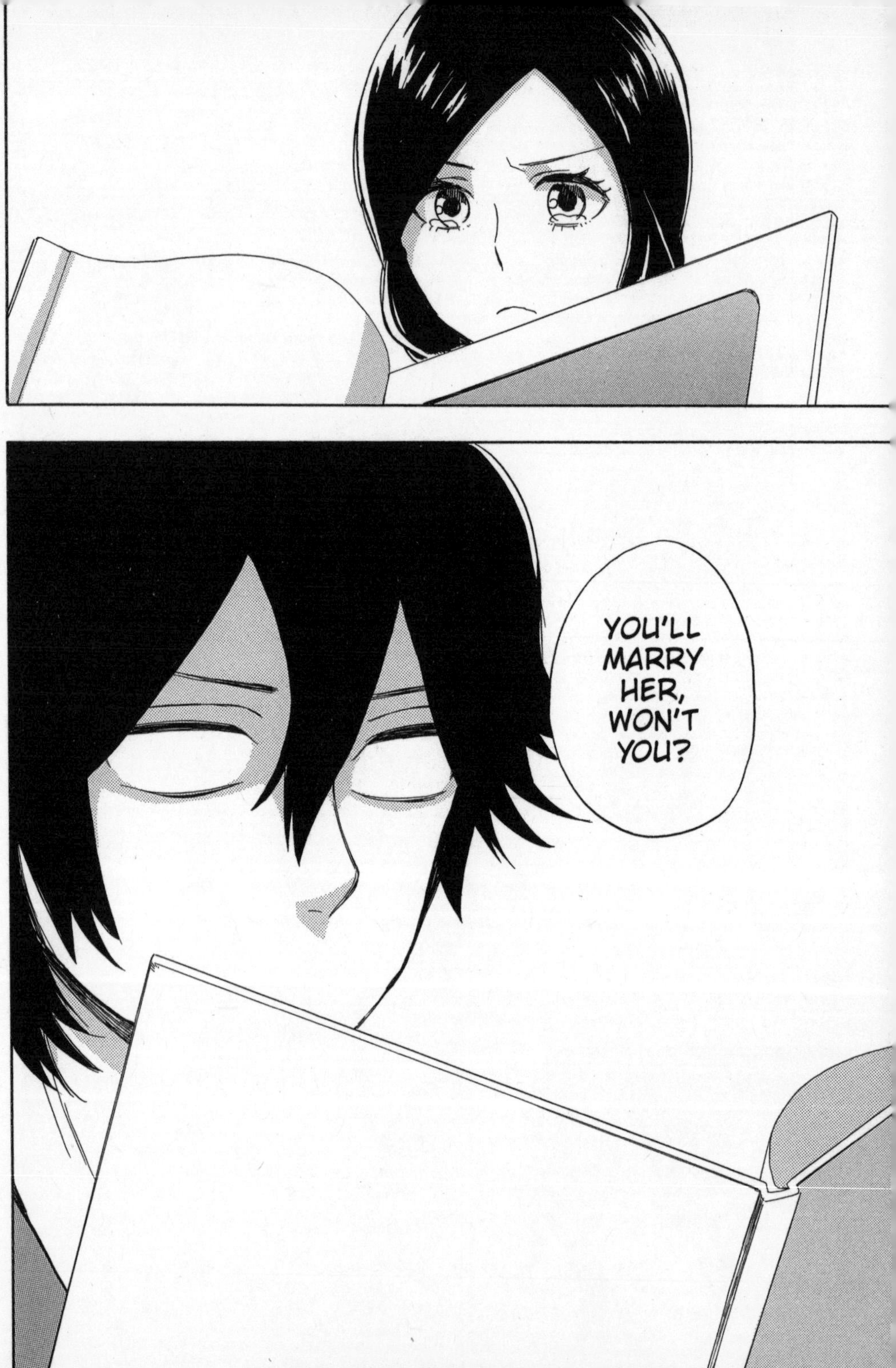
YOU'LL MARRY HER, WON'T YOU?

TO BE CONTINUED IN BARAKAMON 11

TRANSLATION NOTES ·······················

COMMON HONORIFICS

no honorific: Indicates familiarity or closeness; if used without permission or reason, addressing someone in this manner would constitute an insult.

-san: The Japanese equivalent of Mr./Mrs./Miss. If a situation calls for politeness, this is the fail-safe honorific.

-sama: Conveys great respect; may also indicate that the social status of the speaker is lower than that of the addressee.

-kun: Used most often when referring to boys, this indicates affection or familiarity. Occasionally used by older men among their peers, but it may also be used by anyone referring to a person of lower standing.

-chan: An affectionate honorific indicating familiarity used mostly in reference to girls; also used in reference to cute persons or animals of either gender.

-sensei: A Japanese term of respect commonly used for teachers, but can also refer to doctors, writers, and artists. Hence, Village Chief is not implying that Handa is a teacher when he calls him *"sensei."*

Calligraphy: Japanese calligraphy has a long history and tradition, with roots stemming from ancient China. One of the traditions carried over was the Chinese expression of the "Four Treasures," which refers to the brush, ink, paper, and inkstone used in calligraphy. Traditionally, an inkstick—solidified ink—is ground against an inkstone filled with water in order to produce ink with which to write. This time-consuming process helped to teach patience, which is important in the art of calligraphy. However, modern advances have developed a bottled liquid ink, commonly used by beginners and within the Japanese school system.

Gotou Dialect: Many of the villagers, especially the elderly ones, are actually speaking the local Gotou dialect in the original Japanese. This dialect is reflected in the English translation with some of the grammar elements of older Southern American English to give it a more rustic, rural coastal feel without making it too hard to read (it's not meant to replicate any particular American accent exactly). This approach is similar to how dialect is made accessible in Japanese media, including *Barakamon*, because a complete dialect with all of its different vocabulary would be practically incomprehensible to most Tokyo residents.

Yen conversion: While exchange rates fluctuate daily, a convenient conversion estimation is about ¥100 to 1 USD.

PAGE 9

"All kids love the wind!": There's a Japanese saying that goes, "children are children of the wind; adults are children of fire." It basically means children are happy to be outdoors in all weather, while adults are sensitive to the cold (and stay in by the fire).

PAGE 13

"'Mom'? But he's a grown-up!": It's not unusual for parents in Japan to call each other *"otou-san* (Father)" and *"okaa-san* (Mother)," even when their children aren't around. Naru isn't familiar with this though, due to her family circumstances.

PAGE 14

kankoro mochi: A type of soft rice cake with lots of sweet potato mixed in, and a specialty of the Gotou Islands.

mite-tempered: The Japanese phrase used for "short-tempered/impatient" was *"ki no mishikaka,"* which uses a dialect version of the standard Japanese word *"mijikai."*

PAGE 15

Ostrich Club: *Dachou Kurabu* is a Japanese comedy trio who specialize in reaction comedy.

PAGE 24

sweet sake: *Amazake* is a traditional Japanese rice drink that's fermented differently from regular sake to be sweet instead of intoxicating. Since it has little to no alcohol, it's fine for children to drink.

PAGE 37

strained lees: *"Shiborikasu"* in the original Japanese is a term primarily from production of wine, sake, etc., referring to the unwanted solids left over after the precious fermented liquid has been strained out.

PAGE 43

"waltz in": The original Japanese verb Handa used was *"tachi-iri,"* which literally means "enter while standing up." Miwa then plays with the term and asks if they can "enter while sitting *(suwatte-iri),"* which isn't a real word, and the other girls go on from there.

PAGE 51

Hiroshi: Readers of the spin-off prequel series *Handa-kun* (available from Yen Press!) might recognize that Yoshino-sensei is using the story-telling style for that series in this chapter. The original Japanese says, "Hiroshi Kido...Nickname, Hiroshi," but a change from kanji characters to katakana letters doesn't translate well as a "nickname" in English...

PAGE 59

Que●ckle Wipers: Quickle Wipers, made by Japanese corporation Kao, is a brand of replaceable floor wipes used on a standard sweeper, much like Swiffer™ in the United States.

PAGE 61

"Wipin' down others' messes": The saying *"shirinugui"* literally means "wiping ass/butt."

school year's end: In Japan, the end of school is separate from and happens before the graduation ceremony.

PAGE 64

"Hiro-kun": Another reference to the series *Handa-kun*.

PAGE 69

Hiro's controversial hair and speech: Japanese schools are very strict when it comes to rules about dress and appearance. Dying hair even medium brown is not permitted, and bleaching it blond, like Hiroshi did, is so completely against the rules that it marks the person as a delinquent.

PAGE 85

Hiro's sneeze: It's a superstition that, if you sneeze, it means someone is talking about you. That someone usually isn't a narrator though...

PAGE 86

oden: A popular dish throughout Japan, especially in winter, consisting of a variety of ingredients, such as boiled eggs, fish cakes, fried tofu, daikon radish, and more (with regional variations), simmered in a light, soy-flavored *dashi* (fish) broth.

PAGE 93

"Linnerin' Scent of Summer": The Japanese title Naru used was *"Natsu no Nokoriga* (Summer's Lingering Scent)."

middle-aged bottoms: Tama's using Boys' Love terms again—this time, *"ossan uke,"* where a middle-aged man *(ossan)* is the receiving partner *(uke)* in a gay couple.

PAGE 96
snug: The "insult" Kirie uses, "*godinmari,*" tends to have a neutral or positive connotation, like "snug" or "cozy." "Snug" can also mean "sheltered, homey, and living in comfort" though, which also works as a backhanded insult to "genius son" Handa.

PAGE 105
youkan: A type of Japanese sweet traditionally made with red bean paste and sugar, with agar to turn it into a firmly solid jelly. It's usually sold as blocks and served in slices, as we see Handa's mother prepare, and can come in other flavors than red bean.

Shishiya: "*Shishi*" means "lion."

PAGE 109
"tender, loving care": The original phrase used, "*chou yo hana yo* (butterflies and flowers)," is from a saying about how parents love and treasure their children while raising them, even more than butterflies and flowers.

PAGE 117
Ishida and Ohtani: Mitsunari Ishida and Yoshitsugu Ohtani were two commanders in Toyotomi's army during the Warring States period who had a legendary friendship—or possibly more than friendship—which explains Tama's interest.

PAGE 120
"time's tight": The word Naru used, "*ketsu-kacchin,*" is used in the TV business or by comedians to mean, "The next item on the schedule is pressing in/ticking away (so hurry it up)." It's also a tiny bit crude, since the word "*ketsu*" means "buttocks" or "rear."

PAGE 121
"I caught too much, so take this.": It's a common practice in Japan to downplay a gift by saying a variation of, "I had too much extra," so that the other person won't feel obligated to reciprocate. It'd be good for Handa to realize that these are actually gifts though...

PAGE 144
hooks, stops, and sweeps: "*Hane,*" "*tome,*" and "*harai*" are Japanese terms for different ways of finishing a stroke in calligraphy.

PAGE 158
Demon Bride: "*Oniyome*" is a term for a wife who is very strict with her husband.

PAGE 160
ancient writing: An older, curvier style of writing Chinese characters, which is still often used for seal stamps or to give things a more ancient feel.

PAGE 162
fish!: Being an island country that gets so much of its food from the sea, Japan has developed numerous original kanji characters for the wide variety of fish available there, beyond the characters found in Chinese. Most of them have the general kanji for "fish" on the left-hand side, and it's a common challenge to see how many you can remember and write.

PAGE 163
conger eel: The fish word "*anago*" is written without the kanji for "fish," so it doesn't fit with the rest (hence Handa avoiding the subject).

PAGE 185
arranged marriage: The term Handa's mother used was "*omiai,*" or "marriage meeting." Such meetings are arranged between two people interested in marriage and often include their parents. Generally, it's meant as a starting point for courtship, rather than an actual arranged marriage, but there are always exceptions...

BONUS: DANPO THE 10TH

(Translation: Pond)

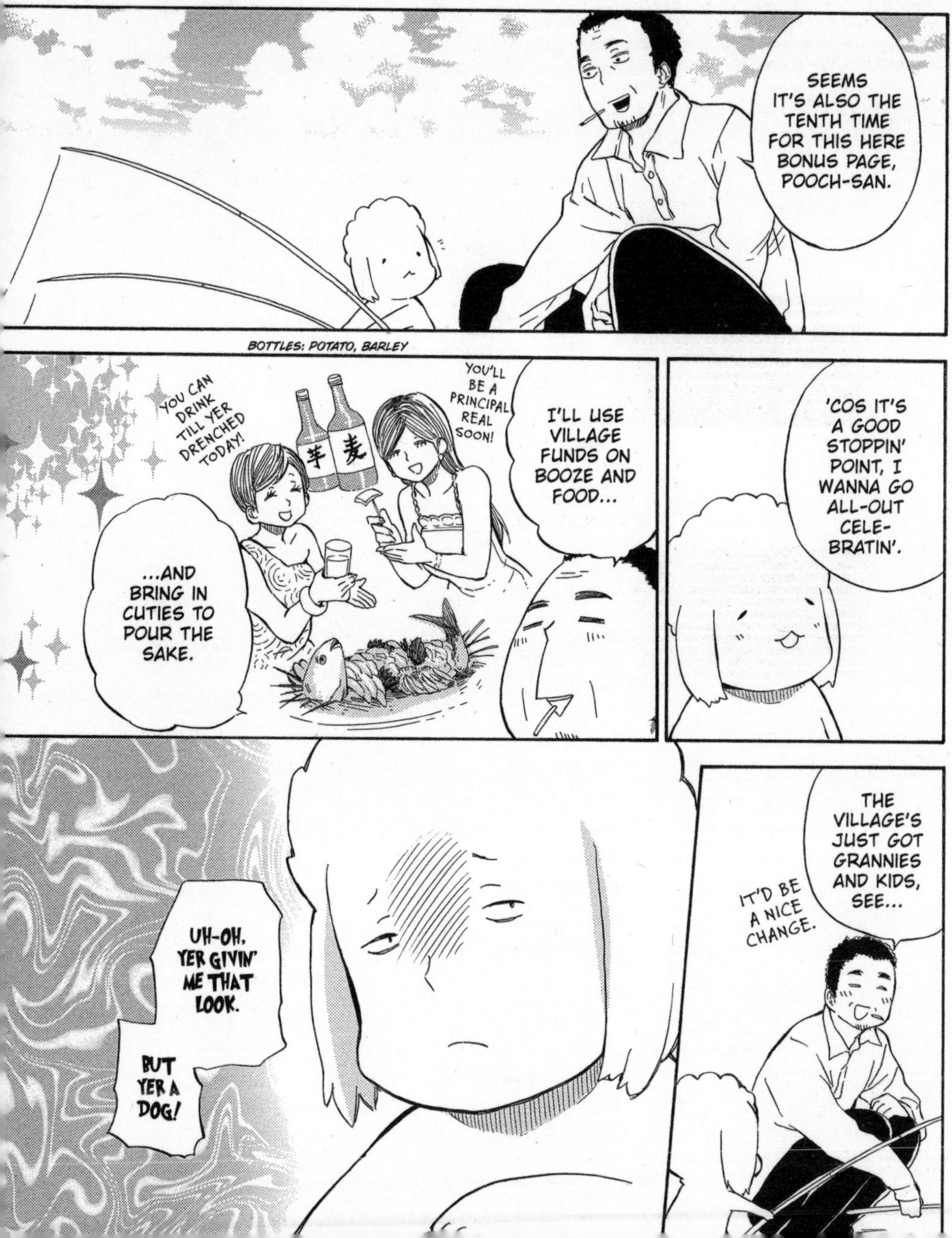
SEEMS IT'S ALSO THE TENTH TIME FOR THIS HERE BONUS PAGE, POOCH-SAN.
'COS IT'S A GOOD STOPPIN' POINT, I WANNA GO ALL-OUT CELE-BRATIN'.
I'LL USE VILLAGE FUNDS ON BOOZE AND FOOD...
YOU'LL BE A PRINCIPAL REAL SOON!
BOTTLES: POTATO, BARLEY
芋
麦
YOU CAN DRINK TILL YER DRENCHED TODAY!
...AND BRING IN CUTIES TO POUR THE SAKE.
THE VILLAGE'S JUST GOT GRANNIES AND KIDS, SEE...
IT'D BE A NICE CHANGE.
UH-OH, YER GIVIN' ME THAT LOOK.
BUT YER A DOG!

BARAKAMON NEWS

Vol.510

BARAKAMON is being simultaneously released in both *Monthly Shonen Gangan* and *Gangan ONLINE*!!

Everyone, thank you very much for buying Volume 10 of *BARAKAMON*! Currently, *BARAKAMON* is running concurrently in two magazines: *Monthly Shonen Gangan*, which goes on sale the 12th of each month, and WEB magazine *Gangan ONLINE*, which updates on Thursday each week. (*BARAKAMON* updates on the third Thursday of each month.) You can read the new chapter in the print magazine a bit earlier than the WEB one. In the print magazine, you can also see bonus color pages not included in the volume release, while, in the WEB magazine, you can see videos, such as commercials. Both can be enjoyed differently than the volume releases, so I think you should try both of them!

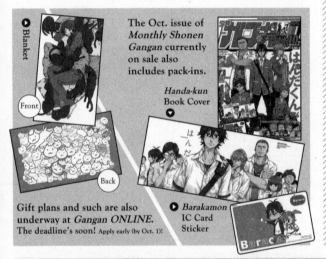

Blanket

Front

Back

The Oct. issue of *Monthly Shonen Gangan* currently on sale also includes pack-ins.

Handa-kun Book Cover

Barakamon IC Card Sticker

Baraca

Gift plans and such are also underway at *Gangan ONLINE*. The deadline's soon! Apply early (by Oct. 1)!

Gangan ONLINE

http://www.ganganonline.com/
[Public Twitter] https://twitter.com/ganganonline

Monthly Shonen Gangan

http://gangan.square-enix.co.jp/
[Public Twitter] https://twitter.com/shonen_gangan

BARAKAMON 11 set for sale in June 2016!

For the latest news, check the *BARAKAMON*/*Handa-kun* public Twitter!

https://twitter.com/go_barakamon

Thanks to all your passionate support, *BARAKAMON* has reached its tenth volume. In order to get back to basics, we went with a Sensei and Naru combo for the cover, just like Volume 1. Feel free to continue to support *BARAKAMON* as it takes its time progressing. Well, then, I sincerely hope to see you all again in Volume 11!

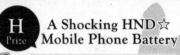

MON 10

SATSUKI YOSHINO

WITHDRAWN

Translation/Adaptation: Krista Shipley, Karie Shipley
Lettering: Lys Blakeslee

Barakamon vol. 10 © 2014 Satsuki Yoshino / SQUARE ENIX CO., LTD. First published in Japan in 2014 by SQUARE ENIX CO., LTD. English translation rights arranged with SQUARE ENIX CO., LTD. and Hachette Book Group through Tuttle-Mori Agency, Inc.

Translation © 2016 by SQUARE ENIX CO., LTD.

Yen Press
Hachette Book Group
1290 Avenue of the Americas
New York, NY 10104

www.HachetteBookGroup.com
www.YenPress.com

Yen Press is an imprint of Hachette Book Group, Inc. The Yen Press name and logo are trademarks of Hachette Book Group, Inc.

Library of Congress Control Number: 2015960109

First Yen Press Edition: April 2016

ISBN: 978-0-316-39348-5

10 9 8 7 6 5 4 3 2 1

BVG

Printed in the United States of America